Psychology of Work and Unemployment

WILEY SERIES IN
PSYCHOLOGY AND PRODUCTIVITY AT WORK

Series Editors
D. J. Oborne and M. M. Gruneberg

The Physical Environment at Work
Edited by D.J. Oborne and M.M. Gruneberg

Hours of Work—Temporal factors in work scheduling
Edited by Simon Folkard and Timothy H. Monk

Computers at Work—A behavioural approach
D. J. Oborne

Psychology of Work and Unemployment
Gordon E. O'Brien

Further titles in preparation

Psychology of Work and Unemployment

Gordon E. O'Brien

School of Social Sciences

Flinders University, Australia

JOHN WILEY & SONS

Chichester · New York · Brisbane · Toronto · Singapore

Library of Congress Cataloging-in-Publication Data:

O'Brien, Gordon E.
   Psychology of work and unemployment.
   (Wiley series in psychology and productivity at work)
   1. Work–Psychological aspects.   2. Psychology
Industrial.   3. Labor supply–Effect of technological
innovations on.   4. Unemployment–Psychological aspects.
Underemployment–Psychological aspects.   I. Title.
II. Series.
   HF5548.8.O19   1986   158.7   85-29604
   ISBN 0 471 10533 3

British Library Cataloguing in Publication Data:

O'Brien, Gordon E.
   Psychology of work and unemployment
   1. Psychology, Industrial
   I. Title   II. Series
   331.1'01'9   HF5548.8
   ISBN 0 471 10533 3

Printed and bound in Great Britain by
Biddles Ltd, Guildford and King's Lynn

Contents

Editorial Foreword to the Series

Gordon O'Brien's book *Psychology of Work and Unemployment*, is a welcome addition to the Psychology and Productivity at Work series. A major thrust of current psychological approaches to organizational psychology is in terms of the critical importance of the nature of the job itself in relation to both satisfaction and productivity. While, of course, such an approach is almost self-evidently valid and has led to major concerns about redesigning jobs with the needs and values of individuals in mind, of itself the approach is simplistic. It is this simplistic nature of current approaches to understanding job attitudes and performance in organizations that O'Brien seeks to rectify in this book. A central theme to his argument is the importance of skill-utilization and under-utilization in relation to understanding both job behaviour and its effect on personality and behaviour. Skill-utilization and under-utilization, of course, cannot be understood in isolation from the total context of work, the nature of skill, the characteristics of job stressors, personality, control and a host of other major factors. Thus O'Brien chooses an interactionalist approach, seeking to examine the ways in which factors interact and change each other.

The book, however, seeks to do more than give an account of factors affecting or affected by work behaviour. It considers the whole gamut from employment to underemployment and reviews the current state of our understanding of unemployment, leisure and retirement. We believe that this is an important book, not only covering thoroughly the psychology of work, leisure and unemployment, but also offering thought-provoking and at times controversial insights into the whole area.

M. M. Gruneberg
D. J. Oborne

Preface

This book is written for employees, managers, social science students and anyone interested in the psychological effect of employment and unemployment on people. The content of the book is unusual in at least three ways. First, unlike most books on managerial psychology, it is concerned about the effects of job structures and work situations upon the performance and personality of employees. Most texts on the management of work organizations concentrate on the motivational functions of leadership but fail to consider how the job situation has shaped the meaning of work for employees. Unless there is information about the psychological function of work for employees, attempts to motivate employees may be misguided. They may recommend managerial practices which may not be relevant to employee needs and values. What employees see as meaningful is a function of their past job experiences and this must be taken into account in understanding their reactions to jobs and managers.

Until recently, it has been assumed that the personality of employees has been predetermined by their early socialization experiences. But now, there is considerable evidence that personality does change during adulthood. One of the main determinants of these changes is the type of work that people do. There is an increasing amount of evidence to support a view which states that people become what they do. If job experiences restrict opportunities for personal control, skill-use and intimacy then employees have diminished capabilities for self-discretion, competence and interpersonal relationships. This diminishes the rate of personal development of employees as well as their job performance.

Thus the focus of this book is employee-oriented as well as management oriented. Working or not-working is a central experience for adults and psychologists have tended to neglect the effects of this experience. This book assembles the available evidence on the psychological importance of work. If work structures do affect personality and task performance they should have a direct effect upon work behaviour, non-work activities such as leisure, and employees' capacity to adjust to a state of unemployment. Two kinds of unemployment are considered. One is involuntary and occurs when employees lose their jobs during their working life. The other is voluntary, at least for many, and occurs when employees reach retirement age. If work structures affect personal capabilities strongly, then unemployment or retirement studies should show significant decrements in personal adjustment.

A second concern of the author is the effect of technological change upon employee and managerial performance. Many have argued that technological change has brought enriched jobs to a few but has largely led to jobs which have become de-skilled. Machines have replaced and taken over many employee skills and consequently it is a misnomer to talk about employment opportunities in the future. Rather, it is suggested, that we are part of an era of underemployment where it has become increasingly difficult for educated employees to find jobs that fully utilize their skills. This view will be examined. It is a problem that affects employees and managers alike. If job changes are not utilizing valued skills of employees it could have long term effects on their personality. For managers, it is a problem of utilizing human sources. It is not just the simple problem of not being able to utilize employee skills at work. It is also a motivational problem. Prolonged experience of empty jobs, it will be maintained, negatively affects employee control beliefs, their work motivation and their beliefs about their own work competence. Efforts to motivate such employees will not be successful if managers just concentrate on contextual issues such as human relations, communication or even pay incentives. If work structures reduce employee effectiveness then only change in work structures will improve their performance.

A third distinctive emphasis is upon unemployment. Rarely do organizational psychologists consider what happens to employees when they lose their jobs. What are the psychological effects? To what extent are the reported effects due to loss of income, and to what extent are they due to loss of job activities? Can the effects of unemployment be remedied by 'education for leisure'?

These are some of the main questions addressed: The approach adopted is an interactional one. The traditional psychological approaches to work behaviour have concentrated on the effects of personal capabilities, motivation and work values upon work performance. They have neglected the effect of work structures and job content upon personal capabilities. A more complete understanding of work behaviour takes account of both the effect of people on work performance as well as the effect of job content and organizational structure upon people. This interactional approach, it will be argued, is required if organizational psychology is to develop beyond a narrow managerial psychology. It is also required for a deeper understanding of the nature of employment, leisure and unemployment.

Acknowledgements

Many people have helped me with this book. My parents taught me to appreciate the strength of organizational structures and the importance of realistic self-direction. Oscar Oeser guided my efforts to measure organizational and job structure. Students at Flinders and Purdue University forced me to be more specific about my ideas. The manuscript was typed with accuracy and patience by Carol McNally and Kay Guest. I am grateful to Christine Tucker, Elmer Zalums and Ralph Horton for their support. For permission to reproduce figures I acknowledge the American Psychological Association, *Administrative Science Quarterly*, Rand McNally and Jossey-Bass.

G. E. O'BRIEN

CHAPTER 1

Work and Personality

> . . the understandings of the greater part of men are necessarily formed by their ordinary employments. The man whose whole life is spent in performing a few simple operations, of which the effects too are, perhaps, always the same, or very nearly the same, has no occasion to exert his understanding, or to exercise his invention in finding out expedients for removing difficulties which never occur. He naturally loses, therefore, the habit of such exertion, and generally becomes as stupid and ignorant as it is possible for a human creature to become.
>
> (Adam Smith, *Wealth of Nations*, 1776, pp. 302–3 in 1976 edition)

It is a common observation that differences between people can be partly understood from their occupations. Schoolteachers, for example, are often inclined to bookishness and an emphasis on following rules and procedures. Engineers are said to be tough-minded and realists while those from the helping professions, such as social work, are characterized by tendermindedness, optimism and idealism. The effects of work on people has been a major theme of modern literature. Writers as diverse as Dickens, Hardy, Lawrence and Zola have explored the effect of modern industrial work on the personality and interpersonal relationships of men and women. Even economists, whose interests have focused on the economic functions of work, have not refrained from speculation about what work does to people. Thus Adam Smith, whose *Wealth of Nations* contributed to the widescale adoption of industrial assembly work, had some forebodings about the human effects of machine production. This is shown in the above quotation. Has modern organizational psychology, which aims to understand human behaviour at work, anything to say about the lasting effects of work structures on employees? In what way do work structures affect performance *and* personality? This book reviews the available information on these questions.

Work, defined generally, is the expenditure of effort in the performance of a task. Hence, work can be done in employment or leisure. Although there is some point to distinguishing between work and employment the common usage of the term, work, refers to employment and this usage will be followed. Perusal of modern texts on industrial and organizational psychology shows that little attention is given to the study of work as a determinant of personality or relatively stable attributes such as values or cognitive styles. Yet, at the same time, the person at work is the object of study. There is an abundance of material on individual work motivation, leader attributes, job satisfaction and work stress. But the theories and research studies, with few exceptions, consider personal attributes in the context of predicting individual and organizational productivity. The person is treated as a component of a system or organization whose goals are to be predicted and maximized. This approach is scientifically legitimate in the sense that productivity is one of the distinctive outputs of any group and its prediction in terms of theories about the joint effect of human resources and organizational structure is an intellectual endeavour amenable to empirical and logical methods. However, this body of knowledge, managerial psychology, says little about the effects of work on personality or stable behavioural dispositions.

Certainly there are some relevant studies but most of these are about temporary states like job satisfaction, stress and motives. There are some writers who use this information to talk about the 'quality' of work life but they do not pursue their quest to the point of asking, 'How does work shape people?' or 'What kind of work structures are necessary to promote personality development?' It is hard, therefore, to avoid a suspicion that organizational psychologists are only interested in the effects of work on people to the extent that these effects can be shown to affect their subsequent performance.

As a consequence, little is known about the functions of work for the individual. This is not only a central question for understanding adult behaviour, it is also important for understanding productivity. Unless we know a great deal about the psychological functions of work for employees it is unlikely that we will achieve much success in predicting work adjustment and productivity.This implies that management psychologists, of whom there are many in North America, will have limited success in predicting individual productivity unless they attempt to collect more information about the reciprocal effects between work structures and personality structures.

Many theories of work motivation, for example, assume that personality is an unchangeable and stable behavioural disposition. Typical research efforts are devoted to showing how differences in work values, personal control and needs for personal growth affect motivation and performance. If these attributes *change* as a result of work experiences, then the effectiveness of these theories will be limited.

This can be illustrated by a brief examination of a current influential theory of work motivation and productivity. This is the job characteristics theory of Hackman and Oldham (1975, 1976, 1980). In one sense this has been a successful theory for it has generated a great deal of research and is frequently taught to students of management and psychology as a useful way of diagnosing whether jobs are motivating or not. Yet the evidence supporting the theory is relatively weak (O'Brien, 1982a; Roberts and Glick, 1981). It is reasonably good at predicting job satisfaction but has been unable to predict productivity.

The theory states that jobs high on certain core dimensions—task identity, task significance, skill-variety, autonomy and feedback—induce experiences of meaningfulness, responsibility and knowledge. These experiences are assumed to be rewarding and to motivate employees toward high levels of productivity and positive evaluations of their job. The degree, however, to which the core job dimensions are experienced as meaningful depends on what is assumed to be a stable personality characteristic—an individual's 'growth need strength'. This is a measure of the degree to which people need to have jobs which enable them to grow and develop.

Those people who wish to express their needs for learning and responsibility on the job are assumed, according to the theory, to be very responsive to jobs that are high on the core dimensions. By contrast, those who are low on growth need strength are considered to be significantly less responsive. These tend to be people who have an instrumental rather than an expressive orientation to work. They prefer jobs that allow them to obtain extrinsic benefits, such as good pay and job security, to jobs which provide intrinsic rewards such as challenge and autonomy. The theory implies that these instrumental-orientated employees are less likely to benefit from improved jobs and, as a matter of strategy, job enrichment should focus on workers with expressive orientations or high growth need strength.

Are these predictions supported? The evidence is considered in detail later (Chapter 4), but the short answer is no. Regardless of growth need strength, employees are satisfied with jobs that provide variety, autonomy, feedback and significance. Furthermore, there is no evidence showing that this personality variable predicts productivity levels either directly or indirectly.

There appear to be three main reasons for this failure. First, like many theories in work psychology, the job characteristics model fails to incorporate structural variables. Productivity and satisfaction can be affected by work structures such as communication, power and cooperation structure (O'Brien, 1984a). No matter how challenging a job is, an employee is not likely to be motivated and productive unless the work group structure gives that employee freedom to do the job in the way he or she desires. Second, the theory does not incorporate individual ability as a variable. This is surprising in that level of ability has frequently been shown to determine productivity and job evaluations. Third, the theory assumes that growth need strength is unrelated to job experiences. However, it is likely that work orientations and needs are shaped by the job. If a job provides no opportunity for using valued skills then the worker is unlikely to see work as a source of personal development. It will be seen as a necessity that requires productive effort commensurate with extrinsic benefits such as pay and security (Lafitte, 1958). The job characteristics theory does not admit this possibility. One of the few longitudinal studies testing the theory did actually report that workers growth need strength increased with job enrichment (Orpen, 1979). Thus job experiences can change this personality variable and hence change an employee's responsiveness to challenging work.

The significance of the effects of the job on work orientations has wider implications. It has become fashionable to label many employees, particularly from blue-collar occupations, as instrumental in their orientations to work. Studies like those of Goldthorpe's are cited as showing that many people just work for money and care little for jobs that offer challenge and opportunities for self-direction (Goldthorpe *et al.*, 1968). The implication for job design theorists like Hackman and Oldham is that such people do not want or need jobs that provide opportunities for psychological growth. This has the effect of authorizing discriminatory policies of job design. Lacking strong evidence which shows growth need strength is independent of work experiences, the restriction of job enrichment interventions to those who are high on growth need strength could deny a considerable number of employees the opportunity to increase their job satisfaction.

It could also deny them the opportunity to develop their personality through their work. Most North American work psychologists assume that work has little effect on personality, without demonstrating that this is actually the case. Obviously this kind of research needs to be done. But it is not going to be done by a research orientation that is dominated by the problem of predicting performance just from personal attributes and task dimensions. Such research is limited because there is no theory of group structure that can be used to explain how outputs like productivity are jointly determined by tasks, personal resources and work structure. It is also limited because this orientation does not ask 'What is the psychological function of work?' If we knew this then we might be in a better position for choosing personality dimensions that do have strong effects on productivity.

These comments are not meant as an attack on psychology for studying management problems. Individual and group productivity is one of the central concerns of organizational psychology. Productivity is an evaluation of how well goals are reached and it is impossible to divorce the study of task behaviour from the study of goal achievement. What is being criticized is the prevalent orientation in organizational psychology which not only concentrates on management problems, but does it without attempting to understand behaviour as a reciprocal interaction between people and social structures. This restricted view of personality within modern organizational psychology has been recently criticized in a similar fashion by Weiss and Adler (1984). The neglect of reciprocal interactions between personality and work structures seem to be due to a narrow definition of the goal of organizational psychology.

PERSONALITY AND ORGANIZATIONAL STRUCTURE

Organizational psychology is commonly defined as the scientific study of human behaviour in work organizations. But what does this mean? It could mean that the field describes and explains individual and organizational processes in terms of the reciprocal interaction between the characteristics of persons who are members of the organization, and the characteristics of the organization of which they are a part. If it did mean this then it would imply that individual work behaviour should be explained by theories which describe the reciprocal or two-way interplay between personality structures and organizational structures. Such theories should ideally, specify the personal characteristics of individuals which are relevant to predicting their work behaviour, as well as specifying a set or organizational characteristics that affect individual behaviour and organizational performance. This would then be followed by an analysis of the processes whereby organizational structures changed personality structure, personality structure changed organizational structure and, finally, the manner in which both structures determined organizational and individual outputs such as productivity.

However, there is no general interactional theory of this kind in contemporary organizational psychology. Most of the theories and methods are very specific and focus on particular problems such as work motivation, leadership and personnel selection. Perhaps this is due to a distrust of grand theories which try to explain everything. More likely it is due to the historical development of the subject. Early researchers tried to balance a desire to be useful to organizations with a desire to develop and promote employee psychological growth. These two main questions have shaped the development of the subject and each question has led a distinctive orientation. The questions are:

1. How do you maximize individual and organizational performance?
2. What are the effects of jobs upon relatively enduring personal characteristics such as values and personality?

The first question addresses management problems while the second is more relevant to the problem of promoting employee welfare. The orientations associated with these two questions can be labelled 'management' and 'humanistic' orientations. Each of these orientations considers legitimate questions but neither is likely to lead to a general theory of organizational behaviour in the way previously described. A management orientation will only consider stable personality characteristics in so far as they predict performance. Thus, individual differences in ability, values and personality are used to predict employee performance. But rarely is the question raised about the effects of jobs and organizations on changing abilities, values and personality.

Conversely, the humanist tradition may examine the effects of jobs on stress, alienation and personality without asking questions about the effects of these personal consequences on employee productivity (Frese, 1982). It may be the case that the long term effects of a job upon a person would change that person's performance. By itself, neither orientation has developed an approach that answers all of the possible questions about organizational behaviour. Part of the problem is that the management orientation assumes that personality is constant while jobs, organizations and outputs change. On the other hand the humanistic orientation assumes that, over time, jobs and structures are constant while employees change.

Both approaches, therefore, are restricted in their ability to describe organizational behaviour in an interactional manner. A true interactional approach requires the specification of reciprocal linkages between personality and organizational structure. The approach so far is abstract. For it to have substance we need:

1. Specification of personality structure.
2. Specification of organizational structure.
3. Identification of empirical relationships connecting the two structures.
4. Identification of the way in which the two structures jointly determine outputs such as individual and organizational performance.
5. Theories specifying the process by which structural relationships change over time.

At present, psychological research has not provided theories of the kind required. Before they can be developed it is necessary to identify the types of relationships connecting jobs to personality structure. In this book some of the evidence needed to specify these relationships will be considered. Personality variables will include all those relatively stable attributes, including abilities, of the individual. As will be seen, there is little consensus on which attributes are important. Organizational structure will refer to the stable relationships connecting persons, positions and tasks (Oeser and Harary, 1962, 1964; Oeser and O'Brien, 1967). In the case of both personality and organizational structure, the elements and relationships selected will depend on the function or purpose of work. For organizations, their function is relatively clear. Organizations are constructed to achieve specific goals such as productivity, profitability or the efficient provision of services. Hence the selection of concepts to define organizational structure will be based on knowing which relationships determine those goals. Thus interpersonal relationships, communication, power, task allocation, assignment rules and task order or precedence can be used to define organizational structure usefully because each of these relationships is known to affect productivity or goal attainment.

But what are the functions of work for the person? There is at present no clear answer to this question. Most writers would agree that work is necessary for survival or income. Beyond this there is disagreement. The function or meaning of work has changed across the centuries, which might suggest that there is no necessary function beyond survival. In that case, theories about the function of work would just reflect changing ideologies and beliefs. On the other hand, some modern psychologists have tried to identify general psychological functions of work. Often, however, they have started with assumptions about the function of work that can be traced to prior ideological or religious beliefs.

THE FUNCTION OF WORK: PAST AND PRESENT

No comprehensive history of the meaning and function of work is available. A short account of changing concepts of work through the ages was written by Tilgher (1930) and it is a useful source on the subject. Although Tilgher does not develop any explanation of why the meaning of work has changed, it appears that a major reason was the desire to provide a meaning that fitted or explained contemporary social structure. Thus, in classical Greece, citizens regarded physical work as a barrier to the search for truth and beauty. Work of this kind enmeshed people in the earthly process of change which distracted them from the contemplation of unchangeable universals. Citizens were free to contemplate while slaves were forced to do physical work. Some respect was given to those who worked on the land for they provided necessities. However, physical work was reserved for lesser beings who were not considered to have the higher attributes of citizens who were deemed capable of personal fulfilment through creative work.

Thus Greek thought on work had a dualistic nature to it. Creative work activities, perhaps what we would call leisure activities, were reserved for an elite while essential physical toil was imposed on slaves. In other seminal cultures, at a later date, the idea of work of any kind as a means of personal fulfilment was dropped. In early Hebrew thought work was considered an honourable activity for all. But work was not a way of salvation or fulfillment. It was a duty and burden imposed on men because of the sin of their ancestors. Elements of this view passed into Christian thought, where work was also considered a worthy activity. It was a Christian duty to work at the tasks required by one's position in society. Work was also important for achieving personal independence and for providing basic necessities for the community of believers.

With the advent of the Protestant reformation, work became a 'calling' and not just a duty. While Luther accepted previous doctrines about work as a penalty for original sin, he also advocated work as a method of serving God. In doing this, he abolished a distinction between religious and worldly activity. One could serve equally well in the role of a labourer as in the role of a priest. Yet this idea of work as a calling had little to do with any theory about the way in which the *content* of work could further personal development. Obedience to the structural demands of the job was a path to personal development or salvation but the actual content of the work seemed unimportant. It was still basically a doctrine of work as a duty necessary to spiritual salvation. Calvin elaborated this doctrine by advocating austerity and thrift. For him, wealth and success at work was a sign that the worker was predestined to the spiritual elect. Such feedback was the proper reward of good work. It was improper to become attached to, or even enjoy, the fruits of labour such as money, property and social status.

Such a work ethic was a congenial one for a new industrial society which required men who accepted work, however unpleasant, as a duty. It was also an ethic especially suited to a capitalist entrepreneur who had to be devoted to work, and the demonstration that his work reflected his spiritual status. This connection between the Protestant work ethic and the rise of capitalism was pointed out by Weber (1930). It was an ethic conducive to industriousness, reliability and the acceptance of managerial authority. It was also a factor contributing to the success of Protestant entrepreneurs. They accumulated wealth which was not dissipated in personal consumption but provided capital necessary for economic growth.

Modern psychological and sociological theories of work have dropped the theistic basis of the Protestant ethic but have still retained the idea of work as a means of personal development. Contemporary views still see work as an individualistic goal-seeking activity which provides experiences necessary for personal development. The major differences between modern twentieth century theorists depends on (i) the *extent* to which they see work as essential to psychological growth, and (ii) the degree to which they emphasize the *content* of work tasks and not just the organizational *structure* within which work activity occurs.

There are two major types of theory. The first to be considered is Freudian theory which sees the structure of work as necessary for both survival and the development of ego functions. This type of theory says little about the potential of work *content* for facilitating psychological growth. This lack, to some extent, is met by self-actualization theories.

FREUDIAN THEORIES OF WORK

The importance of income and structure is a persistent theme in Freudian views of work. Freud's views on work are mainly contained in his *Civilization and Its Discontents* (Freud, 1962). His view of work is a pessimistic one as he views it as a necessity induced by scarcity and the need to survive. The formal structure of work in society also prevented the uninhibited satisfaction of sexual and aggressive instincts. Work structures imposed rules of conduct which required employees to live by a reality and not a pleasure principle. Objective transactions with the physical environment and coworkers were ordered by imposed rules which prevented immediate gratification of instinctual impulses and thus strengthened the internal control mechanism—the ego. Because of these external controls work for men was not a pleasurable activity because, according to Freud, human beings exhibit an inborn tendency to carelessness, irregularity, and unreliability.

Thus for Freud work was an unpleasant necessity for survival and the structure of cooperative work activities had the function of controlling and sublimating sexual and aggressive instincts. This structure had a positive function for the individual in that it allowed him to learn and adapt to the real world and thus contributed to a state of maturity. Maturity was achieved when a person's ego strength was strong enough to direct his activities so that his instincts were satisfied in a socially acceptable form. Furthermore he would not be overwhelmed by external or internal unconscious libidinal demands which, if accepted, would lead to high levels of anxiety. These general functions of work were also accompanied by an interesting comment on the potential negative effects of attachment to work. Freud had a hydraulic view of energy or libido. The quantity of libido is fixed and if a person invests a lot of energy in work then that much less energy is available for love and personal activity.

> Since a man does not have unlimited quantities of physical energy at his disposal, he has to accomplish his tasks by making an expedient distribution of his libido. What he employs for cultural aims he, to a great extent, withdraws from women and sexual life.
>
> (Freud, 1962, p. 50)

This suggests that Freud might have thought that there was an optimal division between work and love but, unfortunately, he does not seem to have expanded his views on this subject. Traditional Freudians, in so far as they discuss work at all, assert that the overt function of work is self-preservation and the covert or latent function is an integrated ego activity that provides direct or indirect ways of satisfying sexual and aggressive instincts (Neff, 1977).

Somewhat consistent with this view is the more recent theory of Jahoda (1981, 1982). While not using Freudian terminology, she has specified a number of functions which the structure of work can serve. Like Freud, she does not consider the content of work, but emphasizes the economic and psychological functions served by the structure of employment. Her work functions were partly based on her observations of the unemployed during the Great Depression. The passivity, distress and resignation in the lives of the unemployed, she attributed to deprivation of income and work structure. This led her to assert that the manifest function of employment is income and the latent functions are time structure, enlargement of social experience, participation in collective purposes, status and identity, and regular activity. All of these latent functions contribute to the ability to participate as mature citizens in our present society. They are thus similar to the reality and ego functions outlined by Freud.

The main similarity between Freud and Jahoda is their emphasis on the importance of income and work structure and their relative neglect of the content of work tasks as a determinant of psychological growth. Neither ask the question of whether differences in task experience can explain differences between employees in their personality or psychological development. Some neo-Freudians did attend to the effect of work tasks. For example, Hendrick (1943) maintained that people had a mastery instinct and gained direct pleasure from tasks that allowed them to be challenged by, and then eventually control, their environment. Also Fromm stressed the importance of work tasks providing autonomy and self-expression (Fromm, 1948, 1968). Influenced by Marx as well as Freud, Fromm maintained that too many tasks in industry did not allow employees to use their human potentialities. Lacking intrinsic rewards and interest in their work, they developed instrumental orientations about work. This meant that work was valued as a means to material rewards. As work came to be seen as a contractual relationship, it generalized to other relationships outside of work. Thus personal relationships in modern society tended to become contractual, cold and lacking authentic experience. Mature and authentic personal relationships depended on people having the experience of being fully themselves. But this was only possible when work provided them with opportunities for being themselves. Fromm provides very general prescriptions about the ideal nature of work. It appears that work, for him, must provide challenge, self-expression and autonomy. If it does not, then it can have serious and stable negative effects on personal adjustment and well-being. Fromm was influenced by Freud but should not be regarded as a Freudian in that he rejected the idea that human development could be understood only by reference to aggressive and sexual instincts.

This can be seen in his views on work for, unlike Freud, he stressed the importance of task content as a determinant of psychological development. Only tasks that fully utilize people's capacities would promote their full potential. In this respect he should be classified with theorists who see work content as being of central importance to personality development.

SELF-ACTUALIZATION THEORIES: PERSONALITY, WORK STRUCTURE AND TASK CONTENT

Whereas Freudian theories about the structure of work and psychological development are conservative in the sense that their application would not require change in the existing content of work tasks, another group of theories arose out of the protest and disillusionment with both the structure of work and the content of work tasks in industrial society. The progress of industrial civilization, for many writers, has been seen as dehumanizing. Before psychology and Karl Marx discovered work alienation there was already present a literature of humanistic protest against the excessive routinization, effort and simplicity of factory tasks (Meakin, 1976). Writers as diverse as Carlyle, Ruskin and Morris had decried a system which locked men into activities devoid of self-expression and joy.

The basic assumption of these writers is that men become what they do. If work tasks allow people to use their skills, make responsible decisions, and learn new skills then their intellectual capacity and life satisfaction will grow, and they will develop healthy self-esteem and a sense of personal control. On the other hand, prolonged experience of tasks that are routine, simple and directed by others will induce dissatisfaction, intellectual rigidity, low self-esteem and a sense of not being in control of their lives. People so affected will feel separated or alienated from what they do. It is not a part of them because it is not fully chosen and does not use their capabilities. With time, the performance of such tasks can change people. From being devalued by their work they gradually come to devalue themselves. Lacking stimulation and challenge, they fail to maintain an active mode of thinking and gradually lose insight into the nature of their needs and the way in which their needs are thwarted by their environment. In this sense they also become separated from their 'true' selves. The most systematic expression of this view about the function and dysfunction of work was made by Marx in his early writings on work alienation (Marx, 1844). According to Marx, man had become alienated from his work, his workers and his own identity by the dehumanization of work in industrial capitalistic society.

What, then, constitutes the alienation of labour? First, the fact that labour is external to the worker, i.e., it does not belong to his intrinsic nature; that in his work, therefore, he does not affirm himself but denies himself, does not feel content but unhappy, does not develop freely his physical and mental energy but mortifies his body and ruins his mind. The worker therefore only feels himself outside his work, and in his work feels outside himself. He feels at home when he is not working, and when he is working he does not feel at home. His labour is therefore not voluntary, but coerced; it is forced labour. It is therefore not the satisfaction of a need; it is merely a means to satisfy needs external to it.

(Marx, 1844, pp. 70, 71 in 1977 edition).

Marx attributes the debasement of workers to segmented, oversimple tasks imposed on employees by owners and managers. Both the nature of the tasks and the organizational structure contributed to alienation and Marx wanted to change both. Implicitly he made no judgement about the relative importance of these two determinants of alienation—task content and work structure. He assumed, somewhat illogically, that the nature of tasks could not be changed from within the existing work systems. Certainly he did not see any evidence that managers were prepared to redesign tasks in order to match worker skills. But that does not mean that capitalistic structures would necessarily lead to job de-skilling. His main reason for recommending abolition of private property and the replacement of owners and shareholders by worker control appeared to be his belief that capitalists would always be motivated by profits. Hence, in order to protect their capital and privileges, they would design tasks to reduce both training costs and workers' capacity to use their knowledge to disturb or undermine the work process.

Apart from his theory about the causes of alienation, Marx does present a simple yet vague theory about the function of work. Work, for him, was a desirable end in itself which had the potential for liberating humanity and restoring 'natural' ties between men and nature. This emphasis on the importance of work for 'self-actualization' is one shared by many modern psychologists. None of the modern work psychologists would accept Marx's ideology but their views resemble Marx's in many ways when they write about work tasks as having the potential for psychological growth or 'self-actualization'.

The self-actualization theories are characterized by a belief that a dominant motive for human behaviour is the drive to express individual skills and capacities in the fullest way. The fully actualized person is someone who has found joy in being what they were potentially capable of being. The main problem with grouping these theories is not only the vagueness of their definitions of self-actualization (e.g., What are the set of human capacities? What are the attributes of tasks that promote self-actualization?) but the differences in the way in which they describe this need or state.

One of the earliest writers was De Man who in 1929 wrote *Joy in Work*. He pointed to a basic impulse towards 'joy in work' and tried to identify the factors that facilitated or hindered this impulse. His analysis was based on his study of German workers. For De Man every worker aims at joy—it is innate.

'Every worker aims at joy in work, just as every human being aims at happiness' (De Man, 1929, p. 11). He found that his German workers could attain joy in mechanized capitalistic factories provided that the work was not too repetitive and fatiguing. The apparent greater dissatisfaction of North

American workers he explained as a cultural problem: 'the moron as an unskilled industrial worker is a specifically American problem' (De Man, 1929, p. 122). Needless to say he rejected the Marxist view that control over work was important. He actually believed that workers had a 'need for subordination'. All that was required to promote joy at work was to design jobs that allowed the worker to satisfy primary instincts of activity, play, curiosity, self assertion and combativeness.

Within Northern American culture the proponents of joy and self-actualization have provided a somewhat different list of instincts and needs. Maslow's theory of human motivation defined a hierarchy of needs which are related by a prepotency principle (Maslow, 1943). Although all needs can operate at once, the saliency or importance of higher needs is increased as lower needs become satisfied. The main needs are physiological, safety, love, esteem and self-actualization. The highest and ultimate need is self-actualization which is defined in a cryptic way as the need to become everything that one is capable of becoming. Self-actualization for Maslow could be accomplished by a person who (i) has work that positively uses his or her capacities, (ii) is free of illness, (iii) is gratified to a 'sufficient' extent in the lower needs, and (iv) is committed to a certain set of values such as truth, uniqueness, wholeness, perfection and self-sufficiency. With tones reminiscent of the Protestant ethic, Maslow claims that the self-actualizing person views his work as a mission or calling and the distinction between work and play disappears.

Maslow did not try to specify in detail the dimensions of tasks that were critical for personal growth. This, together with the difficulty in measuring his needs, has led to few empirical studies that substantiate his theory. This does not mean that his theory is not of value. His hierarchy of needs has some degree of plausibility as judged by common experience but its confirmation still depends on adequate measures for his needs and longitudinal studies of the effect of various task attributes on need fulfilment.

A related theory that did endeavour to specify task attributes necessary for psychological growth is that of Herzberg (1966). Like Maslow, Herzberg emphasized the importance of task experience at work as a determinant of psychological growth. For Herzberg people were productive, satisfied and mentally healthy to the extent that work provided opportunities for achievement, recognition, challenge, responsibility and advancement or learning. It was also desirable that work should provide adequate income, competent supervision and save working conditions, but contextual factors such as these satisfied a different need—a need to avoid pain. If management and workers concentrated on these factors alone, they might succeed in reducing irritations and dissatisfaction but they would not achieve psychological growth in employees. Such growth was necessary before satisfaction, productivity and personal fulfilment could be attained.

Herzberg's theory has received a great deal of attention in the managerial and psychological literature. It probably has generated more research than Maslow's theory, especially as far as it relates to satisfaction and productivity, but its status as a theory of work function is still indeterminate. This is partly due to its very general definitions of psychological growth and its failure to provide objective dimensions of job attributes. Hence its main value at present is as another set of propositions that suggest the way in which the content of work can affect psychological development—whatever this may mean.

THE NEED FOR EVIDENCE

The various theories about the psychological function of work have either been based on limited clinical evidence (e.g. Freud), unrepresentative samples (e.g. Jahoda), or generalizations lacking strong empirical support (e.g. Marx, Maslow, Herzberg). Some of the theories are useful as theories of job satisfaction but job satisfaction is a concept which only refers to a person's evaluation of a job and is not a direct measure of need satisfaction. Although it is reasonable to expect that positive job satisfaction occurs when needs are met, the existence of positive job satisfaction says little, if anything, about which particular needs are met or anything about which aspect of the job is determining satisfaction and need fulfilment.

This is not to deny that current theories are useful as a starting point for thinking about the functions of work. They do provide a list of job variables that could affect stable personality dispositions. These include the structure of work organizations such as power, communication and task allocation as well as the content of jobs such as achievement opportunities, skill-use, recognition, variety and autonomy. As well as the structure of work organizations and the content of jobs, a common factor mentioned is income. Income could affect people's self perceptions, independence and ability to benefit from enriching family and leisure activities. Besides suggesting these general work factors the array of theories provide a large list of personal functions and needs that could be affected. But which ones are important and how are they related to work variables?

One way to start answering this question is to examine the available evidence which shows how jobs can have lasting effects on behaviour, performance and personality (Kohn and Schooler, 1983; Warr, 1983).In order to do this without providing an unconnected body of facts it is necessary to have some frame of reference or guiding assumptions about what are the most important questions. We are more likely to find something if we know what we are looking for. The first assumption to be made is that an understanding of the relationship between work and people is best advanced by studying the point of contact between work organizations and the employee. What an employee does and what the organization requires is a set of tasks. Hence the first and main relationship between a person and work is the relationship between what a person can do and what work tasks require.

Any task, to be performed adequately, requires a set of skilled actions, People are hired for a position because the employer expects them to have the skills required to perform the tasks allocated to the position. Those who are hired, the employees, have skills which may or may not correspond to those required by their tasks. Whether or not a given employee is likely to be productive then is going to be determined by the degree of match between the level of skill required by the job and the level of skill possessed by the individual on those skills which are relevant to task performance. The degree of correspondence is termed job–person match. Assessment of the degree of job–person match and the specification of rules for job selection has traditionally been the main problem of personnel selection.

Yet there is another kind of match which is likely to affect job performance as well as determine the psychological effect of the job on the person. This is person–job match. It is the degree to which skills required by the job match the skills possessed by the person. The immediate experience of a person performing a task is whether the task is easy, challenging or too difficult. If the task is too easy then the person feels under-utilized. If it is too difficult then the experience is one of over-utilization. When a reasonable person–job match occurs the task will be perceived as moderately difficult and challenging. Over time, the same task may produce all three responses. Initial reactions to an apparently difficult task can be modified by on-the-job learning until the task becomes manageable and challenging. Then with repeated experience the job skills become well learned and eventually the task becomes easy. However, for simplicity, it is useful to assume that objective person–job discrepancies are stable and that they induce stable task evaluations.

The person's evaluation of skill-utilization is assumed to be important for a number of reasons. First, in our society people tend to define their identity, self-esteem and personal competence on the basis of what they can do. That is, we define ourselves in terms of our valued skills. If we are asked to do a job that does not use these skills then, in the work environment, there will be inconsistency between how we define ourselves and how the job defines us. A prolonged experience of inconsistency could thus lead a person to change their estimation of their identity, self-esteem or personal competence.

Second, a job that uses skills implicitly gives the user a sense of personal control. When under- or over-utilized we are aware of the extent to which the task limits our actions.Thus employees who are not in jobs well matched to their capabilities might develop personal control orientations which lead them to believe that their lives at work and perhaps outside of work, are prescribed by external factors. This could have implications for their psychological well-being as a moderate belief in personal control seems essential for 'normal' psychological functioning (Lefcourt, 1976; Phares, 1976).

Third, if skill-use changes employees' control beliefs then it could change their productivity. A considerable amount of research, reviewed by O'Brien (1984b) and Spector (1982) suggests that people with high personal control are more productive than those who see their life outcomes as externally determined by other people, social structures, or luck.

Fourth, skill-utilization or skill-use is one of the main predictors of job satisfaction (Locke, 1976; O'Brien, 1982b; Warr, 1983) and thus is a factor which employees use to evaluate the degree to which a job satisfies their needs. It is also possible that work motivation or effort could be adversely affected by poor skill-utilization with subsequent losses in performance.

Finally, the problem of skill-utilization bears on current concerns of sociologists and labour economists about underemployment in the workforce. One of the first social science writers to identify underemployment as a major problem was O'Toole. He led a committee of investigation into the nature of work in the United States. Their findings were presented to the federal government and published in 1973 as *Work in America.* One of the main conclusions was that work, for many, was dissatisfying because it was incommensurate with worker skills, expectations and needs. Furthermore, there were personal costs in unsatisfactory work due to stress and poor physical health. O'Toole was later to admit that some of the evidence used in this report was not rigorous but he was convinced that one of the latent problems of American society was the disparity between the educational level of the workforce and the skill level of the available pool of jobs (O'Toole, 1978).

Underemployment, in this sense, refers to skill-utilization and is one of the various forms of underemployment referred to by economists. Thus, Glyde (1977) has identified one form of underemployment as being 'an involuntary employment condition where workers are in jobs, either part-time or full-time, on which their skills, including formal and work experience training, are technically under-utilized, and thus under-valued relative to those individuals of similar ability who have made equivalent investments in skill development' (Glyde, 1977, p. 246).

Other writers have come to focus on underemployment because of concern about the effects of technological change. Thus, Braverman (1974) has argued that the progressive application of Taylor's principles of scientific management has led to jobs in most sectors of the workforce which deny employees the power to use their mental and physical capacities. If such assertions are true, and they need evaluation, then it is important to study skill-utilization in order to understand the effects of modern job design and technological change.

The remaining chapters of this book will examine the effects of skill-utilization on employee performance, satisfaction and personality. It is not claimed that skill-utilization is the only determinant of these variables. However, the concept is a useful one for organizing the available research. Chapter 2 will consider the general question of underemployment and try to present material which bears on current trends in job design and person–job match. Perhaps this is somewhat unusual for books on organizational psychology which are typically concerned with explaining the processes determining individual behaviour. However, psychologists, in their concern for understanding individual behaviour, are often unaware of the broad pattern of social changes that are affecting behaviour. We may think a particular set of variables are important because they are psychological. Thus, job reactions and performance are often discussed as if they could be understood in terms of individual dispositions such as motivation, values, attitudes and abilities. This may enable prediction of individual differences in behaviour but fail to deal with the broad structural and environmental factors that shape common patterns of behaviour. These factors are typically left to the sociologists. But the problem of understanding behaviour as a joint function of individual and structural attributes is one which requires a marriage between traditional psychological and sociological disciplines.

The third chapter will examine some of the evidence and theory pertaining to the effects of skill-utilization on satisfaction and performance. The remaining chapters will then consider the long term effects of job characteristics, including skill-utilization, on employee behaviour. The main questions to be considered are:

1. In what way do jobs determine stress and anxiety? (Chapter 4)
2. What are the direct positive and negative effects of employment on personality? (Chapter 5, 6)
3. How do these personality changes affect job performance? (Chapter 7)
4. What happens to people when they become unemployed? (Chapters 8, 9)
5. Is it possible for employees to compensate for work deprivations through the constructive use of leisure? (Chapter 10)

All of these questions need to be considered in assessing the function of work for adult personality development. If work does have an important effect on people's lives there should be marked personality dysfunctions when employment is lost; and the effects of work experiences should generalize to non-work behaviour. The final chapter will endeavour to draw together the major findings and consider their implications for job design.

REFERENCES

Braverman. H. (1974). *Labor and Monopoly Capital*, New York: Monthly Review Press

De Man, H. (1929). *Joy in Work*, New York: Holt

Frese, M. (1982). Occupational socialization and psychological development: an underemphasized research perspective in industrial psychology, *Journal of Occupational Psychology*, **55**, 209–24

Freud, S. (1962). *Civilization and its Discontents*, New York: Norton

Fromm, E. (1948). *Man for Himself*, New York: Farrar & Rinehart

Fromm, E. (1968). *The Revolution of Hope: Toward a Humanized Technology*, New York: Harper & Row

Glyde, G.P. (1977). Underemployment: Definition and causes, *Journal of Economic Issues*, **11**, 245–60

Goldthorpe, J.H., Lockwood, D., Bechhofer, F., and Platt, J. (1968). *The Affluent Worker: Industrial Attitudes and Behaviour*, Cambridge: Cambridge University Press

Hackman, J.R., and Oldham, G.R. (1975). Development of the Job Diagnostic Survey *Journal of Applied Psychology*, **60**, 159–70

Hackman, J.R., and Oldham, G.R. (1976). Motivation through the design of work: Test of a theory, *Organizational Behavior and Human Performance*, **16**, 250–79

Hackman, J.R. and Oldham, G.R. (1980). *Work Redesign*, Reading: Addison-Wesley, 1980

Hendrick, I. (1943). Work and the pleasure principle, *The Psychoanalytic Quarterly*, **12**, 311–29

Herzberg, F. (1966). *Work and the Nature of Man*, Cleveland: World Press

Jahoda, M. (1981). Work, employment and unemployment: values, theories and approaches in social research, *American Psychologist*, **35**(2), 184–91

Jahoda, M. (1982). *Employment and Unemployment: A Social-psychological Analysis*, Cambridge: Cambridge University Press

Kohn, M.L., and Schooler, C. (1983). *Work and Personality: An Inquiry into the Impact of Social Stratification*, Norwood, N.J.: Ablex

Lafitte, P. (1958). *Social Structure and Personality in the Factory*, London: Routledge & Kegan Paul

Lefcourt, H.M. (1976). *Locus of Control*, New York: Wiley

Locke, E.A. (1976). The nature and causes of job satisfaction, in M. Dunnette (ed.), *Handbook of Industrial and Organizational Behavior*, Chicago: Rand McNally

Marx, K. (1844). *Economic and Philosophic Manuscripts of 1844*, Moscow: Progress Publishers, (edition published in 1977)

Maslow, A.H. (1943). A theory of human motivation, *Psychological Review*, **50**, 370–96

Meakin, D. (1976). *Man and Work: Literature and Culture in Modern Society*, London: Methuen

Neff, W.S. (1977). *Work and Human Behavior*, 2nd edition, Chicago: Aldine

O'Brien, G.E. (1982a). Evaluation of the job characteristics theory of work attitudes and performance, *Australian Journal of Psychology*, **34**, 383–401

O'Brien, G.E. (1982b). The relative contribution of perceived skill-utilization and other perceived job attributes to the prediction of job satisfaction: a cross-validation study, *Human Relations*, **35**, 219–37

O'Brien, G.E. (1984a). Group productivity, in M. Gruneberg and T. Wall (eds), *Social Psychology and Organizational Behaviour*, Chichester: Wiley

O'Brien, G.E. (1984b). Locus of control, work and retirement, Chapter 2 in H. Lefcourt (ed), *Research with the Locus of Control Construct*, vol. 3, New York: Academic Press

Oeser, O.A., and Harary, F. (1962). A mathematical model for structural role theory, I, *Human Relations*, **15**, 89–109

Oeser, O.A., and Harary, F. (1964). A mathematical model for structural role theory, II, *Human Relations*, **17**, 3-17

Oeser, O.A., and O'Brien, G.E. (1967). A mathematical model for structural role theory, III, The analyses of group tasks, *Human Relations*, **20**, 83–97

Orpen, C. (1979). The effects of job enrichment on employee satisfaction, motivation, involvement, and performance: a field experiment, *Human Relations*, **32**, 189–217

O'Toole, J. (1978). *Work, Learning and the American Future*, San Francisco: Jossey-Bass

Phares, E.J. (1976). *Locus of Control in Personality*, New Jersey: General Learning Press

Roberts, K.H., and Glick, W. (1981). The job characteristics approach to task design: a critical review, *Journal of Applied Psychology*, **66**, 193–217

Smith, A. (1776). *The Wealth of Nations*, Cannan's 1904 edition published in Chicago by University of Chicago Press

Spector, P.E. (1982). Behavior in organization as a function of employees' locus of control, *Psychological Bulletin*, **91**, 482–97

Tilgher, A. (1930). *Work: What it has Meant to Men through the Ages*, New York: Harcourt Brace

U.S. Department of Health, Education and Welfare (1973). *Work in America*, Cambridge, MA: M.I.T. Press

Warr, P. (1983). Work, jobs and unemployment, *Bulletin of the British Psychological Society*, **36**, 305–11

Weber, M. (1930). *The Protestant Ethic and the Spirit of Capitalism*, London: Allen & Unwin

Weiss, H.M., and Adler, S. (1984). Personality and organizational behavior, in B. Straw and L. Cummings (eds), *Research in Organizational Behavior*, vol. 6, Greenwich, Connecticut: JAI Press

CHAPTER 2

Underemployment and Skill-utilization

Managers have always been concerned to find employees who have the necessary skills to do their jobs. It seems obvious why this is so. Qualified employees perform better than those who are unqualified. Successful selection and placement, however, is not just a matter of rejecting unqualified people. Poor performance and low motivation can occur when people are selected who are overqualified. They are capable but the job is too small for them. In this chapter it is maintained that a relatively unrecognized managerial and social problem is handling these people—the underemployed.

The task of selecting qualified workers is rarely a simple one. Successful selection depends on knowing what skills are required by various jobs and the reliable identification of these skills in prospective employees. The measurement of job requirements and employee skills requires training in job analysis as well as training in the measurement of individual skills and capacities. Training of this kind is specialized and is not generally included in traditional management education. One reason for the development of organizational psychology has been the increased demand for psychologists to teach and administer methods of personnel selection as they have developed methods of job analysis and skill measurement.

There is considerable evidence that shows that psychological methods of selection can improve individual and organizational performance (Cascio, 1978; Dunnette and Borman, 1979), but there is hardly a widescale use of psychologists by organizations—even in countries where the status of psychology is relatively high (Ronen, 1980).

To some extent, this is explainable in terms of the initial financial costs of these procedures and the difficulties involved in applying them to small organizations. But these do not appear to be the main reasons. One explanation of the failure of modern managers to use objective methods of selection is their unawareness of the degree to which their organizations provide jobs that do not fully use the valued skills of employees. Furthermore, there is no general awareness by either managers or unions of the extent to which this underemployment of workers produces low productivity, dissatisfaction and detrimental personality effects. The nature of these effects will be considered in later chapters. The purpose of this chapter is to consider the extent to which underemployment is common in modern organizations and the reasons why. Two main explanations of underemployment will be considered. First, that it is due to increasing educational participation and over-education of the workforce. Second, that it is due to progressive de-skilling of jobs through technological change and managerial practices.

The central aim is to understand the nature of underemployment. If it is a widespread problem then it should concern both employers and employees. Failure to utilize human resources efficiently can potentially affect productivity and profits. This may worry the manager more than the employee but the problem has implications for the employee if underemployment also affects work satisfaction, self-esteem and the capacity to enjoy life outside work. This discussion is not primarily concerned with the underemployment of psychologists. Certainly psychologists could profitably be employed in many organizations to manage underemployment but, in some ways, they also have not been able or willing to deal with the problems of underemployment and skill-utilization. As many psychologists and readers might argue at this point that the central problem of industrial and organization psychology has always been the problem of person–job match, including skill–job match, it is necessary to review briefly the contribution of psychology to the problem of skill-use and underemployment. If underemployment and skill-utilization has already been considered in psychology then obviously it will be superfluous to argue that it is a new problem.

INADEQUATE PSYCHOLOGICAL APPROACHES TO SKILL-UTILIZATION

The importance of matching employee skills to the job is not a new insight. Although not trained as a psychologist, Frederic Taylor recognized the importance of matching employee skills to the job in his system of scientific management (Taylor, 1911). His work is more famous for his principles of job analysis and pay incentives which influenced both management practice and engineering psychology. In practice, these principles led to the simplification of work tasks so they could be learned easily, be efficiently performed, and maintain managerial control over the work process. The improved productivity benefited both managers and owners. Employees also were meant to gain through a reduction in fatigue and an increase in their wages as these increased in proportion to their level of productivity. However, his explanation of scientific management makes it clear that the success of his system depended on selecting workers who had the necessary capacities for the job at hand. In his anecdote about pig- iron handling Taylor selected a man who was able to lift heavy weights well and was prepared to work according to the rules of Taylor's system. In short, he had to be strong, accept direction and be motivated by money.

The importance of proper selection was never developed in subsequent writings and applications of scientific management. Nevertheless, Taylor should be given credit for implicitly recognizing the importance of person–job match for both the employer and the employee. Further development of the principle of selection by matching individual capacities to the demands of the job had to wait until efforts of psychologists during the First and Second World Wars when they laid the foundations of the standard method of selection using objective tests (Cascio, 1978; Dunnette, 1966). However, modern selection methods do not always lead to utilization of human capacities at work. There are a number of reasons for this.

First, these methods may identify a person who has the necessary skills to perform a given job but this does not imply that the job uses that person's skills fully. A qualified accountant or a trained physicist may, for example, apply for a job that requires the ability to perform routine clerical duties. They may both have the necessary scores on tests of clerical aptitude and be selected for the job. From the standpoint of the required job skills, they have skills matched to job demands. But this job–person match is not the same as a person–job match. The skills obtained from training in accountancy or physics are not going to be used in a routine clerical job and the new hirees would soon experience low skill-utilization or underemployment. Experienced selection psychologists will often screen out applicants whose previous training indicates that they have interests and valued skills not required in a given job. But too often this does not happen because the typical application of test methods start with the set of job demands and is influenced by pressures to fill the job without a balancing concern for the individual or the potential motivational losses due to under-utilization.

A second difficulty with traditional methods of personnel selection is that they are more concerned with rejecting people with low ability for the job than with rejecting those who have too much ability. This difficulty remains even when the psychologist considers only applicants who have interests and capacities that are congruent with job demands. They might reject and accountant and physicist for a clerical job but consider a female school leaver with an expressed interest in 'working with figures'. She might be given tests of intelligence, arithmetical reasoning and persistence because these capacities had been shown to predict performance at clerical work. Normally, if her scores fell below a designated cut-off point and her interpersonal skills were judged as being adequate then she would be selected. Yet if the applicant's scores on the tests were extremely high, this would be a reason to say that there was both poor job–person match and poor person–job match. The applicant would be overqualified for the job. Texts on psychological selection rarely pay much attention to this form of mismatch because they concentrate on the rejection of those with inadequate skills.

A final reason why the application of objective methods of selection may not lead to skill-utilization is due to the failure of selection psychologists to realize that organizational structure may prevent people from using their skills. A person may find that a job fully utilizes his or her skills *provided* that there is freedom to do the job in the way they think is best. Often this is not possible if the job is closely supervised or the job is designed so that it requires unnecessary collaboration or interaction with others A number of small group studies have shown that the formal arrangement of tasks in a group setting may severely curtail the ability of group members to use their talents (Kabanoff and O'Brien, 1979a,b; O'Brien and Owens, 1969). This occurs even when the abilities of group members are matched to task requirements. But they cannot use these abilities if the power and task structures prevent them from having sufficient influence over the task process. Personnel psychologists, unfortunately, adopt a limited individual-istic approach to selection which assumes that job performance is entirely predictable from individual capacities and motivation. In acting on this as-sumption they unwittingly select people for tasks where, due to the restrict-ing effects of organizational structure, skill-utilization is low.

Apart from selection psychologists, it might also be argued that psychologists concerned with leadership and work motivation have also placed skill-utilization in the foreground of their theories and applications. In some ways this is true but it appears that the direct study of the psychological consequence of skill-utilization and the lack of it—underemployment—was deemed to be too simple to be worth direct investigation. Instead psychologists have devised complex lists of needs that purport to describe the motivational bases of individual behaviour in organizations. Some, like Maslow's need for 'self-actualization' (Maslow, 1943), Herzberg's 'growth' needs (Herzberg, 1966), Hackman and Oldham's 'growth need strength' (Hackman and Oldham, 1980), or Fiedler's leader needs (Fiedler, 1967, 1978) may be operative when there is optimal skill-utilization but none of these theorists ever quantify skill-utilization or show the relationship be-tween need fulfilment and person–job skill match (O'Brien, 1980; O'Brien and Kabanoff, 1981).

In many ways current theories of leadership and motivation resemble those of one of the earliest industrial psychologists—Elton Mayo. Mayo's rather complex theories of leadership, motivation and work organization were developed in Australia and extended after his experience in North America. He is best known for his interpretation of the Hawthorne stud-ies, and his espousement of the 'human relation' approach to management

(Mayo, 1919, 1933, 1945). He advocated considerate and non-directive styles of supervision in order to promote harmony and avoid conflict. And he also advocated the development of strong interpersonal ties between workers as a means of both satisfying various social needs and inducing high productivity.

Yet job design and attention to skill match was never a central feature of Mayo's thought. This, at first sight, is curious because he was very aware that most factories had repetitive and fatiguing jobs that under-utilized workers. He also believed that workers had little control over work procedures. Strangely, he never tied low skill-utilization and low autonomy to the pathological states such as obsessions and preoccupations (reveries) which he frequently detected in factory employees.

In some of his private correspondence he came close to making this connection, as the following quote shows:

> There is no question but that society will have to give back to the worker some opportunity for self-expression in work and self-control. At the same time, it will be necessary to ensure that collaboration and skill in work are adequately conserved.
>
> (Mayo, in a letter to Willets, January 17, 1923: quoted in Trahair, *The Humanist Temper*, 1984, p. 163)

Instead of directly investigating the relationship between skill-match, productivity and psychological development, May constructed a complex and changing theory of work group productivity based on an original amalgamation of ideas from Janet, Freud, Jung and physiological psychology.

Many of his ideas are still embedded in modern theories of leadership and motivation which, like Mayo's, have become complex and, again, like Mayo's, have failed to focus on skill-utilization. Thus Fiedler's contingency model of leadership compares task- and person-oriented leadership in various situations (Fiedler, 1967). It is an empirically based theory which is able to explain, to a slight extent, variations in group performance as a function of leadership style. But it has nothing to say about what a leader should do to improve the productivity and well-being of group members. Skill-match is not mentioned. A similar lack is evident in another popular theory of leadership—the Vroom–Yetton model of leader decision making (Vroom and Yetton, 1973). At least the theories of work motivation mentioned earlier have tried to identify task attributes that promote productivity and psychological health. Unfortunately none of them have focused on skill-utilization (with the notable exception of Kornhauser, 1965).

The reasons for this neglect are not obvious. In the case of Mayo, his biographer (Trahair, 1984) shows how his theory was understandable in terms of his early life experiences in Australia and England. This helps explain his choice of concepts but does not go far in explaining why he neglected task variables in favour of complex and vague psychological factors. One simple reason that seems obvious is that Mayo was trained as a clinical psychologist and therefore predisposed to explain behaviour in terms of intrapersonal dynamics. He actually compared the management of workers to the treatment of shell-shocked soldiers. By comparison, one of the main reasons why contemporary psychologists multiply needs, motives and perceptions in their theories is due to a psychological training that has concentrated on individual processes such as learning, perception and cognition. Having no exposure to a training that fits them to see behaviour as a joint function of personality and social structure (which includes tasks as one of its elements), they necessarily have to explain variations in work behaviour in terms of variations in individual attributes alone. Hence a concept such as skill-utilization, which refers to a relationship between elements of the person and elements of the social structure, is a very difficult one for psychologists to incorporate into their theoretical schemes. So far this has been largely a defence against claims that we are raising a problem that has already been treated and solved in organizational psychology. What is the problem?

THE EVIDENCE ON UNDEREMPLOYMENT

A number of writers have provided evidence that an increasing number of employees are finding that their abilities and training are not being utilized in their jobs. Staines and Quinn (1979) analysed changing attitudes of North American employees to their jobs across an eight-year period from 1969 to 1977. In 1969, 27 per cent of those interviewed reported that they had skills from their experience and training that they would like to use but could not on their present jobs. By 1977, the proportion of employees reporting under-utilization of skills had increased significantly to 36 per cent. Cross-sectional surveys of North American employees in the 1970s have also reported high levels of under-utilization. Duncan and Hoffman (1978) found that 42 per cent of employees felt overeducated for their jobs. A survey of clerical workers reported that the majority believed that their skills were not used and they lacked learning opportunities on the job (Grandjean and Taylor, 1980). A similar finding using a clerical sample was found by Burris (1983a, 1983b). A survey of a representative sample of employees in a large Australian city found that a significant proportion of employes felt that their skills did not match their job demands (O'Brien, Dowling and Kabanoff, 1978). Not only was under-utilization of skills a problem across all sections of the workforce. So also was over-utilization of skills. Over-utilization meant that employees reported that they would like their jobs to require less skill. The percentages of employees reporting under- and over-utilization are shown in Table 2.1.

Over the total sample, 38 per cent of employees felt that they were under-utilized. This was estimated by comparing their estimates of how much they wanted to use their skills and training with their estimates of the degree to which their actual job used their skills and training. A surprising result

TABLE 2.1 Percentage of Australian employees from various occupations reporting mismatch between their skills and those required by their jobs. Total sample = 1383

Occupation	Under-utilized (%)	Matched (%)	Over-utilized (%)
Professional	37	37	26
Managerial/ Administration	33	35	32
Clerical	35	32	33
Sales	40	31	29
Transport/ Communications	29	37	34
Trades	45	29	26
Services	39	26	35

(Adapted from O'Brien, Dowling and Kabanoff, 1978, p.233)

was that 30 per cent of the sample felt that the job required a level of skill-utilization that exceeded their desires. Another interesting result was that there was not much difference between occupations in reported skill mismatch. It is commonly assumed that professional and managerial jobs, requiring the highest degrees of skill and training, should provide the highest opportunity for using skills. However, under-utilization of skills in these occupations is only slightly less than that reported for manual trade and personal service occupations.

EXPLANATIONS OF UNDEREMPLOYMENT

A. Overeducation

Within North America a number of social scientists have tried to explain underemployment in terms of the educational level of the workforce. This argument starts by referring to the increasing educational participation of the workforce. Not only are proportionally more people entering high schools, colleges and universities, they are also being educated for a longer period of time than were their parents. There are two major consequences. First, basic skill levels are rising. Second, increased education leads to higher aspirations for jobs that provide challenge, skill-utilization and personal autonomy.

As there is not a general trend to upgrade the skill level of jobs, the argument concludes that there is an increasing mismatch between aggregate job demands and the skill level of employees. The strength of this argument depends on evidence that shows:

1. Educational attainment is positively correlated with the level of job-related skills.
2. Educational attainment is positively correlated with desires for skill-utilization and personal autonomy.
3. There has been no change in required job skills over time.

As we shall see, not all writers have been able to assemble evidence relevant to all three of these propositions. One of the most articulate of the writers on underemployment and education is O'Toole, who is a social anthropologist by training. His concern about underemployment as a major social problem began with his chairmanship of a task force that submitted a report to the secretary of the U.S. Department of Health, Education and Welfare. This report, published in 1973, was titled *Work in America.* Based on literature reviews and commissioned studies, it examined the way in which work determined the health and social adjustment of employees. Some of these commissioned studies were published in a separate volume (O'Toole, 1974). After finding that a considerable number of North Americans were dissatisfied with their jobs, the original report concluded that this dissatisfaction resulted in lowered productivity, high stress, and poor health both physical and mental. What is most relevant is their explanation of low satisfaction:

> Dull, repetitive, seemingly meaningless tasks, offering little challenge or autonomy, are causing discontent among workers at all occupational levels. This is not so much because work itself has greatly changed, indeed one of the main problems is that work has not changed fast enough to keep up with the rapid and widescale changes in worker attitudes, aspirations and values. A general increase in their educational and economic status had placed many American workers in a position where having an interesting job is now as important as having a job that pays well.
>
> (*Work in America*, 1973, pp. xv, xvi)

The report itself does refer to a limited number of empirical studies to support its conclusions, but is open to criticism in that the range of studies is limited and often the studies themselves are not suitable for making definite causal judgements about the determinants of job satisfaction and performance. This is not to discount the value of the report which was a significant attempt to marshal the available evidence on the relationship between work, health and productivity. Nor are the studies referred to in the report to be discarded for at least they show consistency in finding that job attributes are associated with many indicators of health and performance.

The report did not lead to any significant changes in policy by the U.S. government although it helped to maintain interest in the topics of job satisfaction, underemployment and job enrichment. O'Toole was disappointed in the failure of others to develop a comprehensive theory about the utilization of human resources in the workplace. He was also disappointed by the academic concern with narrow topics and methodological issues. He seemed to be looking for an integration of the social science disciplines of psychology, economics and political science that could be applied to the development of national policies about human resources. In a later book, *Work, Learning and the American Future*, he tried to remedy this lack. He returns to the theme of underemployment and claims that it is a major social problem in both socialist and capitalist nations.

> in socialist and capitalist nations alike, increasing numbers of highly qualified workers are unable to find jobs that require their skills and training. Thus, many individuals do take jobs that can be performed just as adequately by workers who have far lower levels of educational attainment.
>
> (O'Toole, 1977, p. 36)

O'Toole's arguments are not accompanied by much evidence. His conclusions therefore cannot be accepted as a rigorous demonstration of the effects of education on underemployment but are valuable to the extent that he provides a lucid presentation of the possible effects of increasing underemployment on national productivity and employee health. He could be right in his conclusions but further evidence is needed. If he is right then effective management will need to change organizations for the sake of both productivity and employee well-being.

A more quantitative approach was used by Berg (1970). Using United States 1950 and 1960 census data, he identified a drift of higher educated people into jobs with relatively low educational requirements. He measured job requirements using the United States Employment Service's estimates of 'general educational development' (GED). The GED provided ratings on three abilities—reasoning, mathematics and language. He used a somewhat arbitrary method of transforming job GED scores into required years of schooling and then compared the actual educational level of job incumbents with the educational level required by their jobs. He found that, over time, there was an increasing disparity between required and actual educational requirements. This was especially true for relatively highly educated employees. This group were increasingly finding themselves in jobs for which they were overeducated.

Berg extended his analyses in a later publication (Berg, Freedman and Freeman, 1978). Using additional survey material, he found that 23 per cent of employees had jobs which required lower education than that they had actually obtained. Rumberger (1981) examined trends across 1960–76 and found similar results while Freeman (1976) found increasingly low skill-utilization for college graduates.

Berg reported a decrease in the growth of U.S. professional and managerial jobs in the 1970s together with an increase in the number of tertiary students. Associated with these trends was an increase in the number of graduates reporting low skill-utilization. In 1958, 58 per cent of males and 70 per cent of females said that their jobs used 'much of their training'. By 1972 these figures had dropped to 34 per cent for males and 57 per cent for females.

It is difficult to make many firm conclusions from these studies on overeducation. The evidence provides some support for believing that college graduates in the United States are reporting, over time, fewer opportunities for using their abilities and education in the jobs that they are able to find. But it is debatable whether this is due to overeducation if this means that education is increasing their skill levels while required job skills remain constant. The common measure of skill used, the index of general educational development (GED), has not been shown to be a reliable or valid measure of skill (Spenner, 1983). Hence it cannot be accepted either as a measure of skills acquired by education or as a measure of skill required by jobs. If one dispenses with the GED as a measure of skill it is possible to look at the discrepancy between education acquired by job incumbents and the median educational level required for entrance to their jobs. But this discrepancy, which appears to be on the increase, strictly says little about underemployment. Education may not necessarily lead to increases in valued skills or in job-related skills. More evidence is needed. Furthermore, due to the common practice of employers to raise educational standards for entry (credentialism), the use of required education as an index of required skill level is very suspect (Burris, 1983).

Thus the observed association between perceptions of underemployment or poor skill-use and educational mismatch may be attributable to other reasons. It could be due to the fact that level of education is positively associated with higher aspirations or work values. In a longitudinal study of students, it was found that the length of education increased students' desire for skill-utilization, autonomy and variety in their eventual jobs (Dowling and O'Brien, 1981). This suggests that it is possible for increasing education to increase reported underemployment by raising students' expectations or values rather than their objective skill levels. A definite answer requires longitudinal studies which measure education, values, objective skill levels of employees and required skill levels of jobs.

Some writers have claimed that underemployment is not to be understood in terms of education at all. Thus Staines and Quinn (1979), in one of the largest studies on underemployment, found that increases in perceptions of underemployment were unrelated to education.

Workers who feel that their levels of formal education exceed those required by their jobs seem likely to possess skills that cannot be used on their present jobs. 'Overeducation' (or under-utilization of education) might, thus, be expected to increase in tandem with under-utilization of skills. This prediction, however, is not confirmed by the 1969 and 1977 data. Data from these two years show no increase whatsoever in the proportion of workers with more education than their jobs required. Consequently, the increase in perceived underutilization of skills may have originated outside of formal education.

(Staines and Quinn, 1979, p. 9)

One other source, besides education, for understanding underemployment is actual change in the nature of jobs. Instead of people increasing their skills over time, it is possible that jobs might have become progressively de-skilled due to technological change and managerial practices.

B. Underemployment and De-skilling of Jobs

Some theorists (e.g. Braverman, 1974) have suggested that jobs in capitalistic societies are being 'de-skilled' through technological change and deliberate managerial strategies designed to maximize managerial control over the production process. In order to assess this view, it is necessary to find objective information about the changes in the skill level of jobs over time. This information is sparse, despite its obvious relevance for training and manpower planning. Our purpose in this section is to examine the available evidence on the effects of technological change. These changes can lead to de-skilling in two ways. First, it can reduce the skill requirements of existing jobs and, second, it can lead to complete de-skilling by increasing unemployment. One of the best summaries of available evidence on this is assembled by Rothwell and Zegveld (1979).

They initially point out that any considered judgement on the determinants of changing employment patterns has to evaluate whether the determinants are temporary or long-term. As far as unemployment is concerned, the temporary determinants may be due to temporary cyclical factors due to periodic economic slumps which reduce the demand for labour. Long-term determinants are called structural and some of their sources have identified technical change as the main determinant. Technical changes may displace labour in two ways. Whole job processes or industries may change from being labour intensive to machine based by technology which takes over the main productive tasks. Alternatively, the progressive introduction of new pieces of technology into existing labour-based organizations may gradually reduce labour requirement. The net effect of both types of changes should be increasing unemployment. Certainly OECD evidence shows that there is a worldwide increase in unemployment in manufacturing industry. Since 1973 there has been an increase in unemployment up to 1978 and this has continued into the 1980s. From 1950 to 1965 there was a gradual increase in employment, followed by a period of stability (1965–73). The recent increase in unemployment has not been accompanied by a decline in industrial output. There has actually been a growth in output so it is unlikely that increased unemployment can be explained by short-term changes in demand for industrial products. Using a study by Soete on OECD countries, Rothwell and Zegveld identified technical change as a major cause of unemployment. It appears that western countries, due to increased international competition, have increased the rate of job-displacing, labour-saving, technical change. The direct effects of technical change were further examined by Rothwell and Zegveld by case studies of various industries. The majority of industries examined showed de-skilling, 50 per cent showed increasing job loss while, at the same time, there was a need for higher level management skills.

Loss of employment seemed to be especially important for industries and service occupations affected by microprocessors. The main areas affected were textiles, automated manufacturing industries, printing, clerical work, telecommunications and watchmaking. Job losses occurred at both non-managerial and managerial levels. Fewer managers were needed and those that remained tended to have their skill requirements increased. Some potential gains in employment were expected due to the growth of firms able to use modern technology to introduce new, innovative products but no quantitative estimate was made. The general tone of the report, however, is negative. There is occurring job loss due to technological change and this is likely to increase. Furthermore, there is progressive de-skilling.

'There generally exists a growing mismatch between skills and job opportunities.' (Rothwell and Zegveld, 1979, p. 169). Unfortunately, this conclusion is not justified by data that report detailed job analyses or employee skill levels. The evidence is based on case studies of industries and types of technology. Inferences are made about required skill levels on the basis of 'expert' opinions and armchair speculation.

The main forms of technology that could lead to decreases in both underemployment and employment are listed below.

1. *Computers*. Both mainframe and mini-computers can be extensively used in industries to monitor and control a 'continuous-flow' production process. Also numerical control computers are being programmed to do work that was previously performed by skilled tradesmen. As costs of the micro-electronic control elements required are decreasing, they are likely to be introduced quickly into small and medium scale production units.
2. *Computer aided design systems*. These systems allow engineers to use a computer to develop designs and thus reduce time and the use of industrial designers. They can now be linked to computer programs which instruct numerically-controlled tools on how to make the required parts. After the design has been worked out a computer schedules the whole production including ordering raw materials, making the component parts and monitoring the output.

3. *Industrial robots.* Robots are in an early stage of development but their use is increasing in the vehicle building and metal working industries. The obvious advantage of robots is their reliability, precision and cost. Although relatively expensive to introduce, within a few years they can pay their way be eliminating the need for unskilled and semi-skilled workers. The main effect of robots is likely to be unemployment but they could also reduce the skill requirements of the available jobs in factories which use robots.

All of these developments could have the net effect of de-skilling jobs and increasing unemployment. Whether or not they do have these effects has yet to be investigated in a systematic, empirical manner. This is not a conclusion shared by most writers who are concerned with de-skilling of jobs. Most would agree with Braverman (1974) that the process of de-skilling is well advanced and can be readily documented.

Braverman claims that there has been a progressive de-skilling of jobs since the beginning of the industrial revolution. The major impetus for this de-skilling has come from scientific management, as expounded by Frederic Taylor. Unlike the schools associated with Munsterberg and Mayo, Taylor changed the methods of designing jobs. Psychological schools since the 1900s have been concerned not with jobs, according to Braverman, but with the adjustment of workers to jobs designed by industrial engineers. This is something of a simplification as there always has been, within psychology, a critique of job design practices. Nevertheless, it is true that the psychological bias has led to a majority of writers being more concerned about motivation, adjustment and attitudes than with the nature of jobs.

Taylor was motivated by ideology and not by science, according to Braverman. He was seeking 'an answer to the specific problem of how best to control alienated labor—that is to say labor power that is bought and sold' (Braverman, 1974, p. 90). Taylor himself accepted that it was management's right and duty to control workers and the work process. Control of workers was not to exert power for power's sake but to ensure that they did their jobs well. The problem with workers was that they often did not use the best methods of working. Perhaps, more importantly, they were inclined to restrict their output by "systematic soldiering". This practice was one that led workers to restrict their output in order to preserve their own interests. The use of piecework systems of payment often meant that increased output would result in a new rate of payment being introduced to restrict wages. Hence the readjustment of rates led to a rational decision to restrict output because, in the long run, increased effort would not lead to significant increases in money.

To correct this problem, Taylor analysed the jobs done and presented management with a descriptive summary of the knowledge required. He then selected workers, on a rough judgement of capacity, who would follow the most efficient method of doing the job. Management thus assumed control of workers' actions and control of the knowledge required. The worker became and operator who was rewarded with increased wages for his adjustment to the new system.

The consequence of scientific management, Braverman concludes, is the erosion of craftsmanship. Craftsmanship involves both skill in performing a complex set of tasks and detailed knowledge about the tasks and raw materials. Thus craftsmanship was destroyed in two ways. Firstly, the tasks required became less skilled and more segmented. Secondly, the knowledge of the process was given to management. All the worker had to know was the specific procedures required by the de-skilled tasks. Braverman does not give information about skill requirements over time. Rather, he relies on selected descriptions of developments in job analysis such as time and motion studies and modern methods of design.

He does acknowledge one attempt, by Horowitz and Herrenstadt (1966) to review the literature and provide objective information about skill levels and automation. They concluded that there had been little change in skill requirements in the U.S.A between 1949 and 1965. Braverman dismisses their study without argument.

He describes the study as 'useless', 'arid', and 'unrewarding'. This is not argument and the study, because of its range and detail, deserves some comment. A selected number of industries were chosen on the basis of whether there had been significant changes in processes or products between 1949–65. Three manufacturing industries considered were meat-processing, rubber tyres and tubes, and machine-shop trades. The non-manufacturing industries were medical services and banking. Versions of the U.S. employment service's Dictionary of Occupational Titles (DOB) were used to measure work requirements. Job information measured referred to required job training, specific vocational preparation, aptitudes and temperaments required by workers for successful work performance. The measure closest to skill requirements is the worker function rating; the level of skill required for working with people, things or data is ranked on a 7- or 8-point scale.

The measures appear comprehensive but have a number of weaknesses—some of which are acknowledged by the authors. These are:

1. Any change over time may reflect better information and not real changes.
2. The number of occupational titles decreased over time, thus causing doubts about the comparability of some jobs.
3. Aptitudinal requirements are expressed in terms of the extent to which a given proportion of the population contains the aptitude. Hence, changes may be contaminated by overall population changes.

4. Changes in educational requirements may reflect changes in entry standards not changes in the jobs.
5. Worker functions are not rated on any one skill dimension but reflect an imprecise global rating.
6. Unknown rater reliability.
7. Unspecified validation studies of how well the measures actually predict performance.

These difficulties did not prevent the authors from concluding that there was no significant effect of technological change on job skill levels.

Inspection of their results shows a tendency for educational requirements to rise, a small increase in the level of skill required by higher level jobs and a small decrease in the level of skill required by lower level jobs. However, because of the measures used no definite conclusion can be made. The study would have been more useful if the authors had used valid skill measures and had selected industries on the basis of a specific technological innovation, (e.g. computerization) or better still, matched organizations where one had adopted a new technology and the other had not. This study neither supports nor refutes Braverman's thesis.

He preferred a study by Bright (1966) who, after analysing a number of automated factories, constructed a theoretical model that showed how skill requirements varied according to the level of automation. On the basis of his case studies, he postulated that job skill requirements were a function of the degree of automation. Moderate increases in the degree of mechanization would increase skill requirements for operators or process workers as well as for the relatively small number of maintenance and managerial jobs. However, the average skill requirements would fall sharply with large amounts of mechanization.

The work by Bright provides a theoretical model for investigating the effect of technology on skill but, at present, has not been tested. To do this would be difficult because it would require the measurement of the degree of mechanization, together with a detailed examination of job skill requirements. Although his conclusions tend to support Braverman's deskilling thesis, they cannot be accepted as being based on strong evidence. What then is the evidence for Braverman's thesis? Much of his book is based on an historical analysis of the procedures of scientific management and its later development. Some case studies are used to illustrate how deskilling occurs through the Tayloristic redesign of jobs. What is omitted, and this seems crucial, is evidence showing the degree to which these 'scientific management' methods are being employed in industry. Although intuitively plausible, the main thesis is unproven.

On the basis of the small amount of evidence available, Braverman forecasts a new epoch of managerial control and worker enslavement.

> For the worker, the concept of skill is traditionally bound up with craft
> mastery—that is to say, the combination of knowledge of materials and pro-
> cesses with the practised manual dexterities required to carry on a specific
> branch of production. The breakup of craft skills and the reconstruction of
> production as a collective or social process have destroyed the traditional con-
> cept of skill, and opened up only one way for mastery over labour processes to
> develop: in and through scientific, technical and engineering knowledge. But
> the extreme concentration of this knowledge in the hands of management and
> its closely-associated staff organizations has closed this avenue to the working
> population. What is left to workers is a reinterpreted and woefully inadequate
> concept of skill: a specific dexterity, a limited and repetitious operation.
>
> (Braverman, 1974, pp. 444–5)

This loss to the worker cannot, for Braverman, be restored by parliamen-
tary forms of workers' participation or workers' control. These forms still
leave workers dependent on 'experts'. What is necessary is both the return
of technical knowledge to workers and a new collective form of production.

In evaluating Braverman, it is necessary to point out that he is postulating
an 'ideal' model of a process of industrial de-skilling. New technology, in
combination with the principles of scientific management, is introduced in
order to maximize profit and control the labour process. As a result, jobs are
simplified and workers increasingly become operators while knowledge of
the total work process is transferred to management. Dealing with an 'ideal'
model, Braverman is not concerned with exceptions. Although various parts
of the model are illustrated by examples and case studies the evidence is
meagre. The central outcome—decreasing skill requirements—has not been
clearly demonstrated. This is the centre of the model, and if shown to be
true for most non-management workers, has important implications for job
attitudes, performance and personality.

C. Critiques of Braverman

Most sociological criticisms have not focused directly on Braverman's
central question. Apart from a few case studies showing increased skill requirements for some jobs (Jones, 1982) the issues addressed have been tan-
gential. A recent critique illustrates this point. Braverman is criticized for
oversimplifying Marxist theories about the transformation of the capitalist
labour process (Elger, 1982), and overstating the degree of de-skilling in
the nineteenth-century (Penn, 1983). One critic does point out that more
evidence is needed to show either a rise or fall in working class skills but
provides no relevant information (Lee, 1982). The largest critique is contained in the writings of More (1980, 1982) but the discussion does not
directly focus on the evidence for de-skilling. More points out that labels
such as skilled and unskilled may not refer to real skill levels but may be
socially constructed by workers or managers. This point is reasonable and

is substantiated by some examples from nineteenth century Britain. But no way is provided for disentangling 'genuine' from socially constructed skill. It could also be pointed out that arguments based on nineteenth-century industry are not necessarily appropriate for the twentieth century.

Braverman's de-skilling thesis remains as a theory in need of support. Certainly he did not muster sufficient evidence to show that there is a general trend within industrialized societies towards a widespread reduction in job skill requirements. It is possible that such a trend is occurring. It is also possible that the general skill level of jobs is increasing. This is maintained by some writers who believe that automation is eliminating low skilled routine work. The new jobs, they claim, require new and complex skills (Kerr *et al.*, 1969; Bell, 1973). Again, the evidence is incomplete. A recent review of the available studies on changing skill levels at work shows that research is needed which measures changes in job skills across a wide range of occupations (Spenner, 1982). Within particular industries, such as printing, there is evidence for de-skilling (Wallace and Kalleberg, 1982). However, there is also some evidence that technology has recently created jobs that do require high level skills such as computer programming. The fundamental requirement for improved evidence is satisfactory measures of measures of skill. But what is skill?

THE NATURE OF SKILL

Skills are said to be possessed by people. When we say that someone is skilled it generally means that they are able to perform a task well. Skill refers then to some specific actions that are done in order to complete a task.

Considered in this way it is confusing to talk of general skill levels. Skill is specific to a given task. A person can be skilled with respect to driving a car but unskilled with respect to maintaining car engines. Thus a concept of skill which is useful must refer to task attributes. But would not this make discourse about skill impossible? It would if every different task required different skills. But it might be manageable if tasks could be grouped into sets on the basis of the similarity in the actions required.

This could lead to the observation of 'skilled behaviour' which would seek to identify the similarities and differences in required behaviours across a wide range of tasks. At present such an observational programme is in its infancy. One of the reasons it has not developed is the absence of a comprehensive and objective classification of behaviour patterns and task structures.

Another possibility is to link skills to tasks via concepts of aptitude or ability. Psychologists have developed measures of ability which predict job performance. The most detailed information on abilities required for task performance is provided by personnel-selection psychologists but the information is far from complete. Specific abilities have been identified for specific occupations, such as routine clerical jobs, but there is as yet no complete taxonomy of abilities and tasks (Dunnette and Borman, 1979). Psychologists are still trying to identify an economical classification of abilities. There is even less agreement about the way in which tasks can be classified.

If we did have a comprehensive classification of abilities and tasks, it would be possible to identify the abilities required for each type of task. In order to see if an employee used his or her abilities in a given job it would be necessary to first measure the employee's level of ability on each of the abilities $(A_1 - A_N)$.

Ability	Employee ability level	Ability level required for job
A_1	a_1	b_1
A_2	a_2	b_2
.	.	.
.	.	.
.	.	.
A_N	a_n	b_n

We would then, as shown above, enter the level of ability of the employee in a column $(a_1 \ldots a_n)$. By empirical means we would establish the level of ability required to perform the job $(b_1 \ldots b_n)$. The degree of ability-utilization for an employee would be obtained by summing the difference $(a_i - b_i)$ over all abilities, i.e.

$$\sum_{i=1}^{i=n}(a_i - b_i)$$

This might be possible but some difficult problems would be encountered even if ability and job classifications were obtained. Some of these difficulties are:

1. The psychological effect of discrepancies might depend on the degree to which the employee valued each ability.
2. For complex tasks, it is not possible to identify the absolute level of ability required for each task. If, for example, a task requires two abilities, A_1 and A_2, then it is possible for two people to perform the task equally well, even though they have quite different levels of these abilities. One person could do it well with high A_1 and low A_2, while the other does equally well with low A_1 and high A_2.
3. This approach tends to assume that abilities can be equated with skills. However, it is quite possible that someone has the required ability for performing a task but is unable to do that task. Welford (1978, 1980)

has pointed out that there is a fundamental difference between capacities or abilities and task strategies. People with equivalent capacities may differ widely in the efficiency of their strategies or methods for performing tasks. The essence of skilled performance is defined by efficient strategies of task completion and therefore the study of skill must identify both the relationships between abilities and strategies, as well as the relation between strategies and task performance. This objection is hard to argue with but if taken seriously would mean that meaningful discussions of skill-utilization would have to await the outcome of a large and laborious research project investigating the relationships between capacities, strategies and job performance.

Until this information appears and the other difficulties of measuring skill-match objectively are overcome, it is necessary to use imperfect measures of skill-match. This does not prevent us examining the effects of perceived skill-utilization on individual performance and personality. Although perceptions of job attributes are subject to various sources of bias, there is considerable evidence showing that these perceptions largely reflect objective job attributes.

OBJECTIVE AND PERCEIVED JOB ATTRIBUTES

Job Perceptions and Social Cues

The use of measures of perceived skill-utilization as measures of objective skill-utilization assumes that there is a fairly strong correspondence between perceptual and objective measures. Until recently, this assumption was rarely questioned. Most researchers who examined the effects of job content on outcomes such as satisfaction, motivation and performance assumed that employees' perceptions of their jobs reflected objective job characteristics. The simple paradigm used can be depicted schematically. (Figure 2.1).

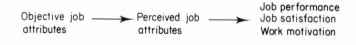

FIGURE 2.1   Paradigm 1

This paradigm assumes that research which shows that perceived job attributes determine job outcomes is a reasonable basis for arguing that objective job attributes determine the same outcomes. Obviously, this depends on a demonstration that there is a strong relationship between perceived and actual job attributes.

The question here is whether employees are capable of accurately describing their jobs. If they say that their jobs do not use their skills, or are boring, or lack opportunities for autonomy, are they responding to their actual jobs? It may be the case that their responses just reflect their mood, personality or the social norms prevalent within their workplace. Some authors have argued that employee perceptions of jobs are social constructions which only partly reflect the objective nature of their jobs (Pfeffer, 1981; Salancik and Pfeffer, 1977, 1978). They maintain that employee descriptions also reflect the information provided by coworkers, supervisors, and employees in other occupations that are used as a frame of reference for making judgements about their own particular jobs.

A number of studies support this social information approach (e.g. Griffin 1983; O'Connor and Barrett, 1980; O'Reilly and Caldwell, 1979; Weiss and Shaw, 1979; White and Mitchell, 1979). Prior information about a job from supervisors or coworkers can affect an individual's perception of a job even after job performance. If this information leads the job incumbents to believe that their jobs are challenging and require initiative, then they are more likely to report that the jobs have autonomy, variety and social significance than those incumbents who are provided with information inducing expectations that the jobs are routine and boring. The extent to which social cues are used to shape job perceptions varies across individuals and dependence on social cues is greatest for those who are low on self-esteem and high on field dependence (Weiss and Shaw, 1979; Weiss and Nowicki, 1981).

These studies suggest that the simple paradigm depicted earlier needs to be modified. The social information studies do not show that the causal relationship between objective and perceived job attributes has to be omitted. None of the studies has shown that job perceptions are social constructions entirely based on informational cues present in the work environment. When objective job attributes are varied as well as social cues both factors have been shown to affect job perceptions (Griffin 1983; O'Reilly and Caldwell, 1979; Weiss and Shaw, 1979; White and Mitchell, 1979).

What social information processing research indicates is that a different paradigm is necessary for understanding the relationship between job attributes and job outcomes. A more adequate paradigm is shown in Figure 2.2. Although not directly varied in any social cue study, ability of the job incumbent is also likely to affect the perception of certain job attributes. If employees are overqualified for a job because of ability they are more likely to describe the job as routine and lacking skill-utilization than those employees whose abilities match job requirements. Another variable that could distort job perceptions which need investigation is the information sources that the employee is exposed to before entering a job setting. Expectations gained from education, training and prior job experiences are likely at least in the short term, to affect employee job descriptions.

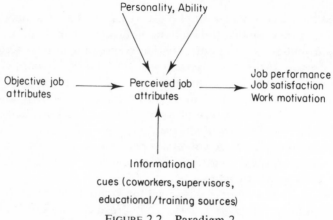

FIGURE 2.2   Paradigm 2

Further information is also needed about the relative contribution of objective job attributes and non-job factors in determining perceived job attributes. Recent reviews of the social information research (Blau and Katerberg, 1982; Thomas and Griffin, 1983) suggests that the degree of correspondence between objective and perceived job attributes depends on factors other than employee personality and social cues. Two important factors are firstly, the length of job experience and secondly, the job attribute being described. Most of the evidence which shows that personality and social cues significantly distort job perceptions comes from short-term laboratory experiments. The subjects are generally placed in a situation where they have to perform novel tasks for a short time and obey the instructions of an experimenter who has considerable power because of his or her professional status. Naturally, subjects are likely to lack the information, time experience and confidence to describe their tasks accurately. Hence, it is not surprising that they are receptive to 'outside' information about the nature of their tasks.

Thomas and Griffin (1983) compared laboratory and field studies and found that the effect of social cues upon job perceptions was much weaker in field studies. In field studies employees had considerable experience with job activities and thus were likely to be resistant to information about their jobs which was inconsistent with evidence derived from their own activity. Hence, attempts by managers, for example, to 'talk up' the job by stressing its significance, importance and challenge are unlikely to alter job perceptions and related work motivation if the employees know from experience that their jobs require little skill and self-direction. However, informational pressures such as these might be more successful in altering perceptions of job attributes which relate, not to the actual content of the job, but rather to the social context in which the job is done. There is some evidence for this assertion as Griffin (1983) found that supervisory cues affected employees' perceptions of social interaction and friendship opportunities more than their perceptions of variety, autonomy and feedback.

In summary, the social information models of task design have not shown that it is unreasonable to assume that employee job perceptions are significantly determined by objective job attributes. However, they do show that these perceptions can be influenced by social cues in the work environment and personality variables such as self-esteem and independence. These social cues and personality factors are likely to have most effect in situations which are novel, unstructured and temporary. They are likely to have the least effect on job perceptions about actual job content made by employees who have had considerable experience with their jobs.

EVIDENCE FOR CORRESPONDENCE BETWEEN OBJECTIVE AND PERCEIVED JOB ATTRIBUTES

The previous section reviewed evidence identifying factors that can distort employee judgements about their jobs. Although this evidence does not show that job perceptions are entirely explainable in terms of social cues and personality, stronger evidence is necessary to show that employee judgements are reasonable, albeit imperfect, indices of objective job characteristics. There are four different types of studies that can be marshalled to support this view. In order, these studies show:

1. A high positive correspondence between employee and expert job descriptions.
2. A high positive correspondence between objective task processes or technology and employee job descriptions.
3. Manipulation of job attributes results in significant changes in employee job descriptions.
4. The relationship between objective job attributes and outcomes such as job satisfaction or work motivation closely corresponds to the relationship, for the same jobs, between perceived job attributes and the same outcome measures.

The evidence for each of these conclusions is reviewed briefly in the following sections.

A. Comparison of Expert and Employee Job Descriptions

Over fifteen studies have compared employee ratings of their job with those made by supervisors, peers or trained observers. The majority of these studies have required both employees and experts to describe the same jobs on the main dimensions of the Job Diagnostic Survey (Hackman and Oldham, 1975, 1976). These dimensions are skill-variety, task significance, task identity, autonomy and feedback. For studies using these dimensions, Fried and Ferris (1984) reported that the median correlation between employee perceptions and expert ratings was 0.63. Using scales measuring skill-utilization and influence, O'Brien (1982c) reported correlations of 0.51 and 0.82 respectively.

It is clear that there are significant and positive correlations between employee and expert judgements but the correlation is not perfect and the degree of agreement depends on the particular job attribute being rated. A major weakness of these types of studies is that they assume that experts are accurate judges of objective job attributes. Like employees their judgements may also reflect, to some extent, bias due to social cues, ability and personality. While these studies lend some support to the view that there is an objective bias to employee job perceptions they cannot be used to claim strong support without additional studies showing high correspondence between expert descriptions and objective job attributes.

B. Technology and Perceived Job Attributes

Organizational technologies vary in the extent that they require routine activities organized by fixed rules about the distribution of people, positions and tasks. Some technologies, such as car assembly lines, have a high proportion of low skill routine tasks. Other technologies, like those utilized by hospitals for patient care, have jobs with relatively high skill and variety. Hence it might be expected that employee job perceptions would vary across technologies. This was shown to be true by Rousseau (1977, 1978) who used Thompson's classification of technologies to describe 19 work units in three different organizations. Thompson (1967) distinguished between long-linked, mediating and intensive technologies. Long-linked or serially independent technologies are exemplified by mass production assembly lines where tasks are simple, structured and performed in a strict order. Mediating technologies also have standardized procedures but the procedures may very depending on the type of input, material or clients. An example would be banks or insurance offices. Finally, intensive technologies have few standardized procedures and modify the work process continuously as the product or goal changes. An example of this technology would be found in research and development organizations.

Rousseau found systematic differences in employee job perceptions across these three kinds of technology. The lowest levels of skill-variety, task identity, task significance and autonomy were reported by employees in long-linked technologies. She also found that job perceptions were stronger predictors of job satisfaction and motivation than technology type. Her analyses supported the conclusion that technology determines employee attitudes indirectly via the direct effects of technology upon employee job perceptions.

Other relevant evidence for the effect of work organization or technology upon employee perceptions comes from some small group studies (Kabanoff and O'Brien, 1979a, 1979b; O'Brien and Owens, 1969). In these experiments, objective skill-utilization was varied by imposing cooperation structures that either facilitated or impeded the use of group member abilities. Collaborative groups, requiring a high degree of task sharing, prevented members from fully using their skills whereas groups requiring coordination or task sequencing facilitated utilization of skills. Perceptions of skill-utilization made by group members were significantly higher in coordinated than in collaborative structures. The studies on technology and job perceptions do show that perceptions vary with objective differences in work organization. However, they do not show the degree of correspondence between perceived and objective job attributes because technology was measured on global attributes of work organizations and not on attributes of specific jobs.

C. Manipulation of Job Attributes

There is considerable evidence from both laboratory and field studies to show that manipulation of objective job attributes produces changes in job perceptions. The large majority of these studies have examined job perceptions as a function of enriched and unenriched jobs. Enriched jobs generally are defined as those where the tasks are high on the component attributes of the Job Diagnostic Survey (Hackman and Oldham, 1975). These dimensions are skill-variety, task identity, task significance, autonomy and feedback. Unenriched jobs are relatively low on these attributes.

Laboratory studies have consistently shown that subjects performing enriched tasks have considerably higher job perceptions with respect to the JDS attributes than subjects performing unenriched tasks (Farr, 1976; Kim, 1980; White and Mitchell, 1979; O'Reilly and Caldwell, 1979; Terborg and Davis, 1982; Umstot, Bell and Mitchell, 1976; Weiss and Shaw, 1979). Similarly, field studies where objective job attributes were manipulated also show consequent variations in job perceptions (Greene, 1981; Griffin, 1983; Orpen, 1979). Few of these studies enable the reader to assess directly the strength of the relationship between objective and perceived job attributes. However, Griffin (1983) reported that objective differences in job attributes accounted for, on average, 41 per cent of the variance in perceived variety, 42 per cent of the variance in perceived autonomy, 43 per cent of the variance in perceived feedback, and 44 per cent of variance in perceived identity or 'wholeness'.

Not all studies have been successful in producing changes across a wide range of job perceptions (Frank and Hackman, 1975; Hackman, Pearce and Wolfe, 1978; Wall and Clegg, 1981). In these studies, the partial success in producing changes in job perceptions could have been due to weak manipulations or the measurement of perceptions too soon after manipulation of objective job attributes. Despite this, the majority of research shows that employees are reasonably accurate in their perception of job changes. One difficulty with this research is that the manipulation of job content is generally made by the investigator using personal judgements about what is enriched or unenriched. Although definite changes in attributes such as variety and autonomy were made, there was no objective measure report of the amount of change. In future, it would be desirable for changes in objective attributes to be measured using indices such as those developed for variety (Globerson and Crossman, 1976) and influence (O'Brien, Biglan and Penna, 1972).

So far all studies have concentrated on the job attributes described by the Job Diagnostic Survey. Hence there is little evidence on the effect of changes in job skill level on perceptions of skill-utilization. Skill-utilization is a central attribute, as has already been maintained, which is not included in the JDS (O'Brien, 1982a, 1982b, 1983). Objective skill-utilization changes when the skills required for a job change while employee skill remains constant. It also changes when required job skills are constant and employee skill changes. Hence objective manipulations must measure required job skills or employee skills or both. One study that did do this manipulated task difficulty by demonstrating that the ability level required to do easy and hard tasks was substantially different (O'Brien and Pere, 1985). When different tasks that varied in required ability were given to the same group of subjects, there were substantial differences in perceived skill-utilization. After controlling for the order of task presentation, perceived skill-utilization was significantly higher for difficult tasks than for relatively easy tasks (Pere, 1981). This study also compared the relative contribution of self-esteem and objective skill-utilization on perceived skill-utilization. Previous research has reported that self-esteem is one of the most important personality variables determining job perceptions. It was found that high self-esteem subjects perceived more skill-utilization than low self-esteem subjects. However, objective differences in tasks were about three times stronger predictors of perceived skill-utilization than self-esteem.

There is a need for more studies that manipulate job attributes in order to assess the accuracy of job perceptions. They should, unlike most studies discussed, measure objective job attributes and establish the degree to which job perceptions are determined by objective, informational and personality factors. At present, there is substantial evidence to show that job perceptions are significantly determined by objective job attributes. The actual strength of this relationship cannot be specified precisely as estimates, when quoted, vary with job attributes, samples and methods. All that can be said is that objective variations in job attributes account for between 20 and 70 per cent of variance in job perceptions.

D. Objective Job Attributes, Perceived Job Attributes and Job Outcomes

A final set of studies provide support for the practice of using perceived job attributes as indices of objective job attributes. These studies show that the relationship between objective attributes and outcomes such as satisfaction and work attributes is similar to that between perceived job attributes and the same outcomes. If perceived job attributes were measures that just reflected mood, personality and social cues then this similarity would not hold.

A number of studies have shown that job attribute/outcome relationships are very similar when job attributes are measured by either experts or observers (objective) or by incumbents (perceived). The major outcome measures in these studies have been job satisfaction and intrinsic work motivation (Algera, 1983; Jenkins, Glick and Gupta, 1983; Kiggundu, 1980; Oldham, 1976; Stone and Porter, 1978). This does not mean that these outcome measures may also determine job perception (Adler, Skov and Salolmini, 1985; Caldwell and O'Reilly, 1982). People who believe they are satisfied tend to rate their jobs as higher in variety, autonomy and significance than those who express dissatisfaction—even though satisfied and dissatisfied respondents perform the same task. Temporary moods of satisfaction can predispose people to see their tasks favourably. But this is not an argument that discredits the correspondence between perceived and objective attributes. Nor does it invalidate the evidence that supports a causal relationship from job attributes to outcome measures such as satisfaction. Rather, it indicates that there is reciprocal causation between job perceptions and outcome measures and at least one study has demonstrated that simultaneous reciprocal causation does occur for employees in 'real' organizations (James and Jones, 1980).

The main aim of the previous sections was to show that it is justifiable to assume that measures of employee job responses, for example, perceived skill-utilization, do reflect objective differences in job attributes. It is too

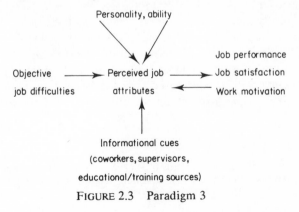

FIGURE 2.3   Paradigm 3

facile to dismiss these perceptual measures because they are also affected by other factors. The whole set of relationships between objective job attributes, perceived attributes and job outcomes is a complex one and requires a complex paradigm. The earlier revised paradigm (Figure 2.2) needs to be amended further on the basis of the research reviewed. A more representative paradigm is shown in Figure 2.3. The two-way arrows represent reciprocal causation. This is not the final word. Subsequent chapters will document the effect of objective and perceived job attributes on personality and ability measures, as well as the reciprocal influence between job attributes and type of information received from the work environment. The main point here though is that there is sufficient evidence to show that self-reports by employees about their jobs do reflect partly the characteristics of their jobs. The association between these two types of measures is substantial although not perfect.

CONCLUSION

This review of underemployment has at least shown that a considerable proportion of the workforce report that their skills are under-utilized. Employee perceptions of under-utilization have been interpreted in various ways. Some writers focus on overeducation while others concentrate on deskilling of jobs. It is likely that both education and job changes affect objective and perceived underemployment. At present, we can conclude that a large proportion of the workforce report that they are underemployed. Their skills are not being fully used in their jobs. Reports of under-utilization may not entirely correspond with the way things really are but it seems reasonable to conclude that employees are reasonably accurate in their perception of the world. Thus it is still possible to proceed by examining the consequences of perceived skill-utilization. There is sufficient evidence to assume that perceived skill-utilization reflects objective skill deficiences in jobs for employees. Furthermore, it is reasonable to assume that perceived skill-utilization is psychologically meaningful. What is seen to be the case, will have psychological effects. But what are these effects? Does the level of skill-utilization reported by employees affect job satisfaction, performance and personality? The effect of underemployment or low skill-utilization upon job satisfaction and performance will be considered in the next chapter. Later chapters will examine the evidence on the effect of skill-match on personality.

REFERENCES

Adler, A., Skov, R.B. and Salolmini, N.J. (1985). Job characteristics and job satisfaction: when cause becomes consequence, *Organizational Behavior and Human Decision Processes*, **35**, 266–78

Algera, J.A. (1983). Objective and perceived task characteristics as a determinant of reactions by task performers, *Journal of Occupational Psychology*, **56**, 95–105
Bell, D. (1973). *The Coming of Post-industrial Society*, New York: Basic Books
Berg, I. (1970). *Education and Jobs: The Great Training Robbery*, New York: Praeger
Berg. I., Freedman, M. and Freeman, M. (1978). *Managers and Work Reform*, New York: Free Press
Blau, G.J. and Katerberg, R. (1982). Toward enhancing research with the social information processing approach to job design, *Academy of Management Review*, **7**, 543–50
Bright, J.R. (1966). The relationship of increasing automation and skill requirements, in National Commission on Technology, Automation and Economic Progress, *The Employment Impact of Technological Change*, Appendix, vol. II to *Technology and the American economy*, Washington, D.C.: U.S. Government Printing Office, pp. 203–21
Braverman, H. (1974). *Labor and monopoly capital: The Degradation of Work in the Twentieth Century*, New York: Monthly Review Press
Burris, B.H. (1983a). The human effects of underemployment, *Social Problems*, **31**, 96–110
Burris, B.H. (1983b). *No Room at the Top. Underemployment and Alienation in the Corporation*, New York: Praeger
Burris, V. (1983). The social and political consequences of overeducation, *American Sociological Review*, **48**, 454–67
Caldwell, D.F. and O'Reilly, C.A. (1982). Task perceptions and job satisfaction: a question of causality, *Journal of Applied Psychology*, **67**, 361–9
Cascio, W.F. (1978). *Applied Psychology in Personnel Management*, Reston, Va.: Reston
Dowling, P. and O'Brien, G.E. (1981). The effects of employment, unemployment and further education upon the work values of school leavers, *Australian Journal of Psychology*, **33**, 185–95
Duncan, G. and Hoffman, S. (1978). The economic value of surplus education, in G. Duncan and D. Morgan (eds), *5000 American Families*, vol. 6, Ann Arbor, Michigan: Institute of Social Research, pp. 223–46
Dunnette, M.D. (1966). *Personnel Selection and Placement*, California: Wadsworth
Dunnette, M. (ed.) (1976). *Handbook of Industrial and Organizational Psychology*, Chicago: Rand McNally
Dunnette, M.D. and Borman, W.C. (1979). Personnel selection and classification systems, *Annual Review of Psychology*, **30**, 477–525
Elger, T. (1982). Braverman, capital accumulation and deskilling. Chapter 2 in S. Wood (ed.), *The Degradation of Work? Skill, Deskilling and the Labour Process*, London: Hutchinson
Farr, J.L. (1976). Task characteristics, reward contingency and intrinsic motivation, *Organizational Behavior and Human Performance*, **16**, 294–307
Fiedler, F.E. (1967). *A Theory of Leadership Effectiveness*, New York: McGraw-Hill
Fiedler, F.E. (1978). The contingency model and the dynamics of the leadership process, in L. Berkowitz (ed.), *Advances in Experimental Social Psychology*, vol. II. New York: Academic Press
Frank, L.L. and Hackman, J.R. (1975). A failure of job enrichment: the case of the change that wasn't, *Journal of Applied Behavioral Science*, **11**, 443–56
Freeman, R.B. (1976). *The Overeducated American*, New York: Academic Press
Fried, Y. and Ferris, G.R. (1984). *The Validity of Hackman and Oldham's Job Char-*

acteristic Model: A Review and Meta-analysis, Champaign-Urbana: Institute of Labor and Industrial Relations, University of Illinois

Globerson, S. and Crossman, E.R.F.W. (1976). Non-repetitive time: An objective index of task variety, *Organizational Behavior and Human Performance,* **17**, 213–40

Grandjean, B. and Taylor, P. (1980). Job satisfaction among female clerical workers: 'Status panic' or the opportunity structure of office work? *Sociology of Work and Occupations,* **7**(1), 33–53.

Greene, C.N. (1981). Some effects of a job enrichment program: a field experiment, *Proceedings of the Academy of Management,* **41**, 281–5

Griffin, R.W. (1983). Objective and social sources of information in rask redesign: a field experiment, *Administrative Science Quarterly,* **28**, 184–200

Hackman, J.R. and Oldham, G.R. (1975). Development of the Job Diagnostic Survey, *Journal of Applied Psychology,* **60**, 159–70

Hackman, J.R. and Oldham, G.R. (1976). Motivation through the design of work: test of a theory, *Organizational Behavior and Human Performance,* **16**, 250–79

Hackman, J.R. and Oldham, G.R (1980). *Work Redesign,* Reading, Mass.: Addison-Wesley

Hackman, G.R., Pearce, J.L. and Wolfe, J.C. (1978). Effects of job changes and job characteristics on work attitudes and behaviors: a naturally occurring quasi-experiment, *Organizational Behavior and Human Performance,* **21**, 289–304

Herzberg, F. (1966). *Work and the Nature of Man,* Cleveland: World Press

Horowitz, M.A. and Herrenstadt, I.L. (1966). Changes in the skill requirements of occupations in selected industries, Appendix. vol. II. *The Employment Impact of Technological Change,* National Commission on Technology, Automation and Economic Progress, Washington, D.C.: U.S. Government Printing Office, pp. 227–87

James, L.R. and Jones, A.P. (1980). Perceived job characteristics and job satisfaction: an examination of reciprocal causation, *Personnel Psychology,* **33**, 97–135

Jenkins, G.D., Glick, W.H. and Gupta, N. (1983). Job characteristics and employee responses, *Proceedings of the Academy of Management,* **43**, 164–8

Jones, B. (1982). Destruction or redistribution of engineering skills? The case of numerical control, Chapter 10 in S. Wood (ed.), *The Degradation of Work? Skill, Deskilling and the Labour Process,* London: Hutchinson

Kabanoff, B. and O'Brien, G.E. (1979a). Cooperation structure and the relationship of leader and member ability to group performance, *Journal of Applied Psychology,* **64**, 526–3

Kabanoff, B. and O'Brien, G.E. (1979b). The effects of task type and cooperation upon group products and performance, *Organizational Behavior and Human Performance,* **23**, 163–81

Kerr, C., Dunlop, J.T., Harbison, F. and Myers, C.A. (1969). *Industrialism and Industrial Man,* New York: Oxford University Press

Kiggundu, M.N. (1980). An empirical test of the theory of job design using multiple job ratings, *Human Relations,* **33**, 339–51

Kim, J.S. (1980). Relationships of personality to perceptual and behavioral responses in stimulating and nonstimulating tasks, *Academy of Management Journal,* **23**, 307–11

Kornhauser, A. (1965). *Mental Health of the Industrial Worker,* New York: Wiley

Lee, D. (1982). Beyond deskilling: Skill, craft and class, Chapter 8 in S. Wood (ed.), *The Degradation of Work? Skill, Deskilling and the Labour Process,* London: Hutchinson

Maslow, A.H. (1943). A theory of human motivation, *Psychological Review*, **50**, 370–96

Mayo, G.E. (1919). *Democracy and Freedom: An Essay in Social Logic*, Melbourne: Macmillan

Mayo, G.E. (1933). *The Human Problems of an Industrial Civilization*, New York: Macmillan

Mayo, G.E. (1945). *The Social Problems of an Industrial Civilization*, Boston: Harvard University

More, C. (1980). *Skill and the English Working Class, 1870–1914*, London: Croom Helm

More, C. (1982). Skill and the survival of apprenticeship, Chapter 6 in S. Wood (ed.), *The Degradation of Work? Skill, Deskilling and the Labour Process*, London: Hutchinson

O'Brien, G.E. (1980). The centrality of skill-utilization for job design, In K. Duncan, M. Gruneberg and D. Wallis (eds.), *Changes in Working Life*, Chichester: Wiley

O'Brien, G.E. (1982a). The relative contribution of perceived skill-utilization and other perceived attributes to the prediction of job satisfaction: a cross- validation study, *Human Relations*, **35**, 219–37

O'Brien, G.E. (1982b). Evaluation of the job characteristics theory of work attitudes and performance, *Australian Journal of Psychology*, **34**, 383–401

O'Brien, G.E. (1982c). The success and failure of employee participation—a longitudinal study, *Work and People*, **8**, 24–8

O'Brien, G.E. (1983). Skill-utilization, skill-variety, and the job characteristics model, *Australian Journal of Psychology*, **35**, 461–8

O'Brien, G.E., Biglan, A. and Penna, J. (1972). Measurement of the distribution of potential influence and participation in groups and organizations, *Journal of Applied Psychology*, **56**, 11-18

O'Brien, G.E., Dowling, P. and Kabanoff, B. (1978). *Work, Health and Leisure*, National Institute of Labour Studies, Working Paper 28, Adelaide: The Flinders University of South Australia

O'Brien, G.E. and Kabanoff, B. (1981). The effects of leadership style and group structure upon small group productivity: a test of a discrepancy theory of effectiveness, *Australian Journal of Psychology*, **33**, 157–68

O'Brien, G.E. and Owens, A.G. (1969). Effects of organizational structure on correlations between member abilities and group productivity, *Journal of Applied Psychology*, **53**, 525–30

O'Brien, G.E. and Pere, T. (1985). The effects of ability, self-esteem and task difficulty on performance and task satisfaction, *Australian Journal of Psychology*, **37**, 309–323.

O'Connor, E.J. and Barrett, G.V. (1980). Informational cues and individual differences as determinants of subjective perceptions of task enrichment, *Academy of Management Journal*, **23**, 697–716

Oldham, G.R. (1976). Job characteristics and internal motivation: the moderating effects of interpersonal individual variables, *Human Relations*, **29**, 559–69

O'Reilly, C.A. and Caldwell, D.F. (1979). Informational influence as a determinant of perceived task characteristics and job satisfaction, *Journal of Applied Psychology*, **64**, 157–65

Orpen, C. (1979). The effect of job enrichment on employee satisfaction, motivation, involvement and performance: a field experiment, *Human Relations*, **32**, 189–217

O'Toole, J. (ed.) (1974). *Work and the Quality of Life*, Cambridge, Mass.: M.I.T. Press

O'Toole, J. (1977). *Work, Learning and the American Future*, San Francisco: Jossey-Bass

Penn, R.D. (1983). Theories of skill and class structure, *Sociological Review*, **31**, 22–38

Pere, T. (1981). *The effects of self-esteem on task performance, satisfaction, and perceptions of skill-utilization*, unpublished B.A. (Hons.) thesis, Flinders University, South Australia

Pfeffer, J. (1981). Management as symbolic action: the creation and maintenance of organizational paradigms, in L.L. Cummings and B.M. Staw (eds), *Research in Organizational Behavior* Vol. 3, Greenwich, Conn.: JAI Press

Ronen, S. (1980). The image of I/O psychology: a cross-national perspective by personnel executives, *Professional Psychology*, **11**, 399–406

Rothwell, R. and Zegveld, W. (1979). *Technical change and employment*, London: Frances Pinter

Rousseau, D.M. (1977). Technological differences in job characteristics, employee satisfaction and motivation: a synthesis of job design research and socio-technical systems theory, *Organizational Behavior and Human Performance*, **19**, 18–42

Rousseau, D.M. (1978). Measures of technology as predictors of employee attitudes, *Journal of Applied Psychology*, **63**, 213–18

Rumberger, R. (1981). *Overeducation in the U.S. Labor Market*, New York: Praeger

Salancik, G.R. and Pfeffer, J. (1977). An examination of need-satisfaction models and job attitudes, *Administrative Science Quarterly*, **22**, 427–56

Salancik, G.R. and Pfeffer, J. (1978). A social information processing approach to job attitudes and task design, *Administrative Science Quarterly*, **23**, 224–53

Spenner, K.I. (1983). Deciphering Prometheus: Temporal change in the skill level of work, *American Sociological Review*, **48**, 824–37

Staines, G. and Quinn, R. (1979). American workers evaluate the quality of their jobs, *Monthly Labor Review*, **102**(1), 3–12

Stone, E.F. and Porter, L.W. (1978). On the use of incumbent-supplied job characteristics data, *Perceptual and Motor Skills*, **46**, 751–8

Taylor, F.W. (1911). *The principles of scientific management*, New York: Harper

Terborg, J.R. and Davis, G.A. (1982). Evaluation of a new method for assessing change in planned job redesign as applied for Hackman and Oldham's Job Characteristic Model, *Organizational Behavior and Human Performance*, **29**, 112–28

Thomas, J. and Griffen, R. (1983). The social information processing model of task design: a review of the literature, *Academy of Management Review*, **8**, 672–82

Thompson, J.D. (1967). *Organizations in Action*, New York: McGraw-Hill

Trahair, R.C.S. (1984). *The Humanist Temper: The Life and Work of Elton Mayo*, New Brunswick: Transaction Books

Umstot, D.D., Bell, C.H. and Mitchell, T.R. (1976). Effects of job enrichment and task goals on satisfaction and productivity: implications to job design, *Journal of Applied Psychology*, **61**, 379–94

U.S. Department of Health, Education and Welfare. (1973). *Work in America*, Cambridge, MA: M.I.T. Press

Vroom, V.H. and Yetton, P.W. (1973). *Leadership and Decision-making*, Pittsburgh: University of Pittsburgh Press

Wall, T.D. and Clegg, C.W. (1981). A longitudinal field study of group work redesign, *Journal of Occupational Behavior*, **2**, 31–49

Wallace, M. and Kalleberg, A.L. (1982). Industrial transformation and the decline of craft: the decomposition of skill in the printing industry, 1931–1978, *American Sociological Review*, **47**, 307–24

Weiss, H.M. and Nowicki, C.E. (1981). Social influences on task satisfaction: model competence and observer field dependence, *Organizational Behavior and Human Performance*, **27**, 345–66

Weiss, H.M. and Shaw, J.B. (1979). Social influences on judgements about tasks, *Organizational Behavior and Human Performance*, **26**, 126–140

Welford, A.T. (1978). Mental work load as a function of demand, capacity, strategy, and skill, *Ergonomics*, **21**, 151–67

Welford, A.T. (1980). On the nature of higher-order skills, *Journal of Occupational Psychology*, **53**, 107–10

White, S.E. and Mitchell, T.R. (1979). Job enrichment versus social cues: a comparison and competitive test, *Journal of Applied Psychology*, **64**, 1–9

CHAPTER 3

Underemployment, Job Satisfaction and Performance

What are the consequences of underemployment for job satisfaction? Some early studies addressed this problem by examining the effects of 'overeducation' or 'overtraining'. Kalleberg and Sorenson (1973) defined overtraining in terms of the discrepancies between workers' educational attainments and the education needed for their jobs. They predicted that overtraining would decrease job satisfaction. This would occur for at least two reasons. First, higher levels of education than those actually required by the job would lead to the under-utilization of valued skills. Second, education increases students' expectations that they will use their acquired skills at work.

Kalleberg and Sorenson measured the educational levels of a large sample of U.S. male office and factory workers and obtained measures of required job education using the US Labor Department's Dictionary of Occupational Titles. Using statistical methods which allowed them to separate out the effects of education, job requirements and overtraining, they found that overtraining reduced job satisfaction and undertraining increased job satisfaction. A similar finding was reported by Quinn and Mandilovitch (1977) using a larger and more representative sample. The most recent study of this type is by Burris (1983) who reanalysed a survey of a national sample of employed persons aged 18 or over in the United States. This study used a scale of General Educational Development (GED), constructed by the U.S. Department of Labor, to measure underemployment. This scale, based on Fine's functional job analysis (1968), attempts to measure the skills required to achieve average performance in various jobs. The scale rates three skills— logical, mathematical and linguistic—separately, using a six point scale. The overall score is set equal to the maximum of each of the three partial scores. Burris made a judgement about the equivalence between GED scores and educational level.

Overeducation was then defined as any situation in which the educational attainment of the respondent exceeded the GED equivalent of his or her present occupation. (p. 457)

Burris found that the level of job satisfaction was significantly related to over- and undereducation. Those undereducated were far more satisfied with their jobs than those reasonably matched while the overeducated were less satisfied. The overeducated workers were disproportionately in unskilled occupations where the average satisfaction levels were low. When education and occupation were controlled, the size of the effect was reduced. Overeducation still negatively predicted job satisfaction. Moderate levels of discrepancy made little difference to job satisfaction. There were no effects of overeducation on political alienation or political leftism.

In the United States the most probable consequence of overeducation is the continued privatization of discontent, leading either to self-blame (low self-esteem, symptoms of psychological distress, etc.) or to individual adaptation through the redefinition of status (elevating the importance of family, leisure and nonwork activities) (p. 465)

The sociological studies then have shown that discrepancy between education levels of employees and education required by the job predicts job satisfaction. Having less education than formally required increases satisfaction while excessive educational qualifications reduce satisfaction. The research still leaves unanswered the role of education as a determinant of job skills and work values. This is important because dissatisfaction would be due to either under-utilization of skills or unrealized values or expectations or both. The studies so far are unable to answer this question because education level could index both skill levels and work values. Furthermore, it has yet to be shown that educational level is positively related to skill level— even for specific skills such as reasoning, mathematics and verbal facility. Nor has it been shown that the index of job requirements (GED) provides the range of skills that are necessary to encompass major job skills. Many jobs, for example, might not require great amounts of these skills for adequate performance. Instead they might require other skills such as eye–hand coordination, persistence and spatial orientation.

SKILL-UTILIZATION AND JOB SATISFACTION

Although most reviews of job satisfaction identify skill use as a major determinant of job satisfaction, this conclusion is largely based on common sense or indirect inference rather than on the findings of studies where skill-utilization has been directly measured.

We shall review the available literature in order to answer three questions.

1. What is the relationship between skill-utilization and job satisfaction?

2. How important is skill-utilization as a predictor of job satisfaction when compared to other factors such as influence, variety and income?
3. To what extent is the relation between skill-utilization and job satisfaction affected by employee work values?

The first study on skill-utilization was made by Kornhauser (1965). In his study of North American automobile workers he found that skill-utilization was the major factor accounting for variations in job satisfaction and 'mental health'. In his study, skill-utilization was defined in terms of the extent to which a job used employee skills. Mental health was measured by a composite of manifest anxiety, self-esteem, hostility, sociability, morale and life-satisfaction. He concluded that

workers' feelings regarding the use of their abilities are unmistakably associated with the superior mental health of the group in higher factory jobs and the poorer mental health at low level jobs.

(Kornhauser, 1965, p. 99)

Kornhauser also took a position relevant to the question of the relative importance of skill-utilization.

this particular set of findings appears to occupy a crucial place among the determinants of the mental health of individual groups when compared to characteristics such as job security, physical conditions, pay, repetitiveness, speed and intensity. (p. 107).

Subsequent research, until recently, failed to follow up these statements. Kornhauser's conclusions needed further research because they were based on crude measures of job characteristics and were derived from a restricted sample. The failure of many job satisfaction theorists to explore the role of skill-utilization is partly explainable by their desire to define job characteristics in terms of needs. Thus Herzberg did not directly measure job attributes, but provided general descriptions of jobs in terms of 'motivators' such as achievement, responsibility, and interest, which satisfied personal growth needs (Herzberg, 1966). Having jobs with interest and responsibility may mean that valued skills are being used but this is not necessarily true.

Similarly, Maslow's idea of self-actualization at work is too broad. It refers both to type of activities and a psychological state where people are being what they are capable of being. Maslow provided no way of describing and measuring job attributes so research based on his theory is of little use for understanding skill-utilization. The degree of 'self-actualization', if it could be measured, may or may not be related to high skill-utilization.

Another reason for failing to examine skill-utilization is the failure of Kornhauser to develop reliable scales. Some theorists, seeking measures of job attributes which were reliable and valid, looked elsewhere for guidance. Thus the recent job characteristics theory of Hackman and Oldham (1975, 1980) used measures that were derived from the work of Turner and Lawrence

(1965). Turner and Lawrence developed a Requisite Task Attribute Index which was a weighted total of six job attributes: variety, autonomy required and optional interaction, responsibility, skill and knowledge.

'Skill and knowledge' was not really skill-utilization but a general concept of skill level measured by asking an employee to estimate the amount of time required to learn his or her job proficiently. Hackman and Oldham used a revised set of measures that included 'skill-variety'—the range of different skills required for a job. Again this seems akin to variety and has nothing to say about skill-match.

One series of studies that did endeavour to measure skill-utilization was conducted with Australian employees (O'Brien, 1980, 1982, 1983). A four-item scale was developed which contained questions about the degree to which the respondent's job used their abilities, training and experience, provided opportunities for learning new jobs, and allowed them to use their training and experience. The response categories for each item were: not at all; very little; some; a reasonable amount; and a great deal. This was a scale of perceived skill-utilization. It was adopted for three main reasons. First, no method was available for measuring objective skill-utilization across a range of jobs. Second, it was likely that employee evaluations were more responsive to what they thought their jobs were than to what they really were. Third, measures of perceived job attributes have substantial, although imperfect, correspondence with objective job attributes (Chapter 2).

Other perceived job attributes were also measured. These included influence over job procedures, variety, pressure and interaction. A fairly representative sample of employees in a large Australian city was selected using multi-stage cluster sampling. These employees were contacted personally and answered questions about their job attributes and job satisfaction. The main results were:

1. Skill-utilization was the strongest predictor of job satisfaction (O'Brien, 1980, 1982). This was based on multiple regression analyses. The weighting or beta coefficient for skill-utilization was significantly greater than the coefficients for the other job attributes.[1]
2. Analyses within occupational categories (professional, administrative, clerical, sales, transport/communication, trades, personal services) show that skill-utilization is the strongest predictor for all occupational groups (Table 3.1).

The results obtained could have been due to similarity in content between the skill-utilization scale and the 18-item facet satisfaction scale. This latter scale did contain items asking about satisfaction with use of abilities, learning opportunities and opportunities for challenge. The analyses were repeated with these items omitted but skill-utilization remained the strongest predictor of satisfaction.

TABLE 3.1   The relative contribution of job attributes to the prediction of job satisfaction

| Occupational category | Sample size N | R^2 | Job attribute beta coefficients | | | | |
			Skill-utiliz-ation	Influ-ence	Variety	Pres-sure	Inter-action
Professional	201	0.61*	0.65*	0.14*	0.08	−0.13*	−0.02
Administrative/ managerial	87	0.53*	0.41*	0.33*	0.30*	−0.23	0.11
Clerical	245	0.54*	0.49*	0.30*	0.08	−0.19*	−0.07
Retail/sales/ insurance	125	0.30*	0.34*	0.22	0.08	−0.17	−0.05
Transport/ communication	85	0.47*	0.53*	0.15	0.03	−0.34*	0.01
Trades (skilled and unskilled)	388	0.52*	0.49*	0.14*	0.15	−0.13*	0.05
Personal services/ recreation	131	0.35*	0.40*	0.06	0.31*	−0.17	−0.09
Total sample	1262	0.70*	0.49*	0.18*	0.14*	−0.18*	−0.01

Notes: 1. The beta coefficient is a measure of the association between a job attribute and job satisfaction when all other attributes are controlled.
2. R^2 is the multiple correlation measuring the degree of association between all attributes combined and job satisfaction.
3. Occupations in mining and armed services were omitted because of small N.
4. *Statistically significant $p < 0.01$.

(from O'Brien, 1982)

The within-occupation analyses also support the assertion that skill-utilization is distinct from skill level. The order of occupations can be assumed to reflect skill level. Professional occupations generally require the greatest amount of training and require the greatest skill while the personal services, such as waiter or cleaner, require the least amount of training and skill. If the association between job satisfaction and skill-utilization was due to occupational differences in skill level, then the regressions conducted within occupational groups should have shown a marked decline in the predictive value of skill-utilization. Skill-utilization cannot be identified with occupational status either. Each employee's occupation was rated on Congalton's status ranking of Australian occupations (Congalton, 1969). This ranking assigns an occupation a number and ranges from 1.61 for a medical doctor to 7.46 for an unskilled labourer. The correlation between skill-utilization and occupational status is −0.31. This indicates that employees in high-status occupations perceived themselves to have higher skill-utilization in their jobs than those in lower status occupations.However, the correlation is not high enough to identify perceived skill-utilization with occupational status.

The primacy of skill-utilization as a predictor of job satisfaction has been replicated with other samples which included clerical workers (O'Brien and Pembroke, 1982), pharmacists (O'Brien and Humphrys, 1982) and another representative sample of occupations (O'Brien, 1983). The last-mentioned study compared the relative importance of skill-utilization and the task attributes defined in Hackman and Oldham's recent job characteristics theory of work motivation (Hackman and Oldham, 1975, 1976). This theory predicts that job satisfaction, intrinsic motivation and performance can be predicted from five job attributes. They are skill-variety, task identity, task significance, autonomy and feedback from the job.

Those attributes are defined as follows:

Skill-variety: the degree to which a job requires a variety of different activities in carrying out the work; which involve the use of a number of different skills andtalents of the person.

Task identity: the degree to which the job requires completion of a 'whole' and identifiable piece of work; that is, doing a job from beginning to end with a visible outcome.

Task significance: the degree to which the job has a substantial impact on the lives or work of other people; whether in the immediate organization, or outside it.

Autonomy: the degree to which the job provides substantial freedom, independence, and discretion to the individual in scheduling the work and in determining the procedures to be used in carrying it out.

Feedback: the degree to which carrying out the work activities required by the job results in the individual obtaining direct and clear information about the effectiveness of his or her performance.

When jobs are high on all these attributes they lead individuals to experience their work as meaningful and capable of providing them with experienced responsibility and knowledge about the actual results of their work activities. The attributes are also used to diagnose the motivating potential of a job. The motivating potential score (MPS) is defined as follows:

$$MPS = \frac{\text{Skill variety} + \text{Task identity} + \text{Task significance}}{3} \times \text{Autonomy} \times \text{Feedback}$$

A very large number of studies have been done using these measures to task attributes. They show that job satisfaction is significantly related to these attributes, separately and in combination (Hackman and Oldham, 1980; O'Brien, 1982; Roberts and Glick, 1981). If skill-utilization is really as important a variable as is claimed for measuring job satisfaction, it should account for significant amounts of the variance in job satisfaction even when Hackman and Oldham's job attributes are controlled for.

A casual inspection of the scales used by Hackman and Oldham suggested that skill-utilization might be measured by their skill-variety scale.[2] At times they interpret the scale as one which measures job challenge. A challenging job is one that fully uses, even stretches, an employee's skills and abilities. These statements are inferred from their discussion of skill-variety.

> When a task requires a person to engage in activities that challenge or stretch his skills and abilities, that task almost invariably is experienced as meaningful by the individual.
>
> (Hackman and Oldham, 1976, p. 257).

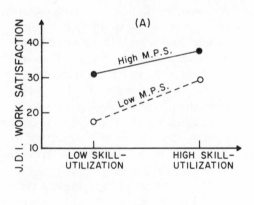

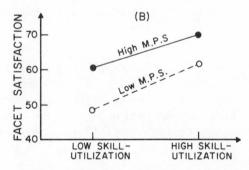

FIGURE 3.1   The relationship between skill-utilization, motivating potential score, and job satisfaction as measured by the Job Descriptive Index (A) or facet satisfaction (B). (From O'Brien, 1983, p. 466)

This assertion may be true but it is not true that skill-variety measures ability or skill-use. The items refer to the variety of tasks and the variety of skills used by the employee in doing a job. They do not ask questions about the degree to which the job *uses* the employee's skill.

In order to show that skill-utilization was different from skill-variety and the other job attributes, all of the scales were given to a representative sample of employees in an Australian city. Job satisfaction was measured by the Job Descriptive Index (Smith, Kendall and Hulin, 1969) and by the 18-item job facet satisfaction scale discussed previously. Using hierarchical multiple regression, the unique variance in job satisfaction accounted for by each job attribute was measured.[3] For both measures of job satisfaction, skill-utilization accounted for a significant amount of the variance in job satisfaction. Skill-variety and autonomy also showed an independent and significant association with job satisfaction. Finally, the motivating potential score (MPS) of each job was calculated and the separate effects of skill-utilization and MPS on job satisfaction were calculated. The results are shown graphically in Figure 3.1.

It was found that both MPS and skill-utilization were significant and independent predictors of job satisfaction. The neglect of skill-utilization by the job characteristics model has important implications for job design. At present, this model does not recommend that job satisfaction and performance should be improved by designing a job so that it requires skills that are reasonably similar to the skills possessed and valued by the employee. Skill-variety is typically increased by combining tasks or establishing direct client relationships if these are relevant to the job (Hackman and Oldham, 1980; Orpen, 1979; Wall and Clegg, 1981). The new tasks added may sometimes involve more skill-utilization but it is probable that they will not because, in practice, it is easier to improve variety than improve skill-utilization.

WORK VALUES, SKILL UTILIZATION AND JOB SATISFACTION

Many writers on work motivation and job satisfaction claim that employees' reactions to their job cannot be predicted from job attributes alone. One reason is that employees differ in their desire for jobs which give them challenge, responsibility and variety. Hence job satisfaction and work motivation may not rise when the scope of the job is enlarged by increasing intrinsic job attributes such as skill-utilization and autonomy. A representative statement of this position is contained in a recent article on job design.

> Whereas efforts to increase job scope are likely to produce substantial gains in job satisfaction and motivation for some individuals, they may only negligibly affect (at least in the short run) the job reactions of others.
>
> (Brousseau, 1983, p. 34)

While not disagreeing that personality differences exist which affect the way in which employees respond to their jobs, it is possible to ask whether these differences have a great effect on job evaluations. This question has substantial implications for theories of job satisfaction and work design. If the effects are large then any theory of job satisfaction should incorporate individual difference factors. Furthermore, application of these theories to job design should be careful to tailor the interventions to the expressed needs or values of the employee. However, if the effects of individual differences are small, then they will not have much practical significance. The preceding discussion has maintained that skill-utilization is a major factor in determining job satisfaction and this means that it should be strongly associated with job satisfaction regardless of employee differences in occupational background, personality and values.

This is a view that probably would not be agreed to by those who have investigated the role of work values in shaping employee job evaluations. Work values, generally defined, are desired psychological states and outcomes. A considerable number of studies have shown that employees do have differences in work values. They differ in the extent to which they adhere to the Protestant work ethic (Hulin and Blood, 1968; Stone, 1975, 1976; Wanous, 1974), desire satisfaction of 'higher' order needs (Hackman and Lawler, 1971; Hackman and Oldham, 1975, 1976), have an instrumental or intrinsic work orientation (Goldthorpe *et al.*, 1969; O'Reilly, 1977) and desire different levels of intrinsic job attributes (Baker and Hanson, 1975; Wall and Payne, 1973). All of these concepts refer to work values because they are measured by asking employees to describe their desired work systems, job attributes and work goals.

Such concepts are generally used to explain the manner in which employees differ in their response in a given type of job. As far as job satisfaction is concerned, the value theories espouse some form of congruency model. They maintain that job satisfaction is a negative linear function of the discrepancy between work values and perceived job attributes. Job satisfaction, it is assumed, will be highest when there is a close similarity, or congruence, between what an employee desires in a job and what he or she experiences in a particular job. In order to test this hypothesis with skill-utilization as a job attribute, a number of studies were conducted which examined the role of 'desired skill-utilization' as a predictor of job satisfaction. Prior analyses of the effect of values indicated that values had a significant but relatively small effect on satisfaction and motivation. This research is discussed in Chapter 5. One possible reason for the smallness of the effect is the general nature of the values measured. It was expected that a very specific value, such as desired skill-utilization, would be more relevant to understanding the skill-utilization/satisfaction relationship.

With a large sample of Australian employees it was found that congruency between desired and perceived skill-utilization was significantly related to job satisfaction (O'Brien and Dowling, 1980). For those people in jobs high in skill-utilization, highest job satisfaction occurred if they reported that they wanted high skill-utilization. People in low-skill-utilization jobs tended to be more satisfied if they wanted low rather than high skill-utilization. However, this interaction effect accounted for about 3 per cent of the variance in job satisfaction, whereas the direct effect of skill-utilization accounted for about 40 per cent. These results suggested that the importance of work values had been overestimated.

One problem with this study, however, was that the mean differences between experienced and desired skill-utilization were fairly small. Perhaps the congruency effect would only appear when this difference was large. To some extent, the average small discrepancy could be due to adaptation. As employees have prolonged experience with a job they change their values to be consistent with their experience. If this happened then there should be a strong positive association between perceived and desired skill-utilization. Actually, the correlation was only 0.16. This hardly supported strong adaptation effects. Nevertheless, it was desirable to find a group of employees who exhibited a range of values as well as general large differences between what they wanted and what they experienced.

Pharmacists were chosen for this second study (Humphrys and O'Brien, 1986; O'Brien and Humphrys, 1982). Pharmacy is an occupation that has undergone a progressive de-skilling. The traditional role of the pharmacist as a compounder of drugs and medicines has been largely replaced by the large drug-manufacturing companies. These companies, through their medical representatives, have displaced the pharmacist as the source of drug knowledge for medical doctors (Kronus, 1976). Thus pharmacists have lost control over the application of their specialized knowledge. Despite this change, pharmacists still receive intensive training in drug pharmacology. As a result of this training, pharmacists could be expected to require high skill-utilization in their work. Hence the majority of pharmacists, at least those working in community shops, would be expected to experience a large discrepancy between their work values and their actual job experiences.

A large sample of 396 Australian pharmacists was surveyed. The questionnaire contained scales measuring perceived skill-utilization. As expected, there was a large discrepancy between perceived and desired skill-utilization. Also, there was no relationship between the scores on these two scales. The correlation was −0.06. Regression analyses showed that, for the total sample, skill-utilization was the main predictor of job satisfaction when compared to job autonomy and variety. There was no interaction effect between desired and perceived skill-utilization—that is, the work value scale (desired skill-utilization) did not moderate the relationship between skill-utilization and job satisfaction. Nor was there any moderating effect of work values when a scale measuring the degree to which pharmacists valued commercial success was substituted in the analysis. There was a small congruency effect for recently qualified pharmacists but this accounted for less than 3 per cent of the variance in job satisfaction. Skill-utilization, by contrast, accounted for 40 per cent of the variance in job satisfaction.

The results of this study, in conjunction with results from previous research (Humphrys, 1981; O'Brien, 1980, 1982; O'Brien and Dowling, 1980; O'Brien and Pembroke, 1982; O'Brien and Stevens, 1981) have two major implications for job satisfaction research. First, skill-utilization is a major determinant of job satisfaction. It determines more variance in job satisfaction scores than influence, variety, pressure or any of the job attributes of Hackman and Oldham's theory.

Second, work values have little effect on the relationship between skill-utilization and satisfaction. This suggests that future research should not persist in trying to establish the role of work values as a central component of job characteristics theories such as that of Hackman and Oldham (1975, 1976, 1980). This model states that an employee's reaction to a job is moderated by his or her higher order need strength. The measure of higher order need strength is based on items that ask the respondent to rate the extent to which he or she *desires* intrinsic job attributes. It is similar then to desired skill-utilization. Evidence, reviewed in Chapter 5, shows that higher order need strength is a very weak moderator of intrinsic job characteristics. The reported interactions between higher-order need strength and job characteristics are very small. Such concepts, at best, seem to have a minor role in predicting job satisfaction. If this was accepted some potentially discriminatory job interventions would not occur. Hackman and Oldham recommend that job redesign be carried out with those who are ready for it. This refers to those with high growth needs or values. The potential benefits of jobs with high intrinsic concept and interest would be denied to the 'unready'—those who report low growth need strength. Yet the research reported here and actually reported by Hackman and Oldham shows that even the 'unready' would receive considerable job satisfaction if their jobs allowed them more opportunities for skill-utilization, variety and autonomy.

DO CHALLENGING TASKS DETERMINE WORK PERFORMANCE?

One of the earliest studies to address this question was by Berlew and Hall (1966). In a study of managers in a large North American corporation they found that managers who started their career with challenging assignments performed better over a 4–5 year period than managers whose initial jobs were less demanding. Another longitudinal study replicated and extended this study with a group of professional engineers (Kaufman, 1974). Engineers whose initial job experience involved challenging work, when compared to those whose initial work was not very demanding, had higher professional competence and performance during their careers. This study also evaluated the relative effect of ability and challenging work on performance. When ability was controlled, challenging work still had a positive effect on subsequent job performance. Those who showed the greatest level of career performance had initial assignments that were challenging, plus high ability.

Berlew and Hall claimed that challenging tasks improved performance because they affected employee goal-setting and motivation. The more successful managers, who had been exposed initially to challenging tasks, internalized the high goals necessary for performance on difficult tasks and generalized these high goals to subsequent tasks. The less successful managers, exposed initially to relatively easy tasks, did not internalize high performance goals and thus expended less effort in their subsequent tasks.

This goal-setting explanation is consistent with both the laboratory and field research on goal-setting (Latham and Baldes, 1975; Latham and Kinnes, 1974; Locke, 1968; Locke *et al.*, 1981). These studies have consistently shown that individuals with difficult and specific goals perform better than individuals with easy or general goals. The explanation of this finding is typically in terms of consistency motivation. The setting of a hard goal motivates an individual to work harder in order to achieve consistency between intentions and behaviour.

This may not be the only reason for high task performance after challenging tasks. It is also possible that high performance is due to the acquisition of a higher level of task skills. Challenging tasks provide more varied and difficult experiences, and therefore require the exercise and development of more skills than easy tasks. Hence later performance on subsequent tasks may reflect different levels of acquired skills. This point was made by Campbell and Ilgen (1976) and they tried to establish the relative effects of goal setting and skill on performance. They found that both initial challenge and goal setting alone affected subsequent performance. They concluded that the effects of initial task difficulty were not attributable to goal setting. Rather, they argued, they were probably due to increased skill or task knowledge. They also extended knowledge of the effects of initial task challenge on subsequent performance by showing that the effects still occurred even if the individual failed the early difficult assignments. Those who failed on initial difficult tasks still out-performed individuals who had initially succeeded at easier tasks.

This suggests that the effects of challenge are independent of the degree of success—at least in initial short-term assignments. This is contrary to the usual practice in organizations. Often individuals are placed initially in positions where tasks are relatively easy so that the individual can enjoy success which is assumed to motivate later performance. The task challenge literature indicates that this may not be the most effective strategy. The detrimental effects of failure may be outweighed by increases in task skills and the internalization of higher performance goals.

A more detailed analysis of the motivational effects of challenge on subsequent performance was made in an experimental study by Taylor (1981). She agreed with Campbell and Ilgen (1976) that challenging tasks could lead to the acquisition of more skill by those who perform them. But she also considered that the motivational effects could involve more than the internalization of higher performance standards.

The motivational processes associated with job challenge could include:

(a) *Performance standards*
New employees given challenging tasks would expect that the organization held high expectations and this expectation would generalize to subsequent tasks.

(b) *Task related attitudes*
High challenge tasks provide intrinsic satisfactions. This is demonstrated in job satisfaction research (O'Brien, 1982). Also the literature on achievement motivation (Atkinson and Feather, 1966; Trope and Brickman, 1975) shows that intrinsic satisfaction is greater on challenging tasks than on non-challenging ones.

But would positive attitudes developed on challenging tasks determine performance on subsequent tasks? Generally, the literature on productivity and job satisfaction shows that these concepts are not strongly related. One reason is that satisfaction may be high because of factors unrelated to task performance (e.g. social relationships, income). Taylor points out that, in the case of persons assigned to high-challenge jobs, the causes of satisfaction would be closely related to job performance.

> Because high performance has yielded much satisfaction in the past, the highly challenged individuals would be expected to be highly motivated to perform well on subsequent assignments. (p. 260)

(c) *Perceptions of skill-competence*
Taylor proposes that individuals assigned to high challenge initial positions will tend to attribute performance to skill competence than those persons assigned to low challenge initial positions.

This is because employees working on challenging jobs receive more positive information about their job skills than those in less difficult jobs. If they do not perform well, those on highly challenging jobs are more likely to attribute it to the difficulty of the task and not their own lack of skill.

All of these factors—higher standards, more positive attitudes and greater perceived skill competence—can separately and together explain why challenging tasks improve later performance. Taylor sought to establish the relative importance of these factors. She also asked a question with practical implications. This was whether the effects of job challenge were only confined to initial tasks? Would challenge, received later, also motivate performance?

With a well-designed experimental study, Taylor confirmed the relationship between challenge and performance. The experience of working on a high challenge versus a low-challenge assignment increased an individual's performance. In addition, the high challenge assignment induced higher performance standards, higher task satisfaction and greater personal attributions to skill.

However, a surprising result was that the effect of later challenge was stronger than that of initial challenge. Taylor suggests that this might be explainable in terms of the negative effects of failure in initial high-challenge tasks. Employee estimates of competence are reduced more by initial failure than failure after relatively successful performance.

In summary, the combined results on the effect of challenge are consistent in showing that high-challenge tasks—ones which fully use employees' skill—induce high performance. This high performance can be explained in terms of both increased knowledge and motivation. High-challenge tasks require more learning and the development of more complex skills. They are also motivating because they encourage the employee to set higher performance standards, produce more positive work evaluations and increase the employee's perception of skill-competence. The effect is not confined to initial tasks set for an entrant to an organization. It seems, from Taylor's work, that the performance increments of later challenge are even stronger than initial challenge.

GROUP STRUCTURE, SKILL-UTILIZATION, AND PERFORMANCE

The previous section showed that the content of the task can have relatively long-term effects on performance. Challenging tasks, which use and extend the skills of employees, induce higher performance than tasks which have low challenge. The main implication for job design then is that organizations should endeavour to construct task systems where the tasks are matched to the skill-repertoire of employees.

However, job design which focuses just on job content and neglects work structure may not always be successful in motivating employees to higher performance. Although a task, considered in isolation, may be challenging to an employee, the formal structure may prevent employees using their skills. One study that illustrates this was conducted by Kabanoff and O'Brien (1979a). Three person groups were formed to perform creative tasks and half the groups had members whose ability level was high on creativity. The groups were considered to have members whose skill-utilization was high since successful performance required high creative ability. The remaining groups had members with relatively low creative ability. It was expected that the high ability groups would have higher performance than the low ability groups.

The main effect of ability on group performance was obtained. However, there was a significant interaction between group (and leader) ability and group structure. Some group structures prevented their leader and members from using their ability. The experiment used four different structures. They were

1. Coacting: all members worked by themselves on their own tasks without cooperating in any way with other group members. There were three component tasks.
2. Collaboration: all group members worked simultaneously on each task while one member recorded the group's ideas.
3. Coordination: each member worked on one task for a third of the time and then passed this task and their products to another group member. This exchange occurred twice so each group member worked on each task for a third of the total time allocated to the group.
4. Collaboration-coordination: group members used the collaborative organization (2) for a third of the time and then used the coordination organization.

It was found that member ability was not related to group productivity in structures which used collaborative structures. The results for leaders are shown in Figure 3.2.

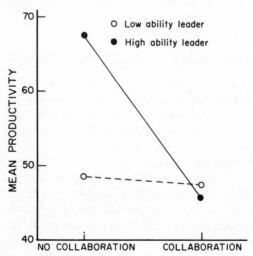

FIGURE 3.2   The effects of task collaboration upon the relationship between leader ability and group performance. (Reprinted from B. Kabanoff and O'Brien Journal of Applied Psychology, **64**, 526–32 Copyright (1979) by the American Psychological Association. Reprinted by permission of the authors

Groups with high-ability leaders performed better than groups with low-ability leaders. However, this effect was confined to groups where the structure did not involve collaborative structures. When collaboration was used group performance decreased and high-ability leaders were unable to use their ability to increase productivity. The dysfunctional effects of collaborative structures for employees performing creative and problem-solving tasks can be understood in terms of the amount of interaction generated. Collaborative groups generate high interaction levels which can:

(i) Maximize the potential for interpersonal conflict (Ilgen and O'Brien, 1974);

(ii) induce social pressures to include all members' contributions— including those with least ability;

(iii) prevent leaders from concentrating on the tasks themselves: much time is required to organize the group processes and handle interaction problems; and

(iv) prevent leaders and members from integrating the ideas produced in the group. The superiority of coordination structures can largely be understood by the fact that these structures allow members to use the diverse contributions of other members, as well as time to integrate these contributions with their own.

The main implication of this study for understanding individual and group performance is that productivity is a function of member resources (e.g. ability), task content and group structure. Further studies are needed to show how structure can affect performance but there are now a considerable number of studies that show that structure can have a very strong effect (O'Brien, 1984). Many of these studies have concentrated on the effects of different types of cooperation (e.g. Hackman, Brousseau and Weiss, 1976; Hewett, O'Brien and Hornik, 1974; Kabanoff and O'Brien, 1979b; O'Brien and Owens, 1969), but other structural relationships can also be important. These other relationships include power, communication and assignment relationships. Future research, then should not only be concerned with the effects of task content on individual performance. It should also identify the way in which work group structures can facilitate or impede the manner in which individuals are able to use their personal resources.

This chapter has shown that it is important for tasks to use employee skills in order to produce both high job satisfaction and performance. Challenging, or high skill-utilization tasks, have general effects on satisfaction and productivity which are only slightly moderated by individual differences in work values or personality. Optimal performance in work organization should occur then if the organization is designed so that component tasks match employee skills and the structure of the organization facilitates the use of these skills.

NOTES

1. The use of multiple regression procedures may not be warranted when the predictors are highly correlated. In this study the average correlation between predictors was about 0.4 and the maximum correlation was 0.53 between skill-utilization and influence. The effect of multicollinearity was assessed using a factor score method and a ridge regression method (Chatterjee and Price, 1977). It was demonstrated that multicollinearity did not affect the stability of the beta coefficients.

2. Hackman and Oldham (1975, 1980) claim that their scale of skill-variety was derived from the earlier work of Turner and Lawrence (1965). Turner and Lawrence developed a Requisite Task Index that included attributes called 'variety' and 'skill and knowledge'. The latter attribute was not really skill-variety (or skill-utilization) as it was measured with one question that asked the employee to estimate the time required to learn the job proficiently. The measure, therefore, is more akin to skill-level. Actually, Hackman and Oldham were not the only people to develop a skill-variety scale. Cooper (1973) used such a scale and he also acknowledges Turner and Lawrence as a source. Cooper's scale is very similar to that of Hackman and Oldham but is not referred to by them.

3. In this study the median correlation between predictors was 0.44. In order to estimate the degree to which multicollinearity could be a problem in these analyses, the variance inflation factor (VIF) for the set of predictors was calculated. The VIF provides an estimate of the effect of multicollinearity on the error between the ordinary least squares estimates and the true values of the regression coefficients (Chatterjee and Price, 1977). The VIF for each beta coefficient, b_i, is equal to $(1-R_i^2)^{-1}$ where R_i^2 is the square of the multiple correlation coefficient from the regression of the i^{TH} predictor on all other predictors. The ratio, R_L, measures the squared error on the least squares coefficients relative to the size of that error if the data were orthogonal

$$R_L = \frac{\sum_{i=1}^{p}(\text{VIF})_i}{p} = \frac{\sum_{i=1}^{p}(1 - R_i^2)^{-1}}{p}$$

where p = number of predictors

The average variance inflation factor was 2.13. Chatterjee and Price assert that VIFs in excess of 10 will result in unstable estimates. Hence the results can reasonably be treated as stable estimates for the sample used.

REFERENCES

Atkinson, J.W. and Feather, N.T. (eds) (1966). *A Theory of Achievement Motivation*, New York: Wiley

Baker, S.H. and Hanson, R. (1975). Job design and worker satisfaction: A challenge to assumptions, *Journal of Occupational Psychology*, **48**, 79–81

Berlew, D. and Hall, D. (1966). Socialization of managers: Effect of expectations on performance, *Administrative Science Quarterly*, **11**, 207–33

Brousseau, K.R. (1983). Toward a dynamic model of job–person relationships: findings, research, questions and implications for work system design, *Academy of Management Review*, **8**, 33–45

Burris, V. (1983). The social and political consequences of overeducation, *American Sociological Review*, **48**, 454–67

Campbell, D.J. and Ilgen, D.R. (1976). Additive effect of task difficulty and goal setting on subsequent task performance, *Journal of Applied Psychology*, **61**, 319–24

Chatterjee, S. and Price, B. (1977). *Regression Analysis by Example*, New York: Wiley

Congalton, A.A. (1969). *Status and Prestige in Australia*, Melbourne: Cheshire

Cooper, R. (1973). Task characteristics and intrinsic motivation, *Human Relations*, **267**, 387–413

Fine, S.A. (1968). The use of the Dictionary of Occupational Titles as a source of estimates of educational and training requirements, *Journal of Human Resources*, **3**, 363–75

Goldethorpe, J.H., Lockwood, D., Beckhofer, F. and Platt, J. (1969), *The Affluent Worker*, Cambridge: Cambridge University Press

Hackman, J.R., Brousseau, K.R. and Weiss, J.A. (1976). The interaction of task design and group performance strategies in determining group effectiveness, *Organizational Behavior and Human Performance*, **16**, 350–65

Hackman, J.R. and Lawler, E.E. (1971). Employee reaction to job characteristics, *Journal of Applied Psychology*, **55**, 259–86

Hackman, J.R. and Oldham, G.R. (1975). Development of the Job Diagnostic Survey, *Journal of Applied Psychology*, **60**, 159–97

Hackman, J.R. and Oldham, G.R. (1976). Motivation through the design of work: test of a theory, *Organizational Behavior and Human Performance*, **16**, 250–79

Hackman, J.R. and Oldham, G.R. (1980). *Work Redesign*, Reading: Addison-Wesley, 1980

Herzberg, F. (1966). *Work and the Nature of Man*, Cleveland: World

Hewett, T.T. O'Brien, G.E. and Hornik, J. (1975). The effects of work organization, leadership style, and member compatibility upon the productivity of small groups working on a manipulative task, *Organizational Behavior and Human Performance*, **11**, 283–301

Hulin, C.L. and Blood, M.R. (1968). Job enlargement, individual differences, and worker responses, *Psychological Bulletin*, **69**, 44–55

Humphrys, P. (1981). The effect of importance upon the relation between perceived job attributes desired job attributes, and job satisfaction, *Australian Journal of Psychology*, **33**, 121–33

Humphrys, P. and O'Brien, G.E. (1986). The relationship between skill-utilization, professional orientation, and job satisfaction for pharmacists. *Journal of Occupational Psychology*, (in press)

Ilgen, D. and O'Brien, G.E. (1974). Leader-member relations in small groups, *Organizational Behavior and Human Performance*, 12, 335–50

Kalleberg, A. and Sorenson, A. (1973). The measurement of the effects of overtraining on job attitudes, *Sociological Methods and Research*, 2, 215–38

Kaufman, H.G. (1974). Relationship of early work challenge to job performance, professional contributions and competence of engineers, *Journal of Applied Psychology*, 59, 377–79

Kabanoff, B. and O'Brien, G.E. (1979a). Cooperative structure and the relationship of leader and member ability to group performance, *Journal of Applied Psychology*, 64, 526–32

Kabanoff, B. and O'Brien, G.E. (1979b). The effects of task type and cooperation upon group products and performance, *Organizational Behavior and Human Performance*, 23, 163–81

Kornhauser, A. (1965). *The Mental Health of the Industrial Worker*, New York: Wiley

Kronus, C.L. (1976). The evolution of occupational power: an historical study of task boundaries between physicians and pharmacists, *Sociology of Work and Occupations*, 3, 3–37

Latham, G. and Baldes, J. (1975). The 'practical significance' of Locke's theory of goal setting, *Journal of Applied Psychology*, 60, 122–24

Latham, G. and Kinnes. S. (1974). Improving performance through training in goal setting, *Journal of Applied Psychology*, 59, 187–91

Locke, E.A. (1968). Toward a theory of task motivation and incentives, *Organizational Behavior and Human Performance*, 31, 157–89

Locke, E.A., Shaw, K.N., Saari, L.M. and Latham, G.P. (1981). Goal setting and task performance: 1969–1980, *Psychological Bulletin*, 90, 125–52

O'Brien, G.E. (1980). The centrality of skill-utilization for job design, Chapter 11 in K. Duncan, M. Gruneberg and D. Wallis (eds), *Changes in Working Life*, Chichester: Wiley

O'Brien, G.E. (1982). The relative contribution of perceived skill-utilization and other perceived job attributes to the prediction of job satisfaction: a cross-validation study, *Human Relations*, 35, 219–23

O'Brien, G.E. (1983). Skill-utilization, skill-variety and the job characteristics model, *Australian Journal of Psychology*, 35, 461–8

O'Brien G.E. (1984). Group productivity, Chapter 3 in M. Gruneberg and T. Wall (eds), *Social Psychology and Organizational Behaviour*, Chichester: Wiley

O'Brien, G.E. and Dowling, P. (1980). The effects of congruency between perceived and desired job attributes upon job satisfaction, *Journal of Occupational Psychology*, 53, 121–30

O'Brien, G.E. and Humphrys, P. (1982). The effects of congruency between work values and perceived job attributes upon the job satisfaction of pharmacists, *Australian Journal of Psychology*, 34, 91–101

O'Brien, G.E. and Owens, A.G. (1969). Effects of organizational structure on correlations between member abilities and group productivity between member abilities and group productivity, *Journal of Applied Psychology*, 532, 525–30

O'Brien, G.E. and Pembroke, M. (1982). Crowding, density and job satisfaction: an examination of reciprocal causation, *Australian Journal of Psychology*, 34, 151–64

O'Brien, G.E. and Stevens, L. (1981). The relationship between perceived influence and job satisfaction among assembly line employees, *Journal of Industrial Relations*, 23, 33–48

O'Reilly, C.A. (1977). Personality-job fit: implications for individual attitudes and performance, *Organizational Behaviour and Human Performance*, **18**, 236–46

Orpen, C. (1979). The effects of job enrichment on employee satisfaction, motivation, involvement, and performance: a field experiment, *Human Relations*, **32**, 189–217

Quinn, R.P. and Mandilovitch, M.S.B. (1977). *Education and Job Satisfaction: a questionable payoff*, NIE Papers in Education and Work, No. 5, Washington, D.C.: National Institute of Education

Roberts, K.H. and Glick, W. (1981). The job characteristics approach to task design: a critical review, *Journal of Applied Psychology*, **66**, 193–217

Smith, P.C., Kendall, L.M. and Hulin, C.L. (1969). *The Measurement of Satisfaction and Retirement*, Chicago: Rand McNally

Stone, E.F. (1975). Job scope, job satisfaction and the Protestant ethic, *Journal of Vocational Behavior*, **7**, 215–44

Stone, E.F. (1976). The moderating effect of work-related valued on the job scope—job satisfaction relationships, *Organizational Behavior and Human Performance*, **15**, 147–67

Taylor, M.S. (1981). The motivational effects of task challenge: a laboratory investigation, *Organizational Behavior and Human Performance*, **27**, 255–78

Trope, C. and Brickman, P. (1975). Difficulty and diagnosticity as determinants of choice among tasks *Journal of Personality and Social Psychology*, **20**, 207–228

Turner, A. and Lawrence, P. (1965). *Industrial Jobs and the Worker*, Cambridge: Harvard University Press

Wall, T.D. and Clegg, C.W. (1981). A longitudinal field study of group work redesign, *Journal of Occupational Behaviour*, **2**, 31–49

Wall, T.D. and Payne, R. (1973). Are deficiency scores deficient? *Journal of Applied Psychology*, **58**, 322–6

Wanous, J.P. (1974). Individual differences and reactions to job characteristics, *Journal of Applied Psychology*, **59**, 616–22

CHAPTER 4

Job Content, Strain and Health

One of the most common themes in the history of work is that work is a necessity and a burden. Although Adam once enjoyed a life where work and play were indistinguishable this was not the paradigm that was passed on to his successors. Instead, the writers on work have seen Adam's state after his disobedience to God as more representative of the human condition. Although some modern psychologists see the content of work as an opportunity for personal fulfilment, hardly anyone has denied that much of the world's work is externally imposed, difficult and capable of causing physical and mental strain.

Hence it is not surprising to find a large amount of research on job dissatisfaction and work strain. This research has been reviewed recently by Cooper and Marshall (1976), Holt (1982), Kasl (1978) and Murrell (1978). This chapter does not aim to provide an exhaustive review of the available studies on work strain but will concentrate on what is known about the association between the content of jobs and subjective feelings of strain. Like all work behaviour and experiences, strain is multiply determined. When someone says that he is fed up or unable to cope at work, his response could be due to a wide range of factors. It could be due to the inability of his job to provide enough money to pay off his debts, a supervisor who is critical of his work, a job that is boring, coworkers who are unpleasant, customers who are too demanding, or a work environment that is dirty, noisy and dangerous. These are just some of the environmental factors that could determine his response. His negative responses may also be related to his own personality. Some people are more likely to grumble than others or are less able to cope with frustration and external demands.

All of these situational and personal factors could determine responses to work and hence attempts to predict strain are always faced with the problem of representing the total field of possible determinants. The research work in this area has not been guided by any consensus about the strategy for un-

72

derstanding strain but, in retrospect, it has passed through three main stages which represent a progression from simple to complex theories. Initially, researchers tried to identify the main factors that could determine strain and health at work. The studies were simple in that they typically focused on one variable (e.g. noise, work load) and showed that variations in this variable were associated with variations in strain measures. These studies are important for identifying predictors of strain but are not adequate to explain individual responses because they also show that a considerable amount of the variation in strain responses cannot be explained by a single factor. People often do not react in the same way to situations which are similar. Thus high noise levels distress some employees but others seem to adapt.

Such findings led to the next stage of research which is the search for 'moderators' of strain responses. Essentially, this stage is represented by studies where strain responses are predicted not by a single variable but by a combination of variables. Thus stress due to noise is explained sometimes in terms of both the level of noise and the amount of control that an employee has over the source of noise. Individuals who have some control over the noise level display lower levels of irritation than those who have no control. Such studies indicated that stress and other responses to the work situation depended on the relation between the individual and the environment. Whether or not employees are able to adapt, depends on external demands and their ability to cope with these demands. So the third stage of research is a relational one where the main problem is to develop measures of match or relationship between personal capabilities and the demands of the workplace. These three stages—identification, moderator and relational—can be used to summarize some of the main findings. But before this can be done some comments need to be made about the concepts of strain and stress.

Definitions of stress are numerous but not always consistent (Holt, 1982). It is a state that may have relatively enduring consequences such as anxiety, depression, lowered performance and poor physical health. As stress can sometimes refer to stressors, or mental states, or the relation between stressors and mental states, the term does not have a useful analytic function. It seems preferable, therefore, to distinguish between strain which refers to various mental states and stressors which are considered to be potential external determinants of strain. Strain should also be distinguished from its consequences. Although this distinction cannot be made precisely, strain refers to experienced tension, dissatisfaction and unpleasantness which, if prolonged, can produce consequences such as personality disorders, poor physical health or lowered job performance.

A large number of factors or stressors have been shown to be associated with the subjective feeling of strain and job dissatisfaction. These are listed in Table 4.1. Most of the studies have been correlational and have found

TABLE 4.1.   Main determinants and consequences of job strain

Determinants (stressors)	Consequences

1. *Job Content*
 	
Machine-pacing
Under-utilization of
  abilities
Over-utilization of
  abilities
Quantitative overload
Low participation in
  job decisions
Time pressures
Monotony
	1. *Behavioural*
	
	Strikes
	Absenteeism
	Lowered performance
	Use of drugs and alcohol
	Increased use of medical
	  services
	Accidents

2. *Organizational structure and policy* Role ambiguity Role conflict Shift work Directive supervision Inequality of pay	2. *Physical health* Hypertension Peptic ulcer Respiratory illness Dermatitis Heart disease
3. *Job environment* Noise Pollution Temperature Poor safety	3. *Psychological health* Depression Anxiety Alcoholism, drug abuse Neurosis Mass psychogenic illness
4. *Non-work factors* Stressful non-work events Family demands Economic insecurity	
5. *Personality* Anxiety Type A syndrome Internal-external control	

that the degree of strain and satisfaction has been significantly associated with variations in these factors. As such they provide some weak evidence in support of causality. Strictly, they have not demonstrated causality in the strongest sense as few studies have been able to observe the consequences of direct changes in stressors. Nevertheless they have identified factors that seem important for predicting strain levels and many have also shown that the prolonged experience strain due to these stressors may generate negative consequences in behaviour, physical health and psychological well-being (Table 4.1), Strain has been related to the physical work environment, the organizational structure and various personality and social attributes of the employee. However, most research has concentrated on the nature of the job.

IDENTIFICATION OF JOB CONTENT STRESSORS

Job content factors refer to the nature of the actual tasks done by employees. The actual attributes used to describe tasks vary considerably across studies but many of the attributes now used were derived from early studies of machine-paced work. The earliest industrial research on stress focused on the deleterious effects of repetitive assembly work on fatigue (e.g. Industrial Health Research Board, 1931). Much of the early work concentrated on ways of reducing fatigue by varying workload and rest periods. Even though many studies showed that machine-pacing could increase strain and fatigue, there was some evidence to show that strain was not always associated with repetitive assembly work. In the United States, Elton Mayo studied the human effects of mechanization (Mayo, 1930). Mayo is commonly referred to as the theorist who advocated the importance of satisfying employee social needs on the basis of his interpretation of the famous Hawthorne studies (Roethlisberger and Dickson, 1939). Part of his own work at the Hawthorne plant measured physiological responses to assembly work. He found that telephone assembly work did not increase arterial tension or heart rate. The high work load of the telephone operators did not cause strain because, according to Mayo, they had the benefit of considerate and sympathetic supervisors who created a 'buoyant' spirit in the operators. Some early work in the United Kingdom also showed that assembly work could be satisfying due to the repetitive nature of the work. Repetition could induce a rhythm or 'traction' that employees found enjoyable (Baldamus, 1961).

Most studies after the 1950s paid more attention to the negative and than to positive responses to machine-paced assembly work. Kornhauser (1965), for example reported that automobile workers frequently complained of strain and boredom. The importance of machine-pacing as a predictor of strain was accentuated by a comparative study of occupations by Caplan, Cobb, French, Harrison and Pinneau (1975). They found that men on a machine-based assembly line reported the most boredom and dissatisfaction with their work. Studies using objective measures of strain have also shown that some types of machine pacing can affect strain. A study of Swedish sawmill workers reported higher rates of cardiovascular disorders among machine-paced than non-machine-paced workers (Frankenhaeuser and Gardell, 1976). Elevated levels of adrenaline and noradrenaline, often assumed to be indicators of cardiac risk, were also found in machine-paced workers.

Most of the studies in the area of machine-pacing do not make clear what it is about these jobs that make them stressful. It could be due to lack of control over the machine, the speed of the work, the lack of opportunity to talk to others, or the under-utilization of skills. An early exception is Kornhauser (1965) who tried to identify the relative importance of the various job and organization factors as predictors of dissatisfaction and mental health. He concluded that under-utilization of skills had the strongest relation to his strain measures and subsequent studies have also emphasized the importance of this variable (French, Caplan and Harrison, 1982; Locke, 1984; O'Brien, 1980; Quinn *et al.*, 1971a,b).

However, control over work procedures also seems to be important. Having a job that uses valued skills can be dissatisfying and can cause strain if the employee does not have influence over work arrangements or decisions affecting the work process. Non-participation in work decisions has frequently been reported as being associated with strain and dissatisfaction (e.g., Quinn and Shepard, 1974) but the results are not always consistent (Wall and Lischeron, 1977).

Besides use of abilities and control over work procedures, the main job content factors associated with strain and satisfaction are variety, task identity, task significance, feedback about performance and pressure (Hackman and Oldham, 1980). Variety refers to the extent that the job involves the repeated performance of the same tasks in the same way. Task identity is typically defined as the extent to which the job is a meaningful one with an identifiable product formed by a series of integrated subtasks. The concept is somewhat vague but extreme examples are used to denote this dimension. An employee fitting one small component to an electric motor would have low task identity whereas his task identity would be high if he assembled the whole motor.

Task significance is defined as the extent to which the task makes a useful contribution to the organization's goals or to societal needs. The final two attributes refer to the extent that the employee receives information about his level of performance (feedback) and the degree to which the work has to be done according to deadlines set by machines or other people (pressure).

All jobs can be described on these content dimensions and research suggests that all are negatively and independently related to strain and job dissatisfaction. Thus jobs are unpleasant to the extent that they do not use valued skills, provide little control over work processes, are monotonous, lack identity and significance, provide little feedback and are performed under conditions of high pressure. Some jobs are low or high on all of these attributes but most jobs vary in the extent to which all of these dimensions are present. Thus, some jobs use few valued skills but provide a high degree of control over work procedures and involve little pressure. Would such jobs produce feelings of strain?

This raises the problem of the relative importance of these attributes. Are some dimensions stronger predictors of strain than others? A related question is that of independence. The contribution of one factor may depend on whether another is present. Having control over work procedures may not induce low strain if the amount of work or pressure is too high.

MODERATOR APPROACHES TO JOB STRAIN

As there is evidence that the strength of the association between single job attributes and measures of strain varies from study to study, later research has examined the interaction between these various dimensions. Studies that have done this are called interactional or moderator studies. The essence of the moderator approach is to show how the effect of one variable on strain is moderated (i.e. increased or decreased) by the presence or absence of another variable. Two studies, typical of this approach, will be considered. Both sought to understand why different strain effects could be observed in individuals who experienced similar job demands. Karasek (1979) found that the effects of job demand or load could not be understood without taking into account the degree to which the job provided control over work procedures. Whereas Karasek focused on the opportunities for control provided by the job, Kobasa (1979) examined control as a personality characteristic. In her study, she found that individuals were able to cope better with job and life stressors without becoming ill if they were internally controlled. Both studies are similar in that they show that the effect of external stressors is partly determined by the control experienced by the employee. Control can be derived either from the structure of the work or from the personal resources of the employee.

A. Job Demands and Decision Latitude

Karasek (1979) maintained that there were two main factors in a job that could produce strain in employees. One factor was the amount and pace of work—job demands. The other was the degree to which the employee was able to control job procedures and use his skills on the job—job decision latitude. Some studies, but not all, had shown that increasing job demands also increased strain responses such as dissatisfaction, exhaustion and depression. A possible reason for these inconsistent results was that job demands would not induce strain if the individual had control over work procedures. This hypothesis mirrors the finding that noise related strain can be reduced when individuals have some control over noise levels (Cohen, 1980).

By describing jobs as high or low demand and high or low decision latitude four types of jobs are generated. These are shown in Figure 4.1.

The highest levels of strain are predicted to occur when there are high

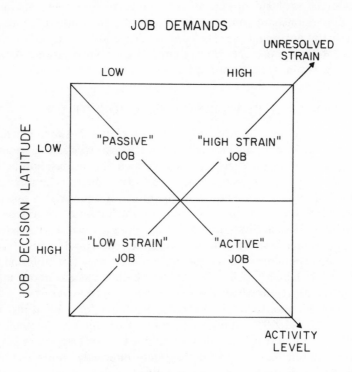

JOB DEMANDS

FIGURE 4.1   Karasek's job strain model. (*Reprinted from Rob A. Karasek, Jr, Job demands, job decision latitude and mental strain: implications for job design,* Administrative Science Quarterly, **24**, 2 (*June 1979*) *by permission of* The Administrative Science Quarterly)

demands and low decision latitude. When the job provides a high degree of decision latitude the incidence of strain effects is reduced even though the job demands may be quite high. Using large samples from both the United States and Sweden, Karasek found that his predictions about the moderating effect of decision latitude were supported. Similar relationships between job factors and strain were found with a variety of measures, including exhaustion, job dissatisfaction and sick days.

The most stressful type of job was one where the employee had a large amount of work to do but did not have much opportunity to use his skills in controlling the work process. The next most stressful job was the 'passive' one where demand and decision latitude were both low. The robustness of these results was shown by using samples from different countries as well as a longitudinal analysis with the Swedish group which showed that changes in job factors over time also changed strain reactions.

These findings summarize the general relationships between strain, decision latitude and job demands. They are important in showing that job strain should be understood in terms of the interaction of job dimensions. High work load does not necessarily produce high strain. It partly depends on other factors. One such factor is decision latitude. Other factors could include social support and personality. Just as increasing decision latitude can ameliorate the strain effect of work load, it is possible that strain could be reduced by increasing social support either at work or in the family. One problem with interpreting Karasek's findings is the meaning of 'decision latitude'. The actual measures combine at least three different job attributes. One is the skill level of the job. Another is the degree to which the job actually uses an employee's valued skills and the third factor is the amount of influence the individual has over job decisions. Conceptually, these are distinct. In practice, it may be the case that jobs with high skill content use employee's skills and provide opportunities for influence but this is not always the case. Karasek reports an imperfect association between the different measures of decision latitude. Skill discretion—which combines skill level and skill-utilization—correlates 0.48 with participation in job decisions. By combining these two different measures to form one scale he assumes that they are measuring the same thing, which clearly they do not. The effect of increasing the skill requirements of a job on strain may be quite different from increasing participation in job decisions but this possibility cannot be analysed by Karasek because they are treated as equivalent concepts.

As skill level was the only measure of decision latitude used with the Swedish sample, it appears that skill level rather than influence is being measured by decision latitude. Thus it is inappropriate to conclude that increases in influence will counteract the negative effects of job demand. Increasing skill-level may also not work. If the skill level is increased above an employee's capabilities then stress could be increased (Czikszentimihalyi, 1975). It appears that decision latitude is meant to measure skill-utilization which is assumed to be indirectly measurable from skill-level. This interpretation is supported by Karasek's discussion of decision latitude. The presence of decision-latitude allows the use of skills and judgement which 'enhances the individual's feeling of efficacy and ability to cope with the environment; it is not a source of stress' (p. 303).

B. Personal Control, Strain and Health

Rotter's internal/external locus of control variable has, in a number of studies, been shown to predict variation in strain responses (O'Brien, 1984; Rotter, 1966). Internally controlled individuals believe, to a large extent, that they are able to achieve their valued goals through their own effort and ability. An opposite belief system is held by externals who believe that most of what they can achieve is determined by other people, fate or chance. Anderson (1977) found that strain induced by economic loss was reported as higher for externally controlled businessmen than for internally controlled businessmen. This study suggested that this was due to the internally controlled individual engaging in more task-relevant behaviour. This increased their productivity and hence reduced the objective reason for their strain. Internals also report less dissatisfaction than externals under conditions of role ambiguity (Organ and Greene, 1974; Keenan and McBain, 1979). These studies suggest that individuals with a reasonable level of 'internal' control beliefs are more able to withstand strain than those who believe that their behaviour is externally controlled. If this is so, then it suggests that those who are externally controlled would be more likely to develop poor physical health as a result of objective strain. This possibility was investigated in a longitudinal study by Kobasa (1979). A number of studies had already shown an association between stressful life experiences and various forms of physical and psychological illness (Dohrenwend and Dohrenwend, 1974, 1978; Gunderson and Rahe, 1974). Kobasa sought to establish the personality factors that would determine whether or not an individual became ill after considerable life-strain. She studied two groups of middle- and upperlevel business executives in the United States. An adaptation of the Holmes and Rahe (1967) Schedule of Recent Life Events was used to measure the degree to which they had experienced stressors. This schedule assigns numbers to life events in proportion to their estimated strain effects and includes events such as death of a spouse, divorce and traffic violations. Kobasa added 15 work-related items, such as geographical transfer of work location and promotion. Starting with a large sample of 896, 86 managers were selected who experienced a high level of stressors *and* a subsequent high level of illness. These were compared with a group of 75 who also reported a high level of stressors but differed in that they reported a low level of illness. All of the executives completed a battery of personality tests, including the Rotter internal-external control scale.

Statistical analysis showed that a small set of related personality measures differentiated or discriminated between the high- and low-illness groups. These measures were interpreted as reflecting a general dimension called 'psychological hardiness'. The low-illness group was high on 'psychological hardiness' whereas the high-illness group was low on hardiness. A hardy individual was defined as having a strong 'commitment to self, an attitude of vigorousness toward the environment, a sense of meaningfulness and an internal locus of control' (Kobasa, 1979, p. 1).

Why should hardiness determine whether experienced strain produced illness? Kobasa maintained that the hardy individual reduces strain through coping behaviour. He does something to his environment and/or restructures his own thought processes. Behavioural activity is designed to change, as much as is possible, the objective situation that induces strain. Cognitive activity often means justifying or rationalizing the stress experience so that it is seen as meaningful and not as just an unavoidable frustration. Thus, a hardy executive, faced with a job transfer that will involve stressful family adjustments, will act in ways designed to minimize strain. Family members might be consulted about the proposed changes and endeavours made to ensure that acceptable accommodation and schooling are provided for the family. The transfer is also made meaningful by seeing it as a necessary step in the career path or as a means of broadening the family's social experience. By contrast, the externally controlled, unhardy, individual would do less to ensure a minimum of family disruption and would be less inclined to fit the transfer into a planned strategy of career achievement. He would therefore be more inclined to see it as a imposed irritation that he can do little about. He remains a passive victim of a stressful life event and thus experiences prolonged strain that, by some unknown physiological mechanism, produces physical illness.

STRAIN AS A FUNCTION OF PERSON–JOB FIT

The moderator approach is an advance on simple studies that basically say that a single factor can determine strain. Whether or not *A* determines stress, according to this approach, depends on factor *B* or *C* or other factors. Yet this approach has limitations of its own. Whether or not a single factor, or combination of factors, determines strain depends on whether these factors are perceived by the employee as threatening his/her ability to cope. Job strain, very generally, depends on the perception of the employee. Perceptions of strain do not have a simple relationship to the amount of objective stressors. There is generally a positive correlation but not at all a perfect one. Whether or not an individual expresses strain depends on his perception of:

(i) the demands of the situation;
(ii) personal capabilities; and
(iii) the degree to which his/her capabilities are adequate in meeting the job demands. From this perspective it is not appropriate to predict work strain from either job attributes or personal capabilities alone. Strain should be understood as a relation between job demands and individual capabilities which include abilities, motivation and personality.

The research strategy implied is one which uses the person–job match paradigm. One of the most extensive investigations using this approach has been that of French and his coworkers (French, Caplan and Harrison, 1982). A simplified version of their research framework is shown in Figure 4.2.

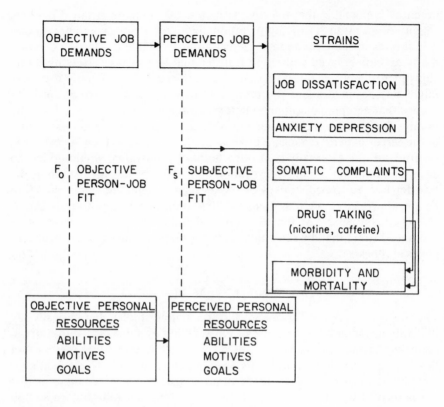

FIGURE 4.2   Person–job fit as a determinant of strain responses (Adapted from French *et al.*, 1982)

In this model, objective job demands are defined very broadly to include anything that the job requires a person to do. These objective job demands determine the employee's perceptions of such demands but the accuracy of the employee's perceptions depend on the closeness of his 'contact with reality'. Similarly, objective measures of an employee's resources for coping with job demands determine his perceptions of his own resources. Employees differ in the accuracy with which they can describe their own resources and they are more accurate as their self-insight or 'accessibility to self' increases. The personal resources include abilities, goals or motives. No detailed classification of resources is provided although they do discuss one motive which they consider important. This is the need for 'self-utilization' which motivates individuals to seek out opportunities to use valued abilities.

In the discussion of strain symptoms it is assumed that they can be determined in a variety of ways. They can be determined by variables in the objective or perceived environment which are perceived to be a threat to physical or psychological stability.

They can also be determined by the degree of match between objective job demands and objective personal resources. However, the main determinant considered, and the only one systematically investigated is the degree of fit between the perceived job demands and the perception of personal resources. Measures of perceived person–job fit were obtained from representatives of 23 occupations. The final sample of 318 male employees in the United States was drawn from a larger pool of subjects in order to equalize the number in each occupation. Various methods of fit were developed but all methods involved subtracting scores on a reported particular job characteristic from scores on desired amounts of this characteristic. Measures of job demands were obtained by asking employees the question 'How much X do you have in your job?' (E). Personal resources were obtained by asking the question 'How much of X would you like?' (P). The degree of fit was measured by $(E-P)$.

The main job attribute considered was job complexity—a general measure of the amount of skill and self-directed effort involved in the job. The actual items were drawn from scales used by Hackman and Lawler (1971), Kohn (1969), and Quinn and Shepard (1974). The strongest predictor of job dissatisfaction, boredom and depression was poor fit on job complexity. Poor fit was measured by the absolute difference, discounting sign, between perceived and desired job complexity. Thus if employees perceived that their job had either too much complexity or too little complexity they reported relatively high levels of dissatisfaction, boredom and depression. However, none of the measures of fit predicted physiological measures of strain such as blood pressure, cholesterol or uric acid levels.

A direct measure of perceived match on abilities, under-utilization, was a significant predictor of job dissatisfaction and boredom. Dissatisfaction and boredom increased with increases in perceived under-utilization.

No correlations were reported between measures of fit on job complexity and under-utilization of abilities so it cannot be inferred that they are overlapping measures. What is reasonably clear is that employees were dissatisfied and bored if their skills were not used in their jobs. They were also dissatisfied if the complexity of the job exceeded their desired levels of complexity. But why did person–job fit affect some measures of strain and not others? French and his associates did not provide a detailed discussion of this but some of the results suggest that the type of strain response depends on the kind of mismatch.

A simple subtractive formula like $E-P$ measures two different types of mismatch. One type occurs when $E < P$ and the person feels that the job is not complex enough or does not use his skills. Another type occurs when $E > P$. Then the employee perceives that the job is too complex and demands a level of ability that is beyond him. French *et als'* results suggest that under-utilization of skills leads to boredom, depression and low satisfaction. Over-utilization of skills also leads to low satisfaction with attendant anxiety but not boredom. This interpretation is supported by the relation of under-utilization with satisfaction and boredom as well as the finding that anxiety is increased when the job is perceived as being too complex.

A. Challenge, Uncertainty and Strain

These findings have been independently found by Csikszentmihalyi (1975) in his investigation of factors that induce creativity in work and play. When people engage in tasks which provide a challenge that is commensurate with their skills they become involved, are creative and often have peak experiences which he terms 'deep flow'. This is a state of enjoyment that has a similarity to states described by other psychologists working in other areas. Some of the early writings of Groos (1901) and Buhler (1930) contained the concept of *Funktionlust*—a state of pleasure achieved when individuals are able to pursue activities that use their physical and sensory potential. Later writers like Hebb (1955) and Berlyne (1960) maintained that tasks must have an element of novelty in order to be enjoyable. For them novelty had the function of stimulating or arousing the organism to an optimal level required for pleasurable and effective performance. They did not specify how much novelty was required for optimal arousal, however. Too much novelty can, it appears, produce panic. However, the kind of novelty that was optimal for arousal was that which the individual saw as challenging. Challenging tasks involve some degree of uncertainty in that the chances of success are reasonable but by no means guaranteed. Other writers like De Charms (1968) stress that enjoyment and task motivation are due to the opportunities that a person has for being in control and being the initiator of the act. These theories identify the characteristics of tasks that are experienced as satisfying but are too general to explain why some tasks are enjoyable and others induce boredom or anxiety. In order to do this, Csikszentmihalyi endeavoured to construct a model based on research which could predict whether enjoyment, boredom or anxiety would be the result of the given task activity. He used a match model, as did French, *et al.* which was based upon the degree of similarity between task challenge and action capabilities. His model is shown in Figure 4.3.

According to Csikszentmihalyi's theory, anxiety results when task challenges exceed an individual's capabilities. If his capabilities are increased but the task is still experienced as too demanding then the experience is one of worry. When challenges are commensurate with skills then the activities induce enjoyment and draw the person into a state of absorption. His term for such tasks is autotelic, meaning that the performance of the tasks is

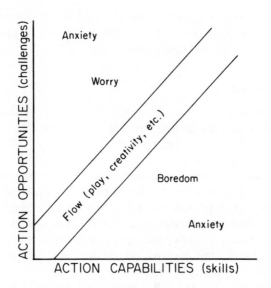

FIGURE 4.3　Model of the flow state. (*From Csikszentmihalyi, 1975, p. 49: reprinted with permission of Jossey-Bass Inc., Publishers*)

self-directing. However, if the individual's skills exceed those required by the task a state of boredom results. As this discrepancy increases boredom is again changed into anxiety. The evidence provided by Csikszentmihalyi only indirectly supports the model. Most of his data was obtained by asking people what it was that made them become engrossed in their play or work. The three most important reasons were:

(i) enjoyment of the experience and the use of skills;
(ii) the activity itself; the pattern, the action, the world it provides;
(iii) development of personal skills.

He also investigated the states that followed when people were prevented from engaging in 'autotelic' activities and showed that they often resulted in either boredom or anxiety, but he did not test his theory directly by exactly measuring personal skills and skills required by the task.

However, the model does provide an explanation of why boredom and depressive affect can appear in some situations and anxiety in others. It also suggests that strain should not be viewed just as an inability to cope with task demands. Strain symptoms can also appear when the individual is quite capable of performing a task.

Very generally, strain can occur when there is a discrepancy between an individual's valued skills and the skills required for effective task performance. Over- or under-utilization of skills will lead to job dissatisfaction.

Boredom and depression appear when the individual is overqualified for the task but anxiety is experienced when there are very large discrepancies between individual skills and task requirements.

B. Reasons for Strain

So far these studies have helped to identify those work situations which are experienced as stressful or dissatisfying. They provide a certain kind of explanation of strain in that, knowing the characteristic of the individual and the task, we can predict whether or not certain kinds of strain reactions will occur. But what makes people anxious, depressed or happy? None of the authors specifically answers this question. Why should ability match be enjoyable and lack of match uncomfortable? One kind of explanation specified that match situations induce an optimal level of arousal. Lacking specific evidence on how some physiological state of arousal is related to emotions and psychological states this explanation has limited value, although further research could make it a useful theory.

A second explanation is that all people have the need to self-actualize or use their potential. But this type of explanation seems circular and far too broad. How do you measure such a need? Typically, it is inferred from behaviour in creative or fulfilling tasks. But you cannot define an explanatory concept just by reference to the behaviour it is meant to explain.

A third explanation is couched in terms of self-identity. Individuals define themselves in terms of what they can do—or think they can do. If work activities use employees' valued abilities then their self-identity is confirmed. Cognitive inconsistency occurs when the specification of required abilities conflicts with self-defined abilities.

There is little evidence that directly supports this type of explanation. Partly this is due, it appears, to the concept of identity being too broad to be manageable. In principle the concept of identity includes the totality of what a person is. As it therefore includes everything that a person, or a social scientist, could think of, it becomes unmanageable as a scientific concept. However, if the concept of self-esteem is used instead of identity then the explanation does become testable. Generally, self-esteem refers to the degree that a person values him- or herself. Measures of self-esteem typically include two types of items. The first type is a simple evaluation of the self on dimensions like good–bad, respect–don't respect or like–dislike. The other type refers to estimates of one's own ability or competence in various situations. These items measure perceived competence and this concept is distinct from a general evaluation of the self which is the core meaning of self-esteem.

Repeated experience in jobs that fail to use valued abilities could lead to discrepancy between one's own estimation of abilities and one's abilities as socially defined. If it is not possible to change the job then pressure toward consistency would lead to lowered estimates of ability. These lowered estimates of ability would lead, in turn, to lowered self-esteem. This means that strain should be studied as a function of the employees' perception of the match between their perceived competence and job elements.

PERSON–JOB FIT, SKILL-UTILIZATION AND STRAIN

The prevailing trend in work strain research has been to define strain as an interactional concept. Strain is an imbalance or lack of fit between job demands and the capabilities of the employee (French, Rogers and Cobb, 1974; French, Caplan and Harrison, 1982; Lofquist and Dawis, 1969; McGrath, 1976). There is some evidence to support this approach but there are qualifications that need to be made. Firstly, the value of the person–job fit explanation has to be demonstrated by showing that measures of fit predict strain better than either job factors or personality/ability factors alone. This has rarely been attempted, the most notable exceptions being Harrison (1976, 1978) and French, Caplan and Harrison (1982). They correlated various strains with perceived job complexity, desired job complexity and the discrepancy between perceived and desired job complexity.

The results of Harrison's analyses are shown in Table 4.2. This table shows that the measure of person-environment fit has some explanatory power over and above the separate effects of perceived and desired complexity. The direct effects of E and P account for 26 per cent of the variance, for

TABLE 4.2. The relationship between strain measures, perceived job complexity and desired job complexity

Strains	Perceived complexity (E)	Desired complexity (P)	Fit $\lvert E - P \rvert$	$\lvert E + P + \lvert E - P \rvert \rvert$ (multiple correlation)
Job dissatisfaction	−0.31	−0.30	0.47	0.50
Boredom	−0.51	−0.34	0.51	0.61
Somatic complaints	NS	NS	0.16	0.18
Anxiety	NS	NS	0.21	0.25
Depression	NS	−0.12	0.22	0.23
Irritation	NS	NS	0.15	0.20

Notes: 1. NS means not statistically significant. All reported correlations are statistically significant.
2. In the regression analyses used to derive the multiple correlations in the last column, the addition of the fit measure significantly increased the multiple correlation based on E and P separately.

From Harrison (1978).

example, in boredom and $|E - P|$ for an additional 11 per cent. But it still is
the case that the direct effects of E and P account for significant variations
in boredom. A strict person–fit model cannot account for this.

Harrison does not comment directly on this problem but admits that the
measures of perceived job complexity and desired complexity may be 'fit'
measures themselves. How an employee perceives his job would be determined by how his own needs for complexity and similarly, his desires for
complexity, could be affected by the amount of complexity he experiences.
Some indirect evidence for his contamination is provided in the data Harrison uses. Perceived complexity (E), correlates 0.41 with $(E - P)$. This
problem of separating out the effect of fit from perceived measures of the
environment and needs seems intractable as long as self-reports are used.
Simple frame-of-reference theory indicates that perceptions of attributes are
determined, not just by the objective properties of the attributes, but also
by relevant comparison standards. In the case of a job, what we perceive
must partly be determined by what we want and, conversely, what we want
is partly determined by what we receive or experience. Although Harrison,
French and Caplan acknowledge that perceptions do not accurately reflect
the objective environment or the objective resources of the employee, they
provide no means of estimating the degree to which these perceptions reflect
objective attributes, defensive biases and contextual biases. Of course, if P
and E are partly fit measures themselves then the $|E - P|$ term underesti-
mates the effects of fits using subjective difference scores. Furthermore, the
use of difference scores themselves is subject to considerable controversy,
particularly when they are highly correlated with the component scores that
are subtracted from each other.

A second difficulty with the person–fit approach is that it tends to think
that fit alone determines strain. Whether it does or not might depend on a
large number of factors such as attributes of the job, personality, and social
support at work and at home.

A third and final difficulty is that these cross-sectional studies show few
effects of fit on physiological measures of strain. No convincing reasons are
given except to suggest that the sample is too large and heterogeneous for
such effects to be identified. However, if there is a robust and strong effect
it should appear. There may be somatic effects but the measures are not
appropriate for detecting them.

A. Skill-utilization as a Direct Measure of Person–Job Fit

The main problem with most of the person-fit measures is that they do not
have a uniform and inclusive set of variables to describe the dimensions on
which match occurs. Many types of needs, motives and abilities are measured
but there is no theory about which is most important. Further research could

proceed in either of two ways. One way would be to construct complex listings of job attributes and get employees to describe their jobs on these dimensions as well as their own competence to deal with these attributes. The relative importance of the various dimensions for determining strain could be established empirically. A problem with this approach is that employees may not be able to describe their jobs or their abilities accurately. Also the large range of internal stressors that have been identified may not be salient to employees because they use few categories in describing their work environment. Although they may say that they feel under strain in their job, this does not mean they can always accurately perceive what it is that is determining these states. This suggests that a simpler approach to understanding strain should get the employees to identify the degree to which their jobs use their skills. This is a judgement that employees are able to make even though they may not be able to specify the actual skills required by the job or the degree to which they possess various skills.

It is then an empirical matter to determine (i) the determinants of skill-utilization, and (ii) the consequences of skill-utilization. Intuitively nearly all of the job content and organizational structure factors can determine skill-utilization. If an employee is pressured by time or people, if he lacks control over work procedures, if there is ambiguity in the specification of

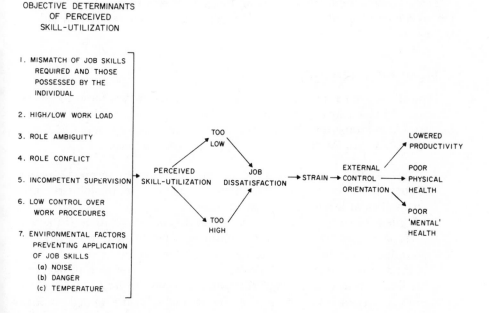

FIGURE 4.4   A model of the relationship between perceived skill-utilization, job strain and job performance

what it is that should be done, if the job is too easy or too hard, then the employee cannot use his skills properly. When this occurs, things are perceived as being out of control and various symptoms and consequences of strain appear. The type of model proposed is outlined in Figure 4.4.

In this model, the directed arrows indicate the proposed causal chain leading from objective situational factors which determine perceived skill utilization to the three major consequences of prolonged strain—lowered productivity, poor physical health and poor 'mental' health. At present, there is little research to show how each of the various situational factors determine perceived skill-utilization. There is some evidence to show that various objective measures of ability misfit determine perceived skill-utilization (e.g. Burris, 1983).

Objective discrepancies between job skills and skills of employees are not the only determinant of skill-utilization. A person may have the necessary skill for a job under 'normal' circumstances, but these skills may not be able to be used if there is a sudden increase or decrease in work loads. The appointment of an incompetent supervisor or the introduction of restrictive formal rules of procedure may also prevent the employees using their skills. Other environmental factors like high noise or temperature may reduce the employee's ability to use his or her capabilities.

There is more research supporting the link between skill-utilization and job satisfaction (Kornhauser, 1965; O'Brien, 1982) which in turn determines feelings of strain (O'Brien, 1980).

B. Strain and Productivity

Typically strain has been directly related to productivity without the specification of a mechanism to explain why it is that high strain induces lowered performance and poorer health. It is probable that prolonged states of strain are associated with lowered individual performance because

1. The objective work situation producing individual strain precludes the fullest use of employee capabilities. This means that the job structure is inefficient in the use of human resources.
2. Feelings of strain reduce satisfaction and hence motivation. If the job is seen as unsatisfying then the employee is less likely to work hard or to allocate maximum time to performing the job duties.
3. Strain, arising from a job with either under- or over skill-utilization, is likely to lead to a belief that there is little the individual can do to achieve intrinsic job rewards. Being unable to use valued abilities at a level that is comfortable induces a feeling of being externally controlled. Persistent experience of strain will then lead to fairly stable beliefs that behaviour at work is externally imposed and controlled.

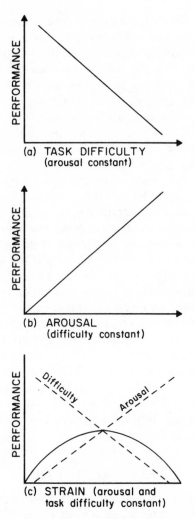

FIGURE 4.5   McGrath's theory of strain and task performance. (*From McGrath, 1976: reprinted with permission from Rand McNally*)

Such an external orientation has been found to reduce work motivation and productivity (O'Brien, 1984; Spector, 1982).

4. Strain increases levels of arousal. This form of explanation has been examined by McGrath (1970, 1976). His review of the literature showed that a frequent assumption was that strain is related to physiological arousal in a positive, linear fashion. Another frequent assumption was that arousal and performance are related in a curvilinear manner such that performance is depressed when arousal is either too

high or too low. McGrath questioned these assumptions because some research has shown that individual performance in groups is related to arousal in a linear and not in a curvilinear fashion (Lowe, 1971). He also concluded that the relation between strain and performance depended on task difficulty as well as arousal. When arousal is constant, performance decreases as task difficulty increases (Figure 4.5a). When difficulty is held constant, performance increases as arousal increases (Figure 4.5b). These relationships can then be used to predict the effect of strain on performance because strain is a joint function of both task difficulty is very high and arousal is also high. Low strain is experienced when the task is easy and arousal is low. Since difficulty and arousal have opposite effects on performance the relationship between performance and strain is curvilinear (Figure 4.5c).

Performance is low when strain is either too high or too low. If performance is low because of low strain then the way of increasing performance is to increase task difficulty or arousal or both. Similarly, if performance is too low because of high strain then the way to increase performance is to reduce task difficulty or arousal or both. The theory provides an elegant explanation for the effects of strain, arousal and task difficulty on performance. It also helps explain why reasonable levels of skill-utilization should maximize performance. This happens because the task provides a challenge to the employee and increases his level of arousal. When the task is too easy the individual is bored and has low arousal and performance drops. Under conditions of over utilization of skills the task is too difficult Arousal may be high but the individual performs poorly because he or she does not have the abilities required.

STRAIN AND HEALTH

The direct effects of strain on physical health have been well documented although the exact way in which cognitive-affective states such as mental strain affect physiological responses is still a matter of research. However, prolonged stress has been found to: (i) lower the effectiveness of the immune system which acts to rid the body of infections (Stein, Keller and Schleifer, 1981); (ii) produce endocrine problems through hypoactivity or hyperactivity (Lipton, 1976); (iii) affect autonomic control with consequent changes in cardiovascular, respiratory, secretory and visceral systems (Lisander, 1979); affect the neurotransmitter and neuroendocrime functions of the brain (Anisman, 1978). These changes can affect health through eating habits and increased use of drugs and alcohol.

The physiological research has suggested that belief about control can mediate the effects of strain on physical health and this supports our view that the effects of strain must be understood in terms of personal control. In his review, Anisman (1978) indicates that the negative physiological effects of strain are not observed when control over strain is possible. By implication this means that strain effects are magnified when the individual is led to believe that personal control is low. Hence if the job situation is one where the employee cannot either change the situation or move to another job then recurrent strain will induce feelings of low personal control. This is the type of situation which Zagans (1982), in his recent review of the strain–health relationship, concludes will maximize the likelihood of illness.

The relation of strain to mental health measures such as self-esteem, anxiety, and depression has been frequently investigated. The relationships are not well understood at present because not all studies show that strain produces low self-esteem, anxiety or depression. Furthermore, it is not clear when strain produces one state rather than another. Sometimes employees under strain report anxiety but not depression and sometimes depression is increased but not anxiety (Broadbent, 1983). If strain is experienced for a relatively short period then self-esteem, anxiety and depression may not have been affected. There may be short-term anxiety states or feelings of depression but these states are not the same as long-term anxiety and depressive syndromes that are generally referred to in theories of strain and mental health. These long-term syndromes may appear in employees whose prolonged experience of strain induce external control beliefs. Research in clinical and social psychology has shown that individuals who feel that they are externally controlled are most at risk for developing depressive and anxiety syndromes (Lefcourt, 1976; Phares, 1976). These studies do not identify the conditions under which anxiety alone or depression alone appear but it seems plausible to expect that future research might show that anxiety responses appear first and depression appears later when behaviour aimed at reducing anxiety is unsuccessful.

CONCLUSION

Research has identified many factors that can be associated with work strain. The content of the job, the organizational structure, as well as the personality and capabilities of the employee can all affect job strain. The results are not always consistent due to the use of different measures, different samples and a failure to take account of the importance of assessing the extent to which strain is temporary or prolonged.

Attempts have been made to integrate the findings by the development of theories of job–person fit. These theories have had the advantage of emphasizing that work strain is not understandable by reference to the objective work environment alone. Whether or not strain occurs depends on the meaning that the individual places on these factors. The common approach of job–person fit theories has been to measure aspects of the perceived environment, such as job complexity, as well as the individuals perception of his own resources. Limited success has been achieved in showing that strain results when the employee is in a situation where perceived resources exceed job demands or when resources are insufficient for job demands.

Strain which is prolonged has been found to lower work productivity and to affect physical and mental health. Further research is needed to understand the mechanisms or processes whereby strain produces these consequences. A simple model was described which outlined the stages in the development of strain and its consequences. Strain, it was maintained, had its strongest effects on behaviour when it was produced by a work situation that was recognized by an employee as over-utilizing or under-utilizing his skills. When the employee was unable to change the situation or his skill levels then the situation was initially perceived as unpleasant and the job became dissatisfying. This dissatisfaction developed into strain due to the perception that individual resources were not being used or that job demands exceeded personal resources.

Being unable to change the situation strain leads to a belief in low personal control. To the extent that this belief in low personal control is induced there follows lowered productivity, physical illness and poor mental health. Although not inconsistent with much of the research on work strain, the model needs to be investigated rigorously. It will also need to be expanded because the various stages or transitions within the model are likely to be affected by other variables such as personality differences and social support. There is a considerable amount of research that shows that social support, either emotional or instrumental, can alleviate work strain (House, 1981). However, some studies have shown that social support can sometimes heighten the experience of strain. Obviously more information is required about how various forms of social support can effect work strain.

What is clear is that work strain can seriously affect work productivity and health. The main implication for reducing strain is to design jobs so that there is a reasonable match between job demands and employee resources. Not only should jobs reasonably match employee skills, they should be perceived as providing skill-utilization.

If there are difficulties in introducing job and structural changes then employees can be helped to handle job strain. This can take two forms. The first way is to train them to recognize their own strain feelings and associated symptoms. This would be a first step in helping them to reduce strain but not sufficient in itself. Once strain has been recognized they could be taught the various ways in which their job environment could be determining their strain. If they have the power they then could take steps to change their job content. If, for example, there is too much work to be done in the time available they should reduce their work load or have some of it delegated. If work procedures are responsible for preventing full utilization of employee skills then supervisors or managers could be asked to alter these procedures. Unfortunately, individuals often have low power in organizations and this accounts for findings that show that employees have little success in coping with occupational strains through attempts to change problem conditions (Pearlin and Schooler, 1978).

If such changes cannot be made then the second type of training could be designed to help employees endure high strain levels. This is obviously not the best solution. The research on locus of control indicates that high strain is less likely to produce poor physical health if employees are 'psychologically hardy' (Kobasa, 1979). Such individuals are concerned about their own personal development, develop life goals, have an active and not a passive orientation to living and believe they have some ability to achieve their goals by personal effort. Yet it may be futile to counsel people to believe in themselves and change their environment when the external constraints on their behaviour are very strong. Counselling designed to increase a sense of personal control and competence will be counter-productive if it does not recognize that objective external control precludes a high degree of personal control. However, what can be productive is counselling that prevents individuals lapsing into a state of believing that everything in their work and non-work environment is beyond their control. Realistic counselling would aid the individual to make accurate identification of those situations where personal action can have an effect and those situations where external constraints preclude individual effort. Strain effects could then be reduced in two ways. Situations capable of being changed would be changed and strain in constrained situations would be accepted, if not thereby reduced. If the employee had an unrealistic belief in his ability to control his work then this would be likely to lead to magnified frustration and strain when the situation severely limits his ability to change the causes of his strain. The main point here is that the resilient individual is not one who believes that everything he wants is achieved by personal effort and ability. Rather it is a person who has developed the insight into his own capabilities and the opportunities that various situations provide for this exercise.

In the long run, strategies for reducing the effects of work strain by changing individual beliefs and behaviour are likely to have little effect when the stressors or environmental factors producing strain are not changed. This is because it is extremely difficult to change personal beliefs by counselling or written texts. It is especially difficult when the beliefs advocated are inappropriate to the situation of the employee.

REFERENCES

Anderson, C.R (1977). Locus of control, coping behaviors, and performance in a stress setting: A longitudinal study, *Journal of Applied Psychology*, **62**, 446–51

Anisman, H. (1978). Neurochemical changes elicited by stress. In H. Anisman and
   G. Bignami (eds), Psychopharmacology of Adversely Motivated Behavior, New
   York: Plenum
Baldamus, W. (1961). Efficiency and effort, London: Tavistock
Berlyne, D.E. (1960). Conflict, Arousal, and Curiosity, New York: McGraw-Hill
Broadbent, D.E. (1983). Some relations between clinical and occupational psychol-
   ogy, unpublished paper. Department of Experimental Psychology, University of
   Oxford
Buhler, K. (1930). Die geistige Entwicklung des Kindes, Jena: Fischer
Burris, V. (1983). The social and political consequences of overeducation, American
   Sociological Review, 48, 454–67
Caplan, R.D., Cobb, S., French, J.R.P., Harrison, R.V. and Pinneau, S.R. (1975).
   Job demands and worker health: Main effects and occupational differences, DHEW
   publication no. 75–160. Washington D.C.: U.S. Government Printing Office
Cohen, S. (1980). After effects of stress on human performance and social behavior:
   a review of research and theory, Psychological Bulletin, 88, 82–108
Cooper, C.L. and Marshall, J. (1976). Occupational sources of stress: A review of
   the literature relating to coronary heart disease and mental ill health, Journal of
   Occupational Psychology. 49, 11–28
Csikszentmihalyi, M. (1975). Beyond Boredom and Anxiety. San Francisco: Jossey-
   Bass
De Charms, R. (1968). Personal Causation, New York: Academic Press
Dohrenwend, B.S. and Dohrenwend, B.P (eds). (1974). Stressful Life Events: Their
   Nature and Effects, New York: Wiley
Dohrenwend, B.S., and Dohrenwend, B.P. (1978). Some issues in research on stress-
   ful life events, Journal of Nervous and Mental Disease, 166, 7–15
Frankenhaeuser, M. and Gardell, B. (1976). Underload and overload in work-
   ing life: outline of a multidisciplinary approach, Journal of Human Stress, 2,
   35–46
French, J.R.P., Caplan, R.D. and Harrison, R.V. (1982). The Mechanisms of Job
   Stress and Strain, Chichester: Wiley
French, J.R.P., Rogers, W. and Cobb, S. (1974). A model of person-environment fit,
   in G.V. Coelho, D.A. Hamburgh and J.E. Adams (eds), Coping and Adaptation,
   New York: Basic Books
Groos, K. (1901). The Play of Man, New York: Appleton
Gunderson, E. and Rahe, R. (eds). (1974). Life Stress and Illness, Springfield, Ill.:
   Thomas
Hackman, J.R. and Lawler, E.E. (1971). Employee reactions to job characteristics,
   Journal of Applied Psychology, 55, 259–86
Hackman, J.R. and Oldham (1980). Work Redesign, Reading, Mass.: Addison-
   Wesley
Harrison, R.V. (1976). Job demands and workers health: person environment misfit,
   Dissertation Abstracts International (University Microfilms #76–19, 150)
Harrison, R.V. (1978). Person-environment fit and job stress, chapter in C.L. Cooper
   and R. Payne (eds), Stress at Work, Chichester: Wiley
Hebb, D.O. (1955). Drives and the CNS, Psychological Review, 62, 243–54
Holmes, T.H. and Rahe, R.H. (1967). The social readjustment rating scale, Journal
   of Psychosomatic Research, 11, 213–8
Holt, R.R. (1982). Occupational stress, chapter 25 in L. Goldberger and S. Breznitz
   (eds), Handbook of Stress, New York: The Free Press
House, J.S. (1981). Work Stress and Social Support, Reading. MA.: Addison-Wesley

Industrial Health Research Board (1931). *Eleventh Annual Report*, London: H.M.S.O.

Karasek, R.A. (1979). Job demands, job decision latitude and mental strain: implications for job design, *Administrative Science Quarterly*, **24**, 285–308

Kasl, S.V. (1978). Epidemiological contributions to the study of work stress, in C.L. Cooper, and R. Payne (eds), *Stress at Work*, Chichester: Wiley

Keenan, A. and McBain, G.D.M. (1979). Effects of type A. Behaviour, intolerance of ambiguity, and locus of control on the relationship between role stress and work-related outcomes, *Journal of Occupational Psychology*, **52**, 277–85

Kobasa, S.C. (1979). Stressful life events, personality, and health: an inquiry into hardiness, *Journal of Personality and Social Psychology*, **37**, 1–11

Kohn, M.L. (1969). *Class and Conformity: A Study in Values*, Homeward, Illinois: Free Press

Kornhauser, A. (1965). *Mental Health of the Industrial Worker*, New York: Wiley

Lefcourt, H.M. (1976). *Locus of Control: Current Trends in Theory and Research*, New York: Wiley

Lipton, M.A. (1976). Behavioral effects of hypothalamic polypeptide hormones in animals and man, in E.J. Sacher (ed.), *Hormones, Behavior and Psychopathology*, New York: Raven

Lisander, B. (1979). Somato-autonomic reactions and their higher control, in C. Brooks, K. Koizumi and A. Sato (eds), *Integrative Functions of the Autonomic Nervous System*, New York: Elsevier

Locke, E.A. (1984). Job satisfaction, in M. Gruneberg and T. Wall (eds), *Social Psychology and Organizational Behaviour*, Chichester: Wiley

Lofquist, L.H. and Dawis, R.V. (1969. *Adjustment to Work*, New York: Appleton-Century-Crofts

Lowe, R. (1971). *Stress, Arousal and Task Performance of Little League Basketball Players*, Unpublished Ph.D. thesis, University of Illinois

Mayo, G.E. (1930). The human effect of mechanization, *American Economic Review Supplement*, **20**, No. 1: reprinted in *Work or Labor*, ed. L. Stein, New York: Arno (1977)

McGrath, J.E. (1970). *Social and Psychological Factors in Stress*, New York: Holt, Rinehart & Winston

McGrath, J.E. (1976). Stress and behavior in organizations, in M.D. Dunnette (ed.), *Handbook of Industrial and Organizational Psychology*, Chicago: Rand McNally

Murrell, H. (1978). *Work Stress and Mental Strain*, Occasional Paper No. 6, Work Research Unit, London

O'Brien, G.E. (1980). The centrality of skill-utilization for job design, in K. Duncan, M. Gruneberg and D. Wallis (eds), *Changes in Working Life*, Chichester: Wiley

O'Brien, G.E. (1982). The relative contribution of perceived skill-utilization and other perceived job attributes to the prediction of job satisfaction: a cross validation study, *Human Relations*, **35**, 219–37

O'Brien, G.E. (1984). Locus of control, work, and retirement, Chapter 2 in H.M. Lefcourt (ed.), *Research with the Locus of Control Construct* vol. 3, New York: Academic Press

Organ, D.W. and Greene, C.N. (1974). Role ambiguity, Locus of control, and work satisfaction, *Journal of Applied Psychology*, **59**, 101–2

Pearlin, L.I. and Schooler, C. (1978). The structure of coping, *Journal of Health and Social Behavior*, **9**, 2–21

Phares, E.J. (1976). *Locus of Control in Personality*, Morristown, N.J.: General Learning Press

Quinn, R.P., Seashore, S., Kahn, R., Mangione, T., Campbell, D., Staines, G. and McCollough, M. (1971a). *Survey of Working Conditions: Final Report on Univariate and Bivariate Tables*, Washington, D.C.: U.S. Government Printing Office

Quinn, R.P., Seashore, S. and Mangione, I. (1971b). *Survey of Working Conditions*, Washington, D.C.: U.S. Government Printing Office

Quinn, R.P., and Shepard, L. (1974). *The 1972-73 Quality of Employment Survey*, Ann Arbor: University of Michigan, Survey Research Center

Roethlisberger, F.J., and Dickson, W.J. (1939). *Management and the Worker*, Cambridge, Mass: Harvard University Press

Rotter, J.B. (1966). Generalized expectancies for internal versus external control of reinforcement, *Psychological Monographs*, **80** (1, Whole No. 609)

Spector, P.E. (1982). Behavior in organizations as a function of employee's locus of control, *Psychological Bulletin*, **91**, 482–97

Stein, M., Keller, S., and Schleifer, S. (1981). The hypothalamus and the immune response in H. Weiner, M. Hofer and A. Strinkard (eds), *Brain, Behavior and Bodily Disease*, New York: Raven

Wall, T.D. and Lischeron, J.A. (1977). *Worker Participation*, Mardenhead, U.K.: McGraw-Hill

Zagans, L.S. (1982). Stress and the development of somatic disorders, Chapter 10 in L. Goldberger and S. Breznitz (eds), *Handbook of Stress*, New York: The Free Press

CHAPTER 5

Job Content and Personality

The previous chapter examined the way in which job content could determine employee strain and physical health. The available research suggests that a mismatch between job demands and personal capabilities could induce strain and strain, if prolonged, could affect physical and psychological health. In considering the mechanism whereby strain could have long term consequences on employees it was suggested that strain determines control beliefs which, in turn, predisposes employees to various physical and psychological illnesses.

This raises the question of the effects of job experiences on personality. If people are required to do jobs which do not 'fit' their capabilities or personality, do they change? At a general level it seems reasonable to expect that changes would occur when the job requires behaviours that do not allow the expression of stable abilities and behavioural dispositions. If what we have to do is inconsistent with what we want to do there will be pressures to change our dispositions in order to relieve the distress or anxiety associated with cognitive inconsistency. This assertion assumes that cognitive inconsistency is an aversive state which people consciously or unconsciously try to avoid.

Before considering mechanisms, such as consistency, as explanations of change it is necessary to examine the evidence showing what kind of change actually occurs. It is possible that tasks which are poorly fitted to the individual will not change personality but just task-related behaviours and attitudes. This is the assumption made by many theories of work motivation which use personality variables to predict employee performance and job satisfaction (e.g. Hackman and Oldham, 1980; Korman, 1976). They assume that the personality of working adults is stable. However, they do study personality–job fit as a determinant of performance, attitudes and work motivation. These theories might require substantial modification if it can be shown that job experiences directly affect personality.

The purpose of this chapter is twofold. The first aim is to outline the various ways in which personality interacts with job structures in determining individual performance. The second aim is to review the studies that show that jobs can have enduring effects on personality. This second aim is important for a number of reasons. These are:

1. Reactions to jobs cannot be properly understood unless we know the psychological functions of work. If personality changes as a function of job experiences then attempts to predict employee performance and motivation from personality variables must take account of these changes.
2. If people do change significantly as a result of job experience, then it indicates that theories of work motivation should be tied to the field of occupational socialization (Frese, 1982). If they have little effect on personality then the area of occupational socialization has little implication for job design or personality functioning.

THE MAJOR AREAS OF WORK AND PERSONALITY

There are three main areas of research into work and personality. The first is the area of job choice which is the domain of vocational psychology. Here job choices, ideal and actual, are studied as a function of abilities, interests, values and general personality structure. The second area is the study of how personality differences determine different responses to similar jobs.

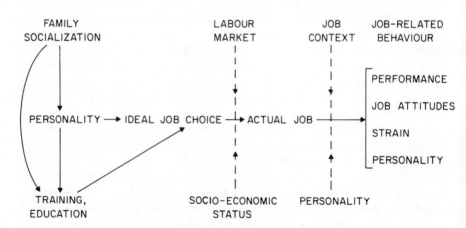

FIGURE 5.1 The relationship between personality, job choice and job content. Labour market conditions and socio-economic status moderate the relationship between job choice and the job actually obtained. Job-related behaviour is directly determined by job content but moderated by job context as well as personality

This has been of interest to those concerned with job design. The third main area is the effect of work structures and job content on personality and general adjustment. The interrelationships between these areas are shown in figure 5.1. Personality, including abilities, is considered to be one of the main determinants of ideal job choice along with family background and education. At the time of job choice for school leavers their personality is determined by socialization experiences. Theories such as Holland's have related personality to ideal job choices but ideal choices, of themselves, are imperfectly related to actual job choices (Holland, 1973, 1976). Whether or not a person gets the job he would like depends on many factors including job availability and the effects of parental and group processes indexed by socio-economic status.

The second area of work–personality relationships concerns the effects of stable personality characteristics on an individual's reaction to the job. Here personality is seen as a determinant of job performance and job attitudes. The final major area is the effect of job structures on personality. If personality changes do occur then it is feasible that these could determine either subsequent job choices, or job performance and the employee's job history within his or her chosen occupation. Since this book is mainly concerned with the relationship between job structures and the individual, attention will be given to the latter two areas.

THE EFFECTS OF INDIVIDUAL DIFFERENCES ON REACTIONS TO JOB CHARACTERISTICS

The current consensus in North American occupational psychology is that there is no one right way of designing jobs. Individual differences in personality, life stage and career plans determine how people react to a given job. If this is true, then it is assuming that there are no 'universal' desirable job structures that will fit people. Put another way, there is no such thing as a 'good' or 'bad' job. Whether or not a given job makes a person productive and fulfilled depends on the person. This seems a position that is extreme and may be a premature reaction to a failure to identify general work needs and general job structures that could meet these needs. While not denying the existence of individual differences, it is possible to consider another viewpoint. There may be general features of jobs that have common effects on people while, at the same time, the strength of these effects is moderated by individual differences. Neither of these positions were held by early theorists on job satisfaction and performance. They assumed that there were general needs or motives that all people try to satisfy in their work. The evidence supporting this view was the frequent observation that certain kinds of jobs produced dissatisfaction in all people. Simple routine jobs were associated with job dissatisfaction, turnover and absenteeism (Blauner, 1964; Herzberg, Mausner and Snyderman, 1959; Walker and Guest, 1952).

Such jobs were prevalent in industries using assembly line procedures and machine technology that reduced the skill content of jobs. Many saw scientific management, derived from the early work of F.W. Taylor, as being responsible for work simplification but it seems that economic forces, new technology and the desire to have a quickly trained, replaceable and controlled workforce all had some independent influence on work simplication.

The response to these findings was the development of job design theories based on the need to have more complex and challenging jobs. A good example is Herzberg's theory of job satisfaction (Herzberg, 1966). According to this theory, jobs had to be enriched if they were to motivate and satisfy employees. In practice, this meant that jobs should provide challenging tasks, achievement opportunities, responsibility, recognition for achievement and feedback. According to Herzberg, all people would respond to these motivating features with increased productivity and satisfaction. This was because psychological growth for all people occurred through developing their needs for autonomy, mastery and achievement through work tasks. A small number would not respond but, for Herzberg, they were abnormal. If they worked only for factors such as money, security and extrinsic incentives they were mentally ill (hygiene seekers).

However, with insight, counselling, and the right experiences they could be changed and learn how their real needs could be met by challenging work tasks. Herzberg's theory, except among Herzberg's associates, has not survived as a dominant theory of job design because:

1. The theory is not clearly stated and therefore difficult to disprove (King, 1970).
2. Evidence relevant to the theory has generally not supported it; the studies that do support it have been criticized because the results are explainable, to some extent, by defensive bias on the part of employees (Vroom, 1964; Locke, 1976).
3. It neglected the evidence that seems to show that there were substantial differences in employee personality and these differences meant that different job structures were required for different people (Hulin and Blood, 1968).
4. It did not provide a method of measuring job attributes. Inferences about the job were made by Herzberg on the basis of content analysis of employees' unstructured comments. Such a method did not ensure that employees were really talking about the same thing and neither did it provide a way of assessing the degree to which job attributes were present.

Two of these deficiencies were overcome in the more recent job characteristics theory (Hackman and Oldham, 1975, 1976, 1980). They provided measurer of central job characteristics (skill-variety, task identity, task significance, autonomy and feedback). In addition, they specified a measure of individual differences, growth need strength, that was meant to distinguish between employees who would respond positively to the presence of the central job characteristics and those who would not.

The main evidence for the importance of personality variables as moderators of the job characteristics—job responses relationship has come from this theory and many would agree with the following summary statement by Brousseau (1983):

> Of the research in this area, the most consistent and convincing evidence has been produced by researchers who have studied the 'moderating' influence of 'higher-order' need strength (or growth need strength) on the relationship between job scope and employees' affective and motivational reaction to their jobs.
>
> (Brousseau, 1983, p. 34)

This is the preferred interpretation of many studies in this area, but it is one that can be questioned. If Brousseau's conclusion is accepted, then we have to assume that only employees with high growth need strength will respond positively to jobs with high amounts of skill-variety, task identity, task significance, autonomy and feedback. Those with low growth need strength do not respond negatively but they 'tend to remain indifferent to the characteristics of their jobs, regardless of how challenging or simple, varied or routine, their jobs happen to be' (Brousseau, 1983, p. 34).

The problem with this conclusion is that it is misleading and, for many studies, untrue. The studies that do show that personality and/or work values affect job responses report very small effects. The effects are statistically significant but account for a very small amount of the variation in response measures such as job satisfaction or intrinsic motivation. Because a result is statistically significant it does not mean that we are dealing with a strong effect. The second problem with this interpretation of personality moderator effects is that it is untrue. People low on growth need strength or equivalent 'need' measures are not indifferent to jobs high on challenge or autonomy. They tend to react quite positively to increases in these task attributes even if slightly less positively than those high on growth need strength.

This criticism of the interpreters of moderator research needs to be documented. To do this, it is necessary to analyse the results. The main purpose of this analysis is to show that individual differences have very little effect on employee responses to jobs that vary in intrinsic dimensions. The conclusion to be drawn from these studies is not the importance of individual variability but the similarity across people in their responses to jobs high or low in challenge, autonomy, identity and meaningfulness.

A. The Unimportance of Individual Differences

A considerable amount of research has sought to establish the role of personality and work values in moderating the relationship between perceived job attributes and job satisfaction. Most of this research has started off by assuming that individual differences would have a considerable effect in moderating the job satisfaction–job attribute relationship. For example, whether an employee was satisfied with a given level of autonomy in a job depended, it was originally thought, on his or her need for autonomy or at least his or her desire for autonomy in the job. This area of investigation appeared promising after early studies by Vroom (1959) and Turner and Lawrence (1965). Vroom found that the association between participation in job decisions and job satisfaction depended on an employee's need for independence. Employees high on independence expressed higher satisfaction with participation than those who were low in independence. Work values or needs were not directly measured in the Turner and Lawrence study but they did find that the association between job satisfaction and job attributes varied as a function of the geographical background of employees. Later studies considered that these results might be attributable to rural and city employees having different work values (Blood and Hulin, 1967; Hulin and Blood, 1968; Susman, 1973). It was suggested that those employees who subscribed to Protestant work values were more likely to enjoy jobs high in challenge than those who rejected the Protestant work values.

Work values refer to desired attributes of an employee's job system and can be either general or specific. General values that have been measured include adherence to the Protestant Work Ethic (Hulin and Blood, 1968; Wanous, 1974; Wollack *et al.*, 1971; Stone, 1975, 1976) work orientation (expressive vs instrumental)(O'Reilly, 1977) and Rokeach's value system (Feather, 1975, 1979). Specific values measure the importance to the employee of potential attributes of the job such as autonomy, variety and skill-utilization. These values are labelled in different ways such as 'higher-order need strength' (Hackman and Lawler, 1971; Brief and Aldag, 1975; Jackson, Paul and Wall, 1981), self-actualization need strength (Sims and Szilagyi, 1976), growth need strength (Hackman and Oldham, 1976, 1980) or desired job attributes (O'Brien and Dowling, 1980; O'Brien and Humphrys, 1982; Porter, 1962).

Although a considerable number of studies have been conducted using these measures, the results have often not been evaluated in terms of the size of moderator effects. If work values make a large difference to the relationship between job satisfaction and job attributes then the accuracy with which job satisfaction can be predicted from job attributes should be considerably improved by estimating job satisfaction as a joint function of job attributes and work values instead of a function of job attributes alone.

TABLE 5.1 Estimates of the size of moderator effects from correlations between job satisfaction and job attributes

Researchers	Sample	Measures Satisfaction	Job attributes	Correlations Low on moderator r	N	High on moderator r	N	Significance of Difference	Estimated Moderator Effect
		Moderator: higher order need strength (Hackman and Lawler, 1971)							
Brief and Aldag (1975)	Corrections employees N = 104. 78% M	General	Variety	0.35		0.47		.	0.004
		Work (JDI)	Variety	0.20		0.63		*	0.046
		General	Autonomy	0.35		0.53		.	0.008
		work (JDI)	Autonomy	0.36		0.62		.	0.017
		General	Task identity	0.33		0.40		.	0.001
		Work (JDI)	Task identity	0.35		0.40		.	0.001
		General	Task feedback	0.36		0.36		.	0.000
		Work (JDI)	Task feedback	0.18		0.52		.	0.029
		General	Product of attributes	0.54		0.56		.	0.000
		General Work (JDI)	Product of attributes	0.33		0.61		.	0.020
Hackman and Lawler (1971)	Telephone company employees and supervisors N = 20	General	Variety × autonomy × task identity × task feedback	0.40	67	0.48	67	*	0.002
Orpen (1979)	Clerical workers	Work (JDI)	Skill-variety	0.14	18	0.19	18	.	0.001
		Work (JDI)	Task identity	0.31	18	0.29	18	.	0.000
		Work (JDI)	Task significance	0.18	18	0.27	18	.	0.002
		Work (JDI)	Autonomy	-0.02	18	0.46	18	*	0.058
		Work (JDI)	Job Feedback	0.09	18	0.28	18	.	0.009
		Work (JDI)	MPS	0.21	18	0.37	18	.	0.006

TABLE 5.1 (Cont.)

Researchers	Sample	Measures		Correlations				Significance of Difference	Estimated Moderator Effect
		Satisfaction	Job attributes	Low on moderator		High on moderator			
				r	N	r	N		
Pokorney, Gilmore and Beehr (1980)	102, 1st-level managers; 71 2nd-level managers	General	Job significance	0.29	54	0.64		*	0.031
			Autonomy	0.23	54	0.42		.	0.009
			Completeness	0.17	54	0.40		.	0.013
			Simplicity	0.09	54	0.34		.	0.016
			Feedback	0.15	54	0.63		*	0.058
Umstot, Bell and Mitchell (1976)	42 heterogeneous 26 f, 16 m	Work (JDI)	Variety	0.73	12	0.70	12	.	0.000
		Work (JDI)	Identity	0.67	12	0.27	12	.	0.040
		Work (JDI)	Significance	0.28	12	0.70	12	.	0.044
		Work (JDI)	Autonomy	0.41	12	0.71	12	.	0.023
		Work (JDI)	Feedback	0.48	12	0.76	12	.	0.020
		Work (JDI)	MPS	0.67	12	0.84	12	.	0.007
Wanous (1974)	Female telephone operators $N = 80$	General	Variety	0.15	37	0.50	37	*	0.031
			Autonomy	−0.09	37	0.59	37	*	0.116
			Task identity	−0.07	37	0.59	37	.	0.034
			Task feedback	0.10	37	0.41	37	.	0.024
Moderator: Protestant Work Ethic									
Aldag and Brief (1975)	Hourly manufacturing employees	General	Skill-variety	−0.29	131	0.04	131	Not reported	0.027
			Task identity	−0.22	131	0.05	131	Not reported	0.018
			Task significance	−0.28	131	0.07	131	Not reported	0.031
			Autonomy	−0.19	131	−0.05	131	Not reported	0.005
			Feedback	−0.18	131	0.09	131	Not reported	0.018

Study	Sample	Measure	Facet	r	N	r	N	Sig.	
Blood (1969)	Students N = 114 Airmen N = 306	Work (JDI)		-0.16	114	0.09	114	.	0.016
		General		-0.17	114	0.22	114	.	0.038
		Work (JDI)		-0.12	306	0.17	306	.	0.021
		General		-0.13	306	0.10	306	.	0.013
Stone (1976)	594 heterogeneous	Work	Job scope	0.51	202	0.39	83	Not reported	0.004
Wanous (1974)	Female telephone operators	Global	Variety	0.10	37	0.41	37	.	0.024
			Autonomy	0.21	37	0.38	37	.	0.007
			Task identity	-0.05	37	0.33	37	.	0.036
			Task feedback	0.22	37	0.24	37	.	0.000
Moderator: personality measures									
Lawler, Hackman and Kaufman (1973)	Telephone operators N = 39 F	General	Changes in variety autonomy	Not reported					
Sims and Sizilagyi (1976)	Paramedical and medical staff	Work (JDI)	Variety	0.34	97	0.55	433	*	0.011
		Work (JDI)	Autonomy	-0.02	97	0.23	433		0.016
		Work (JDI)	Feedback	0.28	97	0.27	433	.	0.000
		Work (JDI)	Task identity	0.19	97	0.19	433	*	0.000
		Work (JDI)	Dealing with others	0.15	97	0.37	433	*	0.012
		Work (JDI)	Friendship	0.03	97	0.31	433	*	0.020

TABLE 5.1 (Cont.)

Researchers	Sample	Measures Satisfaction	Job attributes	Correlations Low on moderator r	N	High on moderator r	N	Significance of Difference	Estimated Moderator Effect
Vroom (1959)	108 delivery company supervisors	General	Participation	0.13	38	0.55	38	Not reported	0.044
				0.53	39	0.03	34	Not reported	0.063
Evans, Kiggunder, and House (1979)	Automobile assembly supervisors and managers	General	MPS	0.11	93	0.42	128	*	0.024
		Work	MPS	-0.10	23	0.40	26	.	0.063
		General	Skill-variety	0.01	95	0.17	118	.	0.006
		Work	Skill-variety	0.07	40	0.12	45	.	0.001
		General	Task identity	-0.10	95	0.25	115	*	0.031
		Work	Task identity	0.10	39	0.26	41	.	0.006
		General	Task significance	0.19	95	0.23	117	.	0.000
		Work	Task significance	-0.12	39	0.51	44	*	0.099
		General	Autonomy	0.16	94	0.26	116	.	0.003
		Work	Autonomy	0.31	39	0.30	44	.	0.000
		General	Feedback	0.03	96	0.30	117	*	0.018
		Work	Feedback	0.00	40	0.21	44	.	0.011
Hackman and Oldham (1975)	Heterogeneous N = 658 59% M	General Security Pay Social Supervisory	JDS	Not reported				?	—
Hackman and Oldham (1976)	Heterogeneous	General satisfaction	MPS	0.32	170	0.49	186	.	0.007

Study	Sample	Change in general satisfaction	Change in MPS	r_{SJ}^L	n	r_{SJ}^H	n		% of variance
Hackman, Pearce and Wolfe (1978)	Bank clerks		Change in MPS	0.16	27	0.30	28	.	0.005
Orpen (1976)	Westerners Tribal Orientation	General		Not reported					–
Sims and Szilagyi (1976)	776 Paramedical staff	General	Variety	0.44	70	0.42	228	.	0.000
		General	Autonomy	0.39	70	0.16	228	*	0.013
		General	Feedback	0.16	70	0.16	228	.	0.000
		General	Task identity	0.29	70	0.19	228	.	0.003
		General	Dealing with others	0.46	70	0.26	228	*	0.010
		General	Friendship	0.17	70	0.19	228	.	0.000

Notes: 1. The estimated moderator effect was calculated using the formula: Effect $= \frac{1}{4}(r_{SJ}^H - r_{SJ}^L)$.(See Note 1.)

2. r_{SJ}^H is the correlation between satisfaction and job attribute scores for groups high on the moderator;

3. r_{SJ}^L is the correlation between satisfaction and job attribute scores low on the moderator.

4. The percentage of variance is obtained by multiplying the effect by 100.

If studies have established this then it is a finding with theoretical and practical importance. It would imply that attempts to improve job satisfaction and performance through changing job attributes would only be successful for employees who have values that are congruent with job content. If work values have little or no effect as moderators then job satisfaction and performance increments might occur by general changes in job attributes and be unaffected by differences in employee work values.

One of the problems in estimating the size of moderator effects is due to differences among studies in the methods of analysis. A common method has involved splitting a sample into two or more subgroups based on differences in subgroup work values. Thus the association between job attributes and job satisfaction has been calculated for groups high and low in work values or need strength. Support for the moderator position has been inferred when the correlations between job attributes and job reactions are greater for the group high on the value measure. These analyses show how the degree of association between job reactions and job attributes varies with work values. This is not quite the same as showing that work values interact with job attributes in determining job reactions. Interaction effects have been found in studies where regression methods have been used to predict job reactions. The predictors include job attributes, work values and a product term obtained by multiplying scores on job attributes and work values.

These studies allow an estimate to be made of the strength of the interaction by examining how much the product term increases the degree to which job reactions can be predicted. For those studies where the effect of values or needs has been measured by comparing the correlation between satisfaction in job attributes for groups high or low in values, the percentage of variance in job reactions attributable to the interaction between job attributes and values has to be calculated by a different method.[1] Table 5.1 summarizes most of the available studies on the effects of work values where the effects are estimated by splitting groups into those high or low on values or needs The final column shows the size of the effect which has been calculated independently. As can be seen, the size of the effect varies from 0.000 to 0.116. Thus, the moderator effects account for between 0 and 11.6 per cent of the variance in job satisfaction. The mean percentage is 1.64 per cent.

Table 5.2 documents the increment in R^2 when the product-term, job attribute × needs/values, is added to the regression. R is the multiple correlation between all predictors and the criterion $R^2 \times 100$ gives the percentage of variance in the criterion accounted for by the predictors. This provides a measure of the strength of the moderator effect. The mean value is 0.0135: i.e. only 1.35 per cent of variance accounted for. Hence differences in needs and work values explain only a very small amount of the variation in job evaluations.

TABLE 5.2 Size of moderator effects estimated by hierarchical regression

Researchers	Sample	N	Job attribute	Moderator	Job satisfaction	ΔR^2 Attributes	ΔR^2 Moderator	Job attribute × moderator
Champoux (1980)	Research and development	Sample 1 Sample 2 Sample 3	Job scope	Growth need strength	General	0.24 0.17* 0.38*	0.002 0.008 0.041*	0.006* 0.067* 0.002
Cherrington and England (1980)	Various	3053	Degree of enrichment	Desired job enrichment	Job attractiveness	not given		<0.01
Ganster (1980)	College students	190	Job scope	Protestant Ethic	Task	not reported		not significant
				GNS	Task	not reported		not significant
				Arousal-seeking	Task	not reported		not significant
				n Achievement	Task	not reported		0.02
Humphrys (1981)	Oil company employees	133	Job scope	Desired job scope	Work (JDI)	0.44*	0.04*	0.04*
			Job scope	Desired job scope	General	0.63*	0.10*	0.02*
Jackson Paul and Wall (1981)	School leavers	215	Job scope	HNS (measured 1 year earlier)	General	not reported		significant
				HNS (measured at same time as job scope)		not reported		significant

TABLE 5.2 (Cont.)

Researchers	Sample	N	Job attribute	Moderator	Job satisfaction	ΔR^2 Attributes	ΔR^2 Moderator	ΔR^2 Job attribute × moderator
O'Brien and Dowling (1980)	Representative city sample	1383	Skill-utilization	Desired Skill-utilization	General	0.38*	0.01	0.01*
			Influence	Desired influence	General	0.24*	0.04*	0.00
			Variety	Desired variety	General	0.19*	0.06*	0.02*
			Interaction	Desired interaction	General	0.02	0.00	0.01*
			Pressure	Desired pressure	General	0.00	0.02*	0.03*
O'Brien and Humphrys (1982)	Pharmacists	281	Skill-utilization	Desired Skill-utilization	General	0.48*	0.00	0.010
			Skill-utilization	Desired Skill-utilization	Work (JDI)	0.31*	0.001	0.006
			Influence	Desired influence	General	0.15*	0.016	0.011
			Influence	Desired influence	Work (JDI)	0.07	0.006	0.002
			Variety	Desired variety	General	0.23*	0.07	0.000
			Variety	Desired variety	Work(JDI)	0.17	0.09	0.010
O'Brien and Stevens (1981)	Assembly line employees	192	Influence	Desired influence	Work (JDI)	0.07*	0.01*	0.001
			Influence	Need for control	Work (JDI)	0.07	0.00	0.000

Study	Sample	N	Challenge measure	Expressive orientation	Work (JDI)			
O'Reilly (1977)	Low status personnel	307	Challenge Challenge	Expressive orientation Instrumental orientation		not reported not reported		0.01 not significant
Peters and Champoux (1979)	Research and development staff	1978	MPS MPS	Growth need strength Growth need strength	General Growth	0.228* 0.398*	0.003* 0.000*	0.002 0.008*
Pokorney, Gilmore and Beehr (1980)	Insurance managers	173	Job significance Autonomy Completeness Simplicity Feedback	Growth Need strength Need strength Need strength Need strength	General General General General General	0.22 0.10 0.08 0.05 0.14	0.00 0.01 0.00 0.01 0.01	0.02 0.01 0.03 0.02 0.08*
Robey (1974)	College Students	60	Job scope (interaction)	Intrinsic extrinsic values	Global	not reported		0.061*
Stone (1980)	Various	594	Job scope	Protestant Work Ethic	General	not reported		0.061*
Stone, Mowday and Porter (1977)	Mixed sample	340	Job scope	n Achievement n Autonomy	Work	0.144* 0.144*	0.106* 0.029*	0.019* 0.000
Vecchio (1980)	National sample	3062	Job quality	Anomie	General	not reported		0.004*

Notes: 1. * Indicates statistical significance $p < 0.05$

2. Percentage of variance in job satisfaction accounted for by the interaction between job attitudes and moderator = ΔR^2 (Change) × 100.

B. The Explanation of Small Moderator Effects

In a recent review that found that there were inconsistent moderator effects (White, 1978) the author concluded that research on moderator effects should cease. This conclusion can be challenged in two ways. Firstly, studies on individual differences that moderate the job attribute–job satisfaction relationship show remarkably consistent results. The size of the moderator effect is consistently small in relation to the size of the job attribute effect. The results appear inconsistent if statistical significance is taken as a criterion. However, the appropriate statistic to use in assessing consistency is the percentage of variance accounted for. In many cases a statistically insignificant result is obtained because the size of the sample is relatively small. With larger samples the effect becomes significant even though the size of the effect remains constant.

The second way in which White's conclusion can be challenged is by asking why the effect size is so small. It is a result that appears novel and counter to common sense. Psychological research in many fields shows that there are individual differences in attitudes, values and personality. These personal characteristics can account for differences in behaviour so why should they not have an effect on job evaluations? Since the appearance of White's review, a number of authors have tried to justify the significance of the moderator problem. These will now be examined.

1. The moderator effect is really large

Peters and Champoux (1979) tried to show that small but significant increments in the percentage of variance accounted for could have theoretical and practical importance. A significant moderator effect, according to them, just showed that there was an effect but said nothing about the predictive utility of moderator variables. Perhaps it could be argued that a significant regression coefficient associated with the moderator product-term is not a direct measure of effect size. However, the increment in R^2 is a direct measure of the size of the moderator effect. Peters and Champoux (1979) tried to show that regression equations, estimated for various levels of a moderator, vary considerably in their predictive utility. Closer examination shows that the variation in predictive utility is not large.

An increase of 50 points in the job attribute (MPS) leads to an increase of 0.43 points in growth satisfaction for the group lowest in need strength and an increase of 0.59 points for those highest in need strength. However, the standard deviation of scores on the growth satisfaction scale is 1.13. Thus the effective difference in increment of growth satisfaction is:

$$\frac{0.59 - 0.43}{1.13} = \frac{0.16}{1.13} = 0.14$$

of a standard deviation. This is hardly a large difference, especially when compared with increments in growth satisfaction that could be expected from increasing job attributes from low to high.

2. The hypothesis has not been properly tested

In another attempt to justify the significance of the moderator effect, Vecchio (1980) maintains that White's (1978) rejection of the moderator effect is not warranted as research has not properly tested the hypothesis. He points out that researchers have not used samples that contain a range of jobs that vary considerably in job quality. This is true for most, but not all, studies. Using a sample of over 3000 male employees he sought to obtain a sample of employees with wide variety in job quality. However, the moderator effect was again small in this study. The size of the effect was only reported for anomie. The increment in R^2 due to the product term was statistically significant but the change in R^2, $\Delta R^2 = 0.004$. Educational level and former residence were also reported as having significant moderator effects. Somewhat curiously, Vecchio concluded 'It can now be more confidently concluded that the moderator hypothesis is a valid descriptive summarization for the labor force'. This conclusion can be challenged.

1. Vecchio has not shown that the size of the effect is large.
2. He has not demonstrated significant effects across a wide range of moderators.
3. Lastly, and later he admits it himself, the effect is significant but of little practical utility.

3. The size of the effect increases with the task specificity of the measure

Cherrington and England (1980) also question White's conclusions: 'the results of these studies are not entirely consistent [but] they were significantly impressive to warrant a closer look'. They claim that the results do show consistency as moderator effects are most likely to be significant when the moderating variable is a specific measure of S's desire for greater enrichment (e.g. Wanous, 1974). The results become less consistent as 'the moderating variable becomes further removed from the individual's preference for specific job factors and becomes a more abstract personality factor'. They endorse Aldag and Brief's (1979) recommendation that 'direct assessment of individual desires is preferable'.

The problem with this is that the size of the effect does not appear to vary with the specificity of the measure (see Tables 5.1 and 5.2). Cherrington and England then used a direct measure of an individual's desire for job enrichment. This measure was summated from responses to three items that asked employees how much responsibility they would like, how closely supervised they would like to be, and how much participation in decision making they desired. They found a significant moderator effect between job attribute–job satisfaction but the associated increment in ΔR^2 was less than 0.01. Therefore, it must be concluded that they have not demonstrated that the effect size is considerably larger when task-specific moderator variables are used.

4. The effect is due to response consistency

Some authors have argued that giving self-report measures at the same point of time could produce a moderator effect because respondents would aim to be consistent (Jackson, Paul and Wall, 1981). Thus someone who says he has low job influence but desires a lot more would feel that he has to report low satisfaction if he is to be consistent. Correspondingly, if he reported low job influence and low desired job influence, he would report relatively high job satisfaction. Thus the observed moderator effect could be due to response consistency effects and not a 'true' effect. Jackson, Paul and Wall (1981), who propose this criticism, appear to conclude that moderator effects have been well established in the literature.

They then question the adequacy of moderator studies and indicate that it is desirable that the moderator variables be measured at different points of time so that consistency effects can be both avoided and estimated. Using 398 16-year-old school leavers they measured higher-order need strength (HONS) by a simple composite of importance scores for the five JDS job attributes, thus paralleling the form used by Hackman and Lawler (1971). The following year they measured HONS again, together with the perceived JDS job attributes. The HONS scores correlated 0.47 ($N = 215$). Using a modified form of moderated regression they reported the following results. Using the HONS obtained at time 1, the standardized regression coefficients for the regression of job attributes or job satisfaction were:

(a)	Low HONS	0.35
(b)	medium HONS	0.56
(c)	high HONS	0.68

The difference in slopes was reported to be statistically significant. The corresponding slopes for the HONS scores given at time 2 were:

(a)	low HONS	0.45
(b)	medium HONS	0.52
(c)	high HONS	0.64

They concluded that their results supported those 'from less methodologically stringent studies'. Although the results provide some evidence to show that response consistency was not producing a moderator effect, the size of the effect is still weak—only 7 per cent of the variance in job satisfaction was accounted for by the interaction between need strength and job attributes.

The main conclusion is that research shows that the large majority of individuals respond positively to jobs high on challenge, skill-utilization and autonomy. Such jobs produce high levels of satisfaction, interest and intrinsic motivation. Individual differences in response do have slight effects in that people who report that they do not desire personal fulfilment in work alone, or have low desires for skill-utilization and autonomy, have slightly lower levels of satisfaction with complex challenging jobs than those with high desires for personal fulfilment and self-directed behaviour. This does not justify an extreme position which maintains that there are no 'good' jobs but what is good for one person is not for another.

This review does not support Brousseau's conclusion:

> These findings showing the moderating effects of growth need strength indicate that there is no universally good job. Whereas efforts to increase job scope are likely to produce substantial gains in job satisfaction and motivation for some individuals, they may only negligibly affect (at least in the short run) the job reactions of others

(Brousseau, 1983, p. 34)

In this quotation Brousseau recognizes that his general conclusion, if not correct, at least may be incorrect when the long-term effects of jobs are considered. This raises the possibility that the job may change individual values and personality. It also suggests that the failure of moderator research to identify individual differences in job responses may partly be due to people adapting themselves to the job. If you have a challenging job you might report, on personality tests, that you value challenge. If you do not have a challenging job, your self-reports of desired challenge could be low. Before examining the direct effects of the job on attitudes, values and personality we shall briefly examine the effects of situational influences on job responses. These influences refer to factors in the work environment apart from the job content.

C. Situational Influences on Job Responses

A number of writers have pointed out that an employee's response to the job may be determined by the work context as well as the job itself and the characteristics of the person (Lawler, 1971; Hackman and Oldham, 1980; Oldham, Hackman and Pearce, 1976; Porter, Lawler and Hackman, 1975). One study (Oldham, Hackman and Pearce, 1976), concluded that employees who are satisfied with contextual factors such as pay, security, interpersonal relations and supervision respond more positively to challenging jobs than employees dissatisfied with these factors. The meaning of these findings is unclear. It could be used to support a Maslow-type interpretation which would postulate that employees will not be motivated or concerned with higher needs such as achievement or skill-utilization until 'lower'needs such as security and adequate income have been met. Alternatively, it could mean that jobs which require skills, responsibility and initiative are not considered satisfying if the workers do not get an equitable salary and due supervisory recognition for their work. The general evidence for the Maslow hierarchy of needs is inconclusive but there is some point to the latter explanation. Some job enrichments may fail when increases in skill and autonomy are not matched by economic rewards. Most employees have learned to expect that autonomy and skill level are, or should be, tied to economic rewards or salary. Many strikes and industrial disputes occur because of perceived inequity in the distribution of income. Unions and employers typically operate on some principle of 'work value'. Jobs have 'income value' for many different reasons including danger, shift requirements, and their contribution to a whole work process, but a main factor is the amount of training and consequent skill requirements of the job. If employees have to spend a long time in an apprenticeship or at an educational institution they incur relative income losses that they expect to be recouped by eventual higher income. The other reasons for associating higher pay to high skill levels are social tradition, increased personal costs of such jobs (number of hours worked or increased strain), and the need to provide social recognition of the importance of the job. Money is not just a pay-packet. It is also a symbol of what the organization or society thinks of the job and the person in it (Lawler, 1971).

RECIPROCAL EFFECTS BETWEEN JOB AND PERSONALITY STRUCTURE

The preceding sections indicate that there are general effects of jobs upon people. Jobs high in skill-utilization, variety, influence and task significance induce high job satisfaction and intrinsic motivation. Very simply, people like jobs that are challenging and meaningful. Because they like them they want to expend more effort on them and want these jobs to continue. This raises the question of why they like these jobs. Do they meet some common need, personality function or aspiration? If they do, then does persistent experience with these jobs promote psychological growth or personality development? Conversely, if jobs are experienced as lacking skill-utilization, influence and meaningfulness do they have a stunting effect on growth and personality?

These questions are of obvious importance but there are relatively few studies that have been designed to answer them. Studies on job structure, job satisfaction and performance abound, but very few look at the relation between jobs and personality. Those that do can be classified into two types. The first type considers how personality change over the life cycle can determine reactions to jobs. The second type directly considers the effects of job content on stable personality attributes. We shall first consider the effect of personality change over the life-cycle on reactions to work.

A. Changes in Personality as a Determinant of Response to Jobs

Some studies in career development are relevant to the problem of understanding how life stages can affect both reaction to work and specific jobs. In a study of managerial careers, Hall and Nougaim (1968) described three temporal stages. The first one is *establishment* when individuals are preoccupied with obtaining security by ensuring that their jobs are established. The second stage is *advancement* when achievement and esteem are important for ensuring that there is advancement to more demanding and responsible jobs. The final stage is one of *maintenance* when security and achievement are guaranteed. Then the individual is free to develop his skills and work interests in a far more autonomous fashion. He or she is not preoccupied with security or achievement as defined by those who judge whether he/she should be promoted but rather by the need to do the job well according to his/her own standards. This study, like others on career development (e.g. Super, *et al.*, 1957) suggests that individuals change in their needs over time. Early in their work life they are most concerned about security, then achievement and promotion in their factory or organization and then, if this is achieved, with intrinsic satisfactions of doing their job to the best of their ability.

This is a fairly loose interpretation of these studies because they do not measure how these various needs change over time. They are inferred or hypothesized from general observations of employee behaviour. Furthermore, these studies do not show that reaction to job content change with time. Some evidence that such changes do occur is provided by Katz (1978a,b). He found that reactions to job scope or complexity varied with the length of time that an individual had been employed in the same job (longevity). During the initial stages of job occupancy, job satisfaction correlated with task significance and feedback but not with autonomy, variety and task identity. For individuals who had been on the job for 1 to 3 years, job satisfaction correlated with all of these task variables. During this 'responsive' stage job satisfaction is highly associated with job performance and turnover. When individuals have been on the same job 10 years or more they become 'unresponsive' to job characteristics. For them, there is no significant relationship between job scope and satisfaction.

The interpretation to be given to these results is not clear. Perhaps, with increased longevity and age, individuals become more concerned with extrinsic rewards, such as income and involvement in non-work activities. A simpler interpretation is possible, however. When people are learning a job they have reasonable opportunities for using their skills regardless of the objective skill level of the job. They are more concerned with getting feedback about their performance and knowing that the job is a worthwhile one. Once the job is learnt, they become responsive to the actual opportunities for regular use of their skills and initiative. They express dissatisfaction if the job does not provide reasonable levels of skill-utilization and autonomy. If the job does not change then on-the-job experiences should increase their skill levels and eventually they will not be challenged very much. After 10 years or so, the job becomes fairly routine to most of them and thus their satisfaction will not be related to their original assessments of job challenge. If this is the case, then Katz's studies indicate that jobs need to be changed as employees increase their skill repertoire. Their personalities may not have changed much nor their desire to exert autonomy and use skills. Their responses to their jobs have changed because the content of their work has not reflected the changes in their skill levels.

B. The Direct Effects of Job Content upon Personality

Most of the organizational research on the effects of job structure upon behaviour has concentrated on performance effects on relatively temporary cognitive or emotional states, such as job satisfaction, job involvement, or strain. While personality measures have sometimes been introduced to explain individual differences in job reactions, studies have only infrequently examined how a job can have enduring effects on personality. This partly reflects a dominant interest in productivity and work motivation. It also is due, in part, to a tendency to believe that personality is largely shaped prior to adulthood and, once shaped, is unlikely to be much affected by social structures. This assumption is being increasingly challenged as evidence accumulates showing that personality changes occur in adults as different life problems are faced (e.g. Vaillant, 1974, 1975; Vaillant and McArthur, 1972).

Furthermore, there is a body of research that shows that work structures can directly affect personality. Table 5.3 summarizes the findings from studies in this area. The studies all agree that the content of the job can significantly determine employees' personality, their intellectual style and their relatively stable desire for enriched work. As a group the studies are impressive because they used large samples from different countries and were mostly longitudinal. Their design and methods of statistical analysis also allowed the researchers to estimate the direction of causal effects. This is important because simple correlational studies which showed an association between job attributes and personality measures could be explained in terms of selection processes. Employees' choice of occupation and job is

TABLE 5.3 The effects of job attributes on stable personal characteristics

Researchers	Sample	Design	Job attributes	Personal characteristics	Results
Andrisani and Nestel (1976)	Representative sample of middle-aged male U.S. employees	Survey 2-year longitudinal	Occupational status	Locus of control (Rotter scale)	Change to higher status jobs increased internal control. Change to lower status jobs decreased internal control.
Brousseau (1978)	116 U.S. engineers, scientists, managers	Survey 6-year longitudinal	Skill-variety Task identity Task significance Autonomy Feedback	Active orientation Philosophical orientation Freedom from depression Self-confidence	Increases in task significance and feedback associated increases in active orientation and decreases in depression
Brousseau and Prince (1981)	176 U.S. engineers, scientists, managers	Survey 7-year longitudinal	Skill-variety Task identity Task significance Autonomy Feedback	Guilford–Zimmerman temperament scales	Increases in task identity and task significance associated with increases in general activity, emotional stability, and friendliness
Kohn and Schooler (1973) Kohn (1976)	3100 male representative U.S. employees	Survey interview Cross-sectional Statistical analysis of causal relationships	Occupational control/self-direction (measured by substantive complexity, closeness of supervision, routinization)	Intellectual flexibility Powerlessness Self-estrangement	Increase in occupational self-direction associated with decrease of powerlessness, self-estrangement and increases in intellectual flexibility

TABLE 5.3   (Cont.)

Researchers	Sample	Design	Job attributes	Personal characteristics	Results
Kohn and Schooler (1978, 1981a,b, 1982)	687 male U.S. representative sample	Survey/interview 10-year longitudinal	Substantive complexity, directive supervision. routinization	Intellectual flexibility Self-direction	Increases in substantive complexity, associated with increased intellectual flexibility and self-direction. Reverse effect for substantive complexity
Miller *et al.,* (1979)	269 employed U.S. females	Survey/interview Cross-sectional Statistical analysis of causality	Occupational self-direction (composite of substantive complexity, directive supervision, routinization)	Intellectual flexibility Fatalism Authoritarian Conservatism	Increases in substantive complexity associated with increases in intellectual flexibility; Routinization increases fatalism and authoritarian conservatism
Mortimer and Lorence (1979)	435 male U.S. College graduates	Survey 10-year longitudinal	Autonomy (decision latitude, challenge)	Self-competence	Autonomy increased competence, after controlling for work values, income and education
O'Brien (1984)	1383 male and female Australian employees	Survey Cross-sectional Statistical analysis of causality	Skill-utilization Influence Income	Internal-external control	Higher levels of skill-utilization and income determine higher levels of internal control

Orpen (1979)	86 clerical South African employees	6-month field experiment	Skill-variety Task identity Task significance Autonomy Feedback	Growth need strength	Increases in combined task attributes associated with increases in growth need strength
Wall and Clegg (1981)	43 male U.K. blue-collar employees	Field experiment $1\frac{1}{2}$ year-longitudinal	Complexity (composite of autonomy, identity, task significance and feedback)	Growth need strength	Increases in complexity led to increases in growth need strength and decreases in psychiatric vulnerability
Tannenbaum (1957)	206 female U.S. clerical employees	Survey 1 year-longitudinal	Participation in decision-making	26 personality traits	Directive structures increased employee dependence, submissiveness, and desired self-direction. Autonomous structures increased self-discipline, competitiveness

partly determined by their interests and personality and hence it could be expected that there would be systematic variations in jobs associated with systematic variations in job content. The majority of studies have controlled this selection effect by using longitudinal designs and statistically controlling pre-employment differences in personality.

The studies are somewhat difficult to summarize, however, as they vary in their method of measuring job attributes and personality. The earlier studies concentrated on very general attributes of jobs such as occupational status (Andrisani and Nestel, 1976), job complexity (Kohn and Schooler, 1973; Kohn, 1976) or gross differences in organizations such as autonomous vs hierarchical structure (Tannenbaum, 1957; Tannenbaum and Allport, 1956). The problem with these job concepts is that they are very broad and do not allow a precise specification of the most important attributes for predicting personality change. What, for example, are the job dimensions indexed by occupational status? Jobs high in occupational status tend to be high on skill level, influence, variety, meaningfulness and income. Are all of these attributes equally important for determining personality? Similarly, complexity of the job could involve a large number of job dimensions. This problem would not be so important if there was a high correlation between the various dimensions used to describe job content. There tend to be significant positive correlations (e.g. Hackman and Oldham, 1975, 1976; O'Brien and Dowling, 1981; O'Brien, 1984), but they are not high enough to say that they are measuring the same general attribute or dimension.

Logic provides another reason for distinguishing job attributes even if there was, for example, a high correlation between job autonomy and income. It is quite possible that personality is determined by income alone. Whether or not it is income or job autonomy that has the effect on personality cannot be determined in studies where income and job autonomy are both indirectly assessed by one general measure. Nevertheless, these early studies do provide a number of important findings. Jobs that allow occupational self-direction induce higher levels of intellectual flexibility and personal control in employees than do jobs that are low on occupational self-direction. Occupational self-direction is the concept used by Kohn and Schooler (1973) and is a composite of job complexity, directiveness of supervision and routinization. Jobs high on these dimensions are likely to be found among those called 'high-status' jobs (Andrisani and Nestel, 1976) and in organizations where employees have a fair amount of autonomy over the organization of their work (Tannenbaum, 1957). Studies reported before 1980 show that employees with jobs that allow them to think for themselves and do a variety of tasks, and which require a relatively high level of skill, tend to be employees who are intellectually flexible, have high self-esteem and a strong belief in their ability to achieve valued goals by personal effort and ability. By contrast, employees who have to endure jobs that are relatively low on autonomy, skill and variety tend to be intellectually less flexible, low in self-esteem and less inclined to believe that their lives are personally controlled. They tend to become conforming and passive and to believe in external control.

Later studies have tried to establish the relative importance of the various job dimensions. Kohn and Schooler (1978, 1981, 1982) and Miller *et al.* (1979) found that the substantive complexity—the degree to which the job required independent thought and action—was far more important than either the degree of close supervision or routinization. Brousseau (1978) found that task significance (the degree to which the job made an important contribution to the task process and/or society) and feedback were more important than variety and autonomy for predicting active orientations and depression. Another recent study (O'Brien, 1984) found that internal control was predicted by skill-utilization and income but not by influence, variety, interaction and pressure.

The combined set of studies, in summary, provide evidence that job content can significantly determine;

1. Intellectual style (Kohn and Schooler, 1973, 1978, 1981, 1982),
2. Depression (Brousseau, 1978; Brousseau and Prince, 1981),
3. Self-competence (Mortimer and Lorence, 1979),
4. Beliefs in internal and external control (Andrisani and Nestel, 1976; O'Brien, 1984),
5. Desires or needs for self-direction, learning and personal accomplishment—growth need strength (Kohn and Schooler, 1981a; Orpen, 1979; Wall and Clegg, 1981).

Confidence in these findings is increased because the majority of the studies were able to control for the effect of job selection or the influence of organization structure on personality differences. There are still a number of problems in this research, however. The main ones are:

1. *Measuring job attributes by self-reports.* All studies have based their measures of job attributes on the structured perceptions of employees. These may be biased to some extent by personality or contextual factors. However, some studies (Kohn and Schooler, 1982; Hackman and Oldham, 1975) have found that there are considerable correlations (averaging about 0.7) between job perceptions and independently rated job attributes. This provides some evidence to show that a considerable amount of the variance in job perceptions reflects objective job differences.
2. *The size of the effects.* Although the effects of job attributes on personality measures are statistically significant, they account for a small

amount of the variance in personality. It is not possible to quantify exactly the strength of the effect in some studies but it appears that job attributes can account for only about 5 per cent of the variance in personality. Given the difficulty in changing personality this may not be surprising. However, it raises the question of the practical utility of the results. Are they big enough to suggest that they will affect the behaviour of the employee at work or outside work?

In response to this query, Kohn and Schooler have argued that small differences occurring over a few years can be magnified through the course of an individual's work history. Thus if an individual is in a job for a few years and benefits in intellectual flexibility and self-control, he or she is likely to be promoted or to seek out a more challenging job. Such a job is likely to further enhance their flexibility and self-control. Conversely, decrements in intellectual flexibility and self-control lead to an individual becoming less able to find challenging work and may lead to demotion to less complex work. The two extreme kinds of patterns can be represented schematically with intellectual flexibility (Figure 5.2). While the differences between A and B at Time 1 are fairly small, they are likely to be much greater at Time 3.

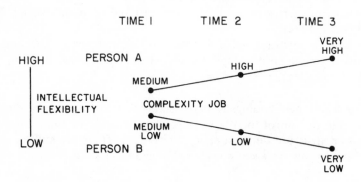

FIGURE 5.2   Changes in intellectual flexibility with time as predicted by Kohn and Schooler's theory. Employees who shift to jobs with increased complexity increase in intellectual flexibility. Employees who shift to jobs with less complexity decrease in intellectual flexibilty

3. *The mechanism whereby jobs affect people.* All of these studies have been primarily concerned with showing that jobs can affect personality. The process whereby job experiences are internalized and influence personality functioning has not been directly investigated. Do jobs, for

instance, that vary in skill-utilization and self-direction induce beliefs about self-competence and personal control at work which, in turn, generalize to non-work settings? What are the most important job dimensions for determining these beliefs? Do beliefs about competence or self-efficacy differ in their consequences from beliefs about self-direction or beliefs in internal/external control?

An attempt to answer some of these questions will be made in the next two chapters where a number of theories about the effects of work on personality will be considered.

NOTE

1.

$$V = \frac{\text{Percentage of variance}}{\text{due to interaction}} = \frac{1}{4} \, (r_{SJ}^H - r_{SJ}^L)^2 \times 100$$

where r_{SJ}^H

is the correlation between job evaluations (S) and job attributes (J) for the group high (H) on value/needs.

and r_{SJ}^L

is the correlation between job evaluations and job attributes for the group low (L) on value/needs.

This formula is derived in O'Brien and Gross (1983).
Thus, if $r_{SJ}^H = 0.6$ and $r_{SJ}^L = 0.5$

$$V = 100 \times \frac{1}{4} \, (0.6 - 0.5)^2 = 100 \times \frac{1}{4} \, (0.1)^2 = 0.0025 \times 100$$
$$= 0.25$$

This means that $\frac{1}{4}$ of 1 per cent of the variation in job satisfaction is attributable to the interaction between job attributes and job satisfaction. As the difference between r_{SJ}^H and r_{SJ}^L might be statistically significant (if the sample is large enough), it is easy to see how a statistically significant difference in correlations may really account for a very small percentage of variance. In this example, the percentage of variance in job satisfaction accounted for by the job attribute is 0.6×100 ($= 36\%$) for the high need group and 25% for the low need group. Thus the effect of job attributes on job satisfaction is at least 100 times more powerful than the interaction with individual differences. Using this formula the size of the moderator effects was estimated, using studies that correlated job attributes and job satisfaction for groups split into high and low growth need strength. The formula is a conservative measure of the size of the moderator effects as it gives the percentage of variance on job satisfaction accounted for by both the direct effects of values and the interaction between job attributes and values.

REFERENCES

Aldag, R.J. and Brief, A.P. (1975). Correlates of work values, *Journal of Applied Psychology*, **60**, 757–60

Andrisani, P. and Nestel, G. (1976). Internal-external control as a contributor and outcome of work experience, *Journal of Applied Psychology*, **76**, 156–65

Blauner, R. (1964). *Alienation and Freedom*, Chicago: University of Chicago Press

Blood, M.R. and Hulin, C.L. (1976). Alienation, environmental characteristics and worker responses, *Journal of Applied Psychology*, **51**, 284–90

Brief, A. and Aldag, R. (1975). Employee reactions to job characteristics: a constructive replication, *Journal of Applied Psychology*, **60**, 182–6

Brousseau, K.R. (1978). Personality and job experience, *Organizational Behavior and Human Performance*, **22**, 235–52

Brousseau, K.R. (1983). Toward a dynamic model of job-person relationships: findings, research questions and implications for work system design, *Academy of Management Review*, **8**, 33–45

Brousseau, K.R. and Prince, J.B. (1981). Job-person dynamics: An extension of longitudinal research, *Journal of Applied Psychology*, **66**, 59–62

Champoux, J.E. (1980). A three sample test of some extensions to the job characteristics model of work motivation, *Academy of Management Journal*, **23**, 466–78

Cherrington, D.J. and England, J.L. (1980). The desire for non-enriched jobs as a moderator of the enrichment-satisfaction relationship, *Organizational Behavior and Human Performance*, **25**, 139–59

Evans, M.G., Kiggunder, M.N. and House, R.J. (1979). A partial test and extension of the job characteristics model of motivation, *Organizational Behavior and Human Performance*, **24**, 354–81

Feather, N.T. (1979). Human values and the work situation: two studies, *Australian Psychologist*, **14**, 131–42

Frese, M. (1982). Occupational socialization and psychological development: an underemphasized research perspective in industrial psychology, *Journal of Occupational Psychology*, **55**, 209–24

Ganster, D.C. (1980). Individual differences and task design: a laboratory experiment, *Organizational Behavior and Human Performance*, **26**, 131–48

Hackman, J.R. and Lawler, E.E. (1971). Employee reactions to job characteristics, *Journal of Applied Psychology*, **55**, 259–86

Hackman, J.R. and Oldham, G.R. (1975). Development of the Job Diagnostic Survey, *Journal of Applied Psychology*, **60**, 159–70

Hackman, J.R. and Oldham, G.R. (1976). Motivation through the design of work: test of a theory, *Organizational Behavior and Human Performance*, **16**, 250–79
Hackman, J.R. and Oldham, G.R. (1980). *Work Redesign*, Reading, Mass.: Addison-Wesley
Hackman, J.R., Pearce, J.L. and Wolfe, J.C. (1978). Effects of changes in job characteristics on work attitudes and behaviors: a naturally occurring quasi-experiment, *Organizational Behavior and Human Performance*, **21**, 289–303
Hall, D.T. and Nougaim, K. (1968). An examination of Maslow's need hierarchy in an organizational setting, *Organizational Behavior and Human Performance*, **3**, 12–35
Herzberg, F. (1966). *Work and the Nature of Man*, Cleveland: World Publishing
Herzberg, F., Mausner, R. and Snyderman, B. (1959). *The Motivation to Work*, New York: Wiley
Holland, J.L. (1973). *Making Vocational Choices: A Theory of Careers*, Englewood Cliffs, N.J.: Prentice-Hall
Holland, J.L. (1976). Vocational preferences, in M.D. Dunnette (ed.), *Handbook of Industrial and Organizational Psychology*, Chicago: Rand McNally
Hulin, C. and Blood, M. (1968). Job enlargement, individual differences and worker responses, *Psychological Bulletin*, **69**, 41–55
Humphrys, P. (1981). The effect of importance upon the relation between perceived job attributes, desired job attributes, and job satisfaction, *Australian Journal of Psychology*, **33**, 121–33
Jackson, P.R., Paul, L.J. and Wall, T. (1981). Individual differences as moderators of reactions to job characteristics, *Journal of Occupational Psychology*, **54**, 1–8
Kabanoff, B. and O'Brien, G.E. (1980). Work and leisure: a task attributes analysis, *Journal of Applied Psychology*, **65**, 595–609
Katz, R. (1978a). Job longevity as a situational factor in job satisfaction, *Administrative Sciences Quarterly*, **23**, 204–23
Katz, R. (1978b). The influence of job longevity on employee reactions to task characteristics, *Human Relations*, **31**, 703–25
King, N. (1970). Clarification and evaluation of the two-factor theory of job satisfaction, *Psychological Bulletin*, **74**, 18–31
Kohn, M.L. (1976). Occupational structure and alienation, *American Journal of Sociology*, **82**, 111–31
Kohn, M.L. and Schooler, C. (1973). Occupational experience and psychological functioning: an assessment of reciprocal effects, *American Sociological Review*, **28**, 97–118
Kohn, M.L. and Schooler, C. (1978). The reciprocal effects of the substantive complexity of work and intellectual flexibility: a longitudinal assessment, *American Journal of Sociology*, **84**, 24–52
Kohn, M.L. and Schooler, C. (1981). Job conditions and intellectual flexibility: a longitudinal assessment of their reciprocal effects, in D.J. Jackson and E.F. Borgatta (eds), *Factor Analysis and Measurement in Sociological Research*, Beverley Hills, Cal.: Sage
Kohn, M.L. and Schooler, C. (1982). Job conditions and personality: a longitudinal assessment of their reciprocal effects, *American Journal of Sociology*, **87**, 1257–85
Korman, A.K. (1976). Hypotheses of work behavior revisited and an extension, *Academy of Management Review*, **1**, 56–63
Kornhauser, A. (1965). *Mental Health of the Industrial Worker*, New York: Wiley
Lawler, E.E. (1971). *Pay and Organizational Effectiveness: A Psychological View*, New York: McGraw-Hill

Lawler, E.E., Hackman, J.R. and Kaufman, S. (1973). Effects of job redesign: a field experiment, *Journal of Applied Social Psychology*, **3**, 49–62

Lefcourt, H. (1976). *Locus of Control: Current Trends in Theory and Research*, New York: Wiley

Locke, E.A. (1976). The nature and causes of job satisfaction, in M. Dunnette (ed.), *Handbook of Industrial and Organizational Behavior*, Chicago: Rand McNally

Maslow, A.H. (1943). A theory of human motivation, *Psychological Review*, **50**, 370–96

Miller, J., Schooler, C., Kohn, M. and Miller, K., (1979). Women and work: the psychological effects of occupational conditions, *American Journal of Sociology*, **85**, 66–94

Mortimer, J.T. and Lorence, J. (1979). Work experience and occupational value socialization: a longitudinal study, *American Journal of Sociology*, **894**, 1361–85

O'Brien, G.E. (1982). Evaluation of the job characteristics theory of work attitudes and performance, *Australian Journal of Psychology*, **34**, 383–401

O'Brien, G E. (1984). Reciprocal effects between locus of control and job attributes, *Australian Journal of Psychology*, **36**, 57–74

O'Brien, G.E. and Dowling, P. (1980). The effects of congruency between perceived and desired job attributes upon job satisfaction, *Journal of Occupational Psychology*, **53**, 121–30

O'Brien, G.E. and Gross, W. (1983). Estimating the size of moderator effects from split-group correlations, unpublished manuscript, The Flinders University of South Australia

O'Brien, G.E. and Humphrys, P. (1982). The effects of congruency between work values and perceived job attributes upon the job satisfaction of pharmacists, *Australian Journal of Psychology*, **34**, 91–101

O'Brien, G.E. and Stevens. K. (1981). The relationship between perceived influence and job satisfaction among assembly line employees, *Journal of Industrial Relations*, **23**, 33–48

Oldham, G.R. (1976). Job characteristics and internal motivation: the moderating effect of interpersonal and individual variables, *Human Relations*, **29**, 559–69

Oldham, G.R., Hackman, J.R. and Pearce, J.L. (1976). Conditions under which employees respond positively to enriched work, *Journal of Applied Psychology*, **61**, 395–403

O'Reilly, C.A. (1977). Personality-job fit: Implications for individual attitudes and performance, *Organizational Behavior and Human Performance*, **18**, 36–46

Orpen, C. (1976). Job enlargement, individual differences and worker responses: a test with black workers in South Africa, *Journal of Cross-Cultural Psychology*, **7**, 473–80

Orpen, C. (1979). The effects of job enrichment on employee satisfaction, motivation, involvement, and performance: a field experiment, *Human Relations*, **32**, 189–217

Peters, W.S. and Champoux, J.E. (1979). The use of moderated regression in job redesign decisions, *Decision Sciences*, **10**, 85–95

Pokorney, J.J., Gilmore, D.C. and Beehr, T. (1980). Job Diagnostic Survey dimensions: moderating effects of growth needs and correspondence with dimensions of job rating form, *Organizational Behavior and Human Performance*, **26**, 222–37

Porter, L.W. (1962). Job attitudes in management: perceived deficiencies in need fulfilment as a function of job level, *Journal of Applied Psychology*, **46** 375–84

Porter, L.W., Lawler, E.E. and Hackman, J.R. (1975). *Behavior in Organizations*, New York: McGraw-Hill

Robey, D. (1974). Task design, work values and worker response: an experimental test, *Organizational Behavior and Human Performance*, **12**, 264–73

Sims, H.P. and Szilagyi, A.D. (1976). Job characteristic relationships: individual and structural moderators, *Organizational Behavior and Human Performance*, **17**, 211–30

Stone, E.F. (1975). Job scope, job satisfaction and the Protestant ethic: A study of enlisted men in the U.S. Navy, *Journal of Vocational Behavior*, **7**, 215–44

Stone, E.F. (1976). The moderating effects of work-related values on the job scope-job satisfaction relationship, *Organizational Behavior and Human Performance*, **15**, 147–67

Stone, E.F., Mowday, R.T. and Porter, L.W. (1977). Higher order need strengths as moderators of the job scope-job satisfaction relationship, *Journal of Applied Psychology*, **62**, 466–70

Super, D., Crites, J., Hummel, R., Moser, H., Overstreet, P. and Warnath, C. (1957). *Vocational Development: A Framework for Research*, New York: Teachers College Press

Susman, G. (1973). Job enlargement: effects of culture on worker responses, *Industrial Relations*, **12**, 1–15

Tannenbaum, A.S. (1957). Personality change as a result of experimental change of environmental conditions, *Journal of Abnormal and Social Psychology*, **55**, 404–6

Tannenbaum, A.S. and Allport, F. (1956). Personality structure and group structure: an interpretive study of their relationships through an event-structured hypothesis, *Journal of Abnormal and Social Psychology*, **53**, 272–80

Turner, A. and Lawrence, P. (1965). *Industrial Jobs and the Worker*. Cambridge, Mass.: Harvard University Press

Umstot, D.D., Bell, C.H. and Mitchell, T.R. (1976). Effects of job enrichment and task goals on satisfaction and productivity: implications for job design, *Journal of Applied Psychology*, **61**, 379–94

Vaillant, G.E. (1974). Natural history of male psychological health. II. Some antecedents of healthy adult adjustment, *Archives of General Psychiatry*, **31**, 15–22

Vaillant, G.E. (1975). Natural history of male psychological health. III. Empirical dimensions of mental health, *Archives of General Psychiatry*, **32**, 420–6

Vaillant, G.E. and McArthur, C.C. (1972). Natural history of male psychological health. I. The adult life cycle from 18–50, *Seminars in Psychiatry*, **4**, 415–27

Vecchio, R.P. (1980). Individual differences as a moderator of the job quality-job satisfaction relationship: Evidence from a national sample, *Organizational Behavior and Human Performance*, **26**, 305–25

Vroom, V. (1959). Some personality determinants of the effects of participation, *Journal of Abnormal and Social Psychology*, **59**, 322–7

Vroom, V. (1964). *Work and Motivation*, New York: Wiley.

Walker, C.R. and Guest, R.H. (1952). *The Man on the Assembly Line*, Cambridge, Mass.: Harvard University Press

Wall, T.D. and Clegg, C.W. (1981). A longitudinal field study of group work redesign, *Journal of Occupational Behaviour*, **2**, 31–49

Wall, T.D., Clegg, C.W. and Jackson, P.R. (1978). An evaluation of the job characteristics model, *Journal of Occupational Psychology*, **51**, 183–96

Wanous, J.P. (1974). Individual differences and reactions to job characteristics, *Journal of Applied Psychology*, **59**, 616–22

White, J.K. (1978). Individual differences in the job quality-worker response relationship: review, integration and comments, *Academy of Management Review*, **3**, 267–80

White, J.K. (1978). Generalizability of individual differences moderators of the participation in decision-making—employee-response relationship, *Academy of Management Journal*, **21**, 36–43

Wollack, S., Goodale, J.G., Wyting, J.P. and Smith, P.C. (1971). Development of the survey of work values, *Journal of Applied Psychology*, **55**, 331–8

CHAPTER 6

Job Content, Alienation and Personal Control

A central problem of most research on work and personality has been the relationship between job content and employee beliefs about personal control. The meaning of the various concepts of personal control differ across studies but it is generally assumed that an individual's sense of personal control is important for understanding adult personality dynamics and task performance. One of the distinctive characteristics of a work environment is that it shapes and constrains behaviour. Employees have to adapt to a collaborative organizational structure which influences their behaviour due to rules about task allocation, task procedures and the distribution of authority. This structure may or may not provide a given employee freedom to control work procedures. Furthermore, the task itself may control the employee's behaviour by limiting opportunities for autonomy and the expression valued skills. Hence one of the most salient factors in a work environment is external control. This is one of the reasons why so many studies have sought to establish the way in which work structures induce stable orientations to control in employees. The simplest approach is to assume that employees, in adapting to a stable control structure, adopt beliefs about control that are congruent with that structure. Those who have high levels of control will come to value high control while those with low control will accept and come to value low control.

This is not the only hypothesis that is of interest to researchers. They have also tried to establish the degree to which work-induced control beliefs affect the behaviour of employees outside work. The question here is whether the control beliefs are specific to the work situation, or do employees internalize them and use them to organize their activities outside work? If they do, then these control beliefs are important for understanding adult personality dynamics. This is the question that is addressed by Kohn and Schooler

(1983) who found that the degree of self-direction allowed an employee in his job directly affected his belief in the efficacy of self-direction. They went on to show that the degree to which an individual was self-directed or conforming generalized to non-work activities such as leisure. Self-directedness also determined intellectual flexibility and various measures of psychological distress.

Others have tried to establish the way in which generalized beliefs about control can affect actual work behaviour. For example, Andrisani and Nestel (1976) found that occupational attainment determined locus of control beliefs and these, in turn, significantly determined occupational attainment. Those who showed greater occupational attainment believed that their life outcomes or satisfactions were largely determined by internal factors such as ability and effort. Those who believed that life outcomes were determined by external factors such as other people or governments did not advance in their career as much as the internally controlled employees. In addition, numerous studies have reported that internal-external control beliefs can affect task performance, job stress and work motivation (Spector, 1982). These latter studies have not shown that work determines control beliefs but clearly they contribute to the view that work structures can determine control beliefs which, in turn, will affect subsequent motivation and performance.

Before looking at these studies and the theories underlying them in some detail, it should be pointed out that the core idea of jobs determining beliefs about personal control is not new. Although not stated with a great deal of clarity, this idea is embedded in Marx's early theory of work alienation. Alienation is a subjective state of employees induced by participation in industrial organizations where the employee has little control over organizational goals, structures and tasks. The state of alienation is a complex syndrome but one of the 'symptoms' is experienced powerlessness (Seeman, 1975, 1983). This suggests that contemporary research work and personal control may provide evidence which would allow an assessment of the validity of some aspects of Marx's early theory of alienation.

This chapter has two main aims. First is to examine in some detail the research which shows that work can determine employee control beliefs. This analysis will involve an assessment of the evidence and the extent to which there are similarities in the various concepts of personal control used by different researchers. It will also try to establish the main structural and job variables that determine personal control. Consideration of the relationship between control beliefs and employee performance will be left to the next chapter. The second aim is to consider the extent to which present research is consistent with Marx's theory of work alienation. This will require a brief exposition of this theory, as well as a recent psychological reformulation of this theory (Kanungo, 1979, 1981, 1982).

WORK ALIENATION

The main source of Marx's theory of work alienation is his *Economic and Philosophic Manuscripts of 1844*. There is some dispute over the question of the consistency of his latter writings on alienation with this early formulation, but we shall assume that the 1844 text is a reasonable source because it is frequently referred to by subsequent writers on alienation and there appears to be no evidence that Marx repudiated the main ideas in this manuscript. The concept of alienation was not original to Marx but he was probably the first writer to show how bureaucratic capitalistic work organizations might produce a state of alienation in skilled and semi-skilled employees.

His concept of work alienation referred to a separation of the worker from the product of his work, his coworkers and himself. In this usage he is consistent with the Latin meaning of *alienare*, which means to separate or take away. Borrowing from Hegel, Marx believed that man had a universal essence which, when fully expressed, led to personal fulfilment and unity with nature and mankind. Expressed in psychological language, he believed that humans had a universal set of needs or capacities which had to be satisfied or utilized in order to achieve personal maturity and solidarity with other humans. He also believed that work was the central human activity necessary for the satisfaction of these needs and capacities. Not all work could satisfy these needs, however. The degree to which workers achieved wholeness depended on the type of work. If the work did not use the employees' capacities and also prevented them from developing meaningful social relationships through the reciprocal transfer of useful products then the employees were cut-off, separated or alienated from their 'true' selves.

The main organization factors that contributed to alienation were:

1. *Lack of ownership of the enterprise.* This deprived workers of the ability to control goals, products and task organization.
2. *Hierarchical control structures.* Most workers did not have autonomy or control over what jobs they did or how they did them. Rather they were directed by a supervisory and managerial group who allocated tasks and defined the way in which they were to be performed.
3. *Job content.* Factory jobs were arduous, simple and repetitive. Natural and acquired skills were under-utilized for the sake of efficiency and managerial control. Workers literally became hired hands and were unable to use their knowledge and mental skills in the performance of simple manual tasks.

The alienated workers, as a result, became unhappy and miserable, felt powerless to control their own destiny, were robbed of life meaning and felt little solidarity with employees or society. Not only was there an awareness of deprivation, there was also in the alienated workers a 'deprivation of awareness' (Touraine, 1967). This meant that the prolonged experience of factory work led the worker to lack of insight into his 'true' needs. Not only did he feel powerless and lost, he was unable to identify what it was that he had lost.

Probably many Marxists would claim that this is a simplistic and overly psychological account of work alienation. It is, however, an account that seeks to express some of Marx's ideas in a form which separates out his ideological and philosophical values and makes them amenable to empirical assessment. This latter aim, I suggest, was once within Marx's programme as he devised the first job satisfaction questionnaire (Marx, 1880). Presumably its purpose was to identify the features of the factory system in the nineteenth century which led to alienation. Unfortunately, the questionnaire was too long, too complex and lacking measures of structure and needs. Apparently, and not unexpectedly, the response rate from workers was extremely poor.

More recently, social scientists have tried to test this theory. One of the most quoted is Blauner's (1964) study which reanalysed Roper's 1947 Fortune Survey of 3000 blue-collar workers drawn from textile, printing, automobile and chemical occupations. He used Seeman's (1959) analysis of alienation which identified four different subjective states: powerlessness, meaninglessness, isolation and self-estrangement. The value of this study is severely limited because Blauner did not have reliable or valid measures of either organizational structure or states of alienation. Thus there is no measure of hierarchical control or job skill requirements. The measures of subjective states also confuse the determinants and consequences of alienation. For example, the questions about powerlessness ask for information about how much control employees have over the work process. This is a measure of perceived control at work and is not the same as the general feeling of powerlessness which is assumed to result *from* perceived lack of control. Finally, the study provided no statistical measures of association between job variables and evaluations of jobs.

Blauner provided a lucid interpretive story using questionnaire responses as illustrations. His conclusions, therefore, are really restatements of Marxist theory which are not substantiated by his research. He inferred that a majority of U.S. blue collar workers were alienated.

> Alienation exists when workers are unable to control their immediate work processes, to develop a sense of purpose and function which connects their jobs to the overall organization of production, to belong to integrated industrial communities, and when they fail to become involved in the activity of work as a mode of personal self-expression.
>
> (Blauner, 1964, p. 15)

There was some evidence to show that a considerable number of workers had little influence over work procedures and found their jobs too simple.

However, they tended to form a minority. Only 25 per cent of the total sample, for example, felt that their job was too simple to bring out their best abilities (p. 205). Work alienation studies up to the 1970s had similar weaknesses to Blauner's. They tended to be interpretive and were not based on reliable or valid measures of job attributes or psychological states. The few studies that did use statistical methods to examine the relationship between job attributes and measures of alienation showed very small associations. This led Seeman (1971) to end his review of these studies with a conclusion that stated that the alienation thesis had little support. This conclusion was reasonable but misleading. The conclusion was justified because studies had not properly formulated a testable theory of alienation and had not used designs or measures that could test the theory. Hence, like many theories in social science, its empirical status is indeterminate. It was inappropriate for Seeman to imply that the evidence was weak and *ipso facto*, so was the theory.

Since Seeman's review there have been few studies that have used the concept of alienation in examining the relationship between work and personality (Seeman, 1983). This seems to be due to the recognition that the concept is too broad to be useful. The preferred strategy has become one of examining the relationship between specific organizational variables (e.g. ownership, job complexity) and specific personal outcomes (e.g. self-directedness). The most systematic research has been that of Kohn and Schooler (1983) and their work will be considered later. First mention should be made of a recent psychological theory of alienation.

Recently, Kanungo (1979, 1982) has interpreted Marx's concept of alienation as a state of low work involvement.

> work involvement is viewed as a generalized cognitive (or belief) state of psychological identification with work insofar as work is perceived to have the potentiality to satisfy one's salient needs and expectations. Likewise, work alienation can be viewed as a generalized cognitive (or belief) state of psychological separation from work insofar as work is perceived to lack the potentiality for satisfying one's salient needs and expectations.
>
> (Kanungo, 1979, p. 131)

His theory of alienation then asserts that the type of alienation exhibited by a worker depends on his or her salient needs. His predictions are summarized in Table 6.1. Although he recommends that involvement in work in general should be distinguished from involvement in a specific job, the needs that predict job and work involvement appear to be the same. He does not provide any evidence showing how the various types of alienation are linked to specific needs. It is difficult to understand how he could because he defines alienation as the absence of job involvement, and measures it by a job involvement scale which makes no reference to isolation, powerlessness or the other aspects of Marxian alienation. The evidence he does present

TABLE 6.1   Job variables and needs producing alienation: according to Kanungo's Theory (1979, 1982)

Type of alienation	Salient need	Jobs blocking need satisfaction
Isolation	Social, belonging	Low sense of membership
Normlessness/meaninglessness	Information/ego-need	Low information/ low responsibility
Powerlessness	Autonomy, control self-esteem (all ego needs)	Low autonomy or responsibility
Estrangement	Self-actualization, Need for achievement	Low skill-utilization and sense of achievement

shows that job involvement—defined as the degree of psychological 'identification' with a job—is positively related to intrinsic work attributes such as autonomy, challenge and participation. This is somewhat confusing as his theory predicts that job involvement would depend on salient needs and intrinsic job factors should only predict job involvement if intrinsic needs are salient. It is clear that Kanungo has not been successful in developing a testable theory of work alienation. It is a theory of job involvement which remains to be tested.

Marx did not write about needs that differ across people and across time. He wrote about complex psychological states that were generated in all people when work separated them from their capacities, products and other people. Kanungo misinterprets Marx by stating that he intended alienation to refer to satisfaction of needs for independence, achievement and power.

> Marx intended to measure alienation in terms of the satisfaction of a single set of needs—the ego needs for independence, achievement and power. In the Marxian formulation, the role of other human needs, such as the physical and social ones, has been completely disregarded.
>
> (Kanungo, 1979, p. 121)

Yet Marx states that certain work structures damaged man physically, mentally and socially. Alienating work:

> does not belong to his intrinsic nature, ... in his work, therefore, he does not affirm himself but denies himself, does not feel content but unhappy, does not develop freely his physical and mental energy but mortifies his body and ruins his mind.
>
> (Marx, 1844, p. 71)

Work, being external, imposed and over-simplified, separates man from himself, the products of his work and his fellow man.

> An immediate consequence of the fact that man is estranged from the product of his labour, from his life activity, from his species-being is the estrangement of man from man.
>
> (Marx, 1844, pp. 74-5)

This separation from others is attributable to two main factors. First, if the employee cannot realize his own potentialities he is limited in his ability to relate to others. Second, if he does not produce goods that are directly related to others' needs, the development of social bonds based on reciprocal need satisfaction cannot be developed. For Marx, the end of perfect work design was not just job involvement. It was nothing less than personal integration, social unity and the production of socially useful products. Marxists, therefore, would see Kanungo's theory as a distortion. It would be seen as being directed at managerial problems of job involvement. It says nothing about changing ownership and low skill jobs. If applied, it would mean that jobs are designed to match reported employee needs. But, if these needs have been shaped by past experiences, then it could lead to the construction of alienated jobs for those employees who report that they are alienated. Thus it is a conservative, psychological theory which perpetuates job design practices that produce alienation. Whether or not we agree with such a view, we must conclude that Kanungo's theory has little to say about alienation and has not generated any evidence that bears on the main manner in which job attitudes determine personal control. The largest set of evidence that is relevant has been assembled by Kohn and his associates.

SUBSTANTIVE COMPLEXITY AND
SELF DIRECTING ORIENTATION

The most extensive research and theory on work and personality is by Kohn and his associates (Kohn, 1969, 1971, 1976, 1980: Kohn and Schooler, Kohn and Schooler, 1969, 1973, 1978, 1981, 1982, 1983; Miller *et al.*,1979). The main conclusion of this research is that work allowing self-direction induces, in the employee, a self-directing orientation that generalizes to task situations outside the work organization. Occupational self-direction is defined in terms of three related but independent concepts. The most important is the substantive complexity of the actual tasks done in the job. Substantive complexity is defined as the degree to which the work requires thought and independent judgement. Work that requires a great deal of thought and allows the employee to make his or her own decisions, provides repeated experiences of self-direction. When little thought and judgement are required the task is done fairly automatically and does not require constant initiative and self-focusing.

However, the potential of the job to provide opportunities for self-direction may be limited by two factors—the closeness of supervision and the degree to which the job is routine. If supervision is too directive then personal autonomy is reduced even though the actual tasks may require complex intellectual and decision skills. Similarly, a job may consist of a fairly complex task but the task is short term and repeated. Initially, the task is experienced as complex but, once learnt, it becomes a monotonous routine. Hence the degree of occupational self-direction in a given job is a function of substantive complexity, closeness of supervision, and what Kohn and Schooler call routinization.

Thus maximum occupational self-direction occurs when the task is complex, supervision is not close and the task procedures are not segmented and predictable. Conversely, very low occupational self-direction is possible when tasks require simple skills, supervision is directive, and the task sequence is routine. The actual degree of occupational self-direction is, according to Kohn and Schooler, significantly related to a wide range of personality variables including intellectual flexibility, self-esteem, fatalism and the valuation of self-direction in all non-work activities. Their conclusions are based on a number of large cross-sectional and longitudinal surveys with representative samples of North American, Italian, Polish and Japanese employees. Before assessing their findings it is useful to trace the development of their ideas as they became refined by both additional information and increasingly sophisticated statistical techniques. As far as possible, this will be a description of their work that is an accurate but condensed version of their theory and findings.

Job Structure, Social Class and Values

Originally, Kohn was interested in the relationship between social class and values. In *Class and Conformity* (Kohn, 1969) he established that the valuation of self-direction varied significantly across different social classes. Social class was conceived as a continuous dimension that reflected an individual's level of education and occupational status or prestige. Using interviews with employed men in North America and Italy, Kohn measured their class position and the degree to which they valued self-direction for their children and for themselves. Self-direction was generally defined as thinking for oneself and was contrasted with following the dictates of external authorities.

This study showed a significant association between class and measures of self-direction and conformity. The higher an employee's social class the more likely he would be to value self-direction for himself and his children. Employees of higher social class also believed that self-direction was possible and effective. The lower an employee's social class the greater was the likelihood that he undervalued self-direction in favour of obedience and conformity to external authority. Furthermore, he would be more likely to believe that conformity was the wisest method of adaptation to an environment providing few opportunities for self-direction.

Other researchers had found similar value differences across levels of social class but Kohn made an original contribution in showing that these class differences could largely be understood in terms of differences in occupational conditions. The small but significant correlation between social class and the father's valuation of self-direction for his children ($r = 0.34$), as well as the correlation between social class and the father's valuation of self-direction for himself ($r = 0.17$) became insignificant when levels of occupational self-direction were partialled out. Occupational self-direction was measured by rating jobs on substantive complexity, closeness of supervision and routinization. Substantive complexity was based on a combination of seven ratings. The initial ratings were the degree of complexity required in working with people, data and things. These three ratings were combined with estimates of the time spent working with people, data and things as well as an overall rating of the complexity or skill level of the job. Closeness of supervision was assigned a score on the basis of ratings of the degree to which the employee was allowed to make his own decisions about the tasks done and the method used in their performance. Routinization was a single rating of the degree to which the tasks were repetitive and predictable.

When these three occupational conditions were statistically controlled, the correlation between social class and self-directed values was reduced by an order of 50–96 per cent. The main occupational condition that reduced the class–value orientation was substantive complexity. Workers of higher social class had jobs that had higher complexity than those from lower social class. In addition, there were significant associations between substantive complexity and a range of values and personality variables. Those with higher substantive complexity valued self-direction in preference to conformity, they had higher self-confidence and were less likely to attribute the cause of life problems to external factors than those with jobs having relatively lower substantive complexity.

The self-direction conformity scores were obtained by asking employees to rank value statements in order of importance. The main statements used to obtain scores on self-direction were 'interest in how and why things work', 'good sense and judgement', and 'ability to face facts squarely'. If these were ranked as being of high importance the individual was labelled self-directed. By contrast an individual was conforming if he gave high priority to 'respectability', 'truthfulness' and 'success'.

This association between work conditions and personality suggested to Kohn and Schooler (1969) that work had a direct effect on employee thought processes. The effect was not confined to the work situation but affected thought and behaviour outside work.

> The conditions of occupational life at high social class levels facilitate interest in the intrinsic qualities of the job, foster a view of self and society that is conducive to believing in the possibilities of rational action toward purposive goals, and promote the valuation of self-direction. The conditions of occupational life at lower social class levels limit men's view of the job primarily to the extrinsic benefits it provides, foster a narrow circumscribed conception of self and society, and promote the positive valuation of conformity to authority
> (Kohn and Schooler, 1969, p. 677)

They recognized that these conclusions were not justified by simple correlational analyses. The association between work and personality variables might have been due to the process of job selection. People who valued self-direction might choose jobs where self-direction was possible. Another possible explanation was that the association was due to unknown job variables which affected both task and personality dimensions. Later studies by Kohn and Schooler tried to establish the direction of causation between work and personality. The first set of studies involved a re-analysis of the data from the 1964 national sample in order to assess the effects of job selection as well as the relative contribution of a range of occupational factors on self-direction, intellectual flexibility and powerlessness.

Re-analysis of the 1964 National Sample

In subsequent articles, Kohn and Schooler (1973) and Kohn (1976) tried to assess the relative importance of a range of job variables on a large number of psychological functions. Not only did they include in their analyses the three measures of occupational self-direction, they also included measures of organizational structure, job pressure and job uncertainty. These latter variables described the environment in which the job was performed whereas measures of occupational self-direction described the actual content of the job. The main structural variables were ownership, the degree of bureaucratization and the employee's position in the formal authority structure. The basic reason for including them was to assess the possibility that the employee's power within the total structure determined the content of his job and hence could explain the association between job content and personality variables. Other environmental factors that could be more important than job content were measures of pressure due to time restrictions, the heaviness of the work and the dirtiness of the workplace. Finally, they included measures of job uncertainty. Uncertainty could affect employees' reactions due to the potential anxiety aroused by job insecurity, the probability of changed jobs and the likelihood of being held responsible for matters outside their control.

The range of dependent variables was extended to include job commitment, job satisfaction, self-esteem, intellectual flexibility and the intellectual demands of employee leisure activities. By using multiple regression it was then possible for Kohn and Schooler to assess the relative importance of the set of job and organizational variables on each aspect of psychological functioning. They also endeavoured to control selection effects by statistically controlling for level of education. Education could determine who acquired various jobs as well as itself being a contributor to intellectual functioning, self orientations and leisure activities.

The results showed that occupational self-direction was still a significant predictor of psychological functioning even when variations in organization structure, pressure, uncertainty and education were controlled. The greater the degree of self-direction required in the job the more likely it was that the occupant would report higher levels of job commitment, job satisfaction, non-work, self-direction, self-esteem and intellectual flexibility.

Kohn and Schooler next concentrated on the problem of reciprocal causation. Choosing intellectual flexibility as a central psychological process they sought to establish whether job conditions determined intellectual flexibility or whether intellectual flexibility determined the type of job attained. Intellectual flexibility was not strictly defined but it was intended to measure the current process of intellectual functioning and was not a measure of any innate or inherited intelligence. Two forms of flexibility were distinguished— perceptual and ideational. The main analyses were performed on ideational flexibility and the level of this concept was operationally defined in terms of a composite of five different tests or ratings. The five indices or instruments were as follows.

1. *Embedded figures test.* This was derived from Witkin's research and required the respondent to differentiate figure from ground in complex colour designs (Witkin *et al.*, 1962).
2. *Hamburger stand problem.* Responses to the following problem were rated. 'Suppose you wanted to open a hamburger stand and there were two locations. What questions would you consider in deciding which of the two locations offer a better business opportunity?'
3. *Cigarette advertisement problem.* Rated scores were obtained for the following problem 'What are all the arguments you can think of for and against allowing cigarette commercials on TV?'
4. *Rating of predisposition to agree.* Ratings were obtained of the extent to which the respondent agreed with questions requiring an 'agree-disagree' response alternative.
5. *Interviewer's rating of intelligence.* This rating was based on the interviewer's general impression of intellectual performance over the course of the entire interview.

Reciprocal causation between ideational flexibility and the substantive complexity of the job was obtained using two stage least squares analysis. This is a relatively complex method of assessing two-way causality between two variables when the data is cross-sectional and there are independent predictors for each of the two variables.

TABLE 6.2   Reciprocal effects between psychological functioning and the substantive complexity of the job

Psychological function	The effects of psychological functions upon substantive complexity	The effect of the substantive complexity of the job upon psychological functions
Intellectual (ideational) flexibility	0.02 (ns)	0.16
Occupational commitment	0.13	0.39
Job satisfaction	−0.07 (ns)	0.14
Self-esteem	0.04	0.10
Intellectual demands of leisure activities	0.14	0.28
Powerlessness	0.03 (ns)	0.25
Self-estrangement	−0.02 (ns)	0.17

Note. (1) ns = not statistically significant.
    (2) The numbers are beta or standardised regression coefficients. The magnitude of these coefficients is interpreted as an estimate of the strength of the effects.

(From Kohn and Schooler, 1973; Kohn, 1976)

A summary of the results is shown in Table 6.2. As can be seen, the effects of the job upon the person are all stronger than the effects of the person upon the job. These results provide somewhat stronger evidence than simple correlations on the direction of causality. The statistical technique is mathematically acceptable provided that a number of stringent assumptions are met. It is unlikely that they were perfectly met but the results did place greater confidence in a 'job determines the man' than a 'man determines the job' hypothesis.

The next step in the confirmation of the effect of job content upon psychological functioning was the collection of longitudinal data which allowed some assessment of the effects of changes in job content upon psychological functioning. The 1973 and 1976 analyses suggested that the main occupational condition that affected psychological functioning was the substantive complexity of the job. Other job conditions, such as closeness of supervision had smaller direct effects while structural factors, such as ownership and power within the organization, had no direct effects but only indirect effects due to the effects on substantive complexity.

At this point Kohn and Schooler were maintaining that job experiences had direct, stable and long-lasting effects on a number of aspects of psychological functioning. In summary, they maintained that the higher the substantive complexity of an employee's job, the higher was that employee's: (i) intellectual flexibility; (ii) commitment to work; (iii) job satisfaction; (iv) self-esteem; (v) leisure quality—rated using criteria of degree of intellectual demand; (vi) self-efficacy (the opposite of powerlessness)—a belief that the employee can achieve desired outcomes by his own behaviour; and (vii) purposefulness and life involvement (the opposite of self-estrangement). These results were obtained for men but they were largely replicated for a sample of married working women (Miller *et al.*, 1978).

C. Longitudinal Analyses of the Effects of Job Content Upon Intellectual Flexibility, Self-directedness and Distress

The preceding analyses had provided some support for Kohn and Schooler's thesis that work directly affected psychological functioning but stronger support awaited the analyses of the effect of job changes over time. In 1974 they obtained further information about work conditions and estimated psychological functioning from about a quarter of the working men (3101) interviewed in 1964. The second sample was drawn to be representative of the original one except that men who had, by 1974, turned 65 years old were excluded. The strength of their analyses was further improved by the use of confirmatory factory analyses and the LISREL programme for evaluating causal models. Confirmatory factor analysis was used to remove the effect of correlated errors. More reliable estimates of causal paths could be obtained after allowing for systematic and random errors of measurement. LISREL also allowed them to evaluate causal models when the expected causal effects were either lagged (over time) or contemporaneous.

The first analysis of the longitudinal data concentrated on intellectual flexibility (Kohn and Schooler, 1981). The main result was that there was a reciprocal causal relationship between substantive complexity and intellectual flexibility. Substantive complexity had a direct, contemporaneous effect on intellectual flexibility. However, intellectual flexibility did not have an immediate effect on job complexity. Prior levels of intellectual flexibility affected the complexity of subsequent jobs. These results were interpreted in terms of the immediate effects of job experiences upon thought processes. If an individual did work that required skill, problem solving and initiative then this mode of thinking generalized to his thought processes outside work. Intellectual flexibility could not affect job complexity immediately because there were structural restraints preventing the large majority of men from changing their jobs. However, those men who possessed intellectual flexibility would be more likely to be promoted or to choose jobs with higher complexity in the future.

The key job condition was substantive complexity. This was the main component of occupational self-direction. Other job conditions could affect the level of substantive complexity and so indirectly affect personality but people were immediately shaped by the content of their work tasks. The longitudinal analyses were extended to include self-directedness and psychological distress (Kohn and Schooler, 1982) and the general pattern of results was similar to that obtained for intellectual flexibility. Generally,there were reciprocal relationships between job conditions and personality. The results are complex but the strongest personality predictor of later job content was intellectual flexibility. Employees who had been relatively high on intellectual flexibility in 1964 were more likely than those who were low on intellectual flexibility to have acquired jobs that were higher on substantive complexity and involve less working hours. A schematic summary of the main causal paths from job conditions to personality is shown in Figure 6.1.

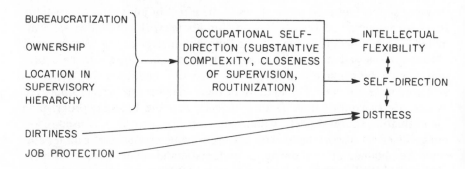

FIGURE 6.1 The main effects of job conditions upon personality. The model is based on Kohn and Schooler's (1982) results. Directed arrows indicate casaul paths. Two-way arrows indicate reciprocal causation

This model shows that bureaucratization (measured by the number of organizational levels), ownership, and position in the supervisory hierarchy, do not directly affect the personality measures. However, they have a small indirect effect because they determine the level of occupational self-direction. The level of occupational self-direction provided in the job directly affects intellectual flexibility and the employee's general valuation of self-direction. Job content had an indirect effect on distress (mainly indexed by self-depreciation, self-confidence and anxiety) because of its effects on intellectual flexibility and self-directedness. Intellectual flexibility and self-directedness have direct or indirect relationships to distress such that those employees highest on flexibility and self-directedness tend to have lower distress.

These effects, according to Kohn (1980), hold regardless of social class, industry, sex and formal organizational structure. The most significant finding is that jobs can affect personality functioning. The mechanism to explain how this happens is only alluded to. It is claimed that people generalize their patterns of thought and behaviour from their jobs to areas outside work. We become what we are allowed to do at work.

> Thus, men who do complex work come to exercise their intellectual prowess not only on the job but also in their non-occupational lives. They become more open to new experience. They come to value self-direction more highly. They even come to engage in more intellectually demanding leisure-time activities.
> (Kohn, 1980, p. 204)

This is an appealing and simple account which allows Kohn to dismiss the role of more complex psychological variables. For example, he sees no need to use a concept of locus of control. Some writers (e.g. Andrisani and Nestel, 1976) suggest that work experiences induce changes in the extent to which individuals perceive that life outcomes are under internal or external control. As many aspects of psychological functioning are related to individual control orientations (Lefcourt, 1976), the concept of locus of control suggests a mechanism whereby work structures could affect a wide range of non-work behaviours. Kohn rejects this approach.

> But why is it necessary to accord so strategic a role to 'locus of control'? Why not say, more directly, that people who do substantially complex work come to think of themselves as capable of doing difficult and challenging tasks ...?
> (Kohn, 1980, p. 204)

D. Evaluation

The programme of research by Kohn and his associates has provided a significant number of findings about the effect of work on personality. The size of the samples, the use of longitudinal data and the sophisticated methods of statistical analyses have allowed them to provide strong support for their general thesis that occupational self-direction can determine intellectual flexibility and self-direction to non-work activities. They were not uncritical of their own work as they recognized that the results needed to be replicated in countries other than the United States. This has led to studies with Polish (Slomczynski, Miller and Kohn, 1981; Miller, Slomczynski and Kohn, 1984) and Japanese (Naoi and Schooler, in press) employees. These studies largely confirm their hypotheses. They plan further research on the problem of generalization, the timing of effects, and the effects of education on personal self-direction (Kohn, 1983). However, the main problems seem to be in the interpretation of their central measures: substantive complexity, intellectual flexibility and self-direction.

1. Substantive complexity

This pivotal dimension of job content is defined and measured as the degree of complexity required in working with data, people and things, It is measured using self-report data but also reflects an objective job dimension as the job ratings correlate quite highly (about 0.70) with independently assessed job complexity. The scales measuring complexity are derived from the U.S. Dictionary of Occupational Titles (United States Department of Labor, 1965). Although the dimension of complexity appears intuitively reasonable because, in our experience, we can order jobs from simple to complex, the concept of complexity says little about the basis of this ordering. What makes a job simple or complex? Is it the level of skill? Inspection of the rating scales indicates that complexity is probably related to skill levels and not to the amount of work or the variety of the work or the amount of autonomy that the employee has over job procedures. For example, the scale rating complexity of work with data goes from lowest complexity, 'reading instructions' to 'synthesizing' which is most complex. Intermediate levels of complexity are defined by 'comparing', 'copying', 'computing', 'compiling', 'analyzing', and 'coordinating'. Such functions appear to reflect increasing skill levels. If it is skill level then what are the main types of skill involved? Even if we allow that it is reasonable to rate overall skill level, there are problems of interpretation. Kohn and Schooler suggest that increases in substantive complexity should be beneficial to all people. But what if the complexity exceeds the capabilities of the employee? Doing a job that is too difficult could lead to anxiety and an associated feeling of being intellectually cramped and over-directed by the demands of the job. At times Kohn and Schooler come close to recognizing that the response to a job is determined by the relation between the objective demands of the job and the employee's capabilities. However, they reject the person–job fit approach and stay with job complexity, a job variable, as the major predictor of psychological functioning (Kohn, 1984).

Challenge is a perception based on the perceived relationship between job requirements and employee skills. When individual skills match or nearly match job requirements then the job is challenging. It seems a mistake to think that individual responses to a job can be inferred from the objective skill requirements of the job alone. At this point, it could be asked why there are empirical relationships between substantive complexity, job attitudes and other complex values and abilities. The explanation proposed is that challenge or skill-utilization is correlated with skill-level or complexity. At present there is no strong evidence to document this. Indirect evidence (Burris, 1983; O'Brien, 1980) shows that a significant proportion of the workforce considers that they are under-employed or are in jobs that do not fully use their skills. Hence, if there were small increases in their job skill levels (or complexity) they should report higher skill-utilization. This then would lead to a positive association between measured skill-level and perceived skill-utilization. If skill levels were increased a large amount, job complexity would increase but skill-utilization would decrease due to over-utilization of skills. The main point is that the skill level of a job is quite distinct from the degree of match between job skills and person skills. However, the relative importance of job skills vs skill-match approaches is a matter for future empirical research.

Another reason for believing that skill-utilization is the important job dimension, which is indirectly indexed by substantive complexity, is the existence of studies that do show that reported skill-utilization has long-term effects on personality measures. Mortimer and Laurence (1979), using a longitudinal design, found that 'work autonomy' determined 'self-competence'. Work autonomy was measured by an instrument which partly measured decision-making latitude but which mainly measured the amount of thinking required and the degree of challenge. While not using longitudinal designs, other studies have shown significant relationships between skill-utilization or challenge and measures of psychological functioning, that appear similar to Kohn and Schooler's measures of self-direction and distress (O'Brien, 1984a,b).

2. Intellectual flexibility *

The problem with this concept is that its meaning is unclear. Certainly the operational meaning is defined by the various tests and ratings used in the studies but what do these measures measure? Problems requiring individuals to think about factors involved in setting up a hamburger stand or to devise arguments for and against cigarette advertising could reflect creativity or divergent thinking or some other cognitive ability. Kohn and Schooler have not yet validated their measure of intellectual flexibility against standard measures of intelligence or cognitive functioning. They do say that it is not a measure of 'basic' intelligence yet one of the instruments used to measure it is a rating of 'intelligence'. Also, Witkin and his associates report significant associations between scores on the embedded figures test, one of the indices of intellectual flexibility, and various tests of intelligence (Witkin et al., 1962).

Intellectual flexibility appears to be measured reliably and appears to reflect some type of intellectual functioning that is stable over time. If it is a measure of the extent to which an individual can devise alternative solutions to open-ended problems or perceive alternative figures in unstructured stimuli, then it is probably related to general intelligence as well as to specific cognitive abilities. It is desirable that the measure of intellectual flexibility be correlated with standard tests of intelligence and tests of cognitive abilities such as those devised by Ekstrom and others (Ekstrom, *et al.*, 1976). If it is related to intelligence, and this has yet to be established, then it raises a difficult problem of interpretation. The reason why measures of intellectual flexibility predict later job content might simply be due to the likelihood that brighter people tend to choose or progress to jobs that use their higher intelligence. These could be jobs of higher skill level. Also the apparent effects of job content on intellectual flexibility might be artefactual. It could just reflect the possibility that brighter people tend to be in jobs of higher skill level. Their intelligence could not, as is shown empirically, change the nature of the job. However, their intelligence is predictable from job content since the job has 'attracted' them because it offers opportunities for using their ability. Kohn and Schooler claim that they have controlled for these selection effects but they have only used measures of education, work orientation and initial intellectual flexibility as controls. Jencks (1972) has shown that education level is only weakly related to intelligence, while work values have yet to be shown to have any relationship to intelligence. If 'intellectual flexibility' has only a weak positive relationship to measures of general intelligence then the selection process explanation of their results has not yet been ruled out.

3. Self-directed orientation

The main problem with this concept is as much with its meaning as the validity of the measures. Across the various studies different measures have been used to measure it. The latest study measures it as a composite of separate measures of 'authoritarian conservatism', personal responsibility for morality, fatalism, trustfulness, self-depreciation and idea-conformity. All of these measures seem to be different but are correlated to a relatively small extent. Assertions are made that a self-directed person is less likely to be authoritarian, more likely to have internal standards of morality, less likely to be fatalistic, self-depreciating and conforming than the conformist type of person but this has not been shown. The assertions are true, largely in virtue of the changing definitions and measures. The actual measures of these traits may be correlated but what do these measures really measure? Very little evidence is presented to show how they actually predict behaviour or how they are related to reliable and valid measures of concepts that appear to measure self-direction (e.g. independence, self-efficacy, locus of control).

These criticisms of the measures do not necessarily jeopardize the major findings. They do indicate that much more work is needed before the findings can be interpreted with a great deal of confidence. Studies should be conducted to investigate the relationship between substantive complexity, skill level and skill-utilization. Other studies should be designed to show what intellectual flexibility is really measuring as well as to show that the effects of jobs on flexibility are not due to the association between job skill level and employee intelligence. Finally, measures of self-direction should be subjected to a process of validation before they can confidently be interpreted as appropriate measures of self-direction.

Kohn and Schooler concluded that job content determined an employee's relatively stable orientation toward self-direction. In turn, personal self-direction directly affected experienced distress and the level of intellectual flexibility. As previously discussed, the meaning of these results depended on the definition of self-directed orientation. This orientation is measured by a diverse set of measures ranging from authoritarian conservatism to fatalism to trustfulness. Although each of these measures may be related to the extent that individuals value self-direction, and are in fact, self-directed, they do not seem similar to each other. For example, authoritarian conservatism is measured by items that ask the respondent to disagree or agree with simple authoritarian practices (e.g. 'Young people should not be allowed to read books that are likely to confuse them' and 'any good leader should be strict with people under him in order to gain their respect'). This scale appears to tap dogmatism and authoritarianism and it is not obvious why it should be considered a measure of self-direction. Dogmatic authoritarian people may prefer to conform more to external authorities than those who are not dogmatic but their dogmatism may also lead them to take action in influencing others when they consider it necessary.

The fatalism scale seems more appropriate to the definition of self-direction as it measures the extent to which respondents believe they are responsible for the solution of their own problems. Such people tend to believe that their life outcomes are largely due to their own abilities or effort. Those who do not believe they are responsible for what happens to them attribute the cause of events not to themselves but to external factors such as luck, fate or other people. This belief in internal or external control is also tapped in Kohn and Schooler's 'self-confidence' scale which is said, in 1982 (but not in 1973), to measure psychological distress and not self-direction.

It is thus difficult to disentangle the meaning of self-direction from the analyses of scales which are based on factor scales and not theory. If the scales had been validated against other scales that have been reliably shown to measure different aspects of self-direction then the measures and meaning of self-direction would be clearer. However, the internal-external control aspect of self-direction has been investigated using a reasonably reliable and valid measure of control beliefs. This measure is Rotter's locus of control scale. If findings obtained using this scale show that job structures can determine control beliefs then this will provide some indirect support for the Kohn and Schooler thesis.

SKILL-UTILIZATION, ALIENATION AND LOCUS OF CONTROL

Locus of control refers to a generalized expectancy about the extent to which reinforcements are under internal or external control. Persons may vary between two extreme orientations. On the one extreme the internally controlled person believes that reinforcements are determined largely by personal effort, ability and initiative, whereas the opposite type is the external who believes that reinforcements are determined largely by other people, social structures, luck or fate. The extent to which a person believes that he or she is internally or externally controlled has commonly been measured using Rotter's Internal-External control scale (Rotter, 1966).

Most studies of work and locus of control have examined the manner in which control orientations determine vocational choices, work motivation, work performance and occupational attainment. Many of these studies have been reviewed elsewhere (O'Brien, 1984; Spector, 1982). Although most studies have problems in design and interpretation, there is considerable agreement in the findings. Internals are more likely than externals to prefer occupations which use their skills and provide autonomy. Whether or not they enter these occupations depends on personal limitations such as ability and external constraints such as job vacancies and the availability of time and money for education and training. Once in a job, internals tend to work harder than externals on jobs that provide opportunities for the use of skill and initiative, they are more satisfied with job content and tend to become more involved in their work. This probably accounts for the finding that internals tend to attain jobs with higher occupational status and income. These studies provide support for the construct validity of the concept of locus of control. They show that locus of control is a significant determinant of organizational behaviour and performance. They do not show how organizational structure and job content determine employee locus of control. Only a few studies bear on this question.

Some field studies on the effect of job content on locus of control fail to come to grips with the problem of measuring job attributes, although they do provide some evidence for inferring that job content does produce changes in locus of control. In a longitudinal study of a representative group of United States male employees aged between 45–59 years, Andrisani and his associates examined the reciprocal effects between occupational status and employee locus of control (Andrisani and Nestel, 1976; Andrisani *et al.*, 1978). As expected, employees who were internally controlled in 1969 tended to have higher occupational status and income in 1971 than those who were externally controlled in 1969. However, this relationship applied only to white males and not to black males. This suggests that the motivating effects of locus of control were blocked for blacks who faced greater external restraints on their ability to progress to jobs with higher status. Reciprocal causation was demonstrated by the finding that employees who increased their occupational status over the two year period became more internally controlled, whereas those whose occupational status declined became more external.

Similar results were found by Frantz (1980) with a United States sample of young males who were interviewed in both 1968 and 1971. Labour market success in private-sector jobs enhanced feelings of internal control during the transition from school to work. Yet one result suggested that success in getting a job and progressing in it depended not on the status of the job but the content of the job. Getting a job in the public sector and progressing in it led to increases in external control. Frantz suggested that this was due to public-sector employees experiencing more bureaucratic restrictions, using less skills and receiving lower wages than employees in private-sector jobs.

Although the previous studies showed that job status could affect locus of control, none of them are able to identify the job attributes that determined it. High status, complex, private-public sector jobs can differ on many dimensions, including level of skill, influence, variety, interaction, pressure, income and the opportunity to use skills. In order to understand why certain jobs are likely to induce an external locus of control, it is necessary to develop a theory about job attributes and the way in which these attributes might determine locus of control.

In a recent study it was hypothesized that the main determinants of control orientations were skill-utilization, influence and income (O'Brien, 1980, 1984b). Skill-utilization was defined as the degree of match between employee skills and skills required by the job. Influence denoted the amount of say that employees had over various aspects of the job including work organization, rest pauses, interaction with employees and supervisors, and the design of the workplace. Both skill-utilization and influence had been shown to be major rewards or satisfactions valued by employees (O'Brien, 1980, 1982; O'Brien and Dowling, 1981). Hence employees who perceived that their jobs had low skill-utilization and influence would expect that their own efforts were not instrumental in obtaining these intrinsic rewards. As external control is the perception that valued rewards cannot be obtained by personal ability and effort, this should mean that employees become externally controlled. By contrast, employees who perceive that their jobs are rewarding as they experience skill-utilization and influence, should become internally controlled. Similarly, to the extent that income is a reward, low

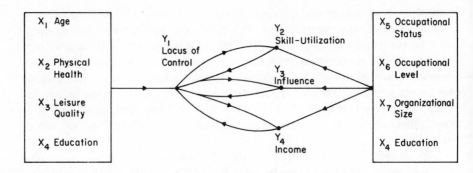

FIGURE 6.2   Reciprocal relationships between skill-utilization, influence, income
and locus of control. (From O'Brien, 1984 p. 61)

income should induce external orientations while high income should induce
internal orientations.

The predicted relationships between locus of control and job attributes
are shown in Figure 6.2. With a large representative sample of Australian
employees it was found that locus of control and skill-utilization were re-
ciprocally determined. The reciprocal relationship was also found for locus
of control and income but not for locus of control and influence. Internals
were more likely to attain jobs high in skill-utilization and income than externals. Employees with jobs high in skill-utilization and income were more
likely to develop internal than external control beliefs, whereas employees
with jobs low on skill-utilization and income were more likely to develop
external than internal control beliefs.

The finding that is most relevant to the present chapter is that skill-
utilization and income determine locus of control. What still has to be explained is why high skill-utilization/income jobs induce more external beliefs.
According to social learning theory (Rotter, 1966; Lefcourt, 1976) individuals are likely to become more internally controlled if they act in a way that
allows them to obtain valued rewards. A major reward of work is job satisfaction, so it would be expected that jobs that are high in job satisfaction would
tend to induce more internal beliefs. Job satisfaction was not included in the
present study but other studies have shown that skill-utilization (O'Brien,
1980, 1982) and income (Lawler, 1971) are important determinants of job
satisfaction. It is also possible that the actual experience of using job relevant
skills is important for maintaining high beliefs in internal control. This explanation is different from the previous one in that it does not assume that
the employee makes a rational judgement about activities and their rewards.
Simply performing activities which are challenging and require self-directed
effort maintains a conviction of personal control.

A somewhat surprising finding was that job influence did not affect locus of control. It was expected that jobs where individuals are able to control their job activities would induce internal control beliefs. However, when skill-utilization and influence were used as joint predictors of locus of control only skill-utilization was a significant predictor. Although influence is negatively correlated with locus of control this relationship disappears when skill-utilization is partialled out. This suggests that the major job determinant of locus of control is not whether an employee can affect decisions about the job environment but rather the content of the job itself. In a work organization, the major task is to do the job and not make decisions about how it should be done (work allocations, speed, rest-pauses, physical conditions). Although jobs that use employee skills tend to be jobs that allow job influence ($r = 0.53$), it is suggested that the regular use of job skills is more important for inducing control beliefs than exercising influence about matters concerning the job environment. For instance, some jobs have relatively high influence but low skill-utilization. A good example is assembly line work in factories where there are extensive opportunities for employee participation in decision making about job context matters. In such work, employees report that they have little control even though they have plenty of opportunities for influence in job procedures and the job environment (O'Brien, 1982; O'Brien and Stevens, 1981). Conversely, some jobs induce reports of high control even though the employees report low influence over job procedures (Csikszentmihalyi, 1975). These jobs are predominantly those involving high skill-utilization. In these studies Rotter's scale was not used to measure control beliefs and so their support for this interpretation of the results is tentative. Further research is needed in field situations where it is possible to observe changes in skill-utilization and influence so that their effect on locus of control can be observed.

Finally, some comment can be made about the smallness of the relationship between job attributes and locus of control. Locus of control is a significant, but not strong, predictor of job attributes. Other personal attributes (e.g. education, ability, work values) and situational factors (e.g. job openings, discrimination) are likely to be stronger determinants of job attributes. Similarly, the job attributes of skill-utilization and income are significant, but not strong, predictors of locus of control. This result indicates that there is support for Seeman's assertion that Marxian theories of work alienation have been overstated (Seeman, 1971). Intrinsic job attributes such as skill-utilization and influence have relatively small effects on beliefs about personal control. Defenders of Marxian views on the effect of work structure upon personal control might argue that employees lack insight into their own control beliefs or that the Rotter scale is not an appropriate scale for measuring locus of control. Both defences would need further research into the manner in which insight and scale content could affect locus of control responses. There has already been considerable discussion on the appropriateness of Rotter's locus of control scale but, so far, no other scale has been developed which measures generalized beliefs about personal control (O'Brien, 1984a). The scale does not sample a wide range of situations and this limits the claim of Rotter that it measures control orientations over all major life spheres. The method of scale scoring also leads to an over-concentration on extreme scores. The most interesting pattern of control scores may not be the internals and externals but rather a middle range score that is obtained by a person who believes in internal control in some situations and external control in other situations.

In summary, this study goes beyond existing research in identifying skill-utilization and income as job attributes that have a reciprocal causal relationship with measures of personal control. Previous research had only shown a reciprocal relationship between global job characteristics, such as occupational status or job complexity, and personal control (Andrisani, 1978; Andrisani and Nestel, 1976; Kohn and Schooler, 1983). The most extensive series of studies has been conducted by Kohn and Schooler who showed that job complexity was the major determinant of personal control. Structural variables such as bureaucratization, ownership and hierarchical level of the employee had smaller and more indirect effects on personal control. Hence the combined groups of studies provide some support for Marxian theories of work alienation if the various measures of personal control are considered to be adequate measures of 'powerlessness'. Despite the problems with the measures of personal control, it is still reasonable to conclude that job content, especially job complexity and skill-utilization, determines measured beliefs about personal control. The next question is whether changes in personal control beliefs lead to changes in employee performance.

REFERENCES

Andrisani, P.J. (1978). Internal-external attitudes, personal initiative and labor market experience, in P.J. Andrisani, E. Applebaum, R. Koppel and R.C. Miljus, *Work Attitudes and Labor Market Experience*, New York: Praeger

Andrisani, P.J., Applebaum, E., Koppel, R, and Miljus, R.C. (1978). *Work Attitudes and Labor Market Experience*, New York: Praeger

Andrisani, P.J. and Nestel, G. (1976). Internal-external control as a contributor and outcome of work experience, *Journal of Applied Psychology*, 76, 156–65

Blauner, R. (1964). *Alienation and Freedom*, Chicago: University of Chicago Press

Burris, V. (1983). The social and political consequences of overeducation, *American Sociological Review*, 48, 454–67

Csikszentmihalyi, M. (1975). *Beyond Boredom and Anxiety*, San Francisco: Jossey-Bass

Ekstrom, R.B., French, J.W., Harman, H.H. and Dermen, D. (1976). *Manual for Kit of Factor Referenced Cognitive Tests*, Princeton: Educational Testing Service

Frantz, R.S. (1980). The effect of early labor market experience upon internal-external locus of control among young male workers, *Journal of Youth and Adolescence*, **9**, 203–10

Jencks, C. (1972). *Inequality: A Reassessment of the Effect of the Family and Schooling in America*, New York: Basic Books

Kanungo, R.N. (1979). The concepts of alienation and involvement revisited, *Psychological Bulletin*, **86**, 119–38

Kanungo, R.N. (1981). Work alienation and involvement: problems and prospects, *International Review of Applied Psychology*, **30**, 1–15

Kanungo, R.N. (1982). *Work Alienation*, New York: Praeger

Kohn, M.L. (1969). *Class and Conformity: A Study in Values*, Homewood, Illinois: Dorsey Press, 2nd ed (1977) published by University of Chicago Press

Kohn, M.L. (1971). Bureaucratic man: a portrait and an interpretation, *American Sociological Review*, **36**, 461–74

Kohn, M.L. (1976) Occupational structure and alienation, *American Journal of Sociology*, **82**, 111–31

Kohn, M.L. (1980). Job complexity and adult personality, in N.J. Smelser and E.H. Eriksen (eds), *Themes of Work and Love in Adulthood*, Cambridge, Mass.: Harvard University Press, pp. 193–210

Kohn, M.L. (1984), Personal communication

Kohn, M.L. and Schooler, C. (1969). Class, occupation and orientation, *American Sociological Review*, **34**, 659–78

Kohn, M.L. and Schooler, C. (1973). Occupational experience and psychological functioning: an assessment of reciprocal effects, *American Sociological Review*, **28**, 97–118

Kohn, M.L. and Schooler, C. (1978). The reciprocal effects of the substantive complexity of work and intellectual flexibility: a longitudinal assessment, *American Journal of Sociology*, **84**, 25–52

Kohn, M.L. and Schooler, C. (1981). Job conditions and intellectual flexibility: A longitudinal assessment of their reciprocal effects, in D.J. Jackson and E.F. Borgatta (eds), *Factor Analysis and Measurement in Sociological Research*, Beverley Hills, California: Sage

Kohn, M.L. and Schooler, C. (1982). Job conditions and personality: a longitudinal assessment of their reciprocal effects, *American Journal of Sociology*, **87**, 1257–85

Kohn, M.L. and Schooler, C. (1983). *Work and Personality: An Inquiry into the Effect of Social Stratification*, Norwood, N.J.: Ablex Publishing Corporation

Lawler, E.E. (1971). *Pay and Organizational Effectiveness: A Psychological Review*, New York: McGraw-Hill

Lefcourt, H. (1976). *Locus of Control: Current Trends in Theory and Research*, New York: Wiley

Marx, K. (1844). *Economic and Philosophic Manuscripts of 1844*, Moscow: Progress Publishers, 1977

Marx, K. (1880). Enquête Ouvrière, *Revue Socialiste*, 20 April

Miller, J., Schooler, C., Kohn, M. and Miller, K. (1979). Women and work: the psychological effects of occupational conditions, *American Journal of Sociology*, **85**, 66–94

Miller, J., Slomczynski, K.M. and Kohn, M.L. (1984). Continuity of learning-generalization throughout adult life: the impact of the job on intellective processes in the United States and Poland, unpublished manuscript

Mortimer, J.T. and Laurence J. (1979). Work experience and occupational value socialization: a longitudinal study, *American Journal of Sociology*, **84**, 1361–85

Naoi, A. and Schooler, C. (in press). Occupational conditions and psychological functioning in Japan, *American Journal of Sociology*

O'Brien, G.E. (1980). The centrality of skill-utilization for job design, in K. Duncan, M. Gruneberg and D. Wallis (eds), *Changes in Working Life*, Chichester: Wiley

O'Brien, G.E. (1981). Locus of control, previous occupation and satisfaction with retirement, *Australian Journal of Psychology*, **33**, 305–18

O'Brien, G.E. (1982). The relative contribution of perceived skill-utilization and other perceived job attributes to the prediction of job satisfaction: a cross validation study, *Human Relations*, **35**, 219–37

O'Brien, G.E. (1984a). Locus of control, work and retirement, Chapter 2 in H.M. Lefcourt (ed.), *Research with the Locus of Control Construct*, Vol. 3, New York: Academic Press

O'Brien, G.E. (1984b). Reciprocal effects between locus of control and job attributes, *Australian Journal of Psychology*, **36**, 57–74

O'Brien, G.E. and Dowling, P. (1980). The effects of congruency between perceived and desired job attributes upon job satisfaction, *Journal of Occupational Psychology*, **53**, 121–30

O'Brien, G.E. and Dowling, P. (1981). Age and job satisfaction, *Australian Psychologist*, **16**, 49–61

O'Brien, G.E. and Stevens, L. (1981). The relationship between perceived influence and job satisfaction among assembly line employees, *Journal of Industrial Relations*, **23**, 33–48

Rotter, J.B. (1966). Generalized expectancies for internal versus external control of reinforcement, *Psychological Monographs*, **80**, (1. Whole No. 609)

Seeman, M. (1959). On the meaning of alienation, *American Sociological Review*, **24**, 783–91

Seeman, M. (1971). The urban alienations: some dubious theses from Marx to Marcuse, *Journal of Personality and Social Psychology*, **19**, 135–43

Seeman, M. (1972). Alienation and engagement, in A. Campbell and P.E. Converse (eds), *The Human Meaning of Social Change*, New York: Russell Sage, pp. 467–527

Seeman, M. (1975). Alienation studies, in A. Inkeles, J. Coleman and N. Smelser (eds), *Annual Review of Sociology*, vol. 1, Palo Alto, Cal.: Annual Reviews, pp. 91–123

Seeman, M. (1983). Alienation motifs in contemporary theorizing: the hidden continuity of the classic themes, *Social Psychology Quarterly*, **46**, 171–84

Slomczynski, K.M., Miller, J. and Kohn, M.L. (1981). Stratification, work and values: a Polish-United States comparison, *American Sociological Review*, **46**, 720–44

Spector, P.E. (1982). Behavior in organizations as a function of employees' locus of control, *Psychological Bulletin*, **91**, 482–97

Touraine, A. (1967). L'Aliénation de l'idéologie à l'analyse, *Sociologie du Travail*, **9**, 192–201

United States Department of Labor (1965). *Dictionary of Occupational Titles*, Washington, D.C.: U.S. Government Printing Office

Witkin, H.A., Dyk, R.B., Faterson, H.F., Goodenough, D.R. and Karp, A. (1962). *Psychological Differentiation: Studies of Development*, New York: Wiley

CHAPTER 7

Personal Control and Work Performance

The studies on the effects of work structure upon personality show that jobs can affect employees' beliefs about personal control and self-direction. These findings are not only important for understanding the relation between work and personality. They are also important for understanding how jobs can motivate people towards high performance. Various concepts of personal control and competence have been independently shown to affect individual performance in groups and organizations. This raises the possibility that certain jobs may lead to progressively lower performance and motivation as they reduce employees' beliefs in control and competence. Conversely, some jobs may act to maintain and enhance performance.

The description of the effects of beliefs about personal control on task performance has been the focus of a number of theories of motivation. Three different kinds of personal control belief have been identified. When an individual performs a task, he or she can have beliefs about:

1. *Control over reinforcements.* The main concept here is Rotter's locus of control (Rotter, 1966). Individuals who believe that their valued reinforcements can be largely attained by their own individual effort and ability are defined as internally controlled. At the other extreme, there are individuals who believe that valued reinforcements are largely determined by other people or external circumstances such as luck or fate (externals). A considerable body of research has investigated the relative performance of internals and externals.
2. *Control over the initiation of behaviour.* De Charms maintains that the most important control belief is whether a person considers himself the originator of task behaviours (an 'origin') or a 'pawn' whose behaviour is initiated or impelled by others (De Charms, 1968, 1976, 1981).
3. *Control over the level of task performance.* Individuals may vary in the degree to which they believe that they can perform various tasks.

159

Bandura has developed an extensive theory based on a concept of 'self-efficacy' (Bandura, 1977, 1982). People who believe that they can achieve high levels of performance on a given task have high 'self-efficacy'. By contrast, those who believe that they are not able or competent to achieve high performance have low 'self-efficacy'. According to Bandura, task performance is significantly related to self-efficacy measures in a positive manner. The higher the score on a measure of self-efficacy the higher the performance. A similar type of belief is the centre of Korman's consistency theory of work motivation. It is termed chronic self-esteem. Self-esteem is here considered a control belief because the common measures of self-esteem have high loadings on items measuring perceived competence. Hence it is possible to interpret Korman's theory as one which shows the conditions under which perceived competence affects task performance.

The first aim of this chapter is to consider the meaning of these three kinds of control belief and to review the evidence which shows how these beliefs can predict work performance. The second aim is to assess the relative importance of these various control beliefs for understanding work performance. Kohn and Schooler's (1982) concept of self-directed orientation will not be considered because, at present, they have not investigated the effect of this orientation on work performance. Also their concept cannot be easily classified into one of the three types. They see their concept as similar to but different from locus of control. Inspection of their measure of self-directedness suggests that it is an amalgam of all types of personal control beliefs.

LOCUS OF CONTROL AND WORK PERFORMANCE

The studies on the effect of work on locus of control show that certain kinds of jobs can affect an employee's relatively enduring beliefs about the determinants of life rewards. Those employees who are most likely to believe that their major life satisfactions are determined by their personal ability and effort have jobs that provide opportunities for using their skills as well as relatively high income. If a person has a low-paying job that does not use his or her skills very much, then that person is likely to believe that major life rewards are largely determined by external factors such as other people, social policies or luck. The evidence for these assertions was presented in Chapter 5.

A different set of studies has shown that employees who believe that they are internally controlled perform better at their jobs than those who are externally controlled.

These studies have shown that internals perform better than externals in situations where the job provides opportunities for initiative and the use of skill. Anderson (1977) used a longitudinal design to evaluate the performance of managers who had to revive their small businesses after their operations had been disrupted by a flood. After two years the performance of internals was superior to that of externals. With an experimental design Ruble (1976) found that internals performed better in participative decision groups than directive leader groups, whereas externals performed better in directive leader groups than in participative groups. There were no main effects of locus of control across situations. Another study found that internals had superior performance to externals in situations where rewards were based on skill (Heisler, 1974). There were no differences in performance between internals and externals when rewards were randomly allocated. Many other studies have looked at the relationship between locus of control and performance and a comprehensive review of their findings has been made by O'Brien (1984) and Spector (1982). Some of the studies are difficult to interpret because of weaknesses in design but the majority report that internals perform better than externals in situations where they have reasonable autonomy over work procedures.

Why do internals tend to perform better than externals? One explanation is that internals put more effort into their work. Compared to externals, internals believe more strongly that effort is related to performance (e.g. Broedling, 1975) and they also have stronger beliefs that their work performance is instrumental in attaining valued rewards (e.g. Lied and Pritchard, 1976).

According to the expectancy theory of work performance (Mitchell, 1974; Vroom, 1964), these beliefs affect performance according to the formula:

$$W = E \times \sum_{j=1}^{n} [I_{ij} \times V_i]$$

where W is predicted effort
   E is the expectancy that effort is associated with performance levels;
   I_{ij} is the instrumentality of performance of the attainment of outcomes;
   V_i is the valence or attractiveness of job outcomes;
and n is the number of outcomes.

According to this formula the predicted effort of internals should be higher than that of externals because they have higher E and I expectations.

Future developments of this model need to take account of three difficulties in the locus of control-performance literature. The first difficulty is that it is not clear whether internals perform better than externals simply because they have higher ability than externals. The second difficulty is that the superiority of internals seems to depend on whether the job allows skill-utilization and influence. Internals seem inclined to put more effort into those tasks requiring high skill-utilization than those requiring low skill-utilization. They also work better in situations where they have relatively high potential influence. By contrast, externals seem inclined to work best in situations that are structured and provide relatively little autonomy and influence. A final difficulty is that the model does not directly incorporate generalized beliefs about control. It assumes that generalized control beliefs will influence specific E and I expectancies and this may not always be true. The situation may be so structured that there is little variation in these beliefs between internals and externals.

If ability, skill-utilization, task influence and generalized control beliefs were built into the formula it should predict performance better than it currently does. Most studies, at present, can account for only about 15 per cent of the variance in task performance. A new formula would also avoid a simplistic approach to work motivation which considers only beliefs and expectations. Obviously for example, locus of control is not the major predictor of work performance. It is an important predictor but ability and task structure can be just as important.

The type of formula required can be generated using Shiflett's (1979) general model

$$P = [T] \times [R]$$

If this model is applied to individual performance—it can be generalized to predict group performance—then:

P is individual performance

$[T]$ is the matrix of situational constraints affecting the utilization of resources (transformers);

and $[R]$ is matrix of task relevant individual resources.

The two main individual resources are ability (a) and motivation (W). The predicted motivation of an individual is calculated from expectancy theory:

$$W = E \times (GE) \times \sum_{j=1}^{n} [I_{ij} V_i]$$

This is the same as the one presented earlier except that GE is the general belief about internal or external control of reinforcement. Thus the individual resource matrix is:

$$[R] = \begin{bmatrix} W \\ a \end{bmatrix}$$

We further assume that the two main job factors constraining people from using ability or motivation are the amount of skill-utilization in their jobs (s) and the potential influence they have over task procedures (p). Skill-utilization might be measured by scales such as those discussed earlier (O'Brien, 1982; O'Brien and Dowling, 1980). Potential influence could be measured by structural indices (O'Brien, Biglan and Penna, 1972). The transformer matrix is

$$[T] = [s \times p]$$

If all measures had a range of 0 →1, then individual productivity is:

$$P = [T] \times [R]$$
$$= [s\ p] \times \begin{bmatrix} W \\ a \end{bmatrix}$$

With matrix multiplication, then:

$$P = (s \times W) + (p \times a)$$

This is a possible theoretical model which needs to be tested. However, it is not inconsistent with the diverse findings on individual productivity. It implies a number of statements which can be presented in the form of recommendations for improving individual performance, as follows.

1. Maximum performance will occur when the task provides high skill-utilization, the employee is motivated, the employee has high ability for the task, and the group structure provides the employee with high potential influence over task procedures.
2. High motivation occurs in individuals with internal rather than external locus of control (*GE* high for internals, low for externals).
3. Since *P* is partly determined by ($s \times W$), the relatively high motivation of internals will not contribute much to performance unless the task provides them with opportunities for skill-use.
4. Since *P* is partly determined by ($p \times a$), individuals of high ability will not contribute much to performance unless they are placed in group structures which allow them to influence the way they use their abilities. This formula may seem unnecessarily complex. The only reply is that the determinants of individual performance are complex. Any theory of performance based on locus of control beliefs alone will be insufficient to explain much of the variance in performance. In the future, advances are only going to be made if we develop models which show how psychological attributes, such as locus of control beliefs, job content and group structure jointly determine performance.

A. What does Rotter's Internal–External Scale Measure?

The large majority of studies have measured these general beliefs or expectancies about control with Rotter's internal–external scale and hence the interpretation of these results depends on knowing what this scale actually measures. The first question is whether the dimension of internal–external control is a personality dimension. Do the scales reflect specific and variable beliefs about the source of reinforcement control or do they tap a basic personality dimension that is fairly stable over time?

The second question is one of scale meaning. Rotter defines locus of control as a generalized expectancy about the extent to which valued reinforcements are controlled by internal or external factors. But is the scale a suitable measure of this generalized expectancy? Some studies have analysed the internal consistency of the scale items and concluded that it is not a pure measure of personal beliefs about control over life reinforcements (Abrahamson, Schludermann and Schludermann, 1973; Cherlin and Bourque, 1974; Collins, 1974; Dixon, McKee and McRae, 1976; Duffy, Shiflett and Downey, 1977; Garza and Widlak, 1977; Gurin, *et al.*, 1969; Levenson, 1974; Mirels, 1970; O'Brien and Kabanoff, 1981; Reid and Ware, 1973; Watson, 1981). Generally, it has been found that the scale is not unidimensional but contains at least two main factors—generally labelled personal control, and system or political control. Items that are situation-free tend to load on the personal control factor, while items referring to political situations tend to load on the system control factor. The personal control items measure the degree to which individuals feel that they are able to make things happen, while the system items tap the individual's beliefs about the efficacy of the individual in shaping political and organizational processes. As it is logically possible for an individual to feel internally controlled, yet also believe he or she is unable to have much control in certain structures, this has led to the apparently reasonable inference that the search for generalized control expectancies should be abandoned. Perceptions of personal control are specific to the type of situation and hence measures of personal control should be developed that are specific to situations. Thus, locus of control measures have been developed for health, affiliation, achievement, retirement and work situations.

Although these developments are feasible the assumption that generalized control beliefs are an illusion is not. The logical inference from the factor-analysis of the Rotter scale is that the scale is not unidimensional and that it is not an adequate measure of generalized control beliefs because it does not canvas beliefs across a large number of situations. It is heavily loaded on educational and political beliefs and therefore neglects many of the common situations such as family, work and leisure, which are encountered in everyday life.

A generalized expectancy is measured on the basis of responses to a range of situations that are commonly experienced by the respondent. Rotter's scale does not do this. It does not include a wide range of situations but it could tap general expectancies because the main 'personal control' factor is derived from situation-free items where the respondent indicates whether life, in general, allows personal reinforcements to be achieved by personal effort.

Yet ambiguity remains in the meaning of the responses to these items. Do they reflect a stable predisposition of the individual or do they measure an individual's perception of his degree of control or influence in actual situations? Of course, actual perceptions of control may determine personal feelings of being in control of reinforcements, but not necessarily. If, for example, an individual is unemployed, he may feel that many of his life satisfactions are no longer under his control (e.g. interesting work, high income) but he may still feel that, within situations where he has freedom of movement, he is capable of achieving what he wants by personal effort. Thus belief in structural determinants of behaviour in some life spheres does not necessarily mean that the person feels externally controlled in all spheres.

A similar point is made by other authors who have suggested that external scorers on the Rotter scale may not really have a generalized belief in external control of reinforcement but may be reporting realistic perceptions of the sources of control in social situations (O'Brien and Kabanoff, 1981; Lange and Tiggemann, 1980; Wong and Sproule, 1984).

B. An Alternative View of Locus of Control

One way of overcoming this problem is to construct a new scale where the individual indicates what he believes determines valued reinforcements in situations where the source of personal outcomes is known. Situations would be classified on the basis of the objective source of determination—personal, structural, and a mixed type, personal-structural. A *personal* situation is one where it is known that individuals largely determine outcomes. An example would be a work situation where the employee works alone. Performance outcomes and personal satisfactions are largely self-determined and unaffected by machines, other people or organizational structure. To some extent, the satisfactions may be affected by the task. If it is too easy or too difficult, major intrinsic satisfactions may be impossible. There is, therefore, no 'pure' personal situation because any interaction will be shaped by tasks, people and the environment. However, if the task is reasonably challenging, (i.e. uses major skills), then what the individual makes of it is within his control. A *structural* situation would be one where the operation of personal effort and skill is minimized by machine demands and directive supervision.

A *mixed situation* could be a semi-autonomous work group where an individual's performance is partly determined by personal effort and partly by the effort of coworkers.

These three types of situation could occur within each of the following common task domains—educational, work, leisure, home, interpersonal and political. If items were devised to cover the domains and types of situations then the predisposition of individuals to select external or internal sources of control could be assessed. Response alternatives could tap four alternative determinants of the outcome: self, non-self (e.g. people, machines, physical conditions), a joint self/non-self factor and chance. If these responses are labelled respectively internal (*I*), external (*E*), mixed (*M*), and chance (*C*), then three main types of respondents can be identified (Table 7.1).

TABLE 7.1   Control response pattern for different situations

Response pattern	Objective Determinants of Outcomes		
	Personal	Structural	Mixed (Personal-Structural)
Internal	*I*	*I*	*I*
Realistic	*I*	*E*	*M*
External	*E* or *C*	*E* or *C*	*E* or *C*

I = internal response.   *E* = external response.
C = chance response.   *M* = mixed response.

The extreme internally controlled individual would choose internal factors across all three types of situation. One response would be accurate but the other two would be distortions. Similarly, the extreme externally controlled individual would have distorted judgements about two situations but would make an accurate external attribution for the structural situation. A third type of person, called realistic, would make an accurate attribution for all three situations.

This classification helps to provide an interpretation of extreme scorers on the Rotter scale, as well as to suggest the characteristics of the middle scorers. The extreme internals on Rotter's scale are what Wong and Sproule (1984) have called idealistic-optimistic controllers. They overestimate their own capability to control and underestimate the strength of external constraints. The extreme externals are unrealistic pessimists who underestimate their capacity to control and overestimate the strength of external constraints. The middle scorers on Rotter scale might be the realists who appreciate that personal control is possible in some situations but not in others.

The realistic individuals are not necessarily the same as Wong and Sproule's 'bilocals' who perceive and desire control from both internal and external loci. The way in which these bilocals are identified does not guarantee that they make realistic assessments about the determinants of personal reinforcements. The items in the Trent Attribution Profile (TAP) refer to undefined situations and it is not possible to assess whether respondents are making realistic responses. This is a problem shared with others who have attempted to classify types of attribution patterns (Lefcourt, 1981; Levenson, 1981; Reid and Ware, 1973, 1974; Paulhus and Christie, 1981). Although these scales identify more complex control orientations than internal/external they are unable to address the problem of whether a given score indicates a respondent's predisposition or an accurate appraisal of reality.

The present formulation of locus of control does not require the abandonment of the concept of a generalized locus of control. It is based on the assumption that a generalized locus of control orientation reflects a stable belief in the individual about his or her ability to change the environment in order to obtain valued rewards. In some ways this is similar to the Freudian idea of ego strength. In psychoanalytic theory the ego is a structure of personality which has the twin function of balancing instinctual drives and internalized rules of conduct, as well as providing means whereby the individual can respond to external demands in order to maintain 'comfortable' levels of need satisfaction and anxiety. To measure this central personality dimension, it is insufficient to have scales that simply describe the individual's perception of the determinant of outcomes in various situations. What is required is an instrument that detects whether the individual is realistic or biased in his expectations about the determinants of his behaviour and rewards. The further advantage of this approach is that it allows one to avoid the trap of thinking that all 'internals' are good, effective people. A moderate level of internality is probably appropriate but extreme internality is likely to be associated with psychopathological states as much as extreme externality. The extreme internal is inflexible, unrealistic and likely to encounter great tension and dissatisfaction when blocked in attempts to use personal effort to gain rewards. If the psychopathology of the extreme external is depression and fatalism, then the psychopathology of the extreme internal is likely to be megalomania, inflexibility and dogmatism.

The preferred personality profile is one of realism where the individual can accurately decide (i) where individual behaviour is externally constrained, and (ii) where individual behaviour is likely to bring personal rewards. Most importantly, the realist will have the flexibility to change his behaviour in accordance with the demands of the situation. At this point, there is a possible connexion to the findings of Kohn and Schooler (1981), 1982). They identified ideational flexibility and self-directing orientation as one of the main consequences of complex work. Flexible people can see alternative courses of action and because of this flexibility they feel greater personal control over their own behaviour. This is one explanation of Kohn and Schooler's finding that flexibility is positively associated with self-direction. High scorers on their measure of self-direction make independent judgement about the appropriate course of action. They do not necessarily think that all problems can be solved by personal will-power or ability. The latter view is more characteristic of the extreme internal. This rigidity reduces the internal's ability to adapt to situations where his control orientation is incompatible with strong structural constraints.

Thus it is proposed that a better formulation of control orientations should be based on the classification of four different cognitive types. Schematically, these are:

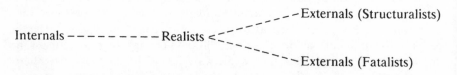

Internals and externals have distorted views of reality. The realist has the highest self-control because he knows when to exert effort and when to accede to external constraints. He fits his response to the situation. Structural externals overestimate the role of structural determinants of behaviour such as power and task structures whereas the fatalist external unrealistically believe that outcomes are dependent on task or fate and ignore the role of personal and structural variables. It is predicted that the 'realists' will show higher performance than extreme internals and externals across task situations which vary in potential influence. At present, this cannot be tested because the available scales are used only to classify people into internals and externals.

PERSONAL CAUSATION

Whatever the method used to measure it, the locus of control concept refers to beliefs about the source of control over reinforcements. It specifically does not refer to:

   (i) beliefs about the control of personal actions;
  (ii) beliefs about competence to do action tasks;
 (iii) beliefs about self-control.

It may be the case that an individual who is very internally controlled also believes that he is determining his own actions and that he is competent as well as generally self-directed, but it is not a logical implication. The relationship between these control beliefs has to be analysed in order to see if these distinctions are clear. The analysis should also try and see if these beliefs have different relationships to behaviour.

The distinction between control over reinforcement and control over behaviour has been made by De Charms (1968, 1976, 1981). Most recently, he illustrated the difference using an example drawn from work situations:

> John Gaffenberg works for the Spildink Printing Company. Until a year ago he was paid a salary and was expected to be at the plant running the printing press from 8.00 a.m. to 5.00 p.m. every work day. Recently, the company installed an incentive bonus system. John can now assure himself of a 10 per cent bonus over his salary if he is never absent from work. If he does miss work, then the bonus diminishes by a function of the number of the number of days he misses.
>
> (De Charms, 1981. p. 337)

For De Charms this is a clear case of the individual being put in a situation where he feels responsible for reinforcement. The emphasis is not on being responsible for his actions, but on the consequences of his actions. Hence he feels 'that the locus of control of reinforcements is internal to himself' (De Charms, p. 337).

Another example gives a situation where the employee feels responsible for his actions rather than the reinforcement or rewards following from his actions:

> Hank Ford works for the Stripgear Motorcar Corporation ... Now the plant is organized into groups of skilled craftsmen who make their own decisions about who does what and about how and in what order they cooperate. They even set their own production quotas. They all contribute to the finished product, which is not released from their group until they are satisfied with it.
>
> (De Charms, 1981, p. 337)

In this situation Hank reports that he likes being able to suggest changes, implement them, and see them work. For De Charms, he now chooses his actions, owns them, and takes responsibility for his part of the group product. The emphasis here is on control of his actions and not their consequences. In De Charm's terminology, Hank is an origin of his actions and not a pawn who is controlled by external factors. Although John has control over his bonus payments he may not necessarily feel in control of his actions. He may think he has no choices in his job and is a pawn of management. The general implication is that knowing a person's perceived locus of control of reinforcement tells us nothing about his experience of personal causation.

Yet is this conclusion really justified? Let us look at the two examples in more detail:

	Control behaviour		*Reinforcement*
Hank	⟶ Work arrangements	⟶	Job satisfaction
John	⟶ Attendance	⟶	Money

John can control the amount of his pay but does it by controlling his own actions. He can decide to go to work or not. The attainment of reinforcement is tied to his control of that part of his work behaviour which relates to attendance. If he had no control over his being able to attend work then he would not feel any control over reinforcement. Certainly he may not feel control over work procedures but there is a logical link between personal causation of work attendance and control of income.

Similarly, Hank may have control over his work arrangements. He feels happy about this, presumably because of intrinsic rewards associated with more control, more skill-utilization (and perhaps more money if he operated on a bonus system). Being more in control of work arrangements, Hank does experience personal causation but, as De Charms indicates, he is happy (satisfied) and would see his personal control resulting in intrinsic job reinforcement. So, in both cases, there is a strong link between control of certain behaviour and feeling in control of reinforcements which are *consequences* of these behaviours.

This does not preclude the possibility that a general feeling of personal causation may not be related to a general belief in control of reinforcements. It does imply though that a person who feels in control of reinforcements will believe he is in control of behaviours that produce these reinforcements. And, of course, the opposite holds. If a person feels in control of his actions he will feel in control of reinforcements that follow these actions. The general point is that the relation between personal control of actions and personal control of reinforcements depends on whether the actions and reinforcements are linked.

A general criticism of De Charms' position is that he assumes that personal action is independent of reinforcements. Yet any action, especially those performed at work, involves some reinforcement. The actor is aware that what is done will be followed by some degree of external reinforcement (e.g. praise, criticism, income, job maintenance) or some internal reinforcement (e.g. satisfaction, dissatisfaction, stress). De Charms defines personal causation as a general and unmeasurable motivational concept which is logically and empirically different from reinforcement.

> In dealing with motives, the feeling of causal efficacy, of being the origin of a change in the environment, of doing something, is the basic universal. The fact that it cannot be measured reliably and hence communicated scientifically sets the problem rather than placing it out of bounds.
>
> (De Charms, 1968, p. 264)

Another problem is that, in a certain sense, the primacy of personal causation is true by definition. A person acts. Someone else can act for a person but this means the action is done by someone else. Sometimes other influences can force a person to move but then it is not an action. We may be transported by a plane. We move but it is not our 'own' movement. We may be pushed and fall. This is not a voluntary movement, an action, but an involuntary movement.

The work of De Charms (1981) does have the effect of highlighting the importance of experience as a determinant of control beliefs. The experience of acting provides reinforcements of a different kind. Most locus of control research emphasizes reinforcements which come *after* actions have been performed. This research demonstrates that internality is shaped by contingencies between actions and consequent reinforcements while externality results from lack of contingency between personal actions and reinforcement. There is not an incompatibility between the two approaches because actions are always associated with some kind of reinforcement. In a work situation, the tasks can be rewarding if they provide the actor with opportunities for skill-use and autonomy (Csikszentmihalyi, 1975; Hackman and Oldham, 1975, 1980; O'Brien, 1982; O'Brien and Dowling, 1980). These task characteristics are major sources of satisfaction (experienced reward) and, when given the opportunity, people choose to continue to work at these tasks (Deci, 1975). They may enjoy being the originator of their own actions but this is because they receive immediate rewards through the task experience.

A. Attributional Bias

There appear to be two reasons why employees in 'good' jobs attribute their rewards to their own efforts and not to the content of the job. Firstly, they have to do the task. Rewards, either through immediate action or later income and recognition, depend on responding to challenges. The individual must decide to engage in the task and, furthermore, must persistently master his resources to meet job requirements. There is thus a component of self-direction. This may not be a repeated cycle of gritting the teeth and saying 'here I go again'. Challenging tasks have their own traction and often the employee becomes pre-occupied with the task. In Csikszentmihalyi's terminology, there is an experience of 'deep-flow'. The person is conscious of being drawn along by the experience but largely sees the process as one of self-determination. The role of the task tends to be underestimated because of the immediacy of the personal experience. The actor engages the task and cognitively attributes the resultant experience as being a consequence of his choice and effort. Perhaps this is due to some form of cultural socialization. When we do enjoyable tasks we think we are in control and that the rewards accrue from our actions. Another form of explanation is possible but rarely voiced. This is that our enjoyment is due to a match or harmony between nature (tasks) and man (skills).

The second reason why employees are more likely to appropriate to themselves the source of their positive experience is attributional bias. Attributional research has commonly found that individuals tend to take personal credit for positive and success experiences and deny personal responsibility for negative and failure experiences (Feather, 1982, 1983; Feather and Simon, 1975). One of the main motivational explanations for this is that individuals distort their interpretations of events in order to enhance and protect the self. Thus, self-esteem is enhanced by attributing positive task experiences to the self and blaming the task (or others) for negative experiences. The degree of distortion probably depends on the individual's desire for personal power. The extreme internally controlled individual sees only himself and not the task structure as being responsible for rewards ('I did it my way'). The realist, while acknowledging that feelings of personal control are partly related to his own efforts, also sees the task as being a necessary (and external) determinant of his rewards.

Thus the answer to the question of why challenging tasks are not seen as an external determinant of behaviour is partly explainable in terms of the behaviours required by the task. To the extent that they require full use of the employees' skills they allow the individual to be self-directed and this self-direction is incorporated as a belief in personal control. The magnitude of this personal control belief can be distorted both by the individual's power need and by the operation of attributional bias. It cannot be assumed that there will be a one-to-one relationship between the amount of behavioural self-direction and internalized self-direction. For some people there will be a realistic assessment of personal control in that they will be aware that the personal control they feel is a joint function of themselves and task opportunities. Others will be deluded to some extent. The most deluded will be those with a strong will to power and a strong desire to believe in their own worth. They are likely to report very high levels of internal control on Rotter's locus of control scale.

SELF-EFFICACY AND SELF-ESTEEM

So far, the two theories of personal control have concentrated on cognitions about the degree to which personal control is exerted over actions and outcomes of actions (reinforcements). Bandura (1977, 1982) and Bandura and Cervone (1983) have argued that such theories neglect efficacy beliefs about personal control that are of central importance for predicting performance levels and the psychological consequences of task performance. Self-efficacy beliefs in Bandura's theory are not beliefs about the likelihood of personal behaviour achieving outcomes. Such outcome beliefs are different from efficacy beliefs which are beliefs about the probability that the actor can successfully perform the behaviour required to produce the outcomes. The distinction between the two types of beliefs is shown in Figure 7.1. These beliefs are separated because it is quite possible for an individual to believe that certain behaviour on his part could produce desired outcomes but, at the same time, also believe that he can not perform the required behaviour. When this happens, the individual may not perform well or at all even though he has a strong belief in personal control of outcomes.

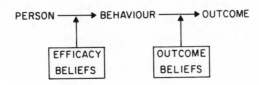

FIGURE 7.1   Representation of the difference between efficacy and outcome beliefs. (From *A. Bandura, self-efficacy: toward a unifying theory of behavioural change,* Psychological review, **84**, *191–215. Copyright 1977 by the American Psychological Association. Reprinted by permission of the author*)

Belief in self-efficacy can affect behaviour in a number of ways. It can affect both the initiation and the persistence of coping or problem solving behaviour. People may not initiate any action if they believe they have low competence or efficacy for the task. Even if they do try to solve the problem or perform a task, low feelings of self-efficacy can determine how much effort they expend and the time they spend on the task. The stronger the perceived self-efficacy the greater the effort expended and the greater is the persistence at the task.

Efficacy beliefs for Bandura may be either general, stable estimates of self competence or they may be specific to particular tasks and situations. Personal mastery experiences which are successful produce some efficacy beliefs which then generalize to other situations. The strongest generalization effects occur for activities which are most closely related to the situations in which self-efficacy was enhanced. Failure in task performance can reduce a belief in self-efficacy which also can generalize to other situations.

Yet self-efficacy beliefs are not shaped by task experience alone. They can be affected by vicarious experience (e.g. watching others perform), verbal persuasion (e.g. suggestion, counselling) and emotional arousal (e.g., relaxation). The relative effects of these methods have been assessed for a range of fearful and defensive behaviours and the most powerful improvements in self-efficacy were obtained through performance training where the subject was given a series of relevant tasks graduated in difficulty. Progressive success improved self-efficacy.

A. Comparison with Other Approaches to Efficacy

Bandura's views differ from others in terms both of the origins of personal efficacy and of the explanation of how it affects behaviour. One of the earliest formulations as by White, (1959) who postulated an 'effectance motive'—an intrinsic drive to explore and manipulate the environment. This motive is activated by novel stimulation and sustained by actions that introduce further novelty into the task situation. Bandura points out a number of difficulties with White's theory:

1. It does not explain how effectance motivation emerges from task activity.
2. The motive is inferred from the behaviour it is meant to explain. 'Without an independent measure of motive strength one cannot tell whether people explore and manipulate things because of a competence motive to do so, or for any number of other reasons' (Bandura, 1977, p. 203).

Bandura sees his approach as preferable because self-efficacy is measured independently from performance. It also makes specific predictions about the occurrence, generality and persistence of coping behaviours. The basis of the predictions is perceived ability:

> People will approach, explore, and try to deal with situations within their self-perceived capabilities, but they will avoid transactions with stressful aspects of their environment they perceive as exceeding their ability.
>
> (Bandura, 1977, p. 203)

Whereas the main problem with effectance motivation is its generality and lack of attention to contextual factors, Bandura sees Rotter's theory of internal-external control as neglecting efficacy beliefs for outcome beliefs. A useful example to illustrate his point is the case of a child who believes that exam grades reflect the level of his performance. In Rotter's view the child would be internally controlled—he believes the outcome is determined by personal ability and effort. However, he may not perform well at, say, an arithmetic exam, as locus of control theory might predict. He may believe he lacks the skill required to perform well. Yet it is quite possible that outcome expectations (internally or externally determined) can mediate the effect of performance on self-efficacy. Whether or not you feel your competence is enhanced by successful performance will depend on whether the performance was due to skill or to external factors.

A final point about self-efficacy theory is that it does not predict that the same mastery experiences will have similar effects for all people. There are two reasons for this. First, people differ in their appraisal of information about their competence and performance. Second, people in a given situation would have different histories of competence. The amount of enhancing experiences would differ as well as the type of situation in which they received them.

Most of the studies designed to test self-efficacy theory have not been done in work situations. Rather, they have concentrated on how training in efficacy can be used to treat people with phobias and health problems. Some have examined achievement situations for children and shown that increases in self-efficacy can improve learning achievement. The only study directly related to work situations was by Locke, *et al.*, (1984). They found that self-efficacy beliefs were positively related to performance on creative tasks. Self-efficacy was measured by subjects' estimated competence to perform the task as well as by their certainty of performing at the estimated level of competence. Self-efficacy appeared directly to affect performance even when ability was controlled. Belief in self-efficacy also indirectly affected performance because those with higher self-efficacy set higher goals and higher goals were positively related to performance. Self-efficacy was related to ability as well as past performance and this study suggests a reciprocal relationship between performance and self-efficacy of the kind illustrated in Figure 7.2.

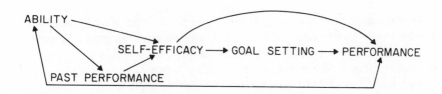

FIGURE 7.2   The relationship between self-efficacy and performance. This model is based on the findings in Locke, *et al.* (1984)

Whether or not self-efficacy theory goes beyond locus of control theory seems to depend on whether it is possible to make a clear distinction between beliefs about response-outcome relationships and beliefs about ability to perform required behaviours. If the outcomes are defined as visible objective rewards then the distinction is clear enough. However, for the most part, Bandura talks of desired outcomes. Then the distinction is not clear. Beliefs about competence can determine your desired outcomes. If you feel lacking in your ability to do a job, then this could shape your desired outcomes. You might think that desirable outcomes are (i) avoiding the sack; (ii) achieving just adequate levels of performance; (iii) reshaping your job, perhaps through delegation, so that you do what you feel able to do well. This point is acknowledged by Bandura himself (Bandura, 1982, p. 140). He admits that expected outcomes cannot be dissociated from performance judgements when the outcomes are 'inherent to the actions'. For him, outcome expectations are independent from efficacy judgements where 'extrinsic outcomes are loosely linked to level or quality of performance'.

This immediately makes us question the applicability of the theory to a work situation where first, extrinsic outcomes are linked to performance. If you do not perform well you get fired—a very drastic outcome—or you earn less or you lose the respect of your coworkers. Extrinsic outcomes such as these are linked to performance. There admittedly are some jobs where, once a position is attained in the organization, you are unlikely to be sacked for poor performance or to lose salary. Tenured academic positions and upper level government positions might fall into this category. But they are not typical and certainly poor performance would still affect some extrinsic outcomes, for example, personal relationships, and level of criticism.

The second difficulty is that work is an activity where intrinsic outcomes are linked to performance. Doing well at a job provides a sense of achievement and a feeling that you are using skills. Since level of performance is also considered by Bandura to determine efficacy beliefs it follows that self-efficacy is then tied to beliefs about the attainment of desired intrinsic rewards.

To the extent that Bandura's theory is confined to perceived outcomes (as it seems to be) and since work activities involve both intrinsic and extrinsic perceived rewards it must be considered that perceptions of self-efficacy at work cannot be disconnected from perceptions of control over rewards (outcomes). Just as De Charms' theory failed to include an analysis of the task situation at work so the applicability of Bandura's to the work situation is also restricted by the same failure. This is not to say that his theory may not be preferable to theories based just on response-outcome expectancies in situations where desired extrinsic outcomes are clearly independent of performance.

It may be useful in some work contexts when there are employees who clearly have the ability to do a job well but fail because they do not believe they really have the ability. Demonstration of their abilities through graduated task performance could improve their performance. Yet it seems unable to deal with the kind of situation that is relevant to understanding the effects of work on personality. If a worker has the ability and believes he has ability but is confronted repeatedly by a task that does not use it what happens to him? His response-outcome expectancies would change. In doing the job he would come to realize that intrinsic rewards (job satisfaction) were not attainable. Yet efficacy beliefs would not change. The task is easy and would simply reinforce his belief that he has abilities far in excess of those required by the job. Thus the main effect, from a cognitive view point, of work is to alter outcome beliefs and not efficacy beliefs. Certainly, efficacy beliefs can change after people have tried various jobs and found what they can and cannot do but the typical problem is how to understand the psychological effects of jobs which remain fairly constant over time. There is one òther major theory of perceived competence and task performance. This has been developed by Korman and, in some respects, is similar to Bandura's self-efficacy theory.

B. Korman's Theory of Self-esteem and Task Performance

Korman's theory of work motivation predicts that the level of task performance achieved by an individual will be consistent with that individual's reported level of competence or chronic self-esteem (Korman, 1968a,b, 1970, 1971a,b, 1976). Persons with high chronic self-esteem perceive themselves as competent and will endeavour to perform at a high level in a task situation. By contrast, those with low chronic self-esteem perceive themselves as lacking competence and unable to achieve need-fulfilment. In task situations they maintain consistency between their self-esteem and task behaviour by performing at relatively low levels of performance. Besides his own studies, Korman cites additional research which shows that high self-esteem subjects perform at higher levels than those with low self-esteem (Aronson and Carlsmith, 1962; Denmark and Guttentag, 1967; Hechler and Weiner, 1974; O'Reilly, 1973). Some recent studies have not found strong support for this prediction (Inkson, 1978; Terborg, Richardson and Pritchard, 1980) while a review of relevant studies concluded that there was some support for Korman's prediction but that the results could be equally well understood in terms of self-enhancement theory (Dipboye, 1977).

Before motivational theories of either a consistency or a self-enhancement type are used to explain self-esteem/performance effects it is necessary first to establish that self-esteem has an effect on performance. A recent review of self-esteem and performance studies (Tharenou, 1979) points out that the design problems in most studies preclude any definite conclusion about the effect of self-esteem on performance. It is also possible that many studies reporting a positive effect of self-esteem on performance do so because the self-esteem measure used is positively correlated with ability. The relatively higher performance of high self-esteem persons compared to those with low self-esteem could be due to their higher levels of task ability. Some evidence for this conjecture comes from a recent study by Terborg, Richardson and Pritchard (1980). A positive correlation between ability and chronic self-esteem was found and the authors recommended that future tests of the self consistency theory should control for ability.

In order to establish whether self-esteem has a direct effect on task performance in a specific situation it is necessary to measure the direct and interactive effects of both self-esteem and ability. Furthermore, if self-esteem effects are found they may be confined to tasks of high rather than low difficulty. As Korman asserted, 'success motivation would be more likely to show up on the hard task' as it 'does not need much success motivation to succeed on the easy task' (Korman, 1970, p. 38).

A recent experimental study did vary self-esteem, ability and task difficulty (O'Brien and Pere, 1985). For both easy and difficult tasks, high self-esteem subjects performed better than low self-esteem subjects. However, when self-esteem and ability were used as joint predictors of performance, self-esteem was unrelated to performance.

At present, most competence theories based on constructs like 'perceived competence' (Korman, 1976) or 'self-efficacy' (Bandura, 1977, 1982) generate ambiguous or inconsistent results. Most studies of self-efficacy *appear* to show that an individual performance is positively related to judgements of ability. However, objective ability is not controlled. When self-efficacy judgements are manipulated this is done by improving the individual's actual skill or mastery. Thus, 'self-efficacy' effects are confounded with actual ability. Also Korman's studies do not control for ability and the reported effects of perceived competence or self-esteem could be due to a correlation between ability and reported competence. A recent review found that the mean correlation across studies between self-reported ability and objective ability was 0.29 (Mabe and West, 1982). This is not high enough to infer that perceived ability is an accurate measure of ability. The correlation is still high enough, however, to suggest that self-efficacy or competence effects may be due to differences in objective ability. Whether or not self-efficacy or perceived competence has an effect on performance cannot be confidently answered until studies examine the joint effects of ability, efficacy and competence upon performance. Locke *et al.*, (1984), in a study previously mentioned, did try to do this and their study suggested that there were self-efficacy effects over and above ability effects on performance. However, more studies are needed before this conclusion can be accepted as a generalization.

CONCLUSION

This chapter reviewed the effect of personal control beliefs on job performance. A substantial number of studies have shown that individuals who have relatively high beliefs in personal control are more motivated, and perform better, than those with relatively weak beliefs in their own ability to control performance and task reinforcements. Hence work performance can be improved if employees are selected who have relatively high control beliefs and furthermore, performance can be maintained and improved if jobs are designed so that employee beliefs in personal control can be raised.

There are two different kinds of control beliefs. One type of belief refers to the degree that employees see that their life outcomes are determined by their own effort or ability. Typically, those who see these outcomes as being largely achieved by their effort or ability are called internals. Those who believe that these outcomes largely result from non-personal attributes, such as government, institutional policies, luck or fate, are termed externals.

There is a reasonable amount of evidence which shows that internals performed better than externals. These results were reviewed and it was shown that the effect of locus of control depended on the type of situation and the ability of the individual. Hence future research should avoid trying to prove the superiority of internals over externals and endeavour to show how locus of control interacts with task content, group structure and ability jointly to determine performance. A simple theoretical model of performance was developed which specified the manner in which locus of control, skill-utilization, influence and ability could determine individual work performance. It was recommended that the common measure of locus of control, Rotter's scale, be revised in order to make it a better measure of generalized expectancies about control. It needs items which sample a wider range of situations, as well as a technique for distinguishing stable personal beliefs from specific perceptions of personal influence in organizations. Finally, it was suggested that the results of locus of control studies should not be interpreted as showing that all 'internals' are best at everything. Extreme internals who believe that all is within their power are likely to be inflexible and uncooperative in their personal style. More research should be devoted to the moderate internal, a 'realist' who is able to differentiate between situations where personal effort is effective and situations where structural factors preclude individual freedom of movement.

The other main type of personal control belief is perceived competence. Competence beliefs tap an employee's belief about his or her ability to perform tasks. Bandura's theory of competence or 'self-efficacy' was reviewed. Some research has shown that self-efficacy beliefs are positively related to performance. Furthermore, self-efficacy beliefs can be strengthened by graduated training, vicarious experience, persuasion and emotional arousal. Examination of research on efficacy and Korman's perceived competence (self-esteem) revealed some difficulties in interpretation. Few studies, showing positive effects of competence/self-efficacy on performance, have controlled for ability. Most studies that did control for ability found no effect of perceived competence on performance. People with high efficacy or perceived competence may perform better than those low on these measures, simply because they have higher ability. Bandura's work suggests a close link between ability and self-efficacy because self-efficacy rises as task experiences allow individuals to raise their ability.

Despite these problems in the personal control-performance literature, it is still reasonable to conclude that job content can determine performance by way of control beliefs. The process by which this occurs still needs to be elucidated. This chapter allows us to go beyond the conclusion of the previous chapters which showed how job content could determine personality, including personal control. It is now possible to conclude that jobs which lead to changes in employee control beliefs can also, under some circumstances, produce changes in employee performance levels.

REFERENCES

Abrahamson, D., Schluderman, S. and Schluderman, E. (1973). Replication of dimensions of locus of control, *Journal of Consulting and Clinical Psychology*, **41**, 320

Anderson, C.R. (1977). Locus of control, coping behaviors and performance in a stress setting: a longitudinal study, *Journal of Applied Psychology*, **62**, 446–51

Aronson, E. and Carlsmith, J.M. (1962). Performance expectancy as a determinant of actual performance, *Journal of Abnormal and Social Psychology*, **65**, 178–82

Bandura, A. (1977). Self-efficacy: toward a unifying theory of behavioral change, *Psychological Review*, **84**, 191–215

Bandura, A. (1982). Self-efficacy mechanism in human agency, *American Psychologist*, **37**, 122–47

Bandura, A. and Cervone, D. (1983). Self-evaluative and self-inefficacy mechanisms governing the motivational effects of goal systems, *Journal of Personality and Social Psychology*, **45**, 1017–28

Broedling, L.A. (1975). Relationships of internal-external control to work motivation and performance in an expectancy model, *Journal of Applied Psychology*, **60**, 65–70

Cherlin, A. and Bourque, L.B. (1974). Dimensionality and reliability of the Rotter I/E scale, *Sociometry*, **37**, 565–82

Collins, B.E. (1974). Four separate components of the Rotter I/E scale: belief in a difficult world, a just world, a predictable world and politically responsive, *Journal of Personality and Social Psychology*, **29**, 381–91

Csikszentmihalyi, M. (1975). *Beyond Boredom and Anxiety*, San Francisco: Jossey-Bass

De Charms, R. (1968). *Personal Causation*, New York: Academic Press

De Charms, R. (1976). *Enhancing Motivation: Change in the Classroom*, New York: Irvington

De Charms, R. (1981). Personal causation and locus of control: two different traditions and two uncorrelated measures, in H.M. Lefcourt (ed.), *Research with the Locus of Control Construct*, vol. 1, New York: Academic Press

Deci, E.L. (1975), *Intrinsic motivation*, New York: Plenum Press

Denmark, F. and Guttentag, M. (1967). Dissonance in the self-concepts of education concepts of college and non-college oriented women, *Journal of Counselling Psychology*, **14**, 113–5

Dipboye, R.L. (1977). A critical review of Korman's self-consistency theory of work motivation and occupational choice, *Organizational Behavior and Human Performance*, **28**, 108–26

Dixon, D.N., McKee, C.S. and McRae. B.C. (1976). Dimensionality of three adult, objective locus of control scores, *Journal of Personality Assessment*, **40**, 310–9

Duffy, P.J., Shiflett, S. and Downey, R.G. (1977). Locus of control: dimensionality and predictability using Likert scales, *Journal of Applied Psychology*, **62**, 214–9

Feather, N.T. (1982). Actions in relation to expected consequences: an overview of research, in N.T. Feather (ed.), *Expectations and Actions: Expectancy-Value Models in Psychology*, Hillsdale, N.J.: Erlbaum

Feather, N.T. (1983). Causal attributions for good and bad outcomes in achievement and affiliation situations, *Australian Journal of Psychology*, **35**, 37–48

Feather, N.T. and Simon, J.G. (1975). Reactions to male and female success and failure in sex-linked occupations, Impressions of personality, causal attributions, and perceived likelihood of different consequences, *Journal of Personality and Social Psychology*, **31**, 20–31

Garza, R.T. and Widlak, F.W. (1977). The validity of locus of control dimensions for Chicano populations, *Journal of Personality Assessment*, **41**, 635–43

Gurin, P., Gurin, G., Lao, R.C. and Beattie, M. (1969). Internal-external control in the motivational dynamics of Negro youth, *Journal of Social Issues*, 25, 25–53

Hackman, J.R. and Oldham, G.R. (1975). Development of the Job Diagnostic Survey, *Journal of Applied Psychology*, **60**, 159–70

Hackman, J.R. and Oldham, G.R. (1980). *Work Redesign*, Reading, Mass.: Addison-Wesley

Hechler, P.D. and Weiner, Y. (1974). Chronic self-esteem as a moderator of performance consequences of expected pay, *Organizational Behavior and Human Performance*, **11**, 97–105

Heisler, W.J. (1974). A performance correlate of personal control beliefs in an organizational context, *Journal of Applied Psychology*, **59**, 504–6

Inkson, J.H.K. (1978). Self-esteem as a moderator of the relationship between job performance and job satisfaction, *Journal of Applied Psychology*, **63**, 243–7

Kohn, M.L. and Schooler, C. (1978). The reciprocal effects of the substantive complexity of work and intellectual flexibility: a longitudinal assessment, *American Journal of Sociology*, **84**, 24–52

Kohn, M.L. and Schooler, C. (1981). Job conditions and intellectual flexibility: a longitudinal assessment of their reciprocal effects, in D.J. Jackson and E.F. Borgatta, *Factor Analysis and Measurement in Sociological Research*, Beverley Hills, Cal.: Sage

Kohn, M.L. and Schooler, C. (1982). Job conditions and personality: a longitudinal assessment of their reciprocal effects, *American Journal of Sociology*, **87**, 1257–85

Korman, A.K. (1966). Self-esteem in vocational choice, *Journal of Applied Psychology*, **50**, 479–86

Korman, A.K. (1967). Relevance of personal need satisfaction for overall satisfaction as a function of self-esteem, *Journal of Applied Psychology*, **51**, 533–8

Korman, A.K. (1968a). Task success, task popularity, and self-esteem as influences on task liking, *Journal of Applied Psychology*, **52**, 484–90

Korman, A.K. (1968b). Self-esteem, social influence and task performance: some tests of a theory, *Proceedings of the 76th annual convention of the American Psychological Association,* 3, 567–68

Korman, A.K. (1970). Toward an hypothesis of work behavior, *Journal of Applied Psychology,* 54, 31–41

Korman, A.K. (1971a). Expectancies as determinants of performance, *Journal of Applied Psychology,* 55, 218–22

Korman, A.K. (1971b). Organizational achievement, aggression and creativity: some suggestions toward an integrated theory, *Organizational Behavior and Human Performance,* 6, 593–613

Korman, A.K. (1974). *The Psychology of Motivation,* New Jersey: Prentice- Hall

Korman, A.K. (1976). Hypotheses of work behavior revisited and an extension, *Academy of Management Review,* 1, 56–63

Lange, R. and Tiggemann, M. (1980). Changes within the Australian population to more external control beliefs, *Australian Psychologist,* 15, 495–7

Lefcourt, H.M. (1981). The construction and development of the multidimensional-multiattributional causality scales, in H.M. Lefcourt (ed.), *Research with the Locus of Control Construct,* vol. 1, New York: Academic Press

Levenson, H. (1974). Activism and powerful others: distinctions within the concept of internal-external control, *Journal of Personality Assessment,* 38, 367–83

Levenson, H. (1981). Differentiating among internality, powerful others and chance, in H.M. Lefcourt (ed.), *Research with the Locus of Control Construct,* vol. 1, New York: Academic Press

Lied, T.R. and Pritchard, R.D. (1976). Relationships between personality variables and components of the expectancy-valence model, *Journal of Applied Psychology,* 61, 463–7

Locke, E.A., Frederick, E., Bobko, P. and Lee, C. (1984). Effect of self-efficacy, goals and task strategies on task performance, *Journal of Applied Psychology,* 69, 241–51

Locke, E.A., Shaw, K.N., Saari, L.M. and Latham, G.P. (1981). Goal-setting and task performance: 1969–1980, *Psychological Bulletin,* 90, 125–52

Mabe, P.A. and West, S.G. (1982). Validity of self-evaluation of ability: a review and meta-analysis, *Journal of Applied Psychology,* 67, 280–96

Mirels, H.L. (1970). Dimensions of internal versus external control, *Journal of Consulting and Clinical Psychology,* 34, 226–8

Mitchell, T.R. (1974). Expectancy models of job satisfaction, occupational preference and effort: a theoretical, methodological, and empirical appraisal, *Psychological Bulletin,* 81, 1053–77

O'Brien, G.E. (1982). The relative contribution of perceived skill-utilization and other perceived job attributes to the prediction of job satisfaction: a cross validation study, *Human Relations,* 35, 219–37

O'Brien, G.E. (1984). Locus of control, work and retirement, Chapter 2 in H. Lefcourt (ed.), *Research with the Locus of Control Construct,* vol. 3, New York: Academic Press

O'Brien, G.E., Biglan, A. and Penna, J. (1972). Measurement of the distribution of potential influence and participation in groups and organizations, *Journal of Applied Psychology,* 56, 11–18

O'Brien, G.E. and Dowling, P. (1980). The effects of congruency between perceived and desired job attributes upon job satisfaction, *Journal of Occupational Psychology,* 53, 121–30

O'Brien, G.E. and Kabanoff, B. (1981). Australian norms and factor analyses of Rotter's internal-external control scale, *Australian Psychologist*, **16**, 184–202

O'Brien, G.E. and Pere, T. (1985). The effects of ability, self-esteem and task difficulty on performance and task satisfaction, *Australian Journal of Psychology*, **37**, 309–323.

O'Reilly, A.P. (1973). Perception of abilities as a determinant of performance, *Journal of Applied Psychology*, **58**, 281–2

Paulhus, D. and Christie, R. (1981). Spheres of control: an interactionist approach to assessment of perceived control, in H.M. Lefcourt (ed.), *Research with the Locus of Control Construct*, vol. 1, New York: Academic Press

Reid, D.W. and Ware, E.E. (1973). Multidimensionality of internal-external control: implications for past and future research, *Canadian Journal of Behavioural Science*, **5**, 264–71

Reid, D.W. and Ware, E.E. (1974). Multidimensionality of internal-external control: addition of a third dimension and non-distinction of self versus others, *Canadian Journal of Behavioural Science*, **6**, 131–42

Rotter, J.B. (1966). Generalized expectancies for internal versus external control of reinforcement, *Psychological Monographs*, **80**, 1–28

Rotter, J.B. (1975). Some properties and misconceptions related to the construct of internal versus external control of reinforcement, *Journal of Consulting and Clinical Psychology*, **43**, 56–67

Ruble, T.L. (1976). Effects of one's locus of control and the opportunity to participate in planning, *Organizational Behavior and Human Performance*, **16**, 63–73

Shiflett, S. (1979). Toward a general model of small group productivity, *Psychological Bulletin*, **86**, 67–79

Spector, P.E. (1982). Behavior in organizations as a function of employees' locus of control, *Psychological Bulletin*, **91**, 482–97

Terborg, J.R., Richardson, P. and Pritchard, R.D. (1980). Person-situation effects in the prediction of ability, self-esteem and reward contingencies, *Journal of Applied Psychology*, **65**, 574–83

Tharenou, P. (1979). Employee self-esteem: a review of the literature, *Journal of Vocational Behavior*, **15**, 316–46

Vroom, V.H. (1964). *Work and Motivation*, New York: Wiley

Watson, J.M. (1981). A note on the dimensionality of the Rotter locus of control scale, *Australian Journal of Psychology*, **33**, 319–30

White, R.W. (1959). Motivation reconsidered: the concept of competence, *Psychological Review*, **66**, 297–333

Wong, P.T.P. and Sproule, C.F. (1984). An attributional analysis of the locus of control construct and the Trent Attribution Profile, Chapter 5 in H.M. Lefcourt (ed.), *Research with the Locus of Control Construct, vol. 3*, New York: Academic Press

CHAPTER 8

The Psychological Effects of Unemployment: Studies of the Great Depression

The evidence considered in previous chapters showed that variations in the nature of work could affect personality and social adjustment. Jobs that restricted opportunities for skill-utilization and a secure income impeded the development of intellectual flexibility and personal control. Even stronger evidence about the effects of work upon people can be obtained from studies of unemployment for it is a state where the individual is dramatically deprived of job income and the opportunity to use valued skills. In examining the unemployment literature there are three main questions which will be considered:

1. How does job loss affect the personality, adjustment and behaviour of the unemployed?
2. To what extent are these effects mediated by prior job experience, personality and social background?
3. To what extent are any psychological effects explainable in terms of economic loss?

The literature of the 1930s will be considered separately from post-war unemployment studies. There are a number of reasons for this. Firstly, it appears that economic factors were involved to a greater degree in the 1930s. Increased affluence since the Depression and the widescale introduction of government unemployment benefits has made the financial difficulties of unemployment less severe in modern times. This is not to say that unemployment effects in the present cannot be explained in terms of poverty. The role of income for the psychological well-being of the modern unemployed will be assessed in the next chapter. It does seem clear, however, that loss of job income was far more severe for the unemployed in the 1930s as few

184

received any regular government pension. Financially they were largely on their own.

A second reason for treating studies from the 1930s separately is due to differences in methodology. The early studies were largely based on interviews and observations whereas latter studies concentrate on the use of standardized questionnaires and complex statistical analysis. In many ways the early studies have poor methodology and this makes it difficult to compare their findings with those of today. Yet they cannot be neglected or dismissed because they had strengths that are lacking in many current studies. They allowed the unemployed to describe their experiences in their own terms without the imposition of the researcher's own theoretical categories. They also generated a number of theories about the effects of job loss which are still useful.

A third and final reason for examining the Depression studies separately is that they differed in occupational background. Present-day unemployment affects people in low, medium and high status occupations, while the unemployed in the Depression were predominantly from semi-skilled and unskilled jobs. They were largely adult males while today there are a considerable number of youth and women who are unemployed. It is important to document the occupational background of the unemployed during the Depression because it appears that the majority lost jobs which had provided them, as a group, with little chance of using skills, and exercising personal autonomy at work.[1] Their jobs were those which, on the basis of previous evidence presented in this book, should have shaped their ability to exercise personal initiative and cope with stress. Hence it was possible that some of the negative consequences of job loss were due to the effects of past job experience.

Corresponding to the questions posed at the beginning, the psychological effects of the Depression will be examined using three main headings. The general effects of unemployment will be assessed through examination of the mood, activities and personal adjustment of the unemployed. Then the way in which these responses were determined by past job experiences will be considered. Finally, the problem of the relative importance of lack of money and lack of job activities will be addressed. The analysis of the Depression literature will show that the simple explanations of the 1930s unemployment literature are not possible. These explanations have assumed that unemployment for the majority led to a decline in psychological adjustment. Furthermore, they have assumed that psychological deprivation was largely due to loss of job activities even though financial strain did play a significant contributory role. This simple deprivation model has persisted due to the influential reviews by Eisenberg and Lazarsfeld (1938) and Johoda (1981, 1982). The present review shows that this picture does not accurately reflect the findings from the 1930s. The experience of unemployment was a traumatic one but there is little evidence that loss of job activities was mainly responsible for distress. The major determinants of distress were economic and the actual degree of distress was shaped by the coping abilities and personality of the unemployed.

GENERAL RESPONSES TO UNEMPLOYMENT

A. Mood and Affective Responses

The most influential studies of the period documented the emotional experiences of the unemployed and mapped changes in these responses as a function of the time employed. There is agreement amongst authors that the emotional response was negative, it became worse with time, and was deeper for those who perceived themselves as having lost more—those with jobs that had relatively secure, interesting and well-paid work. Partly due to its superior methodology and partly due to its greater exposure by general reviews of employment (Eisenberg and Lazarsfeld, 1938; Jahoda, 1979, 1981, 1982), the Marienthal study has been considered the major source of information about the emotional effects of prolonged unemployment (Jahoda, Lazarsfeld and Zeisel, 1933). Using life histories, direct observations and time sheets, the researchers studied the inhabitants of Marienthal, an Austrian village of 1500, during a period of prolonged unemployment. In 1930, the textile factory that provided most employment was closed. At the time of the study, 358 families received some form of unemployment relief, while 93 families had work either in or outside the village. The study did not focus on the unemployed workers so much as on their families.

The mood of the families was classified into four types. These types were designated unbroken, resigned, despairing and apathetic. The unbroken retained a general vitality and hopefulness. Their vitality was shown in the fathers' continued efforts at job-hunting and the maintenance of family activities. Hopefulness was shown in their concentration on future plans. The resigned, by contrast, had no future orientation and had given up making plans. They had restricted their purchases to basic necessities and maintained a relative sense of well-being in caring for their children and maintaining the household. The broken differed from the resigned in their depth of emotional despair. They reported and were observed to express feelings of despair, depression and hopelessness. No attempts were made to find work but they did their best to keep the household in order and look after children. The worst affected were labelled apathetic. These families had no future plans, they neglected themselves and their children, their homes were untidy and unclean, family quarrels were frequent, and many parents seemed to seek escape in alcohol. The number of families in a state of despair and apathy was relatively small. Only 2 per cent of the families were classified as despairing and 5 per cent were apathetic.

In a review of studies up to the mid 1930s, Eisenberg and Lazarsfeld (1938) state that practically all studies conclude that 'unemployment tends to make people more emotionally unstable than they were previous to unemployment' (p. 359). This is quite inappropriate as no studies measured the emotional stability of employees before and after they lost their jobs. Many of the studies reported that the unemployed had negative moods but this hardly means that they were unstable. The unemployed were said to lose a sense of prestige or status (Kardiner, 1936) and also lose self-confidence and morale (Carnegie Trust, 1943; Elderston. 1931; Pilgrim Trust, 1939), while another said that the unemployed were not characterized by feelings of inferiority (Rundquist and Sletto, 1936). In Lancashire and Scotland, Israeli (1935) found the unemployed more depressed than employed groups. Though anxious, the unemployed were not as depressed about the future as mental patients. The lowering of morale was noted in other studies as well (Hall, 1934; Rundquist and Sletto, 1936). It is difficult to make any firm conclusions from these studies. Those studied showed negative moods and attributed it to job loss. However, these negative moods were not the same as long-term personality traits such as depression because the measures were not adequate to measure personality. Furthermore, the direction of causality cannot be established. The studies were cross-sectional and were not capable of showing that mood changes actually did occur after job loss. The main evidence for this is the attribution by the subjects of mood change to their job loss. But it is quite possible that a considerable number of subjects showed negative affect even before job loss.

The importance of job loss as a direct cause of mood is not found in all studies. One of the most detailed studies found that negative feelings were not associated with the loss of job *per se* but rather the state of poverty (Zawadski and Lazarsfeld, 1935). Zawadski and Lazarsfeld analysed 774 biographies submitted by the Polish unemployed in order to obtain a monetary prize. They published only 57 after omitting those that were poorly expressed, colourless, insincere, designed to arouse pity and those from people unemployed more than 10 years. The majority of cases reported prolonged hunger and about a third reported severe cold. At the time of the study, government assistance was paid for only 13 weeks and then they had to rely on their own resources and charity.

The predominant mood expressed was reported to be anger and hopelessness. They were not generally ashamed of their own inability to find work but rather of their misery.

> In only four cases are they ashamed of their own inability and ascribe the cause of the trouble to themselves. Most of them are ashamed, rather, of their misery.
>
> (Zawadski and Lazarsfeld, 1935, p. 238)

Twenty-seven of the fifty-seven reported that they had planned or were planning suicide. This study then shows that the unemployed did not necessarily see their distress as due to the loss of job activities. Certainly job loss meant they were plunged into economic misery which was experienced as distressing. However, this does not justify the conclusion that the loss of job activities caused distress.

Although many authors have quoted Bakke as one of the major sources of the theory of mental changes in unemployment, there is only a small section on mental effects and this is not formalized or based closely on an analysis of his interviews (Bakke, 1933, pp. 62–72). In the section titled 'mental effects', he does assert that the majority of men feel lost. Loss of self-confidence is also felt most strongly by married men whose role as family provider has been undermined. He also reports that mental and physical exhaustion is common. However, this is not attributed directly to job loss but rather to a combination of poor diet and effort expended in unsuccessful job searches. There is no evidence for a theory of stages in Bakke except for one case-study of a driver who was initially hopeful of finding a job. After a few weeks he became depressed and began to blame himself. After 17 weeks he had become 'sullen and despondent'.

The findings, in general, do not support Eisenberg and Lazarsfeld's conclusion that the major affective response to unemployment was emotional instability. Certainly, the dominant response was one of dissatisfaction and frustration. The loss of a job had blocked paths to a secure income and produced strain on personal and financial resources. A minority, under the weight of large economic deprivation, sank to low levels of despair and apathy. However, a majority showed stability and resilience in their effort to hold themselves and their families in a state of reasonable physical and mental health. There is little evidence in the Depression literature of a pre-determined and somewhat inevitable decline into extreme despair and hopelessness. Where this decline occurred, it was often reported to be the result of progressive economic deterioration and concomitant poor physical health. After economic factors, the major factor in producing distress was the feeling of not being useful with its attendant loss of personal status and identity. Few regretted the loss of satisfying work tasks because they had not experienced them. What they regretted in the absence of work was largely the extrinsic factors: income, security, social interaction, external direction and being significant, albeit small parts, of organizations that produced useful social products.

B. The Activities of the Unemployed

There are two different conclusions reached about the activities of the unemployed. One conclusion is that the unemployed were idle and made little use of their time to 'better' themselves through educational, political, religious or craft/hobby activities. The other view is that the unemployed were not idle. Although they had difficulty in structuring their time they worked hard at seeking jobs, managing their meagre income, caring for their children, maintaining social relationships that did not require money, and expanding those normal 'leisure' pursuits that did not require financial expense.

The first view is stated by the Marienthal researchers who found that the majority of the unemployed wasted their time. 'Idleness ruled the day' (Jahoda, Lazarsfeld and Zeisel 1933, p. 73). This conclusion applied to men only as work filled the day of the woman whose spouse was unemployed. By contrast, Bakke in his studies of English and North American unemployed maintains that the unemployed were not idle although he admits their activities were curtailed by economic necessities, a feeling of powerlessness and their past educational and job experiences.

Who is right? One way of answering this is to examine the reports of activity. The Marienthal study examined activity by getting a sample of men to fill in time diaries. Based on time sheets for 80 or 100 men (both figures are mentioned in the text), a frequency table of activities was drawn up. This is shown in Table 8.1.

The table is unsatisfactory in many ways. Idleness is not necessarily inferred from sitting at home (they could be reading/talking about their situation), nor from walking (necessary for exercise), nor from standing around

TABLE 8.1 Activities of the unemployed in Marienthal

	Morning	Afternoon
Idleness (sitting at home, going for a walk, standing around on street, etc.)	35	41
Workmen's Club (Winter—cards/chess, Fine weather—sitting and chatting)	14	16
Inactivity and minor household work (fetching water, shopping)	31	21
Major household work (wood-chopping, child-tending, working in vegetable allotment, mending shoes)	12	15
Looking after children	6	5
Miscellaneous activities (radio, handicrafts)	2	2

From Jahoda, Lazarsfeld and Zeisel (1933)

(they could be maintaining social relationships and receiving emotional support from those in the same situation). From the description of 'minor' household work, they could hardly describe these activities as 'inactive'. Also it is puzzling to find inactivity and minor household work being collapsed into one category. This table hardly provides strong evidence of idleness. Compared to activities engaged in when at work, there is a restriction in the range and variety of pursuits. There was less urgency in their activities as well, which was probably due to the lack of deadlines and the restricted opportunities for leisure in a small factory town.

Nevertheless, they revealed less general activity than Bakke's samples and this seems easily explainable in terms of one thing. Mass unemployment in a single factory town meant that there was no point to job search. To find another job they would have had to leave Marienthal. Bakke's unemployed, on the other hand, engaged in job searches because they lived in relatively large cities. There were many employers and hope was fostered by the observation that the majority of workers were still in employment.

Bakke conducted a more extensive study of unemployment activity in New Haven between 1932 and 1939. As in the Greenwich study he lived amongst the unemployed, using a variety of observational methods including participant observation, a longitudinal analysis of 25 families over the whole period, interviews with 200 'married and together' families in 1933 and a 10 per cent sample of unemployed households in 1938. He checked many of the facts gathered in these interviews with social workers, ministers, public health officials and employers. The results appeared in two books— *Citizens Without Work* and *The Unemployed Worker*—both published in 1940.

In the introduction to *Citizens Without Work* he outlines the main purposes of the study. A central purpose was to assess the self-reliance of the unemployed through an analysis of their activities. In his own words, he was concerned to make 'a reasonable judgement as to the effect of unemployment and unemployment relief on the self-reliance of workers'. His detailed analysis of the activities of the unemployed led him to conclude that there was little use of time for self-development and cultural activities. He explained this in terms of economic deprivation and past experiences. Lack of money forced most to curtail activities where money was necessary (movies, excursions, club attendance, social visits). Activities such as walking, sitting around the home, listening to the radio, chatting and gardening increased when they involved no expenditure. There was no increase in cultural activities such as reading, attending lectures or handicraft. Generally the activities of unemployment were not perceived as leisure because no social role was substituted for the job. It was certainly 'free' time but it had not been voluntarily chosen and the activities were not perceived as leisure because the meaning of 'leisure' depended on the contrast to work activities. However, the main reason for the little use of community facilities for improving skills and knowledge was lack of money and past experience. Work experiences had not provided the working men with any opportunity for self-directed learning and their educational and job training had not equipped them for participative activity. There was a decline in recreational activity but the unemployed were not idle. They continued to seek self-reliance by job-searching and active planning and execution of household chores. They tried to continue with their usual activities but these had to be necessarily curtailed due to financial hardship.

> The plain fact is that the decline in recreation results from a decline in income and only an increased income will make it possible for the unemployed to use their ordinary experience and habits in restoring that leisure-time life to which they have been accustomed.
>
> (Bakke, 1940a, p. 17)

The theme of prior work experiences determining free time is also taken up in the Pilgrim Trust survey. They found general purposelessness in the activities of the unemployed. They noted general apathy towards clubs, educational and social organizations. However, they partly explain it not in terms of idleness or sloth, but rather as a combination of factors including: (i) 'decline of cultural standards'—there was no social norm encouraging personal expansion; (ii) feeling of hopelessness which was not conducive to effort outside that of essential family duties and job-seeking; (iii) character of past jobs—if the unemployed left school early and experienced poor jobs, they were not equipped for self-direction; (iv) poor diet, job-seeking and anxiety made them 'too tired'.

> Work provides for most people the pattern within which their lives are lived and when this pattern is lost they have thrown on them a responsibility which, in the case of most unemployed men, their working lives in no way qualified them to bear—the responsibility for organizing their own existence. They fall in ultimately with some new makeshift pattern.
>
> (Pilgrim Trust, 1938, p. 149)

This is not inconsistent with the findings of the Carnegie Trust study of unemployed youth, of whom 78 per cent obtained non-progressive, unskilled 'blind-alley' employment after leaving school at the age of 14. When they became unemployed they continued reading the same amount and type of material (newspapers, crime, horror magazines), except that it was more often borrowed than bought. They listened to radio in an indiscriminatory way. The cinema and dances were popular as were, to a lesser extent, walking, cycling and football. However, the proportion in the following activities was low; art (less than 3 per cent), handicrafts (5–8 per cent), adult education (2 per cent). The general conclusion from these studies is that the unemployed were not idle. They tried to fill their days with their usual recreational and home activities. These often had to be curtailed due to lack of money and poor health. They had difficulty in forming regular routines because job activities did not exist and their past experience had not equipped them to engage in self-improvement and cultural activities.

B. Political and Religious Activities

Most studies of the 1930s devoted some attention to political activity, possibly because policy-makers wanted to know the extent to which unemployment would induce political protest. Political activity was one possible option for giving direction and hope to people who, in losing a job, lost direction and hope. The other main option was religion, which in principle had the potential for giving meaning to a life which had lost it. Many of the studies reported that political activity was low and roughly commensurate with the degree to which it was engaged in prior to unemployment (Beales and Lambert, 1934; Carnegie, 1943; Jahoda *et al.*, 1933; Bakke, 1940a, b; Pilgrim, 1938; Zawadski and Lazarsfeld, 1935). Thus Jahoda *et al.* (1933), mentioned that political activity was confined largely to a small number of 'political functionaries'. The young unemployed, studied by the Carnegie workers, reported that they had no political commitments or consciousness. Only 6 per cent belonged to trade unions and participation in these union activities was very low. They concluded:

> It is clear that if the unemployed are to be saved from their lot, the struggle will have to be begun by men and women outside their ranks.
>
> (Carnegie Trust, 1943, p. 79)

Explanations for this political inactivity are not considered by most writers. A notable exception was Zawadski and Lazarsfeld. They suggested that protest required the formation of a common cause based on shared communication and action. For the unemployed, however, there was no group coherence.

> the masses cease to exist as such when the social bond—the consciousness of belonging together—does not bind any longer. There remain only scattered, loose, perplexed and hopeless individuals.
>
> (Zawadski and Lazarsfeld, 1935, p. 245)

Further analysis of the reasons for a failure to engage in radical political action is provided by Bakke. One reason is that the repetitive, directed work that the unemployed once had did not encourage in them a belief in the efficacy of self-directed effort. He also provides extra reasons why the culture of the United States did not engender popular working-class protest. For the workers in New Haven neither of the two major parties served the working class alone, unionization was weak and there was a strong social norm that led them to identify any radical idea with unacceptable foreign ways.

The socialistic or radical leaders also failed to understand the experience of the unemployed. They overestimated their capacity for personal control.

More importantly, they did not provide alternative social policies that could be perceived as practicable. They preached the destruction of social and political forms without an alternative. The workers could see the bad effects of their capitalistic system but they were not prepared to jeopardize the good effects by negative protest.

Bakke expands his discussion of the political response of the unemployed by considering why no coherent movement or class consciousness arose from within the ranks of the unemployed. Again he explains that the reasons are apparent when their past work experiences are examined. Work experiences had not fostered any meaningful social associations with workers as a group. Division of functions within factories meant that face-to-face associations were very limited. 'Job consciousness rather than class consciousness is likely to result' (Bakke, 1940a, p. 94). Furthermore, any contact was further limited due to the multicultural background of the workforce. Perhaps the main barrier to protest either in or out of employment was the acceptance by the majority of workers of industrial organization as a cooperative enterprise where they had been assigned tasks with limited direction, skill and personal control.

> The unquestioning assumption that employers and bankers have interests which are eternally opposed to those of workers is not sufficiently widespread to be an active factor in integrating workers' interests and relations in opposition to what might be termed exploitation.
>
> (Bakke, 1940a; p. 97)

Despite this, Bakke says he was still hopeful that working-class consciousness would develop. Nevertheless the evidence that Bakke reports suggests that this hope was a function of Bakke's personal opinions that had been generated in the course of his work.

C. Personality

No definite conclusion can be made about the general effect of unemployment upon the personality of the unemployed from studies of the 1930s. The negative moods of depression, hopelessness and apathy reported by many researchers may have been temporary states that disappeared when economic conditions improved. Although some reviewers such as Eisenberg and Lazarsfeld (1938) concluded that the unemployed were characterized by emotional instability, closer examination of the evidence indicated that this applied to only a minority who experienced extreme economic deprivation. Furthermore, such instability could have been present prior to unemployment. Some researchers made this point clearly. In an appendix to Beales and Lambert (1934), there is an essay by Robb on the medical and psychiatric interpretation of the behaviour of the unemployed. Here Robb indicates that the stress and discouragement generally experienced by the unemployed contributed to psychic and physical illness. However, he concludes that the long-term response is largely, if not entirely, due to the personality of the unemployed prior to job loss. At the beginning of his chapter he makes clear that his conclusions are based on a subset of the unemployed—those who were medically sick. These individuals were discouraged and by this he means that they had lost the will to live. They had lost control of their lives, were driven into themselves and suffered from the constant discrepancy between life as it was and life as they wanted it to be.

> When a man is unemployed, there is no external outlet for his energies. He becomes aware that he is not a free agent. He is impelled to receive a meagre allowance from others—relatives, friends, usually the State. He is driven into himself, experiences an acute sense of isolation, and begins to build his life on the phantasies which spring up in the mind of the bitterly disappointed. He feels hatred against those who have insulted him, humiliated him and compelled him to beg for work. Phantasies of revenge struggle with a sense of importance, phantasies of power with the loss of real ability. Desire and reality are constantly at odds.
>
> (Robb, in Beales and Lambert, 1934, pp. 274-5)

Such was their state, that even the immediate restoration of work would not restore their balance. They needed work 'specially devised with a therapeutic aim'. However, in conclusion he is led to consider why deep withdrawal, aggression, importance and delusions of grandeur were not typical responses. His view is that unemployment was a stress experience that accentuated existing weaknesses in the character of the unemployed. The variety of responses is 'almost entirely dependent on the background exerted to abnormal activity by unemployment'. Unemployment is an acid that works most quickly on those who are already soft and brittle. 'Acid does not bite gold' (Robb, in Beales and Lambert, 1934, p. 286).

This account is remarkable in that it anticipates many of the recent theories and research studies on unemployment where economic deprivation is linked to illness via perceived stress. In some ways it goes further in accentuating the importance of personal resources as a codeterminant of illness. It is one of the few essays of this period which tried to describe how economic deprivation affected the personality dynamics of the unemployed. Most were content to describe the emotional states and activities of the unemployed without trying to establish the degree to which these states were likely to be affected by past experience and prior personality. Thus they were unlikely to consider whether these states were likely to endure when economic prosperity returned. Again, a major exception is the work of Bakke (1933, 1940a,b) who was particularly concerned about the effect of unemployment on the 'self-reliance' of those affected. Bakke observed the discouragement of the unemployed and saw that the strength of this discouragement was a joint function of past work experiences and the amount of economic loss suffered. However, he took issue with those who believed that the unemployed had experienced personality change.

The final chapter of *Citizens Without Work* (1940a) contains Bakke's views on self-reliance and is titled 'Alleged decay of self-reliance'. He maintains that it is inaccurate to depict the unemployed as fatalistic, dependent, inactive and lacking self-reliance. Within the severe external restrictions imposed upon them the unemployed tried to control their own affairs. They showed high levels of self-reliance in job-hunting, stretching their income, obtaining relief, developing a new domestic economy and appraising job opportunities. There were individual differences in the amount of personal control and effort expended but these were explainable in terms of the degree to which the previous work had strengthened their self-reliance. All workers had suffered lack of control over their work activities but had been able to maintains some sense of personal control in the maintenance of their non-work activities. This fostered the self-reliance that Bakke observed in their unemployment activities. However a few, mainly the skilled workers, once had the opportunity to develop extra self-reliance through the intrinsic and extrinsic rewards of their work.

Yet Bakke recognized that the stimulus to self-reliance had been curtailed by unemployment. It was a further restriction of the working-class man's ability to manage his own affairs and develop a sense of competence derived from using his skills and initiative. Fundamentally he is changed because of the tasks that he is enforced to do. Inevitably, tasks that limit personal control will lead to a general decrease in any individual's perception of control.

> The basic cause of this curtailment, however, lies in the nature of the task he must perform and the factors that he must manipulate in the performance. Men become what they practice.
>
> (Bakke, 1940a, p. 282)

D. Conclusion

This brief review of the general response to unemployment indicates that it is a mistake to accept the conventional interpretation of the psychological effects of unemployment in the 1930s. Some of the unemployed did progressively lapse into a permanent state of despair and apathy. However, most accepted their disappointment with resilience. They tried to do what they could to obtain jobs and maintain their families within the constraints imposed by little money and poor health. They were not idle, if this means regular inactivity and laziness. They experienced stress, boredom, anger and despair. But most were not broken by these experiences. Those who suffered most tended to be those with prior vulnerability and those who had lost most in economic terms. These generalizations reflect, in my judgement, the conclusions reached by the majority of writers. Their conclusions, admittedly, are only as good as their methods. In many cases their methods were open to bias because they were not able to assess the degree to which all of the determinants of behaviour in unemployment were present in their samples. Nevertheless, these studies are all that we have to go on. Although there may be doubts about the basis for their conclusions, it should be possible to give a balanced account of what these conclusions actually were.

It is a distortion to say that they found that the loss of job activities led to distress and psychological damage if what is meant is that the job activities were essential for the maintenance of psychological health. Few of the unemployed regretted the loss of unsatisfying work. They did regret the loss of income, a regular time structure and social status. The importance of economic factors for the understanding of unemployment effects will be considered further in a later section. It appears to have been underrated by psychological interpreters. The role of past work experience has also been underrated. The extensive work of Bakke illustrated how work could shape the personal orientations of the unemployed. It suggested that much of the apparent inactivity and negative mood of the unemployed was not a function of job loss alone. It was also a function of past work experiences which left people feeling that they lacked control of their lives. Unemployment just placed extra restrictions on people who were already unhappy and unable to develop their own personal resources.

THE MEDIATING EFFECTS OF PAST JOB EXPERIENCES ON RESPONSES TO UNEMPLOYMENT

Generally the response to a swift change in life circumstances has to be understood in terms of the joint effect of the nature of the change, prior life experiences and the personal characteristics of the persons affected. These characteristics include age, sex, social class, job experience and education. Few studies made more than passing remarks about these mediating factors. The Carnegie study concluded that unemployment experiences were less difficult for the unskilled because they had previously learnt to expect less of life than the skilled. They also speculated that youth would be more affected than adults. 'Lacking the stability of age and experience, they are emotionally more liable to become drifters; (Carnegie Trust, 1943, p. 69).

The Pilgrim study also identified how the wage cycle and marital status of the employed man could affect his adjustment to the economic problem of unemployment. They reported that the manual worker reached his maximum wage in his twenties and then, as he took on family responsibilities, he became progressively poorer until his children had reached economic independence. When they became unemployed the relative loss of income experienced by these groups differs. The married man with children received benefits that approximated his wage much more closely than it did for single men or married men without dependent children.

The only researcher to consider the mediating role of past job content was Bakke (1933, 1934, 1940a,b). He noted that the large majority of the unemployed had been skilled and unskilled employees from manufacturing industries. He suspected that their responses to unemployment would be shaped by their work experiences and devoted a substantial portion of his analysis to a discussion of their work background.

Most references to Bakke's writings on the unemployed in England and the United States refer to his description of personal and family disintegration. He is cited as providing evidence that job deprivation led to a general decline in personal adjustment following the stages of shock, optimism, depression and fatalism. Associated with this personal decline there was a family decline for unemployed married workers from stability to instability, disorganization and readjustment to economic and social deprivation. Although there is a little information on these phases in his four books, it is an inaccurate picture of his own data and interpretations. It certainly was not his purpose to identify general responses to unemployment nor even just to identify the variety of responses. His main purpose was to show that unemployment could not be understood without studying worker's prior experience of employment (O'Brien, 1985). The first parts of two of his most influential books, *The Unemployed Man* (1933) and *The Unemployed Worker* (1940), are devoted to an examination of the prior working environments of unemployed men and how this shaped their perceptions of employment and unemployment.

In the Greenwich study, the first chapter is concerned with a description of employment. The main features of the work done by the skilled and unskilled employees are firstly insecurity, and secondly, external control. Insecurity of employment, he found, was attributed to the continuous replacement of men by machinery, the practice of dismissing young workers when their wages and unemployment insurance became too high, the intrusion of women into factory work, migrating labour, and the prevalence of older men holding on to jobs even when they were eligible for superannuation.

External control of their working lives was perceived, and to some extent, accepted. Control was exerted from without by an impersonal 'they'—the managers, owners and bosses.

> Those who tell him what he may do, how much he may have for his work, and whether he may work at all; those who make the rules which govern his daily routine, the paying of his rent, the buying of his food, and the education of his children.
>
> (Bakke, 1933, p. 9)

This external control was also perceived as being partly responsible for his insecurity in employment and unemployment and most importantly it was essential to an understanding of the unemployed. Bakke detected in his interviews a generalization of external control beliefs in that the worker tended to feel constrained in all life spheres—work and non-work. 'Habit breeds attitudes. When so much of your life is ordered by others, why pretend to be able to do anything yourself with the rest?' (Bakke, 1933, p. 10). Hence the unemployed, because of their past work experiences, are already prepared to admit that they have little responsibility for their own fate. 'It causes the worker to feel a minimum of responsibility for his own fate; for responsibility goes with control' (Bakke, 1933, p. 10).

In such circumstances, it might be expected that these unemployed men would develop a resentment of those in authority and seek support from coworkers in trying to change the situation. This was not the case, as most of his respondents thought that the controllers had special qualifications for their tasks and distrusted any attempts by employee groups to assert themselves because they felt that the working class were not qualified for this role. Thus they not only believed they were externally controlled, but accepted the controllers because they thought they were better qualified. They tended to blame themselves to some extent for unemployment but also, and probably more often, to blame luck and 'any man or group of men belonging to the other world'.

Although, in principle, the unskilled worker had a choice in his type of employment, in practice this was minimal. Financial necessity typically dictated when he left school and what job he applied for. Certainly once the job was accepted he experienced no choice in the type of tasks, his methods and the general organization of the factory.

Having considered the work of men in Greenwich, Bakke was then led to consider the conditions that would have to be met for working-class men to develop moderate levels of personal control. He was careful to point out that the large majority of working men, including those now unemployed, displayed considerable degrees of personal foresight. Within the restraints of the imposed social structure in which they worked and lived, they did exercise control in areas where they were able. Many tried to increase their financial security through 'slate' clubs—informal savings associations commonly run by unions, churches, social clubs and those who frequented public houses. Considerable numbers also tried to plan their children's future and provide for their families through private insurance. Opportunities for improving their jobs through extra training were generally not available but there was some opportunity for improving their working conditions through union membership. The only other way of improving their job opportunities was through cultivating influential members in clubs and lodges.

Bakke states four principles necessary for workers to have a reasonably high degree of personal control.

1. *Rewards must be tangible:* 'the rewards of labour shall be tangible, within possible reach or hope, and fairly sure of coming if the conditions are met' (Bakke, 1933, p. 44).
2. *Rewards must be commensurate with effort:* 'the possible rewards must be worth the price' (Bakke, 1933, p. 45).
3. *Effort must not be degrading:* 'the necessary sacrifice required by foresight must not be degrading' (Bakke, 1933, p. 46).
4. *Opportunities for trial and error.* Workers would not show initiative if they knew the chances of success were low and if their situations did not permit them to learn what is possible by trial and error.

These conditions were rarely met but he does conclude that the skilled workers had a greater chance of developing personal foresight and a sense of personal control. This conclusion was based on his previous analysis (Bakke, 1933, Ch. 1) of the work experience of the two classes of worker. The rewards of work were more tangible to the skilled man because he was more likely to experience steady employment whereas the unskilled man experienced greater insecurity in employment. The latter might enjoy more opportunities for variety but these rewards were overshadowed by unskilled tasks and a greater probability of losing the job despite conscientious effort. His job was limited in tenure because of the greater encroachment of machines into the unskilled area, the temporary nature of many unskilled jobs and the relative surplus of labourers who could replace him if his work was not judged satisfactory by his employer.

Thus the intrinsic and extrinsic rewards of work were greater for the skilled man. His work provided opportunities for trial and error and he also was able to receive further reward for his efforts, by slight advances in responsibility and wages over time. Such opportunities were very infrequent for the unskilled. Finally the extrinsic rewards of work for the skilled—relatively higher wages and greater security—allowed them greater opportunities for controlling and planning their personal and family life.

All of these views precede the description of the unemployed and despite Bakke's insistence that generalizations about the effects of unemployment cannot be made without reference to their prior working environment, few, if any, reviewers have given them any attention. Partly this is due to Bakke's failure to integrate these early chapters with his chapters on the state of unemployment. He does make some cross-references but it is apparent that he expects the reader to assess the psychological response to unemployment, in terms of the unemployeds' previous experience of employment.

As a consequence of low control over past work activities, the unemployed, for Bakke, tended to:

1. Believe and accept that their lives were largely controlled by external factors.

2. Believe that there was little they could do to alter the social structure.
3. Exert personal control in areas where they thought that they had some freedom of movement. Within the family the worker was still able to be self-reliant and make decisions within the restrictions set by his income, education and intellectual ability.
4. See work as having meaning mainly in terms of it being required to gain money. Work itself had some satisfactions in allowing the worker to form friendships with coworkers and gave him some respect as a useful 'producer'. There was pride in craftsmanship and skilled performance for a few but these were reported by men whose training had qualified them for relatively complex jobs requiring them to use their skills.

This is not to say that Bakke did not recognize considerable differences in personality within the working class. He did. But he highlighted some of the common attitudes and orientations which tended to distinguish them from other social classes. Their beliefs in external control affected their mood, their failure to make political protests and their disinclination to choose recreational activities that required self-direction.

The final section of this book, *Citizens Without Work*, is an account of Bakke's theory about the function of work. He goes beyond the description of the behaviour of the unemployed and their perceptions of their state, to state that their goals and personality were shaped by their tasks. All strove to attain personal control and consequent understanding of their lives but this was continuously thwarted by tasks low in skill-utilization, influence and income. These are not Bakke's terms but they seem to reflect reasonably accurately what he said. In his final book. *The Unemployed Worker* (1940b), he returns to an analysis of the world of labour in a way that is very similar to his analysis of the Greenwich industries. In his interviews with a sample of 200 unemployed workers, he infers that they had, in employment, experienced little control. Lack of control came from many sources and did not include only the limited core of skill and autonomy in actual work tasks. They had little or no control over the level and regularity of wages, the introduction of machinery, accidents, the pace and pressure of the work and their declining usefulness to employers as they grew older. This lack of control was doubly painful as they also tended to accept the American work ideology that 'a person gains a standard of living in proportion to his skill and effort and foresight'.

Yet Bakke was obviously puzzled by the fact that the unemployed still valued employment highly and thus discussed the meaning of employment to his sample. Although he did not clearly distinguish in his writing between the meaning of employment and the functions of work, he did separate the statements about employment made by the unemployed from his own inferences about the underlying goals of employment and how these facilitated or impeded the attainment of a universal personality function—the establishment of 'moderate' degrees of personal control. He does implicitly assert that it is a mistake to accept what workers say about work and employment as evidence for any general theory about the function of work. This is clear when he says that what workers and the unemployed say was shaped by their realistic experience. Deprived of control, it is not unexpected that they mention employment as important because it provides some satisfactions— money, social recognition, being the most important. They did not report intrinsic factors, such as autonomy or control, as being important because they had not experienced these factors in their past work.

So, for Bakke, the unemployed were deprived of tasks and money that further prevented them from psychologically growing. Their development had been already stunted by the conditions of their work and this had shaped their responses to unemployment. Despite their general depression, resignation and frustration, they commonly expressed their need for self-reliance, competence and control in the restricted areas open to them. They had not become permanently sad, mad or bad. The main feature of their behaviour was not apathy, fatalism or other psychiatric disturbance, but rather resilience in an impoverished environment.

ECONOMIC FACTORS AND RESPONSES TO UNEMPLOYMENT

If job experiences shaped the response of the unemployed to a life without work it was not the major reason for the stress and distress that they experienced. The literature seems to identify the major stressor as economic deprivation, not the absence of job activities (Bakke, 1933, 1940a,b; Clague, Couper and Bakke, 1934; Dunn, 1934; Kardiner, 1936). Sometimes the Marienthal study is cited as a study which showed that distress was related to the loss of activities, time structure and status. Even Jahoda used her own study to illustrate the latent functions of work for providing time structure, activity and social identity (Jahoda, 1981, 1982). However, the study demonstrates the primacy of economic factors as determinants of distress, as Jahoda does admit in both the original study and her later reviews. Unemployed workers were not happy without structure, activity and status, but severe depression and apathy were not due to their absence. Rather it was strongly correlated with income. 'Thus economic deterioration carries with it an almost incalculable change in the prevailing mood. This fact is intensified by the concomitant decline in health' (Jahoda, Lazarsfeld and Zeisel, 1933, p. 82). The importance of money as a factor is revealed when family mood is classified alongside income received during unemployment (Table 8.2).

Table 8.2 was based on detailed information from 100 families. If the mood progressively becomes more negative as one goes from the unbroken

TABLE 8.2 Classification of family mood and income in Marienthal

Family Mood	N	Income/schillings per month
Unbroken	16	34
Resigned	48	30
Despairing	11	25
Apathetic	25	19

From Jahoda, Lazarsfeld and Zeisel (1933).

to the apathetic group then it is clear that there is a high correlation between mood and income. The process by which income induced affective states was due to poor diet, anxiety over money for rent, clothing and poor family health. The connection between income and psychological state is clearly acknowledged by the authors when, in discussing the income levels of various families, they say 'it also allows us to foresee at approximately what point the deterioration of income will push a family into the next lower category' (Jahoda, Lazarsfeld and Zeisel 1933, p. 81).

The dominant importance of money also allowed them to predict individual differences between families at a given income level. Those who had previously amassed savings gave away to resignation, despair and apathy less quickly. If they had previously shown poor adaptability, however, they deteriorated very quickly. Thus previous income and personality were seen as moderators of the money-mood relationship 'On the whole, those who had been particularly well-off in the past either held out for an especially long time or broke down especially quickly' (Jahoda, Lazarsfeld and Zeisel 1933, p. 96).

This analysis makes it clear that Jahoda is consistent inferring that income is the manifest function of work, but is on shakier ground in inferring the loss of mood, well-being and social action as also being due to latent functions of work in satisfying needs for time-structure, purpose and identity (Jahoda, 1981, 1982). The primacy of economic factors in the Marienthal study was acknowledged by Lazarsfeld in his introduction to the English translation of the book. There he notes that the emotional state of the Marienthal people was born of poverty. Also Jahoda, in a general comment on unemployment in the 1930s, says 'There is no controversy over the fact that the unemployed experienced their condition as restrictive poverty and not just as the loss of regular occupation' (Jahoda, 1982, p. 21). Further documentation of the effects of economic factors is provided by recent studies of the long-term effects of the Depression.

A. Long-term Effects of the Depression

Recently it has become possible to evaluate whether the Depression did produce long-term effects on those who suffered severe economic loss. This is due to the availability of longitudinal data on men and women who experienced the Depression as children or adolescents. These people were part of the Berkeley growth study initiated in the 1920s and originally designed to provide information about psychological development. The data have been used by Elder (1974, 1978, 1981) to assess the effects of social class and of economic deprivation on adult personality and occupational achievement. Unfortunately, the adult male wage-earners who lost their jobs in the Depression were not included in these studies. Little is known about them except the effects of their behaviour on their children. One thing that Elder does report, however, is that those who suffered economic deprivation died earlier that those who were relatively unscathed.

In his first and largest publication, *Children of the Great Depression* (1974), Elder found that the male wage-earners who lost their jobs during the Depression lost their power and status in their marriage relationships. This is consistent with similar findings by Bakke (1940a) and Komarovsky (1940). They were no longer adequate providers for their families and for many families the wife had to become a wage-earner. This was particularly true of the middle-class families as it had always been the case that a considerable number of working-class families had working mothers. Nevertheless, for both working- and middle-class fathers, the loss of earning power meant that they were no longer the main contributor to the economic welfare of the family and this led to lowered self-respect and self-confidence. Since the wife had to take greater control of economic matters there was greater conflict within the family as the husband did not initially give up his prerogative to make budget decisions alone. The behaviour of the husband apparently became more aggressive and unpredictable and consequently he became more emotionally withdrawn from his children who increasingly grew closer to their mothers.

These effects were exacerbated in the families classified as economically deprived. Economic deprivation was not defined in terms of absolute income but as the proportion of income lost as a result of the Depression. Non-deprived status was given to families with less than a 35 per cent decrease in family income between 1929 and 1933.

Elder's Oakland study focused on the subsequent work meanings and occupational attainment of males born in 1920–1 and thus in their early teens during the worst of the Depression years. In later life, the children from deprived families were less likely to be satisfied with the extrinsic aspects of their jobs than non-deprived men, even when their occupational status, intellectual ability and family status were controlled for. It appears that adolescent insecurity, both economic and emotional, had predisposed them to attribute greater value to job security and income. Although social class predicted their adult occupational attainment, with middle-class males having higher attainment than working-class males, deprivation had little effect on occupational attainment. Although the deprived men had some-how overcome their economic and educational disadvantages, the factors that predicted their attainment were different from those that predicted the attainment of the non-deprived. The non-deprived group achieved in pro-portion to their intellectual ability. Need for achievement and family social class were relatively unimportant predictors. By contrast, the main predictors of attainment for deprived males in 1958 were their need for achievement and family social class. This suggests that economically deprived men's at-tainment depended on motivational rather than ability factors. Those who had acquired high aspirations during the Depression were able to overcome relatively poorer education. It seemed that many from this group received from their parents—especially their mothers—pressure and instruction on the importance of attaining jobs with adequate security and income.

In another sample, Elder tried to show that the Oakland men suffered less psychological damage and associated occupational attainment than men who experienced the Depression as young children. Elder and Rockwell (1979) examined the life history of a group of Berkeley men who were born in 1928–9. The Berkeley group had significantly higher intellectual ability and a higher proportion of them came from the middle class. For the Berkeley group, socialization strains due to economic deprivation were experienced as:

  (i) loss of control of desired outcomes, experienced through seemingly inexplicable parental distress and behaviour;
 (ii) social ambiguity or ambivalence manifested through relational un-certainties, conflicts, extreme mood swings and inconsistent disci-pline and demands; and
(iii) relative loss of the father as a nurturant, strong, affirmative male figure.

These stresses were also associated with increased pressure towards oc-cupational and economic achievement. By comparison with the Oakland group, the Berkeley deprived children experienced longer periods of eco-nomic deprivation because the deprived economic status persisted after the Depression. There was a high association between initial economic loss and persistent family hardship in the late 1930s and early 1940s despite an up-surge in the economy due to world war ($r = 0.56$). Although economic deprivation did not directly affect their entrance to tertiary education, it did have a significant indirect effect via persistent family aspirations. Those from deprived working-class families endured persistent family hardship during their teens which led to lowered scholastic aspirations, lowered high school performance and subsequent lowered likelihood of entering college. The middle-class deprived were better able to cover persistent hardship because they had higher intellectual ability and received greater support from other families in maintaining higher educational and occupational aspirations. Thus deprivation led to lowered educational achievement for both working- and middle-class adolescents but the effect was accentuated for the working class.

As far as personality is concerned the general picture is complex but Elder found that family deprivation had no direct effects on personality for the Berkeley group when this was measured in adolescence and at 30 and 40 years of age. Potential deficits in the deprived were compensated for by positive work experiences but some evidence showed that these gains were gained at a cost in personal adjustment. The relatively high achievers from deprived backgrounds, when compared to high achievers from non-deprived backgrounds, reported relatively higher degrees of 'unhealthy' adjustment patterns (brittle ego defences, feeling victimized, aloofness and negativity). These also reported greater general fatigue, more drinking problems and use of psychotherapy.

In a subsequent study of Berkeley women (Elder and Likert, 1982) who were young mothers during the Depression, it was found that their emotional health was significantly related to economic deprivation during that time. However, the effects were moderated by social class. The deprived middle-class women gained in emotional health relative to the non-deprived middle-class women whereas the deprived working-class women decreased in psychological health, assertiveness and helplessness relative to their non-deprived counterparts.

Elder and Likert partly explain this in terms of the greater resources of the deprived middle class. They had more education, intelligence and problem-solving ability than the deprived lower class. These resources helped them to overcome difficulties and increased their personal competence. However, it should be pointed out that the working-class women had less absolute wealth and education, which would have been barriers to their using greater personal resources even if they had possessed them. Also it appears that the psychological gains of the deprived middle class were not just due to their greater use of their personal resources relative to the non-deprived group. A greater proportion of the deprived women took jobs which potentially provided them with added independence and challenge. Gains in competence could be thus attributed to experiences of job mastery. Working-class women participated more in the workforce but it is probable that they did not enjoy mastery experiences at work because, due to their relatively low education, they had jobs low in skill-utilization and autonomy.

CONCLUSION

Elder's work showed that economic deprivation during the Depression and subsequent persistent economic hardship had significant long-term effects on educational achievement and psychological functioning of married women and children. There were considerable differences in the effects of economic factors due to the moderating effects of personal resources and job experiences but economic factors were identified as the most important determinants. This raises a general problem in determining the effects of unemployment during the Depression. Were the observed psychological and physical levels of health to be interpreted as due to economic factors, or the loss of job content or both? Psychologists have tended to understate the importance of economic factors by focusing on the loss of activity, time structure and job prestige. Certainly these factors were salient and were mentioned, at times, by the unemployed as contributing to their mood of discouragement.

Yet, on balance, the researchers attributed the main cause to poverty. The Marienthal researchers were fairly clear on this point. Bakke, too, saw loss of income as the major factor. He acknowledges that loss of the opportunity to exert autonomy and use skill was important for those who had been fortunate in having jobs with such opportunities. However, he described, in detail, how few regretted loss of job content, because their jobs had provided very little opportunity for psychological growth. Even for the skilled men, economic factors were mostly responsible for their decline in well-being. The role of poverty is also mentioned by Beales and Lambert (1934), Broomhill (1978), Carnegie Trust (1943), Pilgrim Trust (1938), Kardiner (1935) and Zawadski and Lazarsfeld (1935). Due to the severity of the prevailing economic conditions it must be concluded that economic and not job content variables must be given primacy in explanations of the psychological effects of unemployment in the 1930s. A major implication of this is that the literature of the Depression cannot be used to support simplistic views about the importance of job activities for psychological health.

NOTE

1. In Britain, job loss during the Depression was concentrated amongst less skilled males in the four basic and structurally declining industries of coal-mining, ship-building, iron and steel, and textiles (Constantine, 1980). One of the largest surveys endeavoured to sample both prosperous and distressed areas in Britain (Pilgrim Trust, 1938). It was found that 57 per cent of the unemployed were over 44 years old. Using government statistics, they found that unemployment was greatest for those in the following occupations: unskilled manual (31%), skilled and semi-skilled (14%), personal services (10%) and sales (8%). The Carnegie survey of unemployed youth in Britain

found a much higher concentration of unemployment in unskilled occupations (Carnegie Trust, 1943): 72% were unskilled, 21% semi-skilled, and only 7% were skilled tradesmen. In Bakke's extensive study in the United States the occupational breakdown was skilled manual 32%, unskilled and semi-skilled 55%, management 13%, farmers 2%, and white-collar jobs 7% (Bakke, 1940a, b). A major European study of the unemployed did not provide an occupational background but the large majority were probably semi-skilled and unskilled factory operatives (Jahoda, Lazarsfeld and Zeisel, 1971). The unemployed in this study previously worked in a large textile factory.

REFERENCES

Bakke, E.W. (1933). *The Unemployed Man: A Social Study*, London: Nisbet
Bakke, E.W. (1940a). *Citizens without Work: A Study of the Effects of Unemployment upon the Workers' Social Relations and Practices*, New Haven: Yale University Press
Bakke, E.W. (1940b). *The Unemployed Worker: A Study of the Task of Making a Living Without a Job*, New Haven: Yale University Press
Beales, H.L. and Lambert, R.S. (eds) (1934). *Memoirs of the Unemployed*, Victor Golancz. (Republished by Yorkshire: The Scholar Press, 1973)
Broomhill, R. (1978). *Unemployed Workers: A Social History of the Great Depression in Adelaide*, St. Lucia: University of Queensland Press
Carnegie Trust (1943). *Disinherited Youth*, Edinburgh: T.& A. Constable
Clague, E., Couper, W.J. and Bakke, E.W. (1934). *After the Shutdown*, New Haven: Yale University Press
Constantine, S. (1980). *Unemployment in Britain between the Wars*, London: Longman
Dunn, M. (1934). Psychiatric treatment of the effects of depression: its possibilities and limitation, *Mental Hygiene*, **18**, 279–86
Eisenberg, P. and Lazarsfeld, P.F. (1938). The psychological effects of unemployment, *Psychological Bulletin*, **35**, 358–90
Elder, G.H. (1974). *Children of the Great Depression*, Chicago: University of Chicago Press
Elder, G.H. (1978). Family history and the life course, in T Hareven (ed.), *Transitions: the Family and the Life course in Historical Perspective*, pp. 17–64, New York: Academic Press
Elder, G. (1981). History and the life course, Chapter 5 in D. Bertaux (ed.), *Biography and Society*, Beverley Hills: Sage
Elder, G.H. and Likert, J.K. (1982). Hard times in women's lives: historical influences across forty years, *American Journal of Sociology*, **88**, 241–69
Elder, G.H. and Rockwell, R.C. (1979). Economic depression and postwar opportunity in men's lives: a study of life patterns and health, in R.G. Simmons (ed.), *Research in Community and Mental Health*, vol. 1, Greenwich, Connect.: J.A.I. Press, pp. 249–303
Elderston, M. (ed.) (1931). *Case Studies of Unemployment*, Philadelphia: University of Pensylvania Press
Garraty, J.A. (1978). *Unemployment in History*, New York: Harper & Row

Hall, O.M. (1934). Attitudes and unemployment, *Archives of Psychology*, **25**, No. 165

Israeli, N. (1935). Distress in the outlook of Lancashire and Scottish unemployed, *Journal of Applied Psychology*, **19**, 67–9

Jahoda, M. (1979). The impact of unemployment in the 1930s and the 1970s, *Bulletin of the British Psychological Society*, **32**, 309–14

Jahoda, M. (1981). Work employment and unemployment: values, theories and approaches in social research, *American Psychologist*, **35**(2) 184–91

Jahoda, M. (1982). *Employment and Unemployment. A Social Psychological Analysis*, Cambridge: Cambridge University Press

Jahoda, M., Lazarsfeld, P.F. and Zeisel, H. (1933). *Marienthal: The Sociography of an Unemployed Community*, London: Tavistock

Kardiner, E. (1936). The role of economic security in the adaptation of the individual, *The Family*, **17**, 187–97

Komarovsky, M. (1940). *The Unemployed Man and his Family: The Effect of Unemployment upon the Status of the Man in 59 Families*, New York: Dryden

O'Brien, G.E. (1985). Distortion in unemployment research: the early studies of Bakke and their implications for current research on employment and unemployment, *Human Relations*, **38**, 877-894.

Pilgrim Trust. (1938). *Men without Work*, Cambridge: Cambridge University Press

Robb, M. (1934). The psychology of the unemployed from the medical point of view, Appendix B in H.L. Beales and R.S. Lambert (eds), *Memoirs of the Unemployed*, Victor Gollancz. (Republished by The Scholar Press, Yorkshire, 1973)

Rundquist, E.A. and Sletto, R.F. (1936). *Personality in the Depression: A Study in the Measurement of Attitudes*, Minneapolis: University of Minnesota Press

Zawadski, B. and Lazarsfeld, P.F. (1935). The psychological consequences of unemployment, *Journal of Social Psychology*, **6**, 224–51d.

CHAPTER 9

The Psychological Effects of Unemployment: Recent Studies

The main purpose of this chapter is to review research of the last decade in order to see if clearer answers can be obtained about the effects of unemployment on psychological development and behavioural disorder. No simple answer to this question was obtained from a review of the literature of the Depression.

Recent social science research is now rediscovering the complexity of the problem of unemployment as reviewers are pointing out that modern studies frequently do not allow clear inferences about the relative importance of job loss and economic loss, or the way in which personality and past experience shape the behaviour of the unemployed (Hartley, 1980b; Hartley and Freyer, 1984). Perhaps some of the confusion could have been avoided if research questions had been based on a careful perusal of the early writers on unemployment.

However, it would be wrong to say that progress has not been made. Recent research has provided some information that enables more definite estimates of the relative importance of various economic and psychological variables in predicting, and thereby understanding, the effects of unemployment. The purpose of this chapter is to review the main studies published in the last twenty years. There are three types of studies. The first is aggregate studies where the role of economic factors in determining physical and psychological health has been investigated by examining variations in community health in relation to variations in unemployment rate. These studies are termed aggregate studies because they do not examine changes over time in individuals but changes in variables that describe the state of large groups or communities.

The second class of studies tries to elucidate the mechanisms whereby gross unemployment rates produce behavioural disorders. In this class of studies it is assumed that unemployment rate, as an economic measure, produces a higher incidence of life stress which in turn produces behavioural changes in the population affected. These studies fall into what may be called the 'stressful life events' tradition. They involve a postulated mechanism which explains the effect of economic changes on individual behaviour but, like the aggregate studies, are based on measures that reflect community levels of economic change and behavioural symptoms. Like the aggregate studies, they are unable to demonstrate that the postulated mechanisms really apply at the individual level. Systematic increases in unemployment may produce increases in reported life stress and subsequent increase in symptoms such as depression and physical illness, but this does not necessarily mean that an individual who loses his or her job will then report life stress and experience illness. In order to show such a process at an individual level, another type of study is needed. This type of study, for want of a better word, will be called 'individual-level' studies and comprise most of the recent studies that are designed to ascertain the psychological effect of unemployment.

AGGREGATE STUDIES: UNEMPLOYMENT RATE AND BEHAVIOURAL DISORDER IN LARGE POPULATIONS

Recent years have seen a revival of interest in the relationship between economic trends and illness, both physical and mental. A major impetus to this movement was the publication of *Mental Illness and the Economy* by Brenner in 1973. Brenner was interested in the relationships between unemployment and mental health admissions. He found that previous research had not been able to reach consistent conclusions. Most of the earlier studies had tried to establish the effect of the Depression on mental health services. Some studies concluded that the Depression had precipitated a small increase in mental illness, but had not had a dominant effect on hospital admissions (Komora and Clark, 1935; Pollock, 1935). Other studies reported no significant increase in admissions during the Depression (Dayton, 1940; Mowrer, 1939). Further studies showed a relatively large increase in mental hospital admissions during the Depression with a decline in years subsequent to 1934 (Dunham, 1959; Malzburg, 1940; Pugh and MacMahon, 1962).

Brenner considered that variation in results could be due to different populations, absence of an objective criterion of unemployment, and a relatively short time span which did not allow investigators to distinguish between long-term trends and short-term effects. Brenner chose to study admissions to mental health institutions in New York State between 1910 and 1967. He found a strong relationship between the employment rate in manufacturing industries and mental illness. As employment decreased, the number of people admitted to mental hospitals increased. During the period of study, the employment rate dropped sharply during the Depression and this was associated with a sharp increase in admissions during the Depression and the few years following it. He considered that one of the major ways in which mental illness was caused was through economic loss. Those who lost their job suffered economic stress which precipitated or induced mental illness. Although his method precluded the study of individual cases, he was able to provide some indirect support for his hypothesis.

If economic loss produced illness then the admission rate should, he argued, be greater for those who experienced most loss. He used an early study by Menderhausen (1946) to identify the groups likely to have experienced most economic loss. Menderhausen found that 'moderately low' and 'high' income people sustained the greatest economic loss during the Depression, whereas 'very low' and 'moderately high' income people showed economic gains. The lowest income groups tended to be the least educated and least skilled members of the labour force and they tended to gain through the replacement of unskilled labour with workers who were even less skilled and accepted even lower wages. The gains of low-income groups were also partly due to the progressive increase in wages of young men who had started on very low wages. Brenner tried to identify this group of low-income earners by means of education level. He assumed that the least skilled had the lowest level of education. The semi-skilled and skilled had somewhat higher levels of education and it was this group that suffered most economic loss due to unemployment. Those who also suffered large losses were the business entrepreneurs who were assumed to have the highest educational levels. This method of identifying groups at risk of economic loss and subsequent illness is not very precise but is reasonable, given that he did not have access to detailed information on occupation and economic loss. Brenner did find that the relationship between admissions and employment rate was highest for those with moderate levels of education (grammar school) and next highest in college-educated. If these groups did actually suffer the most economic loss, then it suggested that the incidence of mental illness in a group of individuals can be predicted from knowledge of their degree of economic loss. At best this is a plausible hypothesis because Brenner's data are unable to establish the relationship directly.

Generally, however, Brenner's results provide strong evidence that unemployment rates have a strong and systematic relationship to mental illness, as measured by admission to psychiatric hospitals. At least two alternative explanations may be used to explain these results. Firstly, that increased unemployment causes, induces or precipitates mental illness. An alternative hypothesis is that intolerance of mental illness grew during periods of economic depression. This intolerance could be expressed through family and social pressures. Families that might have been able to support mentally ill members during times of relative prosperity might have found the burden too great when financial resources were depleted. Also welfare agencies, being overtaxed during periods of economic depression, might have transferred many of their recipients to hospitals if they showed both financial need and behavioural disorders.

Brenner admits that his 1973 study did not rule out this latter possibility. He was then led to identify measures of stress that were not amenable to explanations in terms of family and institutional factors. His subsequent studies examined the relationship between employment rates and the incidence of suicide, homicide, heart disease, liver disease and crimes against persons and property. These behaviours and illnesses were very unlikely to be affected by variations in social tolerance across time. The results are summarized by Brenner (1979). The employment rate was inversely related to cardiovascular disease, mortality, and cirrhosis of the liver. This provides some support for a view that maintained that unemployment induced greater life stress which, in turn, increased heart disease and excessive consumption of alcohol. These diseases did not appear immediately but peaked about two years after a significant decline in the employment rate. Further studies showed a delayed effect of changes in employment rate for suicide rates, homicide, mortality, and crimes against people and property.

The present status of his results is that the employment rate is inversely related to both acute and chronic stress reactions in large populations in the United States, Canada and the United Kingdom. The acute reactions include mental illness, imprisonment, suicide and homicide. They show up within two years of a change in the employment rate. The chronic reactions such as cardiovascular-renal disease, cirrhosis, and total mortality increase after about three years of a change in the unemployment rate. Brenner's results do show that these reactions occur during both increases and decreases in

TABLE 9.1   Percentage change in the 1965 incidence of social pathology as a result of a 1 per cent change in the unemployment rate in the United States (1960–65)

Measure	Percentage increase
Total mortality	1.9
Cardiovascular mortality	1.9
Cirrhosis of the liver mortality	1.9
Suicide	4.1
State mental hospital admissions:	
Males	3.4
Females	4.3
State prison admissions	4.0

Based on Brenner (1979), Table 3, p.169.

the employment rate, but the strength of the relationships is much stronger for decreases in employment. How strong are these relationships? This can be answered by reference to Table 9.1, which is based on Brenner's own tabulations. This table suggests that an increase in unemployment by say 5 per cent in any one year will be followed within about five years by a 9.5 per cent increase in deaths, a 20.5 per cent increase in suicides, and a 20 per cent increase in mental hospital and prison admissions. Whatever the process accounting for these social traumas is does show that unemployment and associated economic loss cannot be ignored as a determinant of physical and mental illness.

UNEMPLOYMENT, LIFE STRESS AND PSYCHOLOGICAL STATES

Before it is possible to explain the aggregate relationship between employment rate and illness in terms of individual stress, it is necessary to show that changes in employment rate actually do produce changes in individual stressors. This has rarely been directly examined although there is a large body of evidence that shows that various life stresses produce illness behaviour. This research is of limited value for understanding the relationship between economic factors, individual stress and illness. The main reason is that most studies combine life changes, such as job loss, marriage, and death of spouse, into one estimate of life stress. Thus if a relationship is found between life stress and illness it is difficult to disentangle the effects of economic and job loss from the effects of other stressors.

A recent study, however, did try to examine the relationship between general economic changes and the extent to which they were associated with changes in individual, financial and work stressors. Catalano and Dooley (1983) surveyed Los Angeles households every three months between 1978 and 1980. They drew 500 households each quarter and asked occupants to indicate those events that had occurred to them during the recent months. The list of events included undesirable job or financial events (e.g. decrease in wages, loss of job, mortgage foreclosed), desirable job or financial events (e.g. increased wages, promotion), and desirable, undesirable or indifferent 'other' events (e.g. arrest, marriage, death in family). They did find that the probability of illness or injury was related to undesirable job and financial events. However, only partial support was found for the expected relationship between the unemployment rate and undesirable job/financial events. This relationship held only for middle-class respondents and not for those from either high or low socio-economic status. To some extent this finding is similar to that of Brenner (1973) who found that those with moderate degrees of education experienced greater mental illness in response to economic contraction. The parallel is viable only if it is assumed that those of lower socio-economic status had moderate education levels. The Catalano and Dooley study still does not provide strong evidence for individual changes in health following individual changes in job/economic state. They did not study individuals over time but changes across different samples at different points of time.

Nevertheless, the study is interesting for a number of reasons. Firstly, it provided some support for the common assumption that economic contraction induced undesirable job or financial events in individuals. Secondly, it suggested that undesirable job or financial events were more strongly related to illness than other desirable or undesirable events.

> Having one or more events not involving health, job or finances increased the odds of being ill or injured by 24% whereas experiencing an undesirable job or financial event nearly doubled the odds of illness or injury.
>
> (Catalano and Dooley, 1983, p. 55)

Thirdly, it found that the young were more likely to be ill or injured than the elderly.

Finally, it suggested that socio-economic class moderated the relationship between financial loss and illness. This latter possibility was briefly discussed in their report. Those from higher socio-economic positions were, it was suggested, cushioned from the effects of job/financial stresses because they had greater financial resources and because their relatively high educational levels meant that they had greater opportunities for finding alternative jobs and income. The explanation of relatively small effects for those from lower socio-economic levels is more problematic. Why is it that economic contraction has relatively small effects on undesirable job experiences on those from lower socio-economic groups? Two alternative but not exclusive explanations are offered. It is possible that those who are chronically ill are likely to have undesirable job experiences regardless of the economy. Thus they are more likely to have undesirable financial experiences and therefore low income. Alternatively, low-income persons could, by virtue of their relatively low education, hold jobs which are unskilled or semi-skilled. They would, therefore, have jobs that are more likely to be insecure and temporary regardless of the economy. Whichever alternative occurs, and probably both do, it seems that those with lowest income have things bad for them whether the economy is working well or not.

INDIVIDUAL-LEVEL STUDIES OF UNEMPLOYMENT AND ECONOMIC LOSS

So far, aggregate and life-stress studies have been considered These studies have established that, at a collective level, the employment rate is significantly and inversely related to individual life strains and subsequent behavioural disorder. Their design is not suited to a demonstration that changes in an individual's situation over time produce changes in that individual's mental and physical states. As unemployment has recently become a visible social problem, a number of studies on individual reactions to unemployment have appeared. Earlier reviews of these studies have been provided by Borrero (1980), Fraser (1981), Hartley and Freyer (1984), Hayes and Nutman (1981), Jahoda (1979, 1981, 1982), Kasl (1979), Macky and Haines (1982), and Warr (1983). The present review is not exhaustive but includes most of the studies published in British, North American and Australian journals up to 1985. The available studies can be divided into four categories depending on whether they are dealing with adults or youth, or use cross-sectional versus longitudinal designs. There are at least two reasons for considering adults and youth separately. The implications of unemployment for adults are likely to be different because they have more financial responsibilities. They are likely to be married and have considerable expenses in maintaining a family and home. The economic impact of unemployment is, therefore, likely to be much greater for adults than youth. Young people have fewer financial money worries and are cushioned from money problems because they live with their parents or receive financial support from them. Secondly, the two groups differ markedly in prior work experience. Young people are relatively new to employment and their reactions to work and unemployment are likely to be affected largely by their recent educational experience. By contrast, the responses of adults are likely to be determined more by their past work experiences.

A. Studies of Adult Unemployment

1. Cross-sectional studies

Cross-sectional studies have compared employed and unemployed men on various measures of personality, health, leisure, mood and psychiatric vulnerability (Table 9.2). These studies have generally not been designed to assess the effects of unemployment, but rather to estimate the major differences between employed and unemployed. Generally the results are more valuable to the extent that multiple measures were obtained. Simple findings, such as that the unemployed have less life satisfaction than the employed, are not very useful unless the studies give some estimate of the relative importance of various predictors in determining life satisfaction. Studies with multiple predictors can, in principle, assess the relative importance of job activities, income, personality, work values and health in determining responses to unemployment. These exploratory studies would then be useful for deciding which variables are to be included in longitudinal studies designed to assess the causal impact of unemployment.

TABLE 9.2   Cross-sectional studies of the psychological effect of unemployment (adults)

Study	Sample	Nature and duration of unemployment	Psychological measures	Comparison group	Statistical control	Results
Hartley (1980a) (UK)	72 applicants (4 female) to government training course for unemployed managers. 59 employed managers	Median time of unemployment = 16.5 weeks	16pF personality inventory	59 employed managers plus 603 employed managers from study by Hartson and Mottram, (1975)	–	Compared to the smaller comparison group unemployed managers scored higher on 3 factors (assertive, conscientious and imaginative). Comparison with larger group showed that unemployed managers were more emotionally stable, conscientious, self-sufficient and controlled but less intelligent
Hepworth (1980) (UK)	78 men on unemployment register	48% unemployed for more than 6 months	Life satisfaction Psychiatric vulnerability (GHQ)	570 employees in engineering firm	Length of unemployment, perceived economic security, occupational status, time unemployed	Length of unemployment inversely related to psychiatric vulnerability and life satisfaction. Semi-skilled and unskilled men lower on life satisfaction and higher on psychiatric vulnerability than those of higher occupational status. Psychiatric vulnerability associated with inability to occupy time

Study	Sample	Employment definition	Variables	Employed	Analysis	Results
O'Brien and Kabanoff (1979) (Australia)	Cluster sample of Adelaide. 1383 employed, 74 unemployed	Continuous and intermittent combined	Stress, work values, locus of control (Rotter) Life satisfaction 'Leisure' attributes	Employed	Differences between 2 groups established by discriminant analysis	Unemployed had poorer health, were more externally controlled, more involved in home duties. The unemployed desired work with less pressure and interaction than that of employed. No significant difference between groups in stress, desired work influence and skill-utilization, life satisfaction or leisure attributes (skill-use, autonomy, variety, interaction, pressure.) Reported stress in unemployed positively correlated with time spent looking for work
Oliver and Pomicter (1981) (USA)	145 automobile workers	'Laid off' in previous year. Time unemployed not stated	Depression	69 laid off in previous year cf. 64 not laid off	–	Depression in laid-off workers predicted by perceived future state of economy, percentage of salary recoverable from union benefits, perceived probability of being laid off again and current employment status. Depression in non-laid-off groups predicted by race, education, mental status and perceived effect of economy on finances

TABLE 9.2 (Cont.)

Study	Sample	Nature and duration of unemployment	Psychological measures	Comparison group	Statistical control	Results
Swinburne (1981) (UK)	20 managerial/ professional males attending training course	15 unemployed between 2–6 months	Emotional response (interview) activities	Nil	Nil	Initial shock reported by 50%. Less than 25% reported anger, shame or loss of status. 13/20 reported difficulty in being self-directed. 19/20 stressed importance of being active. Experience of loss proportional to the degree that occupational identity was very important to self-concept. Majority not in immediate financial difficulty
Trew and Kilpatrick (1983) (UK)	Sample 1 83 males Sample 2 124 males	Sample 1 35% unemployed less than 1 year Sample 2 32% unemployed less than 1 year	Time diary of activities Mental health (GHR)	Comparisons between samples	–	Most imposed a time structure — using domestic tasks. Psychological well-being greatest for those with active, outgoing lifestyle. Well-being lowest with passive, domestic style. Men from high unemployment areas coped better than those from low unemployment areas

Study	Sample	Time	Variables	Comparison group		Findings
Warr (1978) (UK)	Redundant steel workers $N = 1655$ 97%m	6 month follow up after redundancy $E = 891$ $U = 764$	Positive and negative affect Anxiety Life satisfaction	Employed group	Nil	Employed workers higher on positive affect than the unemployed. Unemployed workers had greater negative affect than employed workers. No general difference in anxiety. Degrees of affect moderated by desire to find a job. For unemployed workers, positive affect was least for those with higher work orientation—negative affect was greatest for those unemployed with high work orientation
Warr and Payne (1983) (UK)	203 middle-class and 196 working-class males. Aged 25–34 years	–	'Leisure' behaviour after job loss	–	–	General increases in social contact and book reading after job loss. Activities requiring money decreased. Middle-class men read more than working-class men. Working-class men visited public hotels more
Warr and Jackson (1984) (UK)	954 working-class males	Less than a month to greater than 12 months	Reported health, financial strain Employment commitment	–	–	Length of unemployment associated with deterioration in health and financial strain. Psychological deterioration, financial strain, and commitment to work greatest among middle-aged men

The results show that unemployed people do not differ greatly from the employed on work values and personality. In fact, Hartley (1980a) reported that unemployed managers in the United Kingdom tended to be higher on assertiveness, conscientiousness and imagination. O'Brien and Kabanoff (1979) found that the unemployed had similar desires for work with autonomy and skill-utilization to the employed. These findings suggest that many of those now unemployed are in this state because of unselective retrenchments and not because of failings in work motivation and personality. However, the unemployed did report worse physical health in the Australian study (O'Brien and Kabanoff, 1979). This finding could be attributable either to unemployment or alternatively to poor health which could have led to them becoming unemployed.

The cross-sectional studies generally showed:

1. That the stress and anxiety levels of the unemployed generally were not significantly different from the employed (O'Brien and Kabanoff, 1979; Warr, 1978).
2. Immediate dissatisfaction with being unemployed (Hartley, 1980a; Swinburne, 1981; Warr, 1978).
3. Stress and deteriorating health were correlated with time unemployed (O'Brien and Kabanoff, 1979; Hepworth, 1980; Warr and Jackson, 1984).
4. The degree of negative affect associated with unemployment was greatest for those with higher work orientation (Swinburne, 1981; Warr, 1978).
5. Unemployed men living in areas of high unemployment had better 'mental health' than unemployed men from low-unemployment areas (Trew and Kilpatrick, 1983).
6. Depressive affect in unemployed workers was significantly related to financial loss (Oliver and Pomiter, 1981).
7. Many unemployed reported difficulty in organizing their time but they did structure their time by engaging in domestic and leisure activities (O'Brien and Kabanoff, 1979; Swinburne, 1981; Trew and Kilpatrick, 1983).
8. The unemployed tended to be more externally controlled than the employed (O'Brien and Kabanoff, 1979).

Taken together these results suggest that unemployment is associated with short-term dissatisfaction but not necessarily with changes in relatively stable states of anxiety and stress. Long-term adjustments are likely to be related in a complex way to economic changes, orientations to work, time unemployed, prior work status and the activities undertaken in unemployment. The results certainly do not permit one to assert that the unemployed, as a group, are more depressed, anxious or inactive and have greater personality decrements than the employed. Perhaps this is due to the relatively short period of unemployment experienced by the subjects in these studies. Stable negative states such as depression and external control may only appear after fairly long periods of unemployment. There is more support for a generalization that states that unemployment is associated with immediate dissatisfaction, which is, in turn, partly related to work orientation, feelings of personal control, economic resources and prior job activities. The results suggest, but do not demonstrate, that the amount of dissatisfaction is greatest for those with higher work commitment, interesting jobs, high anxiety and small financial resources. In the short term, dissatisfaction with being unemployed could lead to feelings of depression (as distinct from fairly stable depression), low self-esteem, and an increased belief in external control. If external control beliefs are extreme then psychological health becomes impaired.

2. Longitudinal studies

The hypotheses suggested by the cross-sectional studies can be used to organize longitudinal studies on adult unemployment. These studies are small in number and none of them provide information that is relevant to all of the hypotheses (Table 9.3).

1. *Prior job experiences.* Unlike the early work of Bakke (1933, 1940a,b), no longitudinal study has systematically analyzed the nature of prior work experiences with a view to establishing work attitudes or personality orientations that are likely to determine responses to unemployment. Hartley's (1980c) study suggested that the degree of dissatisfaction is less for those from managerial positions but no comparison group of non-managerial workers was examined. Cohn (1978) did compare responses for unemployed from different occupational backgrounds and found that blue-collar workers were more dissatisfied with job loss. The most relevant study is that by Little (1976) who found that dissatisfaction depended on both the nature of previous work and the career stage of technical-professional workers. Somewhat surprisingly he found that 48 per cent of his sample were not greatly upset by job loss but expressed positive satisfaction. Many saw it as an opportunity to develop themselves and find more suitable jobs. Those who felt fairly positive about job loss were those who had been largely dissatisfied in the job. Dissatisfaction was also related to career stage. Those who were either at the beginning or end of their career were most dissatisfied. To some extent, those with positive feelings about job loss were those who were in mid-career and currently dissatisfied with their present jobs. Fineman (1983) also found that about

TABLE 9.3 Longitudinal studies of the psychological effects of unemployment in adults

Study	Sample	Nature and duration of unemployment	Psychological measures	Comparison group	Statistical control	Results
Aiken, Ferman and Sheppard (1968) (USA)	260 white. 45 black automobile workers	Intermittent and continuous over two years Severity of unemployment measured by Index of Economic Deprivation	Anomia. Life satisfaction	–	Skill level age, time unemployed, education	Anomia increased and life satisfaction decreased with increases in economic deprivation
Cobb and Kasl (1977). Kasl (1979) (USA)	100 males Manufacturing plant	Intermittent and continuous over two years	1. Relative deprivation. 2. Work role deprivation. 3. Self-reported mental health. 4. Physiological measures	Yes. Men in comparable blue-collar jobs	–	Economic deprivation increases with unemployment and decreases with re-employment. Work role deprivations increase with short-term employment—especially 'chance to use one's best skills.' Adaptation to prolonged unemployment as economic deprivation and work role deprivation does not change with time or, for some measures, becomes less.

Author	Sample	Design	Measure			Results
						Depression increases from time of anticipated to actual unemployment. Depression becomes less with prolonged unemployment, Pulse rate and serum cholesterol increase with short unemployment but then decrease with long unemployment
Cohn (1978) (USA)	1080 M and F National panel. Subsample. 543E 537U	1 year or more. All employed 1968. Interviewees again 1969	Dissatisfaction with self (1 item)	Yes Employed sample	No	Unemployment leads to greater self-dissatisfaction. Degree is less for males to the extent that they become involved in housework and ratio of self/wife income. For males, greater dissatisfaction if in blue-collar job. Actually no significant effect of self-satisfaction for white-collar workers. No significant effect for unemployed mothers. Significant effect for childless women. Effects less for unemployed in high unemployment rate areas than for unemployed in low unemployment rate areas

TABLE 9.3 (Cont.)

Study	Sample	Nature and duration of unemployment	Psychological measures	Comparison group	Statistical control	Results
Fineman (1983) (UK)	100 managers and professionals attending government career programme 82% male. 65% married. Av. age = 42years	Mean unemployment time = 6.55 months Follow up 6 months after initial interview	Psychiatric vulnerability (GHQ). Strain Self-esteem. Anxiety	Scale norms for general population	–	Unemployed tended to be slightly higher than general population on psychiatric vulnerability, strain, anxiety. Effects stronger for those dismissed than those who resigned. About one-third felt positive about being unemployed. Subsequent adjustment better if positive social support.
Gore (1978) (USA)	100 terminees blue-collar, 54 rural, 46 urban, 74 controls employed in comparable jobs	44 promptly re-employed 2 years for some. S1 measures 6 weeks before shut-down, S2 1 month after termination S3 6 months after termination S4 1 year after termination S5 2 years after termination. Prospective	Economic deprivation. Depression. Illness symptoms. Cholesterol Support	Employee group as well as terminated group who became re-employed within 6 weeks	No	Cholesterol of the unemployed remained within normal limits. Unsupported employed at Stage 2 had higher cholesterol levels than supported unemployed over all stages. Unemployed reported more illnesses than controls if unsupported (S1 and S2 only). Unemployed non-supported men had higher depression than supported and time unemployed has little effect. Unsupported unemployed men reported greater economic deprivation than supported unemployed men

Hartley (1980c) (UK)	87 unemployed managers. 64 employed managers	Median length of unemployment 16.5 weeks Measures taken 6–10 week intervals	Self-esteem	Employed	—	No difference in self-esteem between employed and unemployed. Self-esteem of unemployed managers did not decline with time
Little (1976)	100 middle-class males. Technical-professional occupations	1–8 weeks— N=33. 9–32, N=28. 33+, N=35	Attitude to loss. Use of time	—	—	48% expressed positive attitudes to job loss—largely due to previous job dissatisfaction and provision of opportunity to find another job and follow interests. Dissatisfaction with job loss highest amongst those at beginning or near end of career. Idleness not a great problem for most (26/100 saw it as a 'real problem'). Attitude to job loss mostly negative for those in poor financial situation
Parnes and King (1977) Parnes (1981) (USA)	234 middle-age males (1977). Same national panel used in 1981. N=1481	Job 'displacement' permanent	Locus of control (adjusted Rotter scale)	Yes. Not displaced group	Various demographic and occupational variables	Displaced workers become more externally controlled than non-displaced. Displaced workers had been less happy with their jobs than non-displaced workers

TABLE 9.3 (Cont.)

Study	Sample	Nature and duration of unemployment	Psychological measures	Comparison group	Statistical control	Results
Pearlin and Lieberman (1979)	2300 cluster sample of Chicago	Incidence of job loss within a 4-year period Duration not stated	Psychological distress scale. (self-report)	–	–	Association between job loss and distress measures increases over period of four years
Stokes and Cochrane (1984) (USA)	Unemployed (Redundant) =48: 31F, 17M. Semi-skilled, unskilled. Control employed = 48	–	Symptoms—physical and psychological, hostility, guilt, self-satisfaction, acceptance by others	Matched employed group	Time	Unemployed had more symptoms, hostility, guilt, less self-satisfaction and less social acceptance than employed. No differences between male and female unemployed

a third of his unemployed British sample of managers were not stressed by unemployment if they had disliked their previous jobs and thought that they had good prospects of finding a better job.

2. *Financial and coping resources.* Three of the studies do show that financial resources predicted dissatisfaction with unemployment (Little, 1976; Aiken, Freeman and Sheppard, 1968; Cohn, 1978) while Kasl (1979) and Cobb and Kasl (1977) in their study found that economic deprivation did increase with unemployment.

Two studies examined the moderating effort of coping resources. Gore (1978) found that social support affected the cholesterol levels, reported illness, depression and economic deprivation of blue-collar unemployed workers. Those who received lower social support had higher cholesterol levels, greater illness, higher depression and more economic deprivation than supported unemployed workers. Fineman (1983) also found that positive social support moderated the effects of unemployment on mental strain and anxiety.

3. *Short-term effects on distress, self-esteem, personal control, depressive effect.* The results on distress are largely consistent. Pearlin and Lieberman (1979) reported a general association between job loss and distress measures which increased over a period of four years. Stokes and Cochrane (1984) compared redundant workers with a matched group of employed workers and found, across six months, that redundant workers exhibited the greatest personal distress. In their study distress was measured by psycho-physiological symptoms, hostility, guilt, self satisfaction and acceptance by others. However, Hartley (1980b) found that there was no significant difference in self-esteem and distress between employed and unemployed managers. Although the study was conducted over a short time period, Cobb and Kasl (1977) provided the most detailed examination of the effects of unemployment on depressive affect. They found depression increased from the time of anticipated unemployment to the time of actual unemployment. Depressive affect then became less with time. Corresponding results were found with physiological measures. Pulse rate and serum cholesterol levels increased with short-term unemployment but then decreased with time unemployed. The only study on personal control was by Parnes (1981) and Parnes and King (1977), who found that unemployment was associated with decrease in personal control, as measured by Rotter's locus of control scale.

These results provide rather meagre information about the effect of unemployment. Some of the results appear inconsistent and probably apparent inconsistencies are attributable to differences in samples, the time unemployed, whether unemployment was continuous or intermittent, measures used, and differences across samples in the availability of financial and social support.

However, some tentative generalizations can be made:

1. Most people who suffer job loss report dissatisfaction with becoming unemployed and experience depressive affect. However, some people view job loss in positive terms, seeing it as an opportunity to develop interests and find better jobs.
2. The strength of long-term effects is fairly small. One study has reported that personal control orientations change with the unemployed becoming more externally controlled. However, it is questionable whether this reflects some personality change or realistic perceptions of the social environment (Chapter 7).
3. The degree of reported dissatisfaction with self or life varies in proportion to financial deprivation and social support. Those with higher financial resources, social support and education tend to be least dissatisfied with their state.
4. Adaptations occur in financial and activity areas. The unemployed tend to find alternative economic resources and reduce expenses. They also tend to find activities which use their skills and express their interests.

B. Studies of Youth Unemployment

1. Cross-sectional studies

Because the financial responsibilities of youth are less than those of most adults it is expected that unemployment affects in youth should be less affected by economic loss. Effects, when observed, should be more confidently related to job loss although economic factors, ideally, should be measured. Unfortunately, no study has so far examined the effects of job loss on the financial situation of youth. Another reason for expecting that youth without work should respond in terms of the meaning attributed to job loss is due to their recent emergence from education. One of the main functions of education is to prepare students for full-time employment. In the course of their education students acquire knowledge and skills which they expect to use in full-time work. They also expect a job will bestow on them social prestige, independence and a bridge to adulthood. The degree to which unemployment is experienced as dissatisfying might therefore be determined by education, work values and the strength of their desire to assume work roles.

Cross-sectional studies of unemployed youth have not directly examined these hypotheses, but have been mainly concerned with depressive affect, depression, self-esteem and the degree to which attributions about the causes of unemployment affect these states. Their focus has been not so much on the relative effect of employment and unemployment but on the predictors of reactions among those who were unemployed (Table 9.4). Two small studies on causal attributions were conducted by Feather and Davenport (1981) and Feather and Barber (1983). In the first study, 60 per cent of the Adelaide unemployed sample of 210 lived at home with their parents. The sample included those who were both continuously and intermittently unemployed. The mean time of unemployment was 31 weeks. Depressive affect was measured on a 1-item scale where subjects indicated whether their mood was glad, very depressed or some point intermediate between these moods. Not surprisingly, those who were most motivated to get a job were higher on depressive affect than those less motivated. The other main finding was that those high on depressive affect were more likely to blame external difficulties (e.g. recession, decline in employment) for their unemployment than themselves. The theoretical significance is not clear. It could have occurred simply because those most motivated to work had found out, through their job searches, that relatively high youth unemployment was indeed due to economic and industrial problems and not to deficiencies in their education or ability. One interesting finding was that nearly half the sample were glad or neutral in depressive affect.

The second study by Feather and Barber (1983) extended the range of measures to include self-esteem and depression scales. The sample had been unemployed longer than the first sample and a majority, 78 per cent, had full-time work experience since leaving school. Like the first study, the degree of depressive affect was greater for those who made external attributions for the cause of unemployment. However, depression was related to time unemployed, internal causal attributions, perceived uncontrollability of unemployment by people, employment importance and self-esteem. A plausible interpretation of these results is that those people who report depressive symptoms are also likely to suffer from low self-esteem, self-blame and a feeling that their circumstances are beyond control. Being a cross-sectional study it is not possible to say that unemployment was responsible for depression as there was no comparison group of employed youth or measures of depression before and after unemployment.

A comparison group was used in a third cross-sectional study by Feather (1982). Here it was found that unemployed males and females had higher depression and lower self-esteem than employed youth. There were few significant differences in groups in attributional style. Unemployed males, but not females, had lower acceptance of the Protestant Work Ethic than employed males but this could be due to differences in the sample on social background, a consequence of unemployment, or a cause of their state of unemployment. Time out of work was not correlated with Protestant Ethic but depression and self-esteem were negatively related to time out of work.

TABLE 9.4 Cross-sectional studies of youth unemployment

Study	Sample	Nature and duration of unemployment	Psychological measures	Comparison group	Statistical control	Results
Feather (1982) (Australia)	32 M, 37 F unemployed (19.9 years mean age). 39 M, 39 F Employed (21.4 years mean age). 80% of all subjects single. 60% lived with parents	Unemployed mean = 31.3 weeks	Attributional style. Self-esteem. Protestant Ethic. Depression	Employed group	Sex	Unemployed males and females had higher depression and lower self-esteem than employed youth. Unemployed males, but not females, had lower Protestant Ethic scores. Few significant differences in attributional style. Unemployed not less likely to attribute internal factors as being more responsible for good and bad events. However, 'apathy' in the unemployed group inferred from rated personal importance of 'good' events. No difference in importance of 'bad' events. Differences in importance between unemployed and employed on 'importance' was greater for males than females. Weeks out of work significantly correlated with self-esteem, and depression but not Protestant Ethic

Study	Sample	Unemployment duration	Variables measured	Control group	Analysis	Findings
Feather and Barber (1983) (Australia)	116 unemployed (64 M, 52 F). Mean age 20.1 years	78% had full-time work experience since leaving school. Mean time unemployed = 57.5 weeks. (median 30.50weeks)	Expectations of success. Depressive affect. Causal attributions for unemployment. Self-esteem. Depression	No	Regression analyses used to establish relative importance of predictors	Depressive effect (1 item) associated with concern about being unemployed and external attribution for cause of unemployment. Unrelated to expectation of success. Depression related to time unemployed, internal attributions, perceived uncontrollability of unemployment by people, employment importance and self-esteem
Feather and Bond (1983) (Australia)	University graduates. 43 unemployed (13 M, 30 F). 255 employed (156 M, 99 F)	Mean unemployment = 27.7 weeks (median 26.50 weeks)	Use of time Employment importance. Self-esteem. Depression	Employed group	None	Employed reported more engagement, direction and routine in their use of time than the unemployed There was no difference in degree of structure (organization). No significant differences in self-esteem but employed were lower on depression. No difference in employment importance. Self-esteem negatively related to depression for both groups. Use of time for unemployed positively related to self-esteem. negatively to depression and negatively to employment importance

TABLE 9.4 (Cont.)

Study	Sample	Nature and duration of unemployment	Psychological measures	Comparison group	Statistical control	Results
Feather and Davenport (1981) (Australia)	150 M, 60 F Youth. Mean age 19.8 years. 96% unmarried. 60% lived at home with parents	Mean unemployment 30.6 weeks. Median 19.7 weeks	Expectation of success. Valence of work. Motivation to work. Causal attributions for unemployment. Depressive affect (1 item 5 pt scale)	No	None	Depressive affect was highest in those most motivated to get a job. Subjects high on depressive affect were also less likely to blame themselves for their unemployment and more likely to blame external difficulties. Work was more attractive to depressed than to relatively non-depressed subjects
Stafford, Jackson and Banks (1980) (UK)	647 school leavers	Interviewed 7 months after leaving school	Mental health (GHQ). Work involvement	Employed	Sex. Ethnic background. Social class Education	Unemployed had poorer mental health than employed. Unemployed with higher work involvement had poorer mental health than those unemployed with lower work involvement

A final study by Feather and Bond (1983) with university graduates reported that the employed showed more task involvement, direction and routine in their tasks. There was no difference in the degree to which their activities were structured. The percentage of variance accounted for by employment status was fairly small and suggests that the unemployed were not inactive but had a little more difficulty in directing their activities—probably because of financial limitations and the fact that the time structure of the employed was imposed by a work organization.

No definite conclusion can be drawn from these studies. Lack of proper sampling methods means that no statement can be made about differences in depression and self-esteem across employed and unemployed groups. The studies do suggest that the effects of unemployment on depressive affect and depression are not great. They also suggest that greatest depression may occur amongst those who most want to work. However, the whole set of studies, except perhaps the one with university students, may simply reflect differences already existing across social class. People from lower social classes are more likely to be unemployed and they already have lower standing on measures of psychological well-being.

One other study did control indirectly for social class by sampling only less qualified youth (Stafford, Jackson and Banks, 1980). Using the General Health Questionnaire (Goldberg, 1972) they found that those unemployed had poorer mental health than the employed. Furthermore, the higher the work involvement of the unemployed the poorer was their mental health score. Again, the direction of causality cannot be established. It does appear that those who most want to work suffer most in terms of mental health. However, this does not necessarily mean that lack of work for the high work-involved group causes their poor mental health. It is possible for this subgroup that another variable, for example, high parental aspirations, determines both high work involvement and poor mental health.

2. Longitudinal studies

A number of longitudinal studies have provided firmer evidence to show that unemployment produces higher levels of psychological distress (Table 9.5). The main measure of psychological distress (sometimes labelled psychiatric morbidity) is Goldberg's General Health Questionnaire (Goldberg, 1972). The short version of this scale asks subjects to report the frequency with which they have experienced various symptoms that are considered to be potential indicators of non-psychotic mental disorder. The symptoms are similar to those used in self-report stress scales (e.g. feeling tired, anxious, depressed, unable to concentrate). Banks and Jackson (1982) found that the unemployed reported higher distress than the employed youth. Two cohorts of youth were interviewed over two and a half years. The effect of job

TABLE 9.5 Longitudinal studies of youth unemployment

Study	Sample	Nature and duration of unemployment	Psychological measures	Comparison group	Statistical control	Results
Banks and Jackson (1983) (UK)	Two cohorts of school leavers Cohort 1 = 647 Cohort 2 = 1096	Interviewed over $2\frac{1}{2}$ years At final interview 67 unemployed (Cohort 1), 77 unemployed (Cohort 2). Unknown time of unemployment and employment	Psychiatric morbidity (GHQ)	Employed	Sex Ethnic group Education	Unemployed had higher psychiatric morbidity than employed. Morbidity increased for those who left school and experienced unemployment while it decreased for those who found employment
Dowling and O'Brien (1981, 1983) (Australia)	65 unemployed 386 employed, 201 students	Mean time unemployed 5.7 months. All groups tested at school then 1 year later	Work values —Desired influence, Desired skill-utilization. Desired variety	Employed and student group	Initial work values as covariates	After 1 year work values of continuing students higher than those unemployed. No significant difference in work values between unemployed and employed groups. Analysis of subgroups in continuous employment and continuous unemployment showed that the employed had greater desire for skill-utilization and variety than the unemployed

Study	Sample	Design	Measures	Comparison group	Control	Results
Gurney (1980a) (Australia)	248 M, 164 F school leavers from 'middle class areas'	4 months. maximum employment. No mean time of unemployment provided	Self-esteem	Employed students	Sex	No change in self-esteem of the unemployed. Significant increase in self-esteem for employed girls alone
Gurney (1980b) (Australia)	248 M, 164 F school leavers from 'middle class areas'	4 months. maximum employment. No mean time of unemployment provided	Eriksonian scale of personal development	Employed students	Sex	Males who found work improved significantly on 'industry-inferiority'. Unemployed males decreased significantly on 'trust-mistrust' and 'initiative-guilt'. Employed girls improved on 'industry-inferiority', 'identity-confusion', and 'intimacy-isolation'
Jackson et al. (1983) (UK)	Two cohorts of school leavers Cohort 1 = 647 Cohort 2 = 780	Interviewed over 3 years At final measurement 89 unemployed in Cohort 1 and 95 in Cohort 2. Unknown time of employment and unemployment	Psychological distress (GHQ). Employment commitment	Employed group	Initial distress	Psychological distress higher for unemployed than employed. Change from employment to unemployment increases distress while change from unemployment to employment decreases distress. Employment commitment moderated these relationships with greatest distress experienced in movement from work to unemployment for those higher in unemployment commitment

TABLE 9.5 (Cont.)

Study	Sample	Nature and duration of unemployment	Psychological measures	Comparison group	Statistical control	Results
Patton and Noller (1984) (Australia)	School leavers (57 M, 56 F)	Up to 5 months unemployment ($N = 21$)	Depression Self-esteem Locus of control	Employed students	Initial scores. Sex	Unemployed increased scores on depression and became more externally controlled. Unemployed also, over time, had decreased self-esteem. After 5 months, unemployed had more depression, externality and lower self-esteem than employed and students
Tiggeman and Winefield (1980) (Australia)	62 M, 39 F, school leavers	6 months maximum unemployment. 23 never employed	Depression Locus of control. Achievement motivation Happiness Self-satisfaction Bored. Lonely	Employed	None	Unemployed, compared to employed, more bored, lonely, unhappy and had lower self-esteem. No significant differences on depression or locus of control
Tiggeman and Winefield (1984) (Australia)	School leavers. 144 unemployed 1 year later (58 M, 86 F). 617 employed (310 M, 307 F)	37.1% unemployed for less than 3 months. 42.9% unemployed for more than 6 months	Self-esteem. Depressive affect. Locus of control. Mood	Employed	Sex	Unemployed had greater negative mood and higher depression than employed. Unemployed girls decreased in self-esteem. No significant effect on locus of control. Differences between employed and unemployed largely due to increases by the employed

status was examined by measuring changes in distress since leaving school. Distress, or morbidity, increased for those who left school and experienced unemployment while it decreased for those who found employment. The results could not be attributed to sample differences in sex, ethnic group and education, as these were reasonably equivalent for both employed and unemployed groups. Using the same measure of distress, Jackson *et al.*, (1983) replicated these results for another group of school leavers who were interviewed over three years. They also showed that employment commitment moderated these relationships with greatest distress being experienced in movement from work to unemployment for those highest in employment commitment.

Although these studies provide stronger evidence for the negative effects of unemployment on young people, there are a number of problems with them. In order, these are:

1. The content of the initial interviews probably made it clear to the respondents that the study was about the effects of employment and unemployment. Hence in subsequent interviews they may have been concerned to respond in ways that they thought were expected. Neither study controlled for testing effects.

2. Neither study is able to say what aspect of unemployment or employment was responsible for change in distress scores. Was it economic factors, loss (or gain) of status, opportunities or lack of them of engaging in tasks that provided experiences in autonomy or skill-utilization?

3. The size of the effect is not considered. Neither study, for example, considers whether the mean scores of the unemployed group on the GHQ placed them at considerable risk of psychiatric disorder. Some estimate of the size of the effect can be inferred from the Jackson *et al.* study. They report correlations between GHQ and employment status which range from 0.28 to 0.46. Thus employment status accounted for between 7.8 and 21.1 per cent of the variance in GHQ. This is quite a modest amount and does not suggest that unemployment had a traumatic effect.

4. Both studies contained, in their unemployed samples, subjects who had never been employed and subjects who had experienced intermittent employment. Logically, it might be possible that increases in distress appeared only for those who had experienced employment. Those who had been continuously unemployed had never had a job so had not enjoyed the potential benefits of income and work activities. Compared to the intermittently unemployed they might have lost less. It would have been desirable for the analyses to have been conducted separately for those who had been continuously and intermittently employed.

These two studies were done in the United Kingdom and the only other longitudinal studies available come from Australian samples. Two studies by Tiggemann and Winefield (1980, 1984) showed that the unemployed had greater depressive affect than the employed. Across the two studies there were inconsistent results. In the first study it was found that the unemployed had lower self-esteem. In the second study ($N = 761$) lower self-esteem occurred for females only. Also the first study reported no significant differences in depression, but the second showed that the unemployed had higher depression than the employed. Perhaps the inconsistency is due to the relatively small size of the first sample and differences in the scales used.

One consistent finding in these two studies was that there was no significant difference between the two groups in locus of control. It was expected that a failure to obtain a valued reward, work, would induce an external locus of control. Another Australian longitudinal study did show significant differences between unemployed, employed and student samples (Patton and Noller, 1984). The unemployed, even after allowing for initial differences in samples prior to leaving school, had higher depression, lower self-esteem and a more external locus of control. While, across these three studies, there was general agreement that unemployed youth had higher depression levels than employed youth the results on locus of control results are inconsistent. Obviously more research is needed to understand how changes in locus of control might be affected by sample differences (e.g. work commitment), length and quality of unemployment.

Two other Australian studies were not concerned with distress but rather with changes in self-esteem, personality development and work values. Gurney (1980a,b) found no difference between employed and unemployed groups on self-esteem. The only significant change reported on self-esteem was an increase by girls who found employment after leaving school. Other analyses found some changes in resolution of Erikson's life stages. Unemployed males decreased significantly on 'trust-mistrust' while employed males and females improved on 'industry-inferiority'. Presumably, the nature of these changes did not affect self-esteem which would have logically been expected from Erikson's theory. This study is not strictly comparable to the others as it used only a 4-month time period—a period which included at least 6 weeks of 'vacation' time. Perhaps the strongest result is not on the short-term effects of unemployment but on the positive effects of employment for female school leavers.

Finally, Dowling and O'Brien (1981) examined changes in work values of school leavers over a period of a year. Using initial work values as covariates they examined the differences between student, employed and unemployed groups after a year. The work values measured were desired skill-utilization, desired influence and desired variety. Continuing students showed a significant rise in work values and their final values were significantly higher than those who were unemployed. There were no significant differences between employed and unemployed groups. In a later analysis (Dowling and O'Brien, 1983), they repeated the analysis with continuously employed and continuously unemployed groups.When this was done the employed showed a greater desire for skill-utilization and variety than the unemployed. This difference was partly due to a slight increase in values for the employed and a slight decrease for the unemployed.

As a set, these studies show that the effect of unemployment on school leavers is to increase their psychological distress. The greatest increase in distress is for those who have relatively higher levels of work commitment. However, the effects of unemployment on self-esteem and locus of control were somewhat inconsistent. The other main finding is that the unemployed slightly decrease their aspirations about the intrinsic characteristics of their ideal job so that these aspirations become significantly lower than those held by students and the continuously employed. So far, it is not possible to explain why the general effect of unemployment on youth is relatively slight. Perhaps it is due to the short time period of unemployment, the availability of unemployment benefits, or the relatively high youth unemployment rates which make self-blame less likely. Other possibilities also occur. If the majority of youth still live at home, then they have added financial and social supports. Future studies may show strong negative effects on personality and values if they use a longer period of unemployment. Nevertheless, short-term unemployment for youth may have subtle effects which are not being picked up by the personality and cognitive scales that are commonly used. The work of Gurney is suggestive. His study is the only one which tried to evaluate the effects of unemployment on psycho-social development. The results show that unemployment may not be causing psychological regression but rather may prevent youth from developing a sense of personal competence that is important for later adult development. The unemployed may be frozen at a particular stage of development, while their employed counterparts are progressing.

THEORETICAL APPROACHES TO UNEMPLOYMENT

The previous review leads to no simple description of the effect of unemployment. The majority of studies show that unemployment produces, in most people, a state of dissatisfaction and distress. The magnitude of this distress depends on previous job experience, work values, financial resources, age, social support, leisure activities and the length of unemployment. No theory is available at present that can encompass the complexity of these findings, although some theoretical frameworks have been used to explain particular types of behaviour such as depression or stress. Perhaps it will be futile to try to understand the implications of unemployment for psychological development by comparing the behaviour of the employed and unemployed. This comparison is somewhat like comparing the effect of schooling and the effects of working in order to understand the transition from school to work. The states being compared are too broad and will lead to a complex mass of results which will not be easily interpreted.

Many studies have concluded that unemployment is a health hazard—the subtle implication being that it is better to be employed than unemployed. But this implication cannot be maintained as a generalization. Previous chapters in this book have documented the negative effects of certain types of employment for stress, physical health and psychological development. Conversely, some studies have reported improvements in mood, health and psychological well-being when employees have become unemployed. The basic question underlying comparisons of the unemployed and employed is rarely asked. This is the question of what is the criterion of mental health, psychological well-being, or happiness? To say that employment is preferable to unemployment begs the question of why it is preferable. In what respects or for what aspect of behaviour? If there was available a sound theory of psychological development which also specified in detail the kind of task experiences that would facilitate constructive forms of development then we would be in a better position to specify what forms of employment and unemployment promote or impede psychological wholeness or integration. It is not possible to say that employment necessarily promotes psychological health because the available evidence disproves this.

Psychologists know very little about the psychological functions of work. They know much more about individual performance and job satisfaction. Yet the search for a unifying set of theories about the relationship between work structures (as they exist in employment and unemployment) seems essential for further progress in the area of unemployment. If we do not know the function of work for personality development how can we understand the dysfunctions of not working? Some writers have recognized this need and have sketched outlines of a psychological theory of employment and unemployment. Other writers, wisely perhaps, have bypassed this problem by developing specific theories that seek to explain a limited number of findings in unemployment research. They will be briefly considered first.

A. Unemployment as a Stressor

The researchers using the aggregate life-stress approach (Brenner, 1973; Catalano and Dooley, 1983) have viewed unemployment as a life stressor which determines mental strain. If this strain is prolonged it leads to physical and psychological illness. The magnitude of the strain effects is determined by various factors including social class and the magnitude of financial loss.

As unemployment continues the effect of high strain is to induce physical and psychiatric illness. This type of model is similar to the one used to explain stress in employment and is capable of explaining the general relationship between employment rates and variations in aggregate measures of population health. It has also been applied to studies of individual unemployment responses by Fineman (1983), who introduced more complexity into the model. He illustrated the potential role of coping behaviours and social support in modifying the degree of strain and anxiety. This kind of explanation seems to work best when attention is focused on the economic deprivations of unemployment, but has difficulty in explaining why the loss of normal work activities should be a stressor. It also provides no mechanism for understanding why strain associated with unemployment should determine or preclude stable changes in health.

B. Expectancy-valence Theory

The studies by Feather and Barber (1983) and Feather and Davenport (1981) have interpreted the degree of negative affect during unemployment in terms of expectancy-value theory. This type of theory has been applied to many areas of psychology and the present status of the theory is reviewed by Feather and others in a recent publication (Feather, 1982). The theory is not so much a specific theory as a general framework for understanding motivated behaviour. It assumes that a person's actions are predictable from the perceived attractiveness (positive valence) or aversiveness (negative valence) of expected outcomes. Individual behaviour and cognitions are a function of the attractiveness of valued outcomes and expectations about the instrumentality of certain behaviours in achieving these outcomes. Thus, Feather and Davenport (1981) found that depressive affect in the unemployed was greatest for those who perceived employment as very attractive and had high expectations of obtaining a job. It appears that a complex theoretical framework was not necessary to explain this finding. However, in principle, the framework could be applied to more complex behaviours if there was an associated theory of work values and a theory linking work values to expectations and behavioural intentions. So far these theories have not been developed so that explanatory power of the expectancy-valence approach is small. Attributional theory has also been used by Feather and his associates to explain variations in depression and depressive affect. This type of theory specifies that the amount of depression displayed by the unemployed will depend on the extent to which the individual attributes unemployment to external causes (e.g. economic factors) or internal causes (e.g. ability). Feather and Davenport (1981) did show that those who were most depressed were more likely to attribute unemployment to external attributions. However, attributions accounted for a small proportion of the variance in depression.

The application of attributional and expectancy theories to unemployment is still at an early stage. Neither the stress nor the expectancy-value approach deals directly with the psychological functions of employment and unemployment. Some other approaches have done this.

C. Jahoda's Functional Theory

Jahoda (1979, 1981, 1982) has recently tried to interpret the experience of unemployment in terms of a framework that is partly derived from Freudian theory. In so far as Freud and his followers consider the function of work, they consider it an economic necessity for survival and as a means whereby the individual learns about reality. Transactions with reality are mediated by the psychic mechanism that can balance instinctual urges, internalized social norms and the demands of the environment. This mechanism is the ego and many of the functions of the psychoanalytic ego are similar to the functions that Jahoda attributes to work. According to Jahoda work imposes a time structure, enlarges social experience to complement close family attachments, unites the individual with collective purposes, provides identity and enjoins activity. Jahoda is careful to point out that these functions may not be genetically based but they are functions that are required in modern civilization. The unemployed can suffer distress when their job activities, which allowed these functions to be fulfilled, are lost. These functions are called latent functions of work and together with the manifest function, income, provide the basis of psychological experience which promotes psychological development.

These functions are very general and not easily amenable to quantification. How much time structure, social purpose and identity is necessary? It is also questionable whether all types of employment satisfy these functions. Time structure is certainly imposed but is dubious if all employment provides a sense of collective purpose, rational and informative social relationships and a positive sense of identity. The explanatory power of these functions to explain personal disintegration in unemployment is also limited. Certainly some of the unemployed Jahoda studied at Marienthal suffered because of lack of income and social purpose. However, lack of suffering can also be encompassed within her framework because it can be attributed to their deliberate efforts in satisfying these requirements. To the extent that both good and bad effects can be incorporated into her framework, the framework can potentially explain too much.

What it does provide is a way of thinking about psychological deprivation in both employment and unemployment. An extension of her approach is Warr's (1983) who, unlike Jahoda, provides measurable concepts to describe 'good' and 'bad' activities. Good activities, whether in employment or unemployment, are those which provide adequate income, variety, goals, decision latitude, skill-use, low threat, interpersonal contact, and valued social position. However, like Jahoda, Warr has not yet specified why such activities are good. Presumably it is because they are associated with psychological well-being. But how does the performance of such activities shape personality in a way that promotes happiness and social adjustment? Some kind of theory of personality structure is necessary for us to understand how task experiences lead to stable behaviour that may be either constructive or destructive. A simple theory proposed by Bakke did attempt to do this.

D. Bakke's Theory of Tasks, Income and Personal Control

In the previous chapter Bakke's research on the unemployed during the Depression was described (Bakke, 1933, 1940a,b). He described the distress of the unemployed in terms of past work experiences, loss of income and reduced personal control over life satisfactions. His theoretical comments were not stated formally but tended to be consistent in emphasizing that task experiences and money shaped personality. He also argued that personal control, as an internalized belief system, was one of the central personality dimensions determined by tasks done in work and leisure. His writings appear to be useful for current research because the concept of personal control has been frequently studied by social and clinical psychologists. Much of the research has been based on Rotter's concept of internal-external control and individual variations in internal/external control have been shown to predict a wide range of behaviours (Lefcourt, 1976; Phares, 1976). By linking unemployment experiences to personal control, Bakke is able to provide a theoretical mechanism for understanding patterns of unemployment behaviour.

Bakke's writings on self-reliance and personal control resemble Rotter's (1966) statements about locus of control. Rotter, as part of his social learning theory, defined locus of control as a generalized expectancy about the extent to which reinforcements were under internal or external control. People described as internal believe that reinforcements are determined largely by personal effort, ability and initiative, whereas people classified as external believe that reinforcements are determined largely by other people, social structures, luck or fate. Much of Bakke's work describes how workers and the unemployed became externally controlled as a result of experience in social structures that determined their tasks, the way in which they were performed, and the type of rewards obtained. To the extent that they believed their lives were externally controlled, they became depressed, apathetic and restricted in their social experience. Some recent studies provide partial support for Bakke's views. A few studies have shown that the unemployed are more external that the employed (Searls, Braucht and Miskimins, 1974; O'Brien and Kabanoff, 1979, 1981; Patton and Noller, 1984), and some have also shown that the unemployed become more external with time (Parnes and King, 1977; Parnes, 1981; Patton and Noller, 1984).

These studies provide a little support for Bakke's theory in so far as they provide information about how the unemployed tend to see their lives as more controlled by external forces (other people, governments, luck, fate) than do those in employment. However, the continued use of Rotter's scale or even the alternative contemporary scales now available are unlikely to address the views of Bakke completely. The first problem is due to the fact that none of these scales adequately measures a generalized expectancy about control because they do not sample a wide range of life-spheres and typically omit items about control in work situations. Secondly, the scales themselves do not permit inferences about the extent to which the external responses made by the unemployed reflect direct perceptions of their specific situation or internalized and stable orientations. A number of writers have already suggested that changes in external locus of control scores may not reflect personality change but rather a shift toward realistic perceptions (Gorman, Jones and Holman, 1980, O'Brien and Kabanoff, 1981; Lange and Tiggemann, 1980). If this is so, then the discovery of the lack of internal control in the unemployed should not be interpreted as a psychological deficit or used to predict their vulnerability to illness or psychiatric disturbance. Bakke recognized this point by showing that his unemployed perceived, accurately in his judgement, that their lives had been further constrained by external factors. Yet this did not necessarily mean that they stopped being personally controlled in situations where they were able to use their skill, effort and foresight. Only a few were found to be apathetic, fatalistic and depressed due to a general belief that there was nothing they could do to achieve valued personal goals.

The majority of unemployed were neither internally controlled nor externally controlled in Rotter's sense but intermediate—believing that they were externally controlled in some situations but not in others. This raises another problem in contemporary locus of control research. The characteristics of middle scores are neglected partly because, in statistical analysis, it is easier to analyse differences in behaviour across two groups rather than three but also due to the strong tendency of North American research to demonstrate that internals are 'good' and externals are 'bad' on indices of performance and psychological adjustment (O'Brien, 1984).

Bakke's findings suggest that both the current concept and the method of measuring personal control should be reformulated. In general terms, the dimensions of control should allow a classification of individuals into at least internals, externals and realists (O'Brien, 1984). Both internals and externals have distorted views of social reality. The internal may show an excessive overestimation of his or her own importance and abilities in believing that, in the face of large external constraints, he or she can get what they want with sufficient motivation, effort and skill. The external distorts reality by refusing to acknowledge that there are some areas of life where personal control is still possible. The realist, on the other hand, has the wisdom to know which situations are amenable to personal control and which are not. Bakke's research indicates that most of his sample were realists in this sense and unemployment had not ruined their capacity for self-reliance but, instead, had delimited the number of life situations where personal control was possible.

This insight should prevent a headlong rush into showing that the unemployed are externally controlled, with its negative overtones of personality disorder. It should also prevent some of the excesses of rehabilitation psychologists who mistakenly believe that most of the unemployed suffer from low personal control and need training or therapy to rectify their lack of responsibility and self-control (Tiffany, Cowan and Tiffany, 1970). Not only does this appear to be an example of 'blaming the victim' syndrome, it also can be associated with a deliberate attempt to leave the labour environment producing unemployment untouched.

> Unfortunately, we feel the major efforts to help the poor will continue to take the form of changing the physical environment rather than designing programs to help them develop their own person resources.
>
> (Tiffany, Cowan and Tiffany, 1970, p. 164)

This interpretation of the problem of the unemployed basically considers that the problem is not the situation but the person. Hence the personality and behaviour of the unemployed need to be changed. This is not an isolated example. In a recent book which contains a reasonable summary of selected studies of unemployment, Hayes and Nutman (1981) seem to be oblivious of the objective reason why the unemployed are depressed when faced with external forces which prevent them working.

> It would appear that many of the unemployed, at this stage, are depressed and downhearted because they are still adopting unrealistic and irrational ideas about how their lives should be.
>
> (Hays and Nutman, 1981, p. 30)

They recommend that the depressed unemployed people undergo rational-emotive therapy so that their cognitions can be changed and they can adjust to their uncomfortable situation. There many be some point in encouraging the unemployed to try and assess what they have to do in order to make a practical realistic adjustment to life without a job. If perceptions of external control are realistic and not generalized to encompass all of their behaviours, then the available studies indicate that the unemployed *do* generally adapt to the constraints of their situation. Teaching them to alter their cognitions would be teaching them to misperceive reality. The only point to Hays and Nutman's treatment would be for those who generalize from perceptions of external control in the area of work to all of their personal existence. This generalization is not a logical extrapolation and it *might* be amenable to rational-emotive therapy or counselling designed, by concrete tasks, to show that certain valued rewards are attainable by personal effort.

E. Bakke and Jahoda

Jahoda sought to explain the psychological effects of unemployment by reference to the functions of employment. She distinguished the manifest function, income, from the latent functions—time structure, social identity, activity and social status. Typically, these functions are not met in unemployment and hence the psychological development of the unemployed worker is impeded. One surprising omission is a discussion of the *content* of work. The writings of Bakke suggest that psychological development of the unemployed worker had already been largely shaped by the content of their work. Semi-skilled and unskilled manual workers had experienced jobs that did not use their skills, gave little opportunity to control task processes and provided minimal income. These jobs had 'damaged' them and produced orientations that explained much of their behaviour in a state of unemployment. Thus many of the behavioural deficits that Jahoda attributes to unemployment may not be attributable to the loss of the job activities, but to past job experience. This hypothesis is not considered at all by Jahoda. Possibly this is due to a reliance on the early Marienthal study which concentrated on the mood and activities of the unemployed without seeking to establish at all the kind of work that the unemployed had previously experienced. Furthermore, Bakke's writings suggest that income and past job experiences could largely explain unemployment behaviour. The question here is not just one of who is right—Bakke or Jahoda—but rather the theoretical and practical consequences of Jahoda's position.

Jahoda is aware that much contemporary work is de-humanizing (Jahoda, 1982). Nevertheless, the theoretical assumptions of her position lead to studies showing the extent to which the unemployed lack time structure, social purpose, meaningful activity and 'well-being'. They do not lead to any consideration of how past employment modifies or even determines adjustment to unemployment. At best there will be studies on the 'well-being' of the unemployed which are disjointed or separated from studies on the 'well-being' of the employed. There will not be an attempt to show how the actual tasks in both states affect psychological functioning nor will there be any studies designed to test Bakke's propositions about the effects of employment upon unemployment behaviour. The practical effect of Jahoda's position is to recommend that the unemployed be given a job—any job.

Bakke does not make any explicit recommendations about the utility of 'poor' jobs for relieving the burdens on the unemployed. He leaves the reader to decide the theoretical and practical implications of his work. Unfortunately he has either not been read, or worse, he has been misread. It appears that present psychological research on unemployment could benefit from a rediscovery of Bakke. The dominant assumptions about unemployment are based on a simple psychological deprivation model that will lead only to descriptive studies. Their findings will only be explained by a theory about the functions of work and employment. Jahoda's theory of latent work functions is not equipped for this role because it omits the crucial element of employment—the content of the tasks. Put another way, it is not possible to ask how the absence of work tasks affects people unless you know the psychological functions of work. This is one of the main insights made by Bakke. It leads to new and difficult questions about the nature of unemployment but they are ones that promise to give new life to an area that tends to concentrate on the negative psychological states induced by unemployment without concomitant examination of the function of task activities for psychological development.

REFERENCES

Aiken, M., Ferman, L.A.. and Sheppard, H.L. (1968). *Economic Failure, Alienation and Extremism*, Ann Arbor, University of Michigan Press

Bakke, E.W. (1933). *The Unemployed Man: A Social Study*, London: Nisbet

Bakke, E.W. (1940a). *Citizens Without Work: A Study of the Effects of Unemployment upon the Workers' Social Relations and Practices*, New Haven: Yale University Press

Bakke, E.W. (1940b). *The Unemployed Worker: A Study of the Task of Making a Living Without a Job*, New Haven: Yale University Press

Banks, M.H. and Jackson, P.R. (1982). Unemployment and risk of minor psychiatric disorder in young people: cross-sectional and longitudinal evidence, *Psychological Medicine*, **12**, 789–98

Borrero, I.M. (1980). Psychological and emotional impact of unemployment, *Journal of Sociology and Social Welfare*, **7**, 916–34

Brenner, M.H. (1973). *Mental Illness and Economy*, Cambridge, Mass.: Harvard University Press.

Brenner, M.H. (1976). *Estimating the Social Costs of National Economic Policy: Implications for Mental and Physical Health and Criminal Aggression*, Joint Economic Committee of Congress, Paper No. 5. Washington, D.C.: U.S. Government Printing Office

Brenner, M.H. (1979). Influence of the social environment on psychopathology: the historic perspective, in J.E. Barrett, R.M. Rose and G.L. Klerman (eds), *Stress and Mental Disorder*, New York: Raven Press

Catalano, R. and Dooley, D. (1977). Economic predictors of depressed mood and stressful life events in a metropolitan community, *Journal of Health and Social Behavior*, **18**, 293–307

Catalano, R. and Dooley, D. (1983). Health effects of economic instability: a test of economic stress hypothesis, *Journal of Health and Social Behavior*, **24**, 41–60

Cobb, S. (1974). Physiological changes in men whose jobs were abolished, *Journal of Psychosomatic Research*, **18**, 245–58

Cobb, S. and Kasl, S.V. (1977). *Termination: The Consequences of Job Loss*, Cincinatti: U.S. Department of Health, Education and Welfare

Cohn, R.M. (1978) The effect of employment status change on self-attitudes, *Social Psychology Quarterly*, **41**, 81–93

Dayton, N.A. (1940). *New Facts on Mental Disorders*, Springfield, Ill.: Charles C. Thomas

Dooley, C. and Catalano, R. (1980). Economic change as a cause of behavioral disorder, *Psychological Bulletin*, **87**, 450–68

Dowling, P. and O'Brien, G.E. (1981). The effects of employment, unemployment and further education upon the work values of school leavers, *Australian Journal of Psychology*, **33**, 185–95

Dowling, P. and O'Brien, G.E. (1983). The work values of unemployed and employed youth: a reply to Rump, *Australian Journal of Psychology*, **35**, 91–6

Dunham, H.W. (1959). *Sociological Theory and Mental Disorder*, Detroit: Wayne State University Press

Feather N.T. (1982). Unemployment and its psychological correlates: a study of depressive symptoms, self-esteem, protestant ethic values, attributional style, and apathy, *Australian Journal of Psychology*, **34**, 309–23

Feather, N,.T. (ed.) (1982). *Expectations and Actions: Expectancy-value Models in Psychology*, Hillsdale, H.J.: Erlbaum

Feather, N.T. and Barber, J.G. (1983). Depressive reactions and unemployment, *Journal of Abnormal Psychology*, **92**, 185–95

Feather, N.T. and Bond, M.J. (1983). Time structure and purposeful activity among employed and unemployed university graduates, *Journal of Occupational Psychology*. **56**, 241–54

Feather, N.T. and Davenport, P.R. (1981) Unemployment and depressive affect: a motivational and attributional analysis, *Journal of Personality and Social Psychology*. **41**, 422–36

Fineman, S. (1983). *White Collar Unemployment*, Chichester: Wiley

Fraser, C. (1981). The social psychology of unemployment, in M. Jeeves (ed.), *Psychology Survey No. 3*, London: George Allen & Unwin

Goldberg, D. (1972). *The Detection of Psychiatric Illness by Questionnaire*, London: Oxford University Press

Gore, S. (1978). The effects of social support in moderating the health consequences of unemployment, *Journal of Health and Social Behavior*, **19**, 157–65

Gorman, R., Jones, L. and Holman, I. (1980). Generalizing American locus of control norms to Australian populations: a warning, *Australian Psychologist*, **15**, 125–7

Gurney, R. (1980a). Does unemployment affect the self-esteem of school leavers? *Australian Journal of Psychology*, **32**, 175–82

Gurney, R. (1980b). The effects of unemployment on the psycho-social development of school leavers, *Journal of Occupational Psychology*, **53**, 205–13

Hartley, J. (1980a). The personality of unemployed managers: myths and measurement, *Personnel Review*, **9**, 12–18

Hartley, J. (1980b). Psychological approaches to unemployment, *Bulletin of the British Psychological Society*, **33**, 412–14

Hartley, J. (1980c). The impact of unemployment upon the self-esteem of managers, *Journal of Occupational Psychology*, **53**, 147–55

Hartley, J. and Freyer, D. (1984). The psychology of unemployment: a critical appraisal, in G. Stephenson and J. Davis (eds), *Progress in Applied Social Psychology*, vol. 2, Chichester: Wiley
Hartston, W.R. and Mottram, R.D. (1975). *Personality Profiles of Managers: A Study of Occupational Differences*, ITRU: Cambridge
Hayes, J. and Nutman, P. (1981). *Understanding the Unemployed: Psychological Effects of Unemployment*, London: Tavistock
Hepworth S.J. (1980). Moderating factors of the psychological impact of unemployment, *Journal of Occupational Psychology*, **53**, 139–46
Jackson, P.R., Stafford, E.M., Banks, M.H. and Warr, P.B. (1983). Unemployment and psychological distress in young people: the moderating role of employment commitment, *Journal of Applied Psychology*, **68**, 525–35
Jahoda, M. (1979). The impact of unemployment in the 1930s and 1970s, *Bulletin of the British Psychological Society*, **32**, 309–14
Jahoda, M. (1981). Work, employment, and unemployment: values, theories and approaches in social research, *American Psychologist*, **36**(2), 184–91
Jahoda, M. (1982). *Employment and Unemployment: A Social-psychological Analysis*, Cambridge: Cambridge University Press
Kasl, S.V. (1979). Changes in mental health status associated with job loss and retirement, in M.E. Barrett, R.M. Rose and G.L. Klerman, (eds), *Stress and Mental Disorder*, New York: Raven Press
Kasl, S.V. and Cobb, S. (1982). Variability of stress effects among men experiencing job loss, Chapter 26 in L. Goldberger and S. Breznitz (eds), *Handbook of Stress: Theoretical and Clinical Aspects*, New York: Free Press
Komora, P.O. and Clark, M.A. (1935). Mental disease in the crisis, *Mental Hygiene*, **19**, 289–301
Lange, R. and Tiggemann, M. (1980). Changes within the Australian population to more external control beliefs, *Australian Psychologist*, **15**, 495–7
Lefcourt, H.M. (1976). *Locus of Control: Current Trends in Theory and Research*, New York: Wiley
Little, C.B. (1976). Technical-professional unemployment: Middle-class adaptability to personal crisis, *Sociological Quarterly*, **17**, 262-74
Macky, K. and Haines, H. (1982). The psychological effects of unemployment: a review of the literature, *New Zealand Journal of Industrial Relations*, **7**, 123-5
Malzberg, B. (1940). *Social and Biological Aspects of Mental Disease*, New York: State Hospitals Press
Menderhausen, H. (1946). *Changes in Income Distribution during the Great Depression*, New York: National Bureau
Mowrer, E.R. (1939). A study of personal disorganization, *American Sociological Review*, **4**, 475–87
O'Brien, G.E. (1984). Locus of control, work, and retirement, in H.M. Lefcourt (ed.), *Research with the Locus of Control Construct*, vol.3, New York: Academic Press
O'Brien, G.E. and Kabanoff, B. (1979). Comparison of unemployed and employed workers on work values, locus of control, and health variables, *Australian Psychologist*, **14**, 143–54
O'Brien, G.E. and Kabanoff, B. (1981). Australian norms and factor analyses of Rotter's internal-external control scale, *Australian Psychologist*, **16** 184–202
Oliver, J.M. and Pomicter, C. (1981). Depression in automotive assembly-line workers as a function of unemployment variables, *American Journal of Community Psychology*, **89**, 507–72

Parnes, H.S. (1981). *Work and Retirement: A Longitudinal Study of Men*, Cambridge, Mass.: The M.L.T. Press

Parnes, H.S. and King, R. (1977). Middle-aged job losers, *Industrial Gerontology*, **4**, 77–95

Patton, W. and Noller, P. (1984). Unemployment and youth: a longitudinal study, *Australian Journal of Psychology*, **36**, 399–413

Pearlin, L.I. and Lieberman, M.A. (1979). Social sources of emotional distress, in R.G. Simmons (ed.), *Research in Community and Mental Health*, Vol. 1, Greenwich, Connect.: J.A.I. Press, pp. 217–48

Phares, E.J. (1976). *Locus of Control in Personality*, Morristown, N.J.: General Learning Press

Pollock, H.M. (1935). The Depression and mental disease in New York State, *American Journal of Psychiatry*, **91**, 736–71

Pugh, T.F. and MacMahon, B. (1962). *Epidemiologic Findings in United States Mental Hospital Data*, Boston: Little & Brown

Rotter, J.B. (1966). Generalized expectancies for internal versus external control of reinforcement, *Psychological Monographs*, **80**, 1–28

Searls, D.J., Braucht, G.N. and Miskimins, R.W. (1974). Work values of the chronically unemployed, *Journal of Applied Psychology*, **59**, 93–5

Stafford, E.M., Jackson, P.R. and Banks, M. (1980). Employment, work involvement and mental health in less qualified young people, *Journal of Occupational Psychology*, **53**, 291–304

Stokes, G. and Cochrane, R. (1984). A study of the psychological effects of redundancy and unemployment, *Journal of Occupational Psychology*, **57**, 309–22

Swinburne, P. (1981). The psychological impact of unemployment on managers and professional staff, *Journal of Occupational Psychology*, **54**, 47–64

Tiffany, D.W., Cowan, J.R. and Tiffany, P.M. (1970). *The Unemployed: A Sociopsychological Portrait*, New Jersey: Prentice-Hall

Tiggemann, M. and Winefield, A.H. (1980). Some psychological effects of unemployment in school leavers, *Australian Journal of Social Issues*, **15**, 269–76

Tiggemann, M. and Winefield, A.H. (1984). The effects of unemployment on the mood, self-esteem, locus of control and depressive affect of school leavers, *Journal of Occupational Psychology*, **57**, 33–42

Trew, K. and Kilpatrick, R. (1983). *The Daily Life of the Unemployed, Department of Psychology*, Queen's University of Belfast

Warr, P.B. (1978). A study of psychological well-being, *British Journal of Psychology*, **69**, 111–21

Warr, P.B. (1983). Work, jobs and unemployment, *Bulletin of the British Psychological Society*, **36**, 305–11

Warr, P.B. and Jackson, P. (1984). Men without jobs: some correlates of age and length of unemployment, *Journal of Occupational Psychology*, **57**, 77–85

Warr, P.B. and Payne, R.L. (1983). Social class and reported changes in behavior after job loss, *Journal of Applied Social Psychology*, **13**, 206–22

CHAPTER 10

Work, Leisure and Retirement

The relationship between work and leisure has a long intellectual history.[1] Classical Greek writers maintained that work was an unfortunate necessity and a matter of sorrow (*ponos*). It prevented the contemplation of truth and beauty that could only be properly engaged in when the individual had free time or leisure that was not intruded upon by physical, clerical and administrative work. In classical Greek society it was only the wealthy citizens and philosophers who were able to follow, without distraction, the pursuit of knowledge and personal fulfilment whereas the slaves and artisans were left, it was thought, at an impoverished level of psychological development.

The creative and recreational function of leisure was stressed by some writers and unionists during the onset of the industrial revolution but the meaning given to terms like 'leisure', 'play', 'recreation and 'free time' during the nineteenth and twentieth centuries depended on particular economic and historical circumstances (Hunnicutt, 1980). Although there is evidence that many workers in nineteenth-century England actually used free time as a means of personal development and as a way of developing working-class culture (Cunningham, 1980; Thompson, 1968), this did not develop into a popular movement due to increasing social control of leisure and political activity. Also those who were working in the new factories had relatively little time and energy for self-directed activity after work.

The public debate about the function of free time emerged only when there was a sharp decrease in working hours. From the beginning of the twentieth century working hours in industrialized nations steadily decreased. The largest decline took place in the first 20 years of the twentieth century. In the United States, for example, the average work week dropped from 58 to 48 hours a week and the decline since then has been slower and now appears to have levelled out at about 40 hours. The increased abundance of free time in the present century generated a debate about the functions of free-time for the working population.[2] Until fairly recently there were

251

few writers, employees and managers who saw free time as a period where people could choose activities that provided them with personal fulfilment denied them at work. The common view was that free time was important for work efficiency and the maintenance of physical health. Politicians and reformers frequently saw free time as an opportunity for employees to improve their health and strengthen family bonds. Businessmen gradually accepted shorter working hours on grounds of efficiency rather than the positive virtues of free time. They were influenced by industrial consultants such as Frederic Taylor who believed that employee efficiency declined after about eight hours work. In the early part of the century the creative personal function of leisure was not a public issue. Some, such as Veblen (1899), actually counselled against increases in leisure since it could lead to employees mimicking the self-indulgent life of 'conspicuous consumption' adopted by capitalist owners.

The positive virtues of leisure were raised by unionists who, after the First World War, campaigned for reduction in hours. Not only would shorter hours, for them, decrease unemployment and raise the value of labour, shorter hours would also compensate men for poor jobs. In the United States, unionists believed that machines and management techniques had reduced the capacity of work to provide psychological growth. Their reaction to these changes in work did not lead to large-scale protests about the negative effects of work but to a demand that leisure be seen as a way of compensating for work that was destroying craftsmanship, personal control and creativity.

The arguments lost their impetus after the Great Depression of the 1930s. This occurred for a number of reasons. One reason was that leisure came to be associated with the misery of unemployment. 'The shorter hour movement and the share-the-work movement were both branded as regressive and cosmetic devices to disguise the tragedy of unemployment by distributing its misery' (Hunnicutt, 1980, p. 207). Furthermore economic growth was seen by economists and businessmen as dependent on increased consumer demand that could only be generated by increased work and wages. According to this view, increases in leisure would militate against economic growth.

Leisure as a social issue has begun to emerge again with the onset of increasing unemployment. Recently Jenkins and Sherman in *The Collapse of Work* (1979) argued that the modern situation requires us to rethink the nature of work and leisure. Recession, technological change and the decline of the manufacturing industries have led to unemployment rates which doom millions of workers to a life where paid employment will not be a possibility. Their adjustment to unemployment is poor because, they argue, their belief in the importance of work prevents them from seeing their increased free time as an opportunity for creative leisure. Their work orientation is not innate but a conditioned response that has been reinforced by education, social pressures and the trade unions. Leisure has not been emphasized as a source of life satisfaction or as an activity that can be constructive for society as well as the person. This does not mean that all that is necessary is the development of leisure.

> There needs to be a revolution in attitudes to match the third industrial revolution. This must primarily be in relation to work and leisure. We need to guarantee security; we need international action and co-operation; we need to re-establish control over our lives and we need to plan our responses to the future.
>
> (Jenkins and Sherman, 1979, p. 173)

Social scientists have also argued that leisure studies are necessary in order to establish its potential for personal development as, and if, working time decreases. We need to identify the quality of leisure that can compensate the individual who may, in the future, have little work to do and that work may be of poor quality (e.g. Dumazedier, 1967; Fourastie, 1965; Emery, 1977).

Others have argued that it is necessary to study leisure in order to understand work. Social scientists have tried to identify the general nature of jobs that could improve the quality of working life. As leisure activities are typically chosen to allow autonomy and personal fulfilment, then the study of leisure activities could help identify the dimension of jobs that, in a sense, could turn work into play or leisure (Csikszentmihalyi, 1975; Dunnette, 1973; Porter, Lawler and Hackman, 1975).

The call for a redirection of orientations towards leisure assumes that reconditioning might be a fairly simple matter of changing self-awareness through public education. However, existing work structures may have left enduring effects on values and personality that will prevent individuals from having the capacity to change their leisure behaviour. Hence another reason for examining leisure is to establish the manner in which work experiences have shaped leisure needs and behaviours. Has work a dominant influence on non-work activities or is there independence between the two sets of activities? Or is it possible that leisure is indeed an unrecognized source of compensation for deprivations at work?

WORK, EMPLOYMENT AND LEISURE

At a general level, work is the exertion of effort in the performance of a task. Hence work can occur either in paid employment, in household maintenance activities, or in the pursuit of hobby or leisure pastimes. Although this distinction between work and employment is frequently made the common usage of the term 'work' refers to paid employment. People 'go to work' and relax in their free time after work. Common usage will be adopted here in the discussion of work–leisure relationships but it is acknowledged that work, in a general sense, is expended during the performance of any task. The problem of distinguishing work activities in employment from activities outside employment has been examined in a variety of ways. The simplest approach has been to define them in terms of the social setting and the meaning ascribed to the activities. Work, in employment, involves the performance of prescribed tasks associated with a position in a work organization. The organization is usually considered to be a work organization if there is a contract specifying that wages are to be paid for a specified amount of work. Whereas activities in work organization are largely imposed and evaluated by agents external to the individual, activities in free time are selected by the individual to satisfy personal goals and needs. The main problem with the separation of activities into those associated with work and free time is that free-time activities include activities not usually associated with leisure. Outside work organizations, people travel to and from home, they sleep, wash, eat and maintain household property. These tasks have the quality of necessity and it is necessary to distinguish them from leisure tasks which are freely chosen, relaxing and pleasurable. This means then that leisure activities are the residual tasks performed after work and maintenance activities.

A contrary view is that leisure cannot be defined by activities and tasks because leisure is a state of mind (De Grazia, 1964; Neulinger, 1974). We are at leisure, according to such views, when we choose activities that result in a state of enjoyment. Thus it is possible for people to be at leisure when they are working for others. Conversely, non-work activities may not be leisure ones even if they are freely chosen. If they become tedious or too stressful they cease to be leisure activities.

This subjective approach has the advantage of looking at work and leisure in a way that could eliminate the value overtones of the distinction between work and leisure. Work activities are not necessarily unpleasant but can become pleasurable if they are experienced as freely chosen, are enjoyable and use one's talents. However, the main disadvantage of this framework is that it makes the study of the relationship between work and leisure extremely difficult. Any given activity may be classified as a leisure activity provided that the mental state of the actor is one of enjoyment in the expression of valued capacities. In order to study leisure it would be necessary to have continuous access to the mental state of the actor and this would be very difficult. And it is doubtful that such peak mental experiences are a stable and continuous product of activities that are freely chosen and challenging. Even our most enjoyable activities often require periods of neutral emotion and even some unpleasantness. A keen gardener may be delighted when contemplating and tending his flowers but is unlikely to be in a state of ecstasy when digging, fertilizing and weeding.

A preferable way of studying the relationship between work and leisure is to define them as tasks performed in different social settings (Kabanoff and O'Brien, 1980). This does not preclude the possibility of investigating the mental states associated with these tasks. The task attribute approach allows comparisons to be made between work and leisure tasks—provided some common task attributes have been defined which allow inferences to be made about their similarities and differences. This is an important advantage because much of the work and leisure literature assumes that people either generalize from or compensate for work activities. But what do they generalize from? And what do they compensate for? Generalization implies similarity in work and leisure activities while compensation implies some form of difference. It is probable that difficulties in integration of the literature in this area are due to the failure of most writers to specify the dimensions on which work and leisure activities can be compared.

The two main hypotheses about the effect of work on leisure attributes are derived from the writings of Engels (1892) and Marx (1844). Engels saw some of the excesses of the nineteenth-century English working man as providing release or compensation for work activities that provided little opportunity for autonomy and self-expression. Drinking and sexual promiscuity were, for Engels, leisure activities that provided some degree of self-expression that compensated for the monotony of simplified and externally controlled work tasks. Engels clearly saw the compensations of the English working class as being self-destructive but later writers have defined compensation as a more positive process whereby employees choose, in leisure, activities which provide creative self-expression that is denied them at work (Kando and Summers, 1971; Parker, 1976).

A contrasting hypothesis is that employees choose leisure activities that are similar to those performed at work. This hypothesis was not stated formally by Marx but it is implicit in some of his writings on alienation from work. For him, the working man had the opportunity to be himself only in leisure since the effects of working separated him from his tasks, his coworkers and knowledge of his inner needs. Powerless to fulfil his needs at work and physically exhausted by his job he tended to choose activities that were consistent with his sense of powerlessness. He did not pursue knowledge or engage in creative political, social or artistic activities. Like his work, his leisure was marked by routine, involved little skill, and was shaped by external influences.There has been some support for both compensation and generalization hypothesis but no studies have been able to identify clearly the conditions under which one or the other hypothesis applies. Mansfield and Evans (1975) found some support for compensation while other studies have found that generalization from work to leisure is the dominant pattern (e.g. Kohn and Schooler, 1973; Kornhauser, 1965; Meissner, 1971; Rousseau, 1978). The relationships between work and leisure appear to be fairly weak

TABLE 10.1 Verbal description of work–leisure groups based on discriminant analysis

Group	Influence	Variety	Attribute pressure	Skill-utilization	Interaction
Low work/low leisure (generalization)	Low income, low intrinsic work orientation, high extrinsic work orientation, low education, male single	Low intrinsic work orientation, high extrinsic work orientation, male, low income, work shorter hours, younger	Low income, low intrinsic work orientation, older, high extrinsic work orientation, children < 15, external	Low income, low intrinsic work orientation, male, external, low education	Male, younger, internal, high income
Low work/high leisure (supplemental compensation)	Female, older, internal, low income, low extrinsic work orientation, children < 15 years	Female, older, internal	Work shorter hours, low extrinsic work orientation, internal, younger, no children < 15 years	Low extrinsic work orientation, work shorter hours, high intrinsic work orientation, younger, low income	Low income, male, children < 15 years

| High work/low leisure (reactive compensation) | Male, younger, external, high income, high extrinsic work orientation, no children < 15 years | Male, younger, external | Work longer hours, single, high extrinsic work orientation, external, older, children < 15 years | High extrinsic work orientation, work longer hours. low intrinsic work orientation, older, high income | Female, older. external. lower income |
| High work/high leisure (generalization) | High income, high intrinsic work orientation, low extrinsic work orientation, high education, female, married | High intrinsic work orientation, low extrinsic work orientation, female, high income, work longer hours, older | High income, high intrinsic work orientation, younger, low extrinsic work orientation, no children < 15, internal | High income, high intrinsic work orientation, female, internal, high education | Male, younger. internal, high income |

From Kabanoff and O'Brien (1980), p. 604.

and this has led some writers to advocate a third interpretation. This is that work and leisure form fairly distinct and independent role systems (Bacon, 1975; Dubin, 1956, 1958, 1973; London, Crandall and Seals, 1977).

The relevance of most of these studies to an understanding of work–leisure relationships can be questioned. Except for the study by Rousseau (1978), no attempt was made to compare work and leisure activities on the same dimensions. Objective comparison of the quality of work and leisure was not possible. The Rousseau study did support the generalization hypothesis but the results could have been due to correlated response errors as respondents described their work and leisure on very similar scales (Kabanoff, 1980).

In order to overcome some of these difficulties, a recent study used different methods to measure the attributes of work and leisure activities (Kabanoff and O'Brien, 1980). Work attributes were measured on skill-utilization, influence, variety, interaction and pressure using self-report ratings developed in earlier studies (O'Brien, 1980, 1982). Leisure activities were identified by employees from a checklist of 93 different activities. All of these activities were classified by independent raters using the same task attributes as were used by respondents to describe their jobs. Thus it was possible to compare directly the respondents' task attributes with rated leisure attributes.

The study was not only designed to assess the degree of similarity in work and leisure attributes. It was also designed to explore the mechanism by which work could affect leisure. The literature on work alienation suggested that work that allowed little skill-utilization and influence could produce a stable belief in external control. Employees with a belief that their life satisfaction was largely determined by other people or luck would be less likely to seek leisure activities that required self-direction—that is, activities high on skill-utilization and influence. They would then be expected to display a generalization pattern in their work and leisure. Such a pattern should also be evident in the work and leisure of those employees who had jobs high on skill-utilization and influence. These jobs encouraged the development of a stable belief in internal control over life satisfaction. Believing that they were capable of achieving personal rewards by choice, effort and other ability, they would choose leisure activities high in skill-utilization and influence.

It was also argued that supplemental compensation for impoverished work might occur for employees who experienced low skill-utilization and influence but had maintained a strong belief in internal control. A final work–leisure pattern was reactive compensation. This would occur when people in relatively demanding jobs that used their skills fully, actively chose leisure that required little personal control and skill.

The correlation between work and leisure attributes for a large sample of Australian employees drawn from a wide range of occupations was quite small. To some extent, this might be interpreted as evidence for a segmentalist position. However, belief in internal or external control, as measured by Rotter's scale (1966), was a significant predictor of leisure attributes. Internals were more likely to choose activities requiring greater skill-utilization, influence, variety and pressure. In order to see if control beliefs distinguished between people who adopted different work-leisure patterns, some further analyses were conducted. Table 10.1 shows the variables that discriminated between the different forms of generalization and compensation.

These results show that the adoption of a given work–leisure pattern is determined by many variables including income, gender, education, marital status, locus of control beliefs and work orientation. In this study work orientation was measured by the relative importance to the employee of intrinsic rewards (e.g. job satisfaction, challenge) compared to extrinsic rewards (e.g. pay, security). However, there is some support for the effect of personal control beliefs on the relationship between work and leisure activities. This is strongest for the attribute of skill-utilization. Employees in low skill-utilization jobs tend to be externally controlled and tend to have low skill-utilization in their leisure. The results are only suggestive of the manner in which the form of work–leisure relationships is formed by control beliefs. The study is a cross sectional one and cannot provide strong evidence to demonstrate that work determines control beliefs which, in turn, determine choice of leisure activities.

Certainly the results cannot be used to support theories that predict a general negative effect of poor-quality jobs on leisure (e.g. Emery, 1977; Gardell, 1976; Meissner, 1971). Many people with poor-quality jobs had high-quality leisure. Whether or not people are generalizers or compensators depends on their personal characteristics. Some of these characteristics, such as control beliefs and work orientation, might depend on the degree to which they have experienced certain types of jobs but longitudinal research is required to demonstrate that work attributes actually determine leisure attributes through a process of personality shaping.[3] It may be argued that it is necessary to establish the function of leisure for different individuals. The task attribute approach to leisure may omit the attributes that individuals, themselves, see as important. Some research on this problem has been conducted and it shows that while there are considerable individual differences in leisure needs, there is also general similarity in the extent to which leisure satisfaction is determined by task attributes.

LEISURE NEEDS AND LEISURE SATISFACTION

Leisure needs are partly shaped by work experiences and partly by other factors such as personality (Crandall, 1980; Kabanoff, 1982; Tinsley, Barrett and Kass, 1977), the social environment (Cheek and Burch, 1976; Kelley,

1978), and demographic variable such as age, sex, marital status and socio-economic standing (e.g. Gentry and Doering, 1979; Kabanoff and O'Brien, 1982; Rapoport and Rapoport, 1975).

The general implication of these results is that an individual's leisure needs can vary considerably. Although this is true it does not necessarily imply that there are no general attributes of leisure activities that are important for all people. The content of the activity may vary but the type of activity may be constant. For example, relaxation may be important for most people but the form of the activity may vary. Some people might relax via reading, others by jogging and others by playing chess. Individual differences in personality, socialization and occupation might determine the form of the activity but the function of the activity might be similar.

A contrary view is that the leisure needs and functions depend on a person's occupation. The generalization or spillover hypothesis would predict, for example, that people who experience low autonomy, skill-utilization and variety in their occupations would choose leisure activities that do not require high levels of autonomy, skill-utilization and variety. Compensation, if of the supplemental kind, would mean that people in lower quality jobs would seek out activities high in autonomy, skill-utilization and variety. If either generalization or compensation hypotheses are confirmed, then it means that there should be considerable differences in leisure needs and leisure satisfaction across various occupations that vary in job quality.

A recent study provided evidence that bears on this problem (Kabanoff, 1982). Using a cluster sample of employed people who were chosen to vary in socio- economic status and occupation, Kabanoff measured the extent to which employees used their leisure to satisfy various needs. The eleven needs are shown in Table 10.2 and were partly derived from Crandall (1980) and partly from an analysis of work needs and satisfactions. People were asked to rate the extent to which they used their leisure time to meet each need. Leisure satisfaction was measured with items from Beard and Ragheb's (1980) leisure satisfaction scale. The scale measures satisfaction with six different aspects of leisure: psychological, educational, social, relaxation, physiological and aesthetic.

Table 10.2 shows the leisure needs ranked from most to least frequent. Autonomy, relaxation and family activity are the most important leisure needs as rated by respondents while esteem, competition and social power are the least important needs. There were only a few occupational differences in leisure needs. Professional employees had higher needs on skill-utilization and autonomy than clerical or blue-collar employees.

Kabanoff recognized that what employees *say* is important in their leisure, does not necessarily predict their satisfaction with leisure. Just as people do not always have insight into what really determines their work satisfaction, so also they may not understand what attributes of their leisure activities predict

TABLE 10.2   Leisure needs and items used to measure them

Leisure needs	Items comprising need scale	Mean	Standard Deviation
1. Autonomy	Organize own projects and activities. Do things you find personally meaningful	6.17	1.66
2. Relaxation	Relax and take it easy. Give mind and body a rest	6.15	1.71
3. Family activity	Bring family closer together. Enjoy family life	6.11	2.17
4. Escape from routine	Get away from responsibilities of everyday life. Have a change from daily routine	5.97	1.14
5. Interaction	Make new friends. Enjoy people's company	5.90	1.78
6. Stimulation	To have new and different experiences. For excitement and stimulation	5.54	1.97
7. Skill-utilization	Use skills and abilities. Develop new skills and abilities	5.51	1.85
8. Health	Keep physically fit for health reasons	4.93	1.92
9. Esteem	Gain respect or admiration of others. Show others what you are capable of	4.26	2.06
10. Challenge/competition	Be involved in competition. Test yourself in difficult or demanding situations	4.18	1.93
11. Leadership/Social power	Organize activities of teams, groups or organizations. To gain positions of leadership	3.28	1.68

Notes : 1. Means based on sample of 210
2. All scales gave range 2–10
3. Median reliability of scales = 0.65 (alpha).
4. Correlation between scales varies from 0.56 to −0.01.

After Kabanoff (1982).

their leisure satisfaction. When leisure needs were correlated with leisure satisfaction it was found that the leisure needs considered, by respondents, to be important were not the most important predictors of leisure satisfaction.

Four leisure needs contributed significantly and positively to leisure satisfaction—skill-utilization, health, interaction, and autonomy, while one is negatively related—esteem. Skill-utilization clearly has the strongest relation to leisure satisfaction accounting for 26% of the total variance.

(Kabanoff, 1982, p. 239)

The dominance of skill-utilization occurred across all occupational groups. There were no significant differences in overall leisure satisfaction between occupations and it is therefore clear that a substantial amount of the variance in leisure satisfaction within occupations was attributable to variations in the capacity of the employee to use leisure to exercise abilities or learn new ones. There were a few interesting sex differences. Females rated interaction needs more highly than males while males tended to rate competition needs more highly. However, for both males and females skill-utilization was a relatively strong predictor of leisure satisfaction.

The major conclusions of this study were that :

1. Individuals tend to rate autonomy, relaxation and family activities as the most important functions of their leisure.
2. The rated importance of leisure needs does not predict leisure satisfaction. Rather leisure satisfaction is high to the extent that leisure activities involve skill-utilization, promote health and allow reasonably high levels of interpersonal contact and autonomy.
3. Occupational differences in leisure needs, leisure satisfaction and sources of leisure satisfaction are not large.

This is contrary to the expectations of those who would promote a generalization or compensation view of leisure. This does not necessarily mean that leisure is unrelated to work activities. Although work activities may have a small direct effect on leisure needs, the attributes of work that determine satisfaction are similar to the attributes of leisure that determine leisure satisfaction. It seems that most people are satisfied with activities, either at work or play, that allow them to use their abilities and provide a reasonable amount of personal control or autonomy. Although skill-utilization and autonomy are important for all occupational groups, there seems to be some characteristics of jobs, or the people who hold them, that make these factors more important. Professional people experience skill-utilization as a very strong predictor of their leisure satisfaction. As professional occupations have the highest level of job skill-utilization (Kabanoff and O'Brien, 1982) it suggests that the regular experience of skill-utilization at work engenders a greater desire for, and appreciation of, skill-utilization outside work.

LEISURE AND RETIREMENT

The previous section showed that the characteristics of job activities that determined job satisfaction were also the characteristics of leisure that determined the leisure satisfaction of employed men and women. It also showed that people were more likely to enjoy leisure to the extent that their jobs provided them with opportunities for skill-utilization and autonomy. These findings on the effect of work activities on non-leisure attributes and leisure enjoyment can be used to understand retirement—which is commonly seen as either voluntary or socially enforced unemployment.

There is a large amount of research on the life satisfaction of retired people (Adams, 1971; Chatfield, 1977; Fine, 1975; Larson, 1978; Lemon, Bengston and Peterson, 1972; Maddox and Eisdorfer, 1962; Markides and Martin, 1979; Medley, 1976; Spreitzer and Snyder, 1973), but few studies have investigated the relationship between the quality of retirement activities and retirement satisfaction. Some authors claim that retirees give the same meaning to leisure as they once gave to work (Havighurst, 1977; Kleemeier, 1961). This could mean that the dimensions of work that gave them satisfaction should also be the dimensions of leisure that predict satisfaction in retirement.

Few studies have directly examined this, although a number of factors have been shown to affect satisfaction and adjustment to retirement. These include health, finances, personality, and amount of interaction and activity (Lemon, Bengston and Peterson 1972; Markides and Martin, 1979). In order to investigate the relationship between leisure quality and satisfaction in retirement it is necessary to have a set of dimensions that define leisure quality as well as a measure of satisfaction that clearly distinguishes satisfaction with activities from satisfaction with health and finances. One study that did attempt this used the dimensions of skill-utilization, influence, variety, pressure and interaction to define leisure quality and separate measures of satisfaction for activities, health and finances (O'Brien, 1981a,b). The main aim was to test the hypothesis that satisfaction with retirement activities was determined by leisure quality. Another aim was to examine the extent to which previous occupation determined overall adjustment to retirement.

Contrary to expectations, it was found that participation in activities requiring skill-utilization and autonomy did not predict satisfaction with activities or life satisfaction. The main predictors of satisfaction for both men and women were the amount of interpersonal interaction experienced and the total number of different activities engaged in. One possible explanation is that retirement, at least in Australian culture, is experienced as a state of social isolation and people are happy to the extent that they have a lot of contact and social activities. Also it could be a period where personal identity has been largely formed. The identity of retirees may be largely shaped by previous work and non-work experiences where the exercise of autonomy and valued skills did contribute to identity and personal adjustment. However, identity based on personal control and skill-use is not salient for those who are no longer employed as society does not judge retirees on their contribution to and involvement in tasks requiring self-direction and personal control. Lacking any strong linkage to social goals and work organization, life meaning is imparted rather by the extent and quality of social interaction. Hence interaction and activity level determines satisfaction with activities. If the number of leisure activities is an index of activity or arousal then the results support those of Markides and Martin (1979). Retirees then are satisfied to the extent that they have a high activity level and meaningful social interactions.

Although interaction and activity level are general determinants of satisfaction with retirement, there are also occupational determinants of retirement satisfaction. Table 10.3 shows how various forms of satisfaction as measured by the Retirement Description Index (Smith, Kendall and Hulin, 1969) are related to occupational type. Retirees from blue-collar occupations had significantly lower satisfaction than those from white-collar occupations on activities, finances and life satisfaction.

TABLE 10.3   Variation in retirement satisfaction as a function of pre-retirement occupation

Occupation	N	Mean retirement satisfaction scores				
		Activities	People	Health	Finance	Life in general
White-collar jobs	103	40.7	43.4	18.3	40.6	58.4
Professional	24	42.4	42.4	20.1	42.4	58.2
Administrative managerial/	14	43.3	41.5	20.2	41.8	58.9
Clerical	30	39.1	44.2	17.3	40.3	47.0
Sales/insurance/ retail	35	39.7	44.5	17.1	38.9	59.4
Blue-collar jobs	142	36.3	41.9	17.0	36.9	53.7
Transport/ communication	18	42.6	44.3	20.5	41.1	57.9
Skilled and unskilled manual labour	78	34.6	41.4	15.8	35.2	51.7
Personal services	46	36.7	41.8	17.5	37.9	55.5

Note: The possible scale range is 0–54 for satisfaction with activities, people and finance. The range for health satisfaction is 0–27 and the range for life satisfaction is 7–70.

From O'Brien (1981).

The only significant differences in leisure attributes were on skill-utilization and the number of leisure activities. Retirees from white-collar occupations had higher skill-utilization and a greater number of activities than those from blue-collar occupations. These differences in leisure attributes may partly explain the difference in retirement satisfaction. However, it does seem that previous occupation also determines satisfaction with retirement because occupation determines income, health and the ability to enjoy retirement. White-collar occupations do have higher income levels than blue-collar occupations and this should explain why there are variations in financial security. However, work experience could also have shaped personality to some extent. Kohn and Schooler (1973, 1978, 1981) have shown that people from occupations with jobs that are intellectually complex and varied are more self-directed and flexible than those from jobs that are relatively low in complexity and variability. To some extent this was due to the effect of personality on job choice. However, even after they controlled for selection effects they found that prolonged job experiences involving self-direction induced stable increases in self-direction and flexibility. This suggests that retirees from white-collar jobs, which involve more complexity and self-direction than blue-collar jobs, would be retirees with the ability to cope more adequately with the stresses associated with retirement. Kohn and Schooler did not investigate this possibility but some evidence to support this interpretation comes from other studies.

These studies have found that adjustment to retirement is partly determined by an individual's locus of control (Kuypers, 1971; Palmore and Luikart, 1972; Reid, Haas and Hawkings, 1977; Reid and Ziegler, 1981). Internally controlled retirees, who believed that their desired goals were largely determined by their own effort, skill and motivation, reported higher levels of contentment and happiness than externally controlled individuals who placed greater emphasis on chance and environmental factors as explanations for their own achievement. The relationship between locus of control and life satisfaction was generally stronger for males than females. One problem with these studies is that they did not control for health. Poor health, either physical or mental, could strongly determine an individual's perception of personal control and the reported association between locus of control and satisfaction could disappear when health is partialled out. Furthermore, the studies did not examine retirees' previous occupations as a determinant of locus of control. If work determines personality, and locus of control is a personality variable, then it is reasonable to expect that work experiences could affect retirement adjustment via personality.

One study examined this possibility (O'Brien, 1981). A large sample of Australian retirees was interviewed and information obtained about their physical health, life stress, locus of control and satisfaction with life in retirement. Those who had been regularly employed prior to their retirement provided information about their occupation. From previous studies with employed samples it was possible to assign to each occupation a score on skill-utilization. These scores had been obtained by estimating the mean amount of skill-utilization reported by employees from a wide range of jobs.

Results showed that, for both males and females, previous occupation determined the degree to which retirees experienced personal control over their lives. If they had held a job which enabled them to use their skills they tended to feel internally controlled and able to use their own initiative in obtaining personally rewarding experiences. However, if they came from occupations which prevented a reasonable amount of skill-utilization, they tended to believe they were externally controlled. They saw that their lives were largely determined by fate or social forces such as government and authority figures. These results held even when reported physical health and stress (mental strain) were controlled.

The relation between locus of control and satisfaction in retirement can be interpreted in terms of what is known about the behavioral correlates of locus of control. Externals, compared to internals, are less efficient users of environmental resources and have greater difficulty in maintaining self-directed activity (Lefcourt, 1976; Phares, 1976). Those in retirement have a considerable amount of free time and thus the success of their activities in achieving personal satisfaction depends, to a large extent, on personal initiative. Hence internals are more likely to seek out congenial activities while externals tend to be locked in, accepting unwanted activities and people, and believing that there is little they can do to make the environment more satisfactory.

However, while this explanation may be true for males, it does not explain why there is a relatively weak relationship between locus of control and life satisfaction for females. Perhaps males experience more free time than females. The majority of females in the Australian study were married and it is likely that they performed a substantial number of domestic tasks before and after retirement. If these tasks were experienced as unfulfilling and boring it could have led to stress or mental strain. If so, this might explain why the main determinant of female dissatisfaction in retirement was mental strain. Sex differences in the relationship between locus of control, skill-utilization and life satisfaction could also be due to a failure to consider domestic activities as work occupations. Greater similarity between men and women might have been found if the occupational skill-utilization measure was based on activities in both home maintenance and paid employment.

The relationship between locus of control and retirement satisfaction suggests a number of ways of improving the experience of retirement. If jobs were designed to give people a reasonable amount of skill-utilization then they would develop a sense of personal control. With moderate levels of personal control they would have the personal competence necessary to shape their environment by choosing tasks that suited their interests and capacities. An internal locus of control could also facilitate adjustment by allowing people to seek out and develop alternative methods of coping with the stresses caused by financial worries, isolation and failing health. There is, however, a major problem in understanding the adjustment of retirees. The attributes of their activities such as skill-utilization and autonomy do not predict adjustment. This is a surprising result. One possible explanation is that there is little variation in retiree activities and so it is statistically difficult to find an association between leisure attributes and adjustment. Another interpretation is that satisfactory retirement activities should not only use valued skills but be socially useful. Many writers have pointed out that western societies fail to provide retirees with activities that use their skills and are socially useful (e.g. Parker, 1982). Many retirement activities such as chess, golf or gardening may use considerable skill. Yet these may be unsatisfactory as occupations because the elderly do not feel they contribute to society. Some cultures, such as Australian aboriginal culture, integrate the elderly into the social fabric by giving them senior administrative positions and making them the guardians and teachers of social history and religion. The main implication of this is that future research on retirees should examine the social role that they are required to fill and the extent to which their adjustment, or lack of it, is due to tasks which lack social significance.

NOTES

1. An outline of the changing meaning of work and leisure in history is presented by Tilgher (1930).

2. Although many claim that this is the beginning of the age of leisure there has been little change within industrialized countries in the amount of time spent on work and leisure in the last thirty years (Evans, 1975). Leisure time might have increased if non-work time devoted to household maintenance activities (e.g. cooking, cleaning) had declined. However, this does not seem to have happened as household maintenance has not declined much despite the availability of time-saving devices and take-away food outlets (Linder, 1970; Vanek, 1974). Increased income over this period has, it appears, been used to buy increasing quantities of household goods that require time to purchase and time to instal and maintain. Also, the time available for leisure has been restricted within households due to the increased number of married women who have entered the workforce.

3. Leisure time and leisure quality may be determined as much by working hours as by work content. There has been some experimentation with

changing work schedules but the effects on leisure, productivity and social adjustment have not often been systematically evaluated.

The two main innovations have been flexible working hours and compression of the five-day working week into four days. The results on flexitime are difficult to interpret as conclusions are often based on observation of changes within a particular group of employees without comparison to comparable control groups. The few studies with control designs suggest that flexitime has no adverse effects on productivity and can improve the satisfaction of employees whose work schedules conflict with home duties and shopping opportunities. As a general solution for improvement in leisure and productivity it is clearly inadequate.

The four-day week has been investigated experimentally by a number of psychologists in the United States and Canada (Goodale and Aagard, 1975; Ivanavich, 1974; Ivanavich and Lyon, 1977; Nord and Costigan, 1973; Steward and Larsen, 1971). The effects of a compressed work-week are complicated but some broad generalizations can be tentatively made. In the short term employees respond favourably to the four-day week and there are no adverse effects on productivity. Occasionally improvement in productivity is reported.

The quality of leisure activities is most likely to be improved if the four working days are continuous, thus providing a three-day period of freetime. However, it appears that this also results in employes spending more money on consumer and leisure goods. In the long term productivity is unaffected but a significant minority of employees report negative effects on sleep, home life and fatigue. Older workers are most affected by fatigue while many workers find that they have little home involvement or contact on working days. The results so far suggest that not all workers experience favourable effects from a compressed work week. There is a general increase in leisure quality but certain classes of employees also experience extra fatigue and poor family contact.

The main implication for leisure is that a small reduction in hours per day is unlikely to affect leisure patterns as most of the extra time is likely to be spent on household maintenance and passive leisure activities such as watching television. This suggests that the leisure benefits of a 35- or 30-hour week may only be realized if it is associated with the introduction of a three- or four-day working week.

REFERENCES

Adams, D. (1971). Correlates of satisfaction among the elderly, *Gerontologist*, **11**, 64–8

Bacon, A.W. (1975). Leisure and the alienated worker: a critical assessment of three radical theories of work and leisure, *Journal of Leisure Research*, **7**, 179–90

Beard, J.G. and Ragheb, M.G. (1980). Measuring leisure satisfaction, *Journal of Leisure Research,* **12,** 20–33

Chatfield, W. (1977). Economic and sociological factors influencing life satisfaction of the aged, *Journal of Gerontology,* **32,** 593–9

Cheek, N.H., and Burch, W.R. (1976). *The Social Organization of Leisure in Human Society,* New York: Harper & Row

Crandall, R. (1980). Motivations for leisure, *Journal of Leisure Research,* **12,** 45–54

Csikszentmihalyi, M. (1975). *Beyond Boredom and Anxiety,* San Francisco: Jossey-Bass

Cunningham, H., (1980). *Leisure in the Industrial Revolution,* London: Croom Helm

De Grazia, S. (1964). *Of Time, Work and Leisure,* New York: Doubleday

Dubin, R. (1956). Industrial workers' worlds: a study in the central life interests of industrial workers, *Social Problems,* **4,** 131-42

Dubin, R. (1958). *The World of Work: Industrial Society and Human Relations,* Englewood Cliffs, N.J.: Prentice-Hall

Dubin, R. (1973). Work and non-work: institutional perspectives, in M.D. Dunnette (ed.), *Work and Non-work in the Year 2001,* Monterey, Cal.: Brooks/Cole

Dumazedier, J. (1967). *Toward a Society of Leisure,* New York: Free Press

Dunnette, M.D. (ed.) (1973). *Work and Non-work in the Year 2001,* Monterey, Cal.: Brooks/Cole

Emery, F.E. (1977). *Futures We Are In,* The Hague: Nijhoff

Engels, F. (1892). *The Condition of the Working Class in England in 1844,* London: Allen & Unwin

Evans, A. (1975). *Hours of Work in Industrialised Countries,* Geneva: I.L.O.

Fine, M. (1975). Interrelationships among mobility, health, and attitudinal variables in an urban elderly population, *Human Relations,* **28,** 451–74

Fourastie, J. (1965). *Les 40,000 heures,* Paris: Gonthier

Gardell, B. (1976). Relations at work and their influence on non-work activities: an analysis of a socio-political problem in affluent societies, *Human Relations,* **29,** 885–904

Gentry, J.W. and Doering, M. (1979). Sex role orientation and leisure, *Journal of Leisure Research,* **11,** 102–11

Goodale, J.G. and Aagaard, A.K. (1975). Factors relating to varying reactions to the 4-day workweek, *Journal of Applied Psychology,* **60,** 33-88

Havighurst, R.J. (1977). Life-style and leisure patterns in the later years, in R.A. Kalish (ed.), *The Later Years: Social Applications of Gerontology,* Monterey, Calif.: Brooks/Cole

Hunnicutt, B. (1980). Historical attitudes toward the increase of free time in the twentieth century: time for work, for leisure, or as unemployment, *Society and Leisure,* **3,** 195-215

Ivanavich, J.M. (1974). Effect of the shorter work-week on selected satisfaction and performance measures, *Journal of Applied Psychology,* **59,** 717–21

Ivanavich, J.M. and Lyon, H.C. (1977). The shortened workweek: a field experiment, *Journal of Applied Psychology,* **62,** 34–7

Jenkins, C. and Sherman, B. (1979). *The Collapse of Work,* London: Eyre Methuen

Kabanoff, B. (1980). Work and non-work: a review of models, methods, and findings, *Psychological Bulletin,* **88,** 60–77

Kabanoff, B. (1982). Occupational and sex differences in leisure needs and leisure satisfaction, *Journal of Occupational Behaviour,* **3,** 233–45

Kabanoff, B. (1981). Validation of a task attributes description of leisure, *Australian Journal of Psychology,* **33,** 383–91

Kabanoff, B. and O'Brien, G.E. (1980). Work and leisure: a task attributes analysis, *Journal of Applied Psychology*, **65**, 596–609

Kabanoff, B. and O'Brien, G.E. (1982). Relationships between work and leisure attributes of occupational and sex groups in Australia, *Australian Journal of Psychology*, **34**, 165–82

Kando, T. and Summers, W. (1971). The impact of work on leisure, *Pacific Sociological Review*, **14**, 310–27

Kelley, J.R. (1978). Situational and social factors in leisure decisions, *Pacific Sociological Review*, **21**, 313-30

Kleemeier, R.W. (ed.) (1961). *Aging and Leisure*, New York: Oxford University Press

Kohn, M.L. and Schooler, C. (1973). Occupational experience and psychological functioning: an assessment of reciprocal effects, *American Sociological Review*, **28**, 97–118

Kohn, M.L. and Schooler, C. (1978). The reciprocal effects of the substantive complexity of work and intellectual flexibility: a longitudinal assessment, *American Journal of Sociology*, **84**, 24-52

Kohn, M.L. and Schooler, C. (1981). Job conditions and intellectual flexibility: a longitudinal assessment of their reciprocal effects, in D.J. Jackson and E.F. Borgatta, *Factor Analysis and Measurement in Sociological Research*, Beverley Hills, Cal.: Sage

Kornhauser, A.W. (1965). *Mental Health of the Industrial Worker*, New York: Wiley

Kuypers, J.A. (1971). Internal-external locus of control and ego functioning correlates in the elderly, *Gerontologist*, **12**, 168–73

Larson, R. (1978). Thirty years of research on subjective well-being of older Americans, *Journal of Gerontology*, **33**, 109-25

Lefcourt, H. (1976). *Locus of Control: Current Trends in Theory and Research*, New York: Wiley

Lemon, B., Bengston, V. and Peterson, J. (1972). An exploration of the activity theory of aging: activity types and life satisfaction among inmovers to a retirement community, *Journal of Gerontology*, **27**, 511–23

Linder, S.B. (1970). *The Harried Leisure Class*, New York: Columbia University

London, M., Crandall, R. and Seals, G.W. (1977). The contribution of job and leisure satisfaction to the quality of life, *Journal of Applied Psychology*, **62**, 328–34

Maddox, G. and Eisdorfer, C. (1962). Some correlates of activity and morale among the elderly, *Social Forces*, **41**, 254–60

Mansfield, R. and Evans, M.G. (1975). Work and non-work in two occupational groups, *Industrial Relations*, **6**, 48–54

Markides, K. and Martin, H. (1979). A causal model of life satisfaction among the elderly, *Journal of Gerontology*, **34**, 86–93

Marx, K. (1844). *Economic and Philosophic Manuscripts of 1844*, Moscow: Progress Publishers (edition published in 1977)

Medley, M.L. (1976). Satisfaction with life among persons 65 years and older, *Journal of Gerontology*, **31**, 448–55

Meissner, M. (1971). The long arm of the job: a study of work and leisure, *Industrial Relations*, **10**, 239–60

Neulinger, J. (1974). *The Psychology of Leisure*, Springfield, Ill.: Charles C. Thomas, 1974

Nord, W.R. and Costigan, R. (1973). Worker adjustment to the 4-day week: a longitudinal study, *Journal of Applied Psychology*, **53**, 60–6

O'Brien, G.E. (1980). The centrality of skill-utilization for job design, in K. Duncan, M. Gruneberg and D. Wallis (eds), *Changes in Working Life*, Chichester,: Wiley

O'Brien, G.E. (1981a). Leisure attributes and retirement satisfaction, *Journal of Applied Psychology*, **66**, 371–84

O'Brien, G.E. (1981b). Locus of control, previous occupation and satisfaction with retirement, *Australian Journal of Psychology*, **33**, 305–18

O'Brien, G.E. (1982). The relative contribution of perceived skill-utilization and other perceived job attributes to the prediction of job satisfaction: a cross-validation study, *Human Relations*, **35**, 219–37

Palmore, E. and Luikart, C. (1972). Health and social factors related to life satisfaction, *Journal of Health and Social Behavior*, **13**, 68–80

Parker, S. (1976). *The Sociology of Leisure*, London: George Allen & Unwin

Parker, S. (1982). *Work and Retirement*, London: George Allen & Unwin

Parker, S. (1983). *Leisure and Work*, London: George Allen & Unwin

Phares, E.J. (1976). *Locus of Control in Personality*, New Jersey: General Learning Press

Porter, L.W. Lawler, E.E. and Hackman, J.R. (1975). *Behavior in Organizations*, New York: McGraw-Hill

Rapoport, R. and Rapoport, R.N. (1975). *Leisure and the Family Life Cycle*, London: Routledge

Reid, D., Haas, G. and Hawkings, D. (1977). Locus of desired control and positive self-concepts of the elderly, *Journal of Gerontology*, **32**, 441–50

Reid, D.W. and Zeigler, M. (1981). The Desired Control measure and adjustment among the elderly, in H.M. Lefcourt (ed.), *Research with the Locus of Control Construct*, vol. 1, New York: Academic Press

Rotter, J.B. (1966). Generalized expectancies for internal versus external control of reinforcement, *Psychological Monographs*, **80** (1 Whole No. 609)

Rousseau, D.M. (1978). Relationship of work to nonwork, *Journal of Applied Psychology*, **63**, 513–17

Smith, P., Kendall, L. and Hulin, C. (1969). *The Measurement of Satisfaction in Work and Retirement*, Chicago: Rand McNally

Spreitzer, E. and Snyder, E. (1973). Correlates of life satisfaction among the aged, *Journal of Gerontology*, **29**, 454–8

Steward, G.V. and Larsen, J.M. (1971). A 4 day–3 day per week application to a continuous production operation, *Management of Personnel Quarterly*, **10**, 13–20

Thompson, E.P. (1968). *The Making of the English Working Class*, Harmondsworth: Penguin Books

Tilgher, A. (1930). *Work: What it has Meant to Men Through the Ages*, New York: Harcourt Brace

Tinsley, H.E.A., Barrett, T.C. and Kass, R.A. (1977). Leisure activities and need satisfaction, *Journal of Leisure Research*, **9**, 111–20

Vanek, J. (1974). Time spent on housework, *Scientific American*, **231**, 116-20

Veblen, T. (1899). *The Theory of the Leisure Class*, New York: MacMillan

CHAPTER 11

Working and Not Working

It is right and necessary that all men should have work to do which shall be worth doing, and be of itself pleasant to do: and which should be done under such conditions as would make it neither overwearisome nor overanxious. Turn that claim about as I may... I cannot find that it is an exorbitant claim; yet... if Society would or could admit it, the face of the world could be changed.
(William Morris, Collected Works, vol. 23, (1910–15) p. 194

This book began with a quotation by Adam Smith. His words showed that he understood that jobs lacking skill-utilization affected the workers' intellectual functioning, identity and social adjustment. However, his economic principles did not lead him to recommend that industrial organization should design jobs which used a reasonable amount of employee skills. He was too impressed with the economic advantages of segmented tasks and, as well, he thought that the negative effects of such tasks on people could be rectified by education. He recommended sending the working class to parish schools where they could improve their intellectual capacities, self-discipline and sense of responsibility. In effect, this is what society has done. Educational participation has steadily increased while a majority of employees have remained in jobs which are too small for their capacities.

The net result has been to exacerbate the problem of underemployment. Despite the emergence of new technologies, which some promised would eliminate low-skill jobs, there seems to have been a slow but steady increase in the number of employees who report low skill-utilization. These under-employed workers are not found only in blue-collar jobs. They are also found in clerical, managerial and some professional occupations. The effect of prolonged experience in low-complexity, low skill-utilization jobs has consequences for both the personality of employees as well as organizational performance. The main effect of empty jobs has been a general restriction in employees' sense of personal control. The evidence supports a general model of work-induced personal dysfunction which posits a causal chain linking poor skill-utilization to stress and extreme beliefs in external control. In turn, employees who believe that most of their rewards in life (at work and outside work) are outside their control tend to be less productive, less healthy and more likely to develop anxiety and depressive illnesses (Chapter 4).

Along the way a number of qualifications were made about the generality of these effects and the interpretation given to various measures of job attributes and personality. These qualifications did not affect the general conclusion that low skill-utilization or underemployment affected the job performance and mental health of a very sizeable proportion of the workforce in industrialized countries. The psychological effects of underemployment were compared to the general effects of unemployment—which is a state of extremely low skill-utilization. It was suggested that a great deal of the distress amongst the unemployed was due to poverty. If this is true, then it is quite possible that a person would experience greater distress in poor employment than in being unemployed with an income equivalent to his job wage.

The problem of underemployment is not just a problem relevant to employee-oriented psychologists and policy-makers concerned with minimizing physical and psychological ill-health. It is also a managerial problem. One of management's functions is to maximize the use of human resources for the purpose of productivity. Underemployment implies that employee skills are not being used as they should be. It also implies that management will have considerable difficulty in motivating employees who, because of their job experiences, lack self-direction and involvement in their work. Even unemployment can be a management problem. Prolonged unemployment can rob people of even a moderate sense of personal control. Hence if they are able to get a job, they may not have the required motivation to perform well. A few studies on the work performance of the long-term unemployed have shown that it requires considerable skill on the part of management if they are to obtain effective job performance from those employees who were previously unemployed (Friedlander and Greenberg, 1971; Goodman, Salipante and Paransky, 1973).

The main aims of this chapter are, first, to examine ways in which underemployment can be reduced and second, to provide a theory of the process whereby person–job match could facilitate psychological development. This will be an attempt to link personality or identity structure with organizational structure. Third, we will examine the way in which an uncritical belief in the efficacy of personal control has affected the adjustment and performance of managers. This will involve an analysis of the disadvantages of an individualistic work ethic and the way in which its promulgation has been furthered by managerial psychology. It will be argued that the overvaluation of extreme internal beliefs by managers and psychologists has prevented a proper understanding of work–personality relationships and hindered the development of adequate theories of job reform. Finally, this will lead to a brief discussion of the future of work and the future of work psychology.

METHODS OF IMPROVING PERSON–JOB MATCH

One of the main conclusions of this book is that jobs should be designed so that employee skills are fully utilized. If jobs provided opportunities for skill-utilization it would enable employees to achieve greater satisfaction in their work and a realistic sense of personal control. Work would not be boring or stressful but a way of confirming and extending a positive self-identity through the use of valued skills. Organizational performance would also rise if person–job match was adopted as a principle of job design. This would be due to better use of human resources, lowering of job-related stress, and higher levels of intrinsic job motivation induced by challenging jobs.

A. Selection and Placement

The most direct way in which organizations can improve person–job match is by hiring people whose valued skills will be fully utilized in their work. Thus an essential and basic step is job analysis. A selection programme, whether it is based on psychological tests, interviews, work sample or management assessment centres, will not be successful unless it is derived from a careful analysis of the skills required in various jobs. Although not without shortcomings (Chapter 2), current psychological methods of job analysis can provide a reasonable basis for describing jobs in terms of required personal skills (McCormick, 1979). The next step in selection is to measure applicant skills and interests. In the traditional psychological method of selection, the skills and interests measured could be those inferred from a careful job analysis and then subsequently demonstrated to predict job performance. This does not automatically guarantee person–job match as the procedure does not measure the applicant's whole repertoire of skills.

Reasonable use of selection methods requires that organizations adopt realistic job requirements. Demanding that successful applicants have skills and credentials which are not really needed for successful performance will distort person–job match and will eventually produce low employee motivation and performance. If a reasonable set of job requirements is stated, the next step is to reject applicants who have either insufficient or excessive skill for the job. Sufficient attention has not been given to the problem of overqualified employees. Partly this is due to a belief that the organization may eventually benefit from having employees with talent. After learning to do an initial unchallenging job these employees, it is sometimes argued, will be capable of achieving promotion to jobs with greater skill levels. This may be a reasonable strategy if the initial job does not last long *and* the organization provides frequent opportunities for promotion or transfer. The main disadvantage of this approach is that an initial unchallenging job can dampen work motivation, and depress later performance (Berlew and Hall, 1966). If the overqualified employee cannot easily advance to new positions then there will be dissatisfaction, problems of absenteeism, and performance levels which might be lower than those that could have been reached by less skilled, but better matched, employees.

Selection and placement is not a technique that should be confined to the assessment of new employees. Ideally it should be a continuous process as employee skills change with job experience. Jobs which were once challenging to an employee may become boring and routine when the required skills have been mastered. Challenge from the job can only be maintained if the job is changed or the employee is placed in another job which requires higher skill. When existing jobs are difficult to change, some organizations find it useful to assess employee skills and attitudes regularly and, when necessary, to place employees in jobs providing higher skill-utilization. So far, this kind of continuous assessment and placement has been largely confined to managerial jobs.

B. Job Redesign

When existing jobs fail to use employee skills they should be redesigned so that employees are able to use their valued job skills. Herzberg (1966) was one of the first researchers to show that changes in job content could improve employee motivation and performance. Unfortunately, he did not provide a precise method of assessing job dimensions and employee skills. He did stress the importance of interest, responsibility and achievement for a job to be motivating but he did not provide any measurement techniques which would allow a quantitative assessment of the degree to which the skill level of a job had to be increased to a given employee.

A more detailed approach to job design is that of Hackman and Oldham (1980). Their theory has been discussed elsewhere (Chapters 1 and 5). The approach has basically two propositions.

1. Motivation and performance will be improved if job variety, identity, significance, autonomy and feedback are raised.
2. Individual differences between employees in their need to satisfy 'higher-order' needs will moderate the effects of job enrichment. In effect, this becomes a recommendation to confine job enrichment to those who have high scores on a measure of 'higher-order need strength'.

There are five main problems with this theory of job redesign. First, it has not been demonstrated that it raises productivity—although it does improve job satisfaction and motivation (O'Brien, 1982). Second, it neglects skill-utilization. Although Hackman and Oldham (1980), claim that increases in their job characteristics will make jobs more challenging, they do not measure or increase the match between employee skills and skills required by the job (Chapter 3). Third, the job design procedures do not specify that wages should be altered if employees are given more autonomy. It may be possible that certain changes in autonomy could improve skill-utilization. For example, if it meant giving an employee responsibility for quality control when previously he only produced a product, it could reasonably increase skill-utilization. In cultures where unionization is strong, increases in skill and autonomy could lead to employees requesting increased pay. Increased skill-utilization may not produce desired effects on motivation and performance unless there is an agreement between management and employees on the correspondence between skill levels and pay rates. Hackman and Oldham (1980) do consider pay satisfaction as a possible moderator of job attitudes but this is not the same as linking income directly to job attributes. Where there are strong expectations that skill level will be tied to wage rates, even job redesigns based on skill-utilization will not be effective unless they are accompanied by acceptable changes in wage rates.

A fourth difficulty is the discriminatory application of job design. The evidence on the effects of individual differences on responses to Hackman and Oldham's job characteristics is very weak (Chapter 5). Regardless of need strength, personality and work values, the large majority of employees respond positively to jobs that use their skills and provide them with some control over their own work procedures. That some do report that they have low desires for autonomy and self-determination is not denied. But it is probable that they respond in this way because they have experienced poor jobs in the past, do not expect any changes in the future, and have become accustomed to evaluating the worth of jobs in terms of financial benefits. It may take more time for those employees to be consciously aware of the centrality of skill-utilization in determining their job attitudes but the available evidence indicates that they are motivated by jobs which use their skills even though they might maintain that extrinsic benefits, such as money, are what they are predominantly concerned about (Chapter 3).

A final difficulty with Hackman and Oldham's approach is that they assume that person–job match will be obtained solely by rebuilding individual jobs. A job may be rebuilt but the organizational context may prevent skill-utilization (O'Brien and Owens, 1969; Kabanoff and O'Brien, 1979a). The division of labour, for example, in a work team may be inefficient for the type of task. Team members may, in principle, have tasks that use their skills but the interaction requirements of the task structure may prevent them being able to use their skills. This, of course, is not a criticism just of Hackman and Oldham's method. It also applies to any psychological theories of job design which neglect the organizational structure that 'surrounds' a job. This discussion does not necessarily imply the abandonment of the job characteristic approach. In the future, there is a reasonable possibility that it could improve motivation and performance provided that it:

(i) incorporated skill-utilization as a central job characteristic;
(ii) directly linked job characteristics to wage levels; and,
(iii) specified the group structures that would maximize group productivity and member skill-utilization.

One type of job design that appears to meet these requirements involves the formation of semi-autonomous work groups. This approach has been developed by social scientists from the Tavistock Institute (Emery and Trist, 1960; Rice, 1958). It involves the introduction of all or most of the following changes:

(i) the selection of a reasonable 'natural' or complete work unit;
(ii) allocation of this work unit to a set of workers;
(iii) training of workers in skills required for the various tasks;
(iv) allocation to the group of responsibility for work organization, output and quality;
(v) assignment of supervisory staff to consultant rather than directive roles;
(vi) regular feedback to groups on performance;
(vii) partial linking of wage levels to group performance.

A large majority of studies on semi-autonomous work groups report positive increases in productivity and work attitudes (Srivasta *et al.*, 1974). Any of the above factors could be responsible for the positive effects. Some critics have argued that the main variable producing group performance is the pay rate as positive effects are only observed when groups are given pay incentives (Carey, 1979). Others have suggested that the effectiveness of these groups is limited to lower level employees and does not basically change power structures or job content (Bolweg, 1976). Typically, supporters of semi-autonomous groups argue that these groups do satisfy general needs for autonomy, learning and skill-use (e.g. Emery and Phillips, 1976), but so far the research has not been able to support this interpretation. What is needed is more research that disentangles the relative importance of changes in job content, group structure and income level. If it was shown that semi-autonomous groups improved skill-utilization by changing job content and work structure it would provide stronger evidence for a person–job match interpretation. This would still not be sufficient evidence to support the view that person–job match is the reason why semi-autonomous groups are effective. This requires evidence showing that skill-utilization, autonomous group structure and pay incentives have separate as well as interactive effects on performance and motivation.

C. Employee Participation in Decision-making

A frequently discussed method of improving the utilization of human resources in organizations is employee participation. One of the problems in trying to summarize research and theory on employee participation in decision-making is that the term is used in different ways and the form of participation varies considerably both across and within cultures (Dachler and Wilpert, 1978; Wall and Lisceron, 1977). In the United States, employee participation in managerial decision-making tends to be recommended as a management technique that may be useful for improving motivation and productivity in certain circumstances. In other countries, like Norway, employee participation is discussed more in terms of industrial democracy. It may involve consultation, semi-autonomous work groups, work committees or representation of employees on senior management committees. All of these forms of participation may be involved. They are justified not only as a means of improving productivity but also as a method for improving the quality of working life. This is achieved by allowing workers to use their skills in making decisions about what they do and how they do it. Typically, it is also discussed within a political context where it is seen as a way of achieving consistency in decision-making forms within an avowed democratic culture. In Eastern European nations it is also considered as a political form whereby, in principle, workers can control the production process. Thus, in Yugoslavia, employee participation means self-management of the organization by employees.

In general, employee participation outside North America refers to fairly formalized groups involving employees and managers which range from consultative groups, small work or action committees to direct representation of employees on advisory or management boards. These groups could improve job satisfaction and productivity if, following the previous discussions, they allowed employees to achieve higher levels of skill-utilization by changing both job content and the formal structure of work groups in a way that was consistent with task requirements.

The evidence on their effectiveness is often difficult to interpret as the groups differ in decision type, distribution of power and frequency of meeting. Also, there is often inadequate evaluation of job changes, satisfaction and productivity. However, some evaluation is possible due to the publication of studies in Yugoslavia (Kolaja, 1965; Broekmeyer, 1968; Obradovic, 1970), Israel (Rosenstein, 1970), West Germany (Roberts, 1973), Norway

(Emery and Thorsrud, 1976) and Holland (Mulder, 1971; Van der Velden, 1965). It appears that employee-management groups frequently encounter difficulties such as:

1. Participation by employees in decision-making often has not led to increased influence. As a result, they have not produced desired changes in jobs or management practices.
2. Employee representatives often do not have the information, training and skill to contribute significantly to decision-making. The power of managers, technical experts and administrators has consequently been enhanced because group methods have induced greater employee commitment to management decisions. It seems that group-decision techniques can be a powerful way of inducing conformity in those who experience uncertainty.
3. Employees who are elected representatives can have difficulty in representing the views of their work group. Unless they are trained in gathering and integrating diverse viewpoints, the gulf between representatives and employees may become as wide as the gulf between employees and managers.

The general implication is that employee participation can be an effective method of achieving person–job match only if it allows the utilization of human resources within the work group. Under-utilization of resources can occur in two ways. Either the process of decision-making prevents the participants from fully using their expertise or the decisions made do not lead to job changes that allow employees to use their personal resources.

Joint decision-making may lead to poor-quality decisions and possibly poor motivation when the process does not allow members to consider alternative solutions. One dysfunctional process of this kind was described by Janis (1972) as 'group-think'. This refers to cohesive groups where there are pressures toward consensus rather than quality solutions. In employee-management groups, high cohesiveness may not be such a common thing but it could occur when members are chosen by management on the basis of their personal compatibility rather than ability. If people like each other there are induced pressures to agree with each other. These pressures may be strengthened by selective information-gathering, overt criticism of dissent and the suppression of information by self-appointed 'mindguards'. Janis recommends that leaders of group decision-making groups remain impartial initially, focus on the problem and deliberately assign the role of 'critical-evaluator' to each group member.

This may increase the likelihood of various alternative solutions being considered but will not necessarily improve the quality of the solution in comparison to the solution of the most able member. Some studies have shown that a high degree of face-to-face collaboration may actually lower performance on problem-solving and creative tasks. This occurs because the amount of interaction required prevents the effective integration of member contributions. This was illustrated in the studies of Kabanoff and O'Brien (1979a,b) which varied the degree to which tasks were shared within a group. The positive effects of coordination and the negative effects of too much collaboration have also been demonstrated in some recent studies of group judgement and decision-making. These studies are discussed more fully elsewhere (O'Brien, 1984) and include nominal group techniques (Delbecq, Van der Ven and Gustafson, 1975), delphi methods (Linstone and Turoff, 1975) and social judgement analysis (Hammond *et al.*, 1977; Rohrbaugh, 1979, 1981). All of these studies show that the quality of the group decision depends on the type of task structure employed. Participation should, then, not be considered as just face-to-face decision making. If it is, then members will be less able to use their abilities and skills than in groups where decision-making procedures allow for some period of information-sharing through a process of coordination.

Sometimes it is proposed that real improvement in job content will be achieved only when employees have part or full ownership of an enterprise. From the available research it appears that ownership does not guarantee power equalization or significant improvements in job complexity or skill-utilization (Kohn and Schooler, 1983; Toscano, 1983). In principle, it would seem to strengthen employee power but whether job satisfaction and productivity are improved depends on the type of ownership and whether employees have sufficient knowledge of the principles of job design. Some research reports that ownership increases employee participation (e.g. Long, 1978a,b) but other studies report that is not always true (e.g. Zwerdling, 1980; Hammer and Stern, 1980). At present it seems that producer cooperatives, where employee ownership of capital is directly linked to employee control of the enterprise, is more likely to improve participation than indirect ownership through share purchases. However, even producer cooperatives may not ensure high skill-utilization because appointed managerial experts may introduce engineering principles of job design that do not recognize the value of person–job match.

The importance of skill-utilization as a concomitant of employee participation can be illustrated by two major studies. The first studied the development of various forms of participation in a biscuit and confectionery factory over a period of six years (O'Brien, 1983a). Initially, a controlled experiment compared sections using participatory work groups with sections where supervisors had total control over work procedures. Job satisfaction improved significantly in the participatory sections but not productivity. Satisfaction increases were due to small increases in influence but the main predictor of job satisfaction was skill-utilization. The resulting job-satisfaction levels in the participatory groups were still quite low and this was attributable to the failure of the work groups to initiate any changes in the skill content of jobs. Later on, the factory introduced a management-employee representative committee. This improved communication, factory conditions and satisfaction with management. It did not lead to any changes in job content and job satisfaction was low. Workers still felt under-utilized in their jobs. Basically, the representative groups led to improvement in job context variables such as supervisory style, canteen facilities and safety but job content changes would have required the alteration or removal of the assembly line technology—a step that management were unable to make.

By contrast, another set of studies conducted by an international research team reported improvements in productivity and satisfaction when participation led to improvements in skill-utilization (D10, 1983; Heller *et al.*, 1977; Koopman *et al.*, 1981). These studies also showed that the effectiveness of participation depended on other variables such as type of decision, goal clarity and phase of decision-making. Participation was more effective with tactical or work operation decisions than with strategic or policy decisions. The developmental phases, compared to finalization or implementation phases, showed greater positive benefits of participation. Finally, participation was more likely to lead to better performance and skill-utilization when the goal had low/medium clarity than when the goal had high clarity. These two sets of studies together provide support for the general thesis that skill-utilization is a necessary, although not sufficient, condition for employee participation to produce both increased performance and job satisfaction.

PERSONAL IDENTITY AND PERSON–JOB MATCH

Many theories of human motivation discussed in this book have tried to explain work behaviour in terms of general human needs for personal control and competence. They assume that all people have a need to determine their life course and, in the process, to complete tasks that use their valued skills and abilities. A general problem with the concept of need is that it does not seem to have explanatory value. If people do try to maximize personal control and the use of their valued skills, does it add anything to our understanding by saying that they have a 'need' for control and skill-use? The existence of such needs cannot be demonstrated except by reference to the behaviours that the 'needs' were meant to explain. If it is argued that 'needs' are theoretical constructs that do not exist but are useful fictions that allow us to explain complex patterns of behaviour, then these needs should explain more than the behaviours they are inferred from. To say that employees try to obtain control over work procedures because they have a need for control or power does not add anything to our knowledge. If they want to maximize power or skill-use then why do some people not seek power or challenging work? To say, as some theorists do (e.g. Maslow) that they are fixated or operate at other need levels seems unconvincing. It could lead to a strategy of identifying more and more needs as we find exceptions to the exercise of power, competence or 'self-actualizing' needs.

The concept of need may be useful as an element in a theory of intrapersonal structure but it is not sufficient unless there are other elements and relationships specified to give meaning to 'intrapersonal' structure. Furthermore, the changes in behaviour over time should be seen as the result of the effects of the organization upon the person as well as the effects of the person upon the organization.

In order to expand these statements it is necessary to specify what is meant by organizational structure and personality structure. Furthermore, the specification should use concepts that allow comparison or linkage between the structures. Sociologists have long taken as their central theme that the organization of personality or self-concepts reflects the organization of social structure but they have never been able to solve the problem of measurement of structure. Unfortunately the author is not about to provide the final solution to this problem, but an attempt will be made to describe some potentially useful ways of describing structure, as well as a general theory about the interaction between personality and work structure. The approach taken ignores many other theories about the self or personality system and organizational behaviour.

At the beginning it was said that the point of contact between a person and the organization was the task. The tasks that we do are associated with our work role. They are elements of the role structure. They are given to us because they are associated with our assigned position in the organization. They have been allocated to us and partly define the external structure which constrains our behaviour. The total structure can be described in terms of the totality of relationships that connect us to our position and tasks. As an example, consider the role of a section manager (Figure 11.1).

The formal role of a manger is then defined by the immediate relations impinging on his position. These relationships can be defined using the elements and relationships of structural role theory (Oeser and Harary, 1962, 1964; Oeser and O'Brien, 1967). The basic organizational elements are persons, positions and tasks. The relationships between these three elements constitute the formal and informal relationships that serve to describe the total structure as well as each person's role. In the example given (Figure 11.1), the formal role of the section manager is defined by:

1. The assignment relationship—the selection rule which specifies the abilities required for the position.
2. The power relationship—the direction of the authority relationships impinging on the position. The two adjacent positions to the section

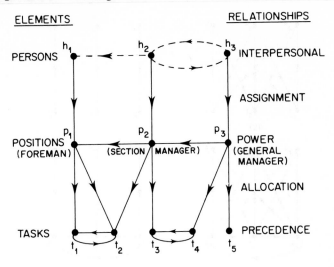

FIGURE 11.1 Informal and formal role relationships for a section manager

manager in this case are that of the foreman over whom he has legitimate authority and that of the general manager whose position has
legitimate authority over the section manager.
3. Task allocation relationships—the section manager is allocated tasks
t_1 and t_3.
4. Task precedence relationship—the lines connecting the tasks specify
the order in which the tasks are performed.

These four relationships define the formal role of the manager. They account for the broad pattern of his behaviour and variations in the particular
pattern of relationships can affect the level of his performance. His total role
also includes the interpersonal or informal relationships which inevitably develop in any organization. People come to like or dislike each other to some
extent and such informal relationships can facilitate or impede task performance. The total set of relationships impinging on any person's position in
an organization defines the objective field or social structure that determines
that person's experience of work.

Are there corresponding intrapersonal elements and relationships that reflect this external structure? One way of approaching this is to follow the
sociologists of the structural interactional school (e.g. Stryker, 1980), and define personality in terms of identity. Individual identity, or self-concept, is a
set of internalized roles and the existing identity at any point of time reflects
the structure of external roles. These capabilities, which broadly mirror the
five types of external relationships, are:

1. Interpersonal capabilities—if our role experience has led to close affectional relationships then we see ourselves as capable of intimacy.
2. Task abilities or competencies—the performance of tasks determines our perceptions of competence. Our task capabilities, or competency, are a complex set of cognitions of what we are capable of doing (i.e. what tasks we can do well and what tasks are beyond us). These cognitions are formed both by external assignment relationships as well as by the task allocation and precedence relationships.
3. Control capabilities—repeated experience of authority structures has shaped us so that we are 'used to' various degrees of directing or being directed. The total set of control capabilities is not likely to be a simple judgement like 'I am dominant' or 'I am dependent'. Rather our experience will lead to complex cognitions of the form 'In situations of such and such kind (i.e. with specified types of people, positions and tasks) I can exercise control and power to a certain degree'.

Knowledge of a person's cognitions about these capabilities defines his or her identity. Our identity or self-image is our perceived capability for experiencing and receiving intimacy, task competence and control in situations which are significant to us. When we become involved in a work structure our identity or self-image may or may not be consistent with our identity as defined by the organization. An incongruent person–situation match occurs in the example of Table 11.1. This would be a case where an employee experiences great inconsistency between his personal identity and the identity defined for him by the organization.

TABLE 11.1   An incongruent person–situation match

Capabilities	Identity (internalized role)	Organization role (Externally imposed)
Intimacy	Capable of close interpersonal relationships	Close interpersonal relationships not required
Task competence	Valued skills are X, Y, Z (intellectual, manipulative interpersonal skills)	Skills X, Y, Z not required or at a level of those skills far below those of which the employee is capable
Control	Can direct activities of others Can direct own task activities	Not required to direct others Own work activities closely directed by others

In principle, and this would be a project for further research, the degree of inconsistency could be quantified. Individual capabilities could be quantified to form a personal identity vector. (PI)

$$PI = \begin{array}{l} \text{Intimacy} \\ \text{Skill–competence} \\ \text{Control} \end{array} \begin{bmatrix} i \\ p \\ c \end{bmatrix}$$

The level of capabilities for an individual for intimacy, skill-competence, and control are i, p, and c, respectively. A comparable social identity vector, reflecting external role requirements, would be SI.

$$SI = \begin{array}{l} \text{Required intimacy} \\ \text{Required skill–competence} \\ \text{Required control} \end{array} \begin{bmatrix} I \\ P \\ C \end{bmatrix}$$

Using matrix operations, it would be possible to develop indices of these three organizational requirements. The required intimacy index would reflect the density of informal relationships (e.g. communications, liking) that surround the person in the organization. The skill–competence index would be based on the task allocation and precedence relationships. The task allocation relationship would be weighted by the level of skill required for each task as well as the relative time devoted to each task. Finally, the required control index would depend on all the structural relationships. The amount of control that an employee has depends on his allocated tasks, the way in which they are organized, his formal authority, and his standing in the network of informal relationships. A suitable index for control or index has already been developed (O'Brien, Biglan, and Penna, 1972).

If the variables in both the personal identity and social identity vectors were measured on commensurate scales, then the overall degree of match could be measured. One possible measure of match that quantifies the similarity of the two vectors is:

$$\text{Match} = (I-i)^2 + (S-p)^2 + (C-c)^2$$

If there is a discrepancy in structures the individual will first try to achieve consistency by changing the structure. Sometimes this is possible but in most hierarchical organizations the structure is fairly rigid. Employees cannot easily change their jobs, the control structure or the intensity of interpersonal relationships. Great discrepancies which cannot be reduced by structural changes often cause people to leave and find a 'better' job. But if this is not possible, the only way in which consistency can be reduced is to change self-image or personal identity. In doing this, the person reacts to the impact of the environment and the reality of external control. The strongest reinforcement or reward—to be one's self—is limited. If the pressure towards consistency leads to a great devaluation of one's capabilities then the perception of external control is high. This seems to be the process that accounts for the effect of low job skill-utilization on external control beliefs (Chapter 6). An external control belief is not just due to a restriction of perceived control capabilities. It is due to restriction of our perceived capabilities for intimacy, task competence and control. Another implication is that a given structure will affect people differently. It may match some people's capabilities but not others because individuals differ in their capabilities. There is no need to specify that all people want to maximize intimacy, ability or control. However, it is assumed that these capabilities are meaningful to all. To live, we have to relate in some way to others, we have to do tasks that use skills, and we have to direct our activities and be directed by others. The exact amount of capability we have on these three dimensions is determined by our genetic background and socialization experiences. Genetic factors are probably most important for determining the limits of our task ability but could determine our interpersonal temperaments and predilection for control as well. Socialization through the family, school and work organizations shapes our ability to relate to people, trains us in task skills and shapes our beliefs in self-determination. Thus when we encounter a new work organization, we do have an identity formed by inheritance and our past roles. Our concern is not to explain how these identities are formed prior to work but rather to explain what happens to personal identity when we encounter work structures. High levels of inconsistency, it is proposed, lead to anxiety and life dissatisfaction. If prolonged, inconsistency leads to strong beliefs in external control. For the individual with high external control beliefs which are generalized across major life situations the result is poor performance, distress and poor health in comparison to those who can validate their identity in matched organizations. These more fortunate individuals are able to believe that they are being themselves and, in being free to be themselves, have some degree of personal control over their destiny. This does not mean that they see themselves as internally controlled in all situations. What they are capable of doing is limited by their own capabilities and circumscribed by the organizational structure. We are not free to achieve anything we want. We are limited by ourselves and the requirement to participate with others in organizations in order to achieve shared personal and social goals.

A. Integration of Personal Capabilities

A problem with the person–organization match theory is that of personal integration. A person's capabilities might be well matched to his position in the organization but there may be lack of balance in his level of capabilities. But what does balance mean? Balance between intimacy, competency and personal control cannot be readily quantified. It does not refer to equal capabilities on these three dimensions. Although all people need to exercise them, there are obviously wide individual differences in the extent to which people can express love, competence and personal control. Perhaps integration is a better word. It refers to compatibility between capabilities. Incompatibility would occur when an individual's control beliefs are incompatible with intimacy or competence. A manager or worker, for example, may strongly believe in his or her ability to achieve personal control over his interpersonal environment and in so doing fail to allow the growth of mutuality in private relationships. Any close personal relationship requires some degree of mutual dependence and this cannot be achieved if one partner believes that he or she can dictate and control the course of a relationship. Similarly, people who strongly believe in their ability to achieve any goals they wish may find themselves attempting tasks which are beyond their ability and eventually suffer feelings of lack of competency. Balance or integration between these three universal capabilities has to be inferred from detailed observation of individual lifestyles. If a person's expressed capabilities on one dimension are diminished by their capabilities on one or both of the other dimensions he or she does not have integrated or balanced identity.

Much of this book has been about the way in which employment and unemployment foster competence and personal control. Social relationships which may be the basis of intimacy capabilities have hardly been mentioned. Elton Mayo and followers of the human relations approach to management would not approve. Employment does involve personal or informal relationships with people, but except for the helping professions, interpersonal contact is not the purpose of employment. The primary element of work structure is the task and the performance of tasks involves skills and self-direction to varying degrees. Hence the experience of work is most likely to shape competence and personal control.

However, work can affect intimacy capabilities indirectly by creating imbalance or disintegration in identity. Work may generate levels of task competence and personal control which reduce employee capabilities for close personal relationships. Many writers have maintained that the rise of bureaucratic industrial organizations has been associated with a decline in social cohesion and the ability to form close personal relationships (e.g. Rubenstein, 1978).

There is some evidence showing that extreme unrealistic beliefs in competence (too high or too low) and personal control (too internal or too external) can lead to poor personal adjustment which in turn affects personal relationships (e.g. Korman, 1980; Lefcourt, 1976). Since work can shape these beliefs, it therefore can affect personal relationships. Not much more can be said until more studies are done on the reciprocal effects between work experiences and interpersonal capabilities. These are likely to show that work-induced beliefs do affect the depth and form of personal relation-ships. But it is not suggested that 'right' work experiences will produce total integration of the personal identity. It may facilitate it but it seems that ul-timately integration can be achieved only by the individual. Fulfilling work will not automatically produce personal integration but it could be one path that an individual uses or has to use while seeking integration, insight and meaning.

B. Cultural Relativity

It may be suggested at this point that intimacy, competence and control capabilities are culturally determined and therefore given levels of these capabilities should have different consequences in different cultures. It is true that beliefs and values are shaped differently across cultures. With re-spect to work values and beliefs about the desirability of personal compe-tency and personal control, there is evidence that cultures differ consid-erably (Hofstede, 1980; Tannenbaum, 1960; Weisz, Rothbaum and Black-burn, 1984). North American culture, for example, values internal control, personal achievement and self-sufficiency more than does Japanese culture where there is high valuation given to group solidarity and achievement through the group.

Such differences are not disputed. However, it is not logical to conclude that the same beliefs have different personal consequences. Holding an ex-treme belief in external control can have similar consequences in North America and Japan. This is substantiated to some extent by Hofstede's study of international differences in work-related values. He correlated beliefs and values with various measures of personal and social adjustment and found quite a large number of significant correlations. Individualism, for example, correlated -0.51 with neuroticism across all countries. If the consequences of individualism varied with country, then there should not be high correlations between beliefs and consequences. So cultural relativity may not be a strong argument against a theory about the psychological effects of extreme levels on the dimensions of intimacy, competence and personal control. As far as the work-personality thesis goes, there is substantial evidence that the effects of job content on personal control and psychological distress are similar across cultures that vary widely in work values (Kohn and Schooler, 1983).

THE NEGATIVE EFFECTS ON EXTREME INTERNAL CONTROL BELIEFS ON MANAGERIAL BEHAVIOUR

A person with extreme internal control beliefs exhibits a behavioural pat-tern of high task activity and striving. In many ways the pattern resembles that shown by both the successful entrepreneural manager who is high on achievement motivation and the Type A personality who thrives on active competitive pursuit of challenging goals. The person with a very low score on Rotter's scale believes that practically all of his or her valued reinforcements can be gained by sufficient effort, knowledge and planning. It is not surprising then that many organizational psychologists have recommended that these individuals be placed in leadership positions or given tasks that challenge them (Spector, 1982). They seem to be self-motivated, more likely to seek information relevant to problem-solving, less likely to accept conformist solutions and better able to deal with stress and unstructured work assignments. This superiority of internally controlled employees over externally controlled employees does not imply, however, that all internals perform better than externals. In this section, it will be argued that extreme internal control beliefs can reduce managerial performance. Furthermore extreme internal control beliefs can have negative consequences for personal adjustment. Using the terminology of the previous section, we shall argue that extreme internals are likely to have low personal integration.

As far as managers are concerned, it seems that large North American organizations require these characteristics in managers. Miner analysed the role requirements of managers in large bureaucratic organizations in North America and identified six main role prescriptions (Miner, 1978). These were:

    (i) a positive attitude toward authority;
    (ii) a desire to compete;
    (iii) assertiveness;
    (iv) a strong desire to exercise power;
    (v) a desire to stand out (be an actor);
    (vi) a tolerance of routine administrative functions.

The successful managers, in studies based on his role-motivation theory, were those who possessed these attributes. They believed that they were capable of achieving personal and organizational goals by their own efforts. Furthermore, it seemed that they believed that organizations were structured so that it was possible to achieve these goals. But were they really successful? Most of the supporting studies use occupancy of senior positions as an index of performance. However, being promoted is not necessarily the result of effective performance. Sometimes people are 'kicked upstairs' because they are incompetent. Sometimes promotion occurs because the manager displays the attitudes and behaviours that an organization assumes, without evidence, are the hallmarks of a good manager. In North America, assertive individualism is the personal counterpart of corporate free enterprise. By definition, the successful individual is one who strongly believes in the efficacy of personal effort and control. He or she also believes that organizations provide freedom of movement which allows individual goals to be achieved when they are actively pursued. Yet there is reason to query the truth of these two beliefs. The first belief, if held in extreme, can lead to poor organizational performance and poor personal adjustment. The second belief is unrealistic and leads to conservatism.

A. Internal Control and Performance

An extreme internal belief is likely to lead to frustration when external obstacles block the individual's attempt at self-determination. Attempts to reduce this frustration could result in dysfunctional behaviour in organizations when it leads to assertiveness rather than compromise with the external demands—whether these be group members' beliefs or rigid organizational structures such as power or task relationships. The studies conducted on internal control and organizational behaviour have not distinguished between extreme and moderate internals, hence it is not possible to document these views with much evidence. However, there is evidence to show that the performance of internals is only superior to externals when the situation is not tightly structured (Dossett, Latham and Mitchell, 1979; Keller and Holland, 1978; Ruble, 1976; Yukl and Latham, 1978; Szilagyi, Sims and Keller, 1976). When organizations are large and formal with fairly clear specifications of power relationships and task allocation these high internal beliefs do not improve the performance of employees. If organizational tasks require negotiation and compromise then internals actually perform worse than externals (Bigoness, 1976). Therefore, the results of studies on employee locus of control and performance need to be qualified. While it is true that the majority of studies show that internals perform better than externals, this is due to researchers using fairly unstructured organizations and groups where it is possible for self-determination to have an effect. However most organizations, particularly large manufacturing and bureaucratic public service organizations, do not provide many positions where a great deal of personal autonomy can be expressed. Thus a person with high internal control beliefs would experience limitation in his quest for personal task goals.

These limitations could have personal consequences for the high internal who seeks to maintain an illusion of personal control. They could lead to an unrealistic use of ego defences such as denial, rationalization and intellectualization (Donovan and O'Leary, 1983). The barriers would be denied or explained away. Alternatively the barriers could be accepted at the cost of high personal stress. There appear to be no studies on the joint effect of internal control and rigid work roles on stress and health, but with respect to personal striving, high internals are similar to Type A personalities who are susceptible to coronary heart disease. Yet another strategy of the blocked internal would be to enhance his or her power through drugs (McClelland, 1975) and there are quite a few studies which show that alcoholics tend to be more internal than external (Gozali and Sloan, 1971; Goss and Morosko, 1970; Gross and Nerviano, 1972; Oziel, Obitz and Keyson, 1972; Weissbach, Vogler and Compton, 1976).

B. Personal Control, Managerial Success and Personal Failure

Some managers maintain this strong belief in personal control because they are regularly able to attain positions which provide them with great personal power. But the majority come to a point in their career when they realize that they are blocked by environmental factors and limitations in their own capacities. What happens then? They appear to suffer an identity crisis which Korman describes as a state of personal and social alienation (Korman, 1980). In his theory of career success and personal failure, based on interviews with North American managers, managerial alienation produced feelings of disinterest in work, and high dissatisfaction with both the job and life.

The factors producing these feelings of distress and detachment are partly situational and partly developmental. By the time managers achieve a reasonable amount of success—judged by status, income and security of tenure—they are in their mid-life stage where the physical signs of aging bear witness to the limitations of personal control. Not only are energy and ability declining, there is also an increased awareness that some personal goals will not be reached. Their organization frequently makes clear that their career progress will be limited. Not everyone is going to be in the highest echelons of management. Korman sees these factors contributing to a sense of external control which is especially painful to managers whose whole education and career have been spent believing in the efficacy of internal control. Not only have aging and blocked career goals induced external control feelings. A by-product of career striving has been the underdevelopment of interpersonal relationships. There are few friends, and often the quality of family life has been impoverished by an absence of intimacy. More likely than not, the internally controlled manager who turns to his wife and children as a means of restoring his esteem and sense of personal power finds that he is not equipped to strengthen affectional ties that have been weakened by neglect. Thus a sense of interpersonal incompetence further reinforces a belief in external control.

Korman refers to instances where the 'alienated' manager, unable to bear the contradictions between life as experienced and life as he prefers to see it, suffers severe emotional illnesses, physical ill health and even suicide. The remedy proposed by Korman is the provision of career counselling, flexibility in organizations for career changes and psychological counselling to promote self-acceptance and flexibility. In terms of the categories mentioned in earlier chapters, the extreme internals have to become 'realists'. They have to acknowledge that not all valued personal goals are attainable by personal striving. They also have to acknowledge the limitations in their own capacities and recognize where their behaviour is inevitably limited by other people and organizational structures.

Korman's solutions are basically short-term strategies which may be useful for those managers who either want assistance in finding jobs that suit their control orientations or guidance and counselling that would lead to more realistic beliefs. Yet psychological treatment can be little more than a band-aid. The problem of extreme internality is caused by societal values and reinforced by the family and educational experience of many professionals in western capitalistic societies.

INTERNAL CONTROL AND CONSERVATISM IN MANAGEMENT AND MANAGERIAL PSYCHOLOGY

A person who has a very low score on the Rotter internal-external score believes in high personal control as well as the ability to control the environment. Factor analyses of the scale have typically identified two subscales. One measures a belief in the person's ability to achieve valued goals. The other scale measures the extent to which the environment allows personal effort to have an effect. As Gurin, Gurin and Morrison (1978) have argued, there is an in-built conservatism in the scale. Very low scorers believe that organizations are structured so that the cream always rises to the top. If people fail to realize their goals it is not due to environmental factors such as low income, unrewarding jobs, deterministic technology or entrenched power interests. Rather it is due to lack of effort, resilience and ability. People with such beliefs are generally conservative in the sense that they see no need to change organizations. If a subordinate performs poorly or shows distress, they are more likely to want to change the person than the structure. This kind of belief is reinforced for many North American managers by managerial psychology texts where the manager is taught techniques for changing the attitudes and motivations of employees. Organizational performance, it is implied, is largely a matter of changing people, not structures. There is hardly any reference to changing organizational variables such as task content, power structures or monetary incentives. This is overstating the trend somewhat, because management are taught principles of job design and the use of financial incentives to motivate employees.

However, the psychological theories of job design (e.g. Hackman and Oldham, 1980; Herzberg, 1966), teach managers to change jobs so that the extreme internal can operate. Thus Hackman and Oldham (1980) recommend that job design will only be successful for individuals high on 'growth need strength'. These are the ones who believe in the efficacy and desirability of high self-direction. The distribution of power and money is also discussed in many texts. But the discussion makes it clear that these are techniques for motivating employees. Power-sharing becomes participation in decision-making where the employee is typically consulted but not offered real power even in decisions that vitally affect the way he does his job. The idealogical basis of the North American participation research is revealed in the typical presentation of the Coch and French (1948) study. Nearly all North American texts of managerial psychology present this study as an outstanding example of how participation in decision-making produces employees who are more committed and more productive. Yet the study is severely flawed, as has been pointed out by Gardner (1977). The study was concerned with the problem of overcoming employee resistance to change. Directive management had found that changes in the way pyjamas were folded, pressed and examined by employees led to dissatisfaction, higher turnover and decreased productivity. Coch and French decided to use Kurt Lewin's technique of attitude change to overcome this resistance. Two kinds of participatory procedures were used. One involved consultation with workers about the changes needed. The changes required were presented and employees allowed to voice their opinions. Apparently convinced of the need for change, employees allowed some representatives to meet with management and learn the new procedures. These representatives then taught the changes to other members of the group.

The other participatory condition was the same except that all employees were taught the new procedures. The control group were just informed of the required changes. All groups were paid on an individual piece-rate basis. The results reported significant superiority in productivity and motivation of both participatory groups over the control group. Most texts repeat the conclusion of Yukl : 'It is clear that participation had a beneficial effect on productivity' (Yukl, 1981, p.211). What is wrong with this conclusion? The general criticism is that there were no statistical tests of significance and there were many other factors, besides participation, that could have accounted for the results. The dramatic presentation, training, increased pay as a result of trained performance, differences in type of work and differences in group size across conditions were all factors that were weighted in favour of the participatory groups. Anyhow, it was not really participation in decision-making. Lewin's technique was one of changing attitudes and the interventions of Coch and French did just this. Employees were committed more to management's directives. The actual changes adopted did not at all reflect any change that might have been suggested by employees. Influence was not shared.

We are not arguing here that employees must have more influence in all management decisions. We are arguing that management psychology is not concerned about altering power structures, task structures or pay structures. Yet there is considerable evidence that employee and group performance can be greatly affected by changes in these structural variables (O'Brien, 1984). In their own interests—to show how productivity can be maximized—industrial psychologists should take structures seriously. Instead they are concerned with changing the attitudes and motivations of employees. It is assumed that the structure of an organization is given and has little effect on personality and motivation. There are no theories of group performance in North American psychology which seek to explain how the total set of structural relationships (assignment, authority, task allocation, task precedence) affect performance.

Partly this neglect is due to an individualistic definition of the nature of psychology. It is also due to a belief that organizations provide avenues for personal fulfilment that are not blocked by the nature of tasks, the distribution of power, or the amount of income payable. The hidden argument is that performance decrements, if they occur, must be explainable in terms of individual unwillingness to be self-determined.

The neglect of structure is widespread in North American psychology even when theories claim to be interactional. A good example is Fiedler's contingency model of leadership (Fiedler, 1967, 1978). This theory goes beyond trying to predict leadership performance from traits such as ability and personality. It claims that leadership effectiveness is a function of the interaction of the leader's style and the group situation. The group situation is defined in terms of leader member relations, task structure and leader power. It reads, to the uncritical, as a theory that indeed says that productivity partly depends on the situation.

But it does not. What the theory actually says is that a person-oriented leader performs better than a task-oriented leader when the situation affords the leader moderate amounts of situational control. When situational control by the leader is very high or very low, it is the task-oriented leader who performs best. Thus it is really a theory of relative leader effectiveness. It does not say how the structure affects performance of a group. If Fiedler believes that structural variables 'contaminate' the performance measures, he typically adjusts performance before he correlates leadership style with group performance. As far as it goes, the theory has reasonable support and the author has contributed to its validation (Fiedler, O'Brien and Ilgen, 1969; O'Brien, 1969; Strube and Garcia, 1981). But it is essentially about two types of leaders who are both concerned with maximizing their personal control: one through task achievement and the other through interpersonal relationships. The leadership style measure, when compared to structural variables such as task structure, accounts for a minute percentage of the variance in productivity (Hewett, O'Brien and Hornik, 1974; Ilgen and O'Brien, 1974; O'Brien and Kabanoff, 1979). Consequently, when leaders are trained to alter the situation to 'fit' their style they will often actually depress performance because the new structure is not appropriate for the task at hand (Kabanoff, 1981). Hence even this theory fits the pattern of changing behaviour and not structure. In this case, Fiedler does not try to change the motivational structure of the leaders but he does try to change their behaviour and he seems quite oblivious to the possibility that these behavioural changes could have negative consequences for group performance and subordinate motivation.

THE FUTURE OF WORK AND WORK PSYCHOLOGY

The growth of capitalism has been associated with a shift in human work motivation. The nature of this motivation was documented by Weber when he showed that the characteristics of ascetic Protestants were especially suitable for personal advancement within capitalistic work structures. Some of the important features of this Protestant Ethic were rationality, self-control, avoidance of interpersonal relationships, thrift, hard work and a belief that personalsuccess in business was a sure sign of being part of the spiritual elect.

In later times, the theistic overtones were replaced with a belief that personal success at work was the central way for people, especially males, to achieve personal identity and psychological fulfilment. The net cultural effect was that, in Reisman's terms, industrial societies promoted an 'inner-directed' rather than an 'outer-directed' personality (Reisman, 1950). Pre-industrial societies had been 'outer-directed' in the sense that a person's worth and identity were dependent on that person's assigned position. The individual's self-concept was a reflection of his or her position and personal worth was not so much a function of what the individual did as it was of what others judged the individual to be. Industrial capitalism, on the other hand, fostered a fierce self-control that had two ways of expressing itself. First, control was expressed over inner impulses. Interpersonal ties and personality were repressed. Second, control over work processes was enjoined in an individualistic manner so that character could be purified and material success could be gained.

The consequences in the long run would seem to be a population increasingly polarized into the extreme internals–the political, scientific and managerial elite—and a majority of extreme externals. These are people who have low skill-utilization jobs, passive leisure and a life of immediate gratification and material acquisitiveness. The number of passive extreme externals is also added to as the incidence of long-term unemployment increases. This may sound extreme and pessimistic. Obviously there are a lot of people with flexible control orientations, satisfying work, good interpersonal relationships and the ability to integrate their activities through the adoption of some philosophy or religion not based on work activity alone.

Yet there are trends that have been identified in this book which can result in more and more people being pushed into the extreme internal or external control patterns. Technological change for many is leading to simplified jobs with low skill-utilization and low income. The evidence, although not as strong as it could be, shows that the personal consequences for employees in these situations are external control beliefs which induce mental and physical illness. An increasing number of people are finding that technological and economic changes mean unemployment. As Bakke found in the 1930's, a majority of the unemployed now show resilience in an environment constricted by poverty and an absence of identity-confirming tasks. But if sufficient income and meaningful work outside employment is not provided, then the accurate perception of external control is likely to lead, with time, to a general passivity that signals the introjection of external control. The preferable psychological solution is employment that allows skill-use and provides adequate income (O'Brien and Kabanoff, 1979; Warr, 1983). A more difficult alternative is to change educational and social ideologies so that unemployment is not stigmatized. To implement such a policy requires much more than training for leisure. Many who are now adults have already been deeply ingrained with a work ethic and, in addition, their capacity to use leisure has been affected by their work experiences (Kabanoff and O'Brien, 1980). If unemployment increases in the future, the psychological health of the unemployed is likely to be improved by education and training for non-employment positions in society. These positions should provide adequate income and opportunities to do tasks that allow development of individual capacities for intimacy, competence and moderate levels of personal control.

An easier solution, but nonetheless difficult and idealistic, is to change the goals and tasks of work organizations. The major goals of modern organizations are defined by productivity and associated economic criteria of profitability or cost/benefit ratios. If these goals are attained, it is assumed that employees and society will benefit through the generation of wealth and material security. There is little evidence to support this 'trickle down' theory. Certainly this century has seen a general improvement in material standards of living for a majority of people in highly industrialized nations. But this increase has not extended to all and for those who have benefited materially, it has frequently been at the expense of psychological growth. Technological advances have been associated with losses in task competence and personal control due either to work simplification or to the abolition of jobs. The ethic of personal control has only been lived by those in a minority of positions where autonomy and task challenge are part of the job description. Considerable numbers of managers in such positions have been socialized into an overestimation of personal control which has limited their capacity for intimacy, cooperation and flexibility.

In their endeavour to be useful and relevant to modern organizational life industrial psychologists have, unwittingly perhaps, contributed to these problems. Rarely have they expressed explicit willingness to be servants of power but they have adopted management problems and have reinforced an ideology of individual achievement and self-direction. Particularly in the United States, there has been an insensitivity to the limiting effects of a group structure on both individual and group performance. Hardly any text examines the long-term effects of jobs on employee personality or even the effects of group structure on performance. Instead there are hosts of theories on work motivation and leadership. The predominant concern is productivity and the theories all imply applications which assist the manager to change reluctant employees into self-motivated automatons. These theories are conservative in at least three ways. First, they help maintain existing structures by emphasizing the need to change people—either managers or employees. Situational variables are recognized but only in the sense that different situations will require different personal changes. Some theories (e.g. Fiedler, 1978; Hackman and Oldham, 1980) do appear to recommend structural changes but, in practice, these are only slight changes in variables such as variety, feedback, participation or leader–member relations.

The second way in which North American managerial psychology is conservative is through its perpetuation of a belief that organizations have fluid structures which allow internally controlled individuals to achieve what they really want. They may frequently imply that individual behaviour depends on the situation but there are very few theorists who bother to analyse situations. In effect, they assume that situational constraints are less important for productivity than individual characteristics. By espousing the desirability of unlimited achievement and internal control motivations they inadvertently select and train people to believe that success is entirely within themselves. Personal control which is tempered by the realization that much work is constrained by rigid organizational and task structures is a necessary component of a mature personality. But uncritical motivational theories endorse a dogmatic belief in personal control that is dysfunctional for most organizations and most individuals. The conservative impact of this orientation is that personal and organizational failure tend to be blamed on the individual and not on the structure.

A final way in which the current managerial psychology is conservative then is its labelling and stigmatization of employees who resist attempts to shape them to existing organizational structures. Employees who come to a realistic assessment that their jobs have little skill content and severely restrict their personal control, come to accept this as a fact of life. When they describe their jobs as just offering money, security or good physical conditions it is often because that is all their jobs could possibly offer. In a neglected study of the effects of industrial jobs, Lafitte (1958), was one of the first industrial psychologists to point out that worker responses are largely shaped by imposed structure.

Lafitte rejected narrow motivational theories of work behaviour which assumed that work organizations were flexible cooperative systems that could be bonded by informed and considerate management practices. Rather, he saw organizations as being directed by a managerial class which had interests opposed to the psychological well-being of employees. His Australian workers did report reasonably high levels of job satisfaction but this was a defensive adjustment on their part. They evaluated their jobs in terms of what was realistic and not in terms of an ideal utopia. They appreciated jobs that provided good physical conditions, income and some personal independence but never expected to achieve personal fulfilment at work. Furthermore, and this was not made explicit by Lafitte, their evaluations were defensive because they saw their own personal rewards from work as entirely extrinsic, They emphasized pay and conditions because this was all they had left to bargain about.

Lafitte's main point was that many factory workers were shaped by repetitive simple tasks performed within an autocratic power structure. They did not seek personal fulfilment because they expected that the industrial system would not change. They did seek money, security and some considerateness from managers. In contrast to this interpretation is the common labelling of such employees as mentally ill hygiene seekers (Herzberg, 1966), intrinsic or instrumentally oriented (Goldthorpe *et al.*, 1969) or as unfortunate individuals who do not seek the satisfaction of 'higher-order' needs (Hackman and Oldham, 1980). The effect of this labelling is that psychologists are advised not to enrich the jobs of these employees. It is easily assumed that they display stable dispositions which will not be responsive to challenging work. There is now sufficient evidence to show that many employees have shaped their attitudes, beliefs and personalities in order to cope with existing work structures and retain the income associated with their job positions. Hence it is discriminatory even to suggest that these people would not eventually learn to enjoy the opportunities for growth that enriched work would allow.

As Adam Smith observed, people at work are shaped by what they do. It was not surprising, given his adherence to work simplification, that he did not recommend changing work content. The best he could suggest was further education for the working class in order to counteract the negative intellectual and character effects of industrial-work. However, the problem of underemployment has not been solved by increased education. It has been worsened because educational levels are rising without associated rises in the skill level of jobs. The problem is unlikely to be solved by minor tinkering with jobs which leaves skill-match discrepancies untouched. Nor will it be solved by procedures called employee participation or participation in management decision-making. There is little evidence that such procedures provide employees with any influence over job content. There seems little likelihood that organizations will change their principles of job design themselves in order to improve personal development and productivity. The only possibility there is reason to be optimistic about is that of legislation to ensure that jobs are designed to fit employee capabilities. If sufficient evidence is collected and made public about negative health and personality effects of certain jobs, then social protest might lead to legal prescriptions similar to those adopted for physical safety. The collection and dissemination of this information is not likely to be done by present managerial psychology. A new approach is necessary. It requires the development of a psychology that is more sensitive to the effect of jobs on people. This sensitivity is also required if organizational psychology is to live up to its promise of studying the reciprocal interaction between the person and the work environment.

REFERENCES

Berlew, D.E. and Hall, D.T. (1966). The socialization of managers: effects of expectations on performance, *Administrative Science Quarterly*, **11**, 207–23
Bigoness. W.J. (1976). Effects of locus of control and style of third party intervention upon bargaining behavior, *Journal of Applied Psychology*, **61**, 305–12
Bolweg, J.F. (1976). *Job Design and Industrial Democracy*, Leiden: Nijhoff
Broekmeyer, M.J. (1968). *De arbeidsraad in Zuidslavie*, Neppel: Book
Carey, A. (1979). Norwegian experiments on democracy at work: a critique and a contribution to reflexive sociology, *Australian and New Zealand Journal of Sociology*, **15**, 13–23
Coch, L. and French, J.R.P. (1948). Overcoming resistance to change, *Human Relations*, **1**, 512–32
Dachler, H.P. and Wilpert, B. (1978). Conceptual dimensions and boundaries of participation in organizations: a critical evaluation, *Administrative Science Quarterly*, **23**, 1–39
Delbecq, A.L., Van der Ven, A.H. and Gustafson, D.H. (1975). *Group Techniques for Program Planning*, Glenview, Ill: Scott Foresman
DIO International Research Team (1983). A contingency model of participative decision making: an analysis of 56 decisions in three Dutch organizations, *Journal of Occupational Psychology*, **56**, 1-18
Donavan, D.M. and O'Leary, M.R. (1983). Control orientation, drinking behavior, and alcoholism, Chapter 4 in H.M. Lefcourt (ed.), *Research with the Locus of Control Construct*, vol. 2, New York: Academic Press
Dossett, D.L., Latham, G.P. and Mitchell, T.R. (1979). The effects of assigned versus participatively set goals, knowledge of results and individual differences when goal difficulty is held constant, *Journal of Applied Psychology*, **64**, 291–8
Emery, F.E. and Phillips, C. (1976). *Living at Work*, Canberra: Australian Government Publishing Service

Emery, F.E. and Thorsrad, E. (1976). _Democracy at Work_, Leiden: Nijhoff
Emery, F.E. and Trist, E.L. (1960). Socio-technical systems, in Churchman, C.W. and Verhulst, M. (eds), _Management Sciences, Models and Techniques_, vol. 2, London: Pergamon Press
Fiedler, F.E. (1967). _A Theory of Leadership Effectiveness_, New York: McGraw Hill
Fiedler, F.E. (1978). The contingency model and the dynamics of the leadership process, in L. Berkowitz (ed.), _Advances in Experimental Social Psychology_, vol. 11, New York: Academic Press
Fiedler, F.E., O'Brien, G.E. and Ilgen, D. (1969). The effect of leadership style upon the performance and adjustment of volunteer teams operating on a stressful foreign environment, _Human Relations_, 22, 503–14
Friedlander, F. and Greenberg, S. (1971). Effects of job training, attitudes and organization climates on the performance of the hard-core unemployed, _Journal of Applied Psychology_, 55, 287-95
Gardner, G. (1977). Workers' participation: a critical analysis of Coch and French, _Human Relations_, 30, 1071–8
Goldthorpe, J.H., Lockwood, D., Bechhoffer, F. and Platt, J. (1969). _The Affluent Worker in the Class Structure_, Cambridge: Cambridge University Press.
Goodman, P., Salipante, P. and Paransky, H. (1973). Hiring, training and retraining the hard-core unemployed, _Journal of Applied Psychology_, 58, 23–33
Goss, A. and Morosko, T.E. (1970). Relation between a dimension of internal-external control and the MMPI with alcoholics, _Journal of Consulting and Clinical Psychology_, 34, 189–92
Gozali, J. and Sloan, J. (1971). Control orientation as a personality dimension among alcoholics, _Quarterly Journal of Studies on Alcohol_, 32, 159–61
Gross, W.F. and Nerviano, V.J. (1972). Note on the control orientation of alcoholics, _Psychological Report_, 31, 406
Gurin, P., Gurin, G. and Morrison, B.M. (1978). Personal and ideological aspects of internal and external control, _Social Psychology_, 41, 275–96
Hackman, J.R. and Oldham, G.R. (1980). _Work Redesign_, Reading, Mass.: Addison-Wesley
Hammer, T. and Stern, R. (1980). Employee ownership: implications for the organizational distribution of power, _Academy of Management Journal_, 21, 78–100
Hammond, K.R., Rohrbaugh, J., Mumpower, J. and Adelman, L. (1977). Social judgement theory: applications in policy formation, in Kaplan, M.F. and Schwartz, S. (eds), _Human Judgement and Decision Processes in Applied Setting_, New York: Academic Press
Heller, F.W., Drenth, P.J.D., Koopman, P. and Rus, V. (1977). A longitudinal study in participative decision-making, _Human Relations_, 30, 567–87
Herzberg, F. (1966). _Work and the Nature of Man_, Cleveland, Ohio: World
Hewett, T.T., O'Brien, G.E. and Hornik, J. (1974). The effects of work organization, leadership style, and member compatibility upon the productivity of small groups working on a manipulative task, _Organizational Behavior and Human Performance_, 11, 283–301
Hofstede, G. (1980). _Culture's Consequences: International Differences in Work-Related Values_, Beverly Hills, Cal.: Sage
Ilgen, D.R. and O'Brien, G.E. (1974). Leader–member relations in small groups, _Organizational Behavior and Human Performance_, 12, 335–50
Janis, I.L. (1972). _Victims of Groupthink_, Boston: Houghton Mifflin
Kabanoff, B. (1981). A critique of leader-match, _Personal Psychology_, 34, 749–64

Kabanoff, B. and O'Brien, G.E. (1979a). Cooperation structure and the relationship of leader and member ability to group performance, *Journal of Applied Psychology*, **64**, 526–32

Kabanoff, B. and O'Brien, G.E. (1979b). The effects of task type and cooperation upon group products and performance, *Organizational Behavior and Human Performance*, **23**, 163–81

Kabanoff, B. and O'Brien, G.E. (1980). Work and leisure: a task attributes analysis, *Journal of Applied Psychology*, **65**, 595–609

Keller, R.T. and Holland, W.E. (1978). Individual characteristics of innovativeness and communication in research and development organizations, *Journal of Applied Psychology*, **63**, 759–62

Kohn, M.L. and Schooler, C. (1983). *Work and Personality*, Norwood, N.J.: Ablex

Kolaja, J. (1965). *Workers' Councils: The Yugoslav Experience*, London: Tavistock

Koopman, P.L., Drenth, P.J.D., Bus, F.B.M., Kruyswijk, A.J. and Wierdsma, A.F.M. (1981). Content, process, and effects of participative decision making on the shop floor: three cases in the Netherlands, *Human Relations*, **34**, 657–76

Korman, A.K. (1980). *Career Success/Personal Failure*, Englewood Cliffs, N.J.: Prentice-Hall

Lafitte, P. (1958). *Social Structure and Personality in a Factory*, London: Routledge and Kegan Paul

Lefcourt, H. (1976). *Locus of Control: Current Trends in Theory and Research*, New York: Wiley

Linstone, H.A. and Turoff, M. (1975). *The Dephi Methods: Techniques and Applications*, Reading, Mass.: Addison-Wesley

Long, R. (1978a). The effects of employee ownership on organizational identification, employee job attitudes, and organizational performance: a tentative framework and empirical findings, *Human Relations*, **31**, 29–48

Long, R. (1978b). The relative effects of share ownership vs. control on job attitudes in an employee owned company, *Human Relations*, **31**, 753–63

McClelland, D.C. (1965). N-achievement and entrepreneurship: a longitudinal study, *Journal of Personality and Social Psychology*, **1**, 389–92

McClelland, D. (1975). *Power: The Inner Experience*, New York: Irvington

McCormick, E.J. (1979). *Job Analysis: Methods and Applications*, New York: American Management Association

Miner, J. (1978). Twenty years of research on role motivation theory, *Personnel Psychology*, **31**, 739–60

Mitchell, T. (1973). Motivation and participation, *Academy of Management Journal*, **16**, 660–79

Morris, W. (1910–15). *Collected Works*, vol. 23, Longman: London

Mulder, M. (1971). Power equalization through participation? *Administrative Science Quarterly*, **16**, 31–8

Obradovic, J. (1970). Participation and work attitudes in Yugoslavia, *Industrial Relations*, **9**, 161–9

O'Brien, G.E. (1969). Group structure and the measurement of potential leader influence, *Australian Journal of Psychology*, **21**, 277–89

O'Brien, G.E. (1982). Evaluation of the job characteristics theory of work attitudes and performance, *Australian Journal of Psychology*, **34**, 383–401

O'Brien, G.E. (1983a). *Employee Participation in an Assembly Line Factory*, Canberra: Australian Government Publishing Service

O'Brien, G.E. (1983b). Skill-utilization, skill-variety, and the job characteristics model, *Australian Journal of Psychology*, **35**, 461–8

O'Brien, G.E. (1984). Group productivity, Chapter 3 in Gruneberg, M. and Wall, T. (eds), Social Psychology and Organizational Behaviour, Chichester: Wiley

O'Brien, G.E., Biglan, A. and Penna, J. (1972). Measurement of the distribution of potential influence and participation in groups and organizations, Journal of Applied Psychology, 56, 11–18.

O'Brien, G.E. and Kabanoff, B. (1979). Comparison of unemployed and employed workers on work values, locus of control, and health variables, Australian Psychologist, 14, 143–54

O'Brien, G.E. and Kabanoff, B. (1981). The effects of leadership style and group structure upon small group productivity: a test of a discrepancy theory of leader effectiveness, Australian Journal of Psychology, 33, 157–68

O'Brien, G.E. and Owens, A.G. (1969). Effects of organizational structure on correlations between member abilities and group productivity. Journal of Applied Psychology, 53, 525–30.

Oeser, O.A. and Harary, F. (1962). A mathematical model for structural role theory, I. Human Relations, 15, 89–109

Oeser, O.A. and Harary, F. (1964). A mathematical model for structural role theory, II, Human Relations, 17, 3–17

Oeser, O.A. and O'Brien, G.E. (1967). A mathematical model for structural role theory, III, The analyses of group tasks, Human Relations, 20, 83–97

Oziel, L.J., Obitz, F.W. and Keyson, M. (1972). General and specific perceived locus of control in alcoholics, Psychological Reports, 30, 957–8

Reisman, D. (1950). The Lonely Crowd, New Haven, Conn.: Yale University Press

Rice, A.K. (1958). Productivity and Social Organization, London: Tavistock

Roberts, I.L. (1973). The Works Constitution Acts and industrial relations in West Germany: implications for the United Kingdom, British Journal of Industrial Relations, 11, 338–67

Rohrbaugh, J. (1979). Improving the quality of group judgement: social judgement analysis and the Delphi technique, Organizational Behavior and Human Performance, 24, 73–92

Rohrbaugh, J. (1981). Improving the quality of group judgement: social judgement analysis and the nominal group technique, Organizational Behavior and Human Performance, 28, 272–88

Rosenstein, E. (1970). Histadrut's search for a participation programme, Industrial Relations, 9, 170–86

Rubenstein, D. (1978). Love and work, Sociological Review, 26, 5–25

Ruble, T.L. (1976). Effects of one's locus of control and the opportunity to participate in planning, Organizational Behavior and Human Performance, 16, 63–73

Spector, P.E. (1982). Behavior in organizations as a function of employees' locus of control, Psychological Bulletin, 91, 482–97

Srivasta, S. et al. (1974). Productivity, Industrial Organization and Job Satisfaction: Policy Development and Implementation, unpublished report to the National Science Foundation, Case Western Reserve University

Strube, M.J. and Garcia, J.E. (1981). A meta-analytic investigation of Fiedler's contingency model of leadership effectiveness, Psychological Bulletin, 90, 307–21

Stryker, S. (1980). Symbolic Interactionism: A Social Structural Version, Menlo Park, Cal.: Benjamin/Cummings

Szilagyi, A.D., Sims, H.P. and Keller, R.T. (1976). Role dynamics, locus of control, and employee attitudes and behavior, Academy of Management Journal, 19, 259–76

Tannenbaum, A. (1980). Organizational psychology, Chapter 7 in H.C. Triandis and R.W. Brislin, *Handbook of Cross-cultural Psychology*, vol. 5, Boston: Allyn & Bacon

Toscano, D.J. (1983). Toward a typology of employee ownership, *Human Relations*, **36**, 581–602

Van der Velden, H.A. (1965). Feiteljik functroneren van vier ondernemingovraden, *Institute of Social Psychology*, University of Utrecht.

Wall, T.D. and Lischeron, T.A. (1977). *Worker Participation*, Berkshire: McGraw Hill

Warr, P. (1983). Work, jobs and unemployment, *Bulletin of the British Psychological Society*, **36**, 305–11

Weissbach, T.A., Vogler, R.E. and Compton, J.V. (1976). Comments on the relationship between locus of control and alcohol abuse, *Journal of Clinical Psychology*, **32**, 484–6

Weisz, J.R., Rothbaum, F.M. and Blackburn, T.C. (1984). Standing out and standing in: the psychology of control in America and Japan, *American Psychologist*, **39**, 955–69

Yukl, G.A. (1981). *Leadership in Organizations*, Englewood Cliffs, N.J.: Prentice-Hall

Yukl, G.A. and Latham, G.P. (1978). Interrelationships among employee participation, individual differences, goal difficulty, goal acceptance, goal instrumentality, and performance, *Personnel Psychology*, **31**, 305–23

Zwerdling, D. (1980). *Workplace Democracy*, New York: Harper & Row

Author Index

Subject Index